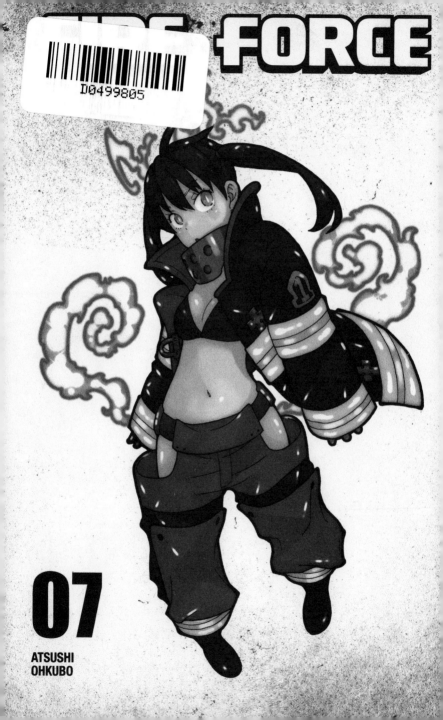

FORCE

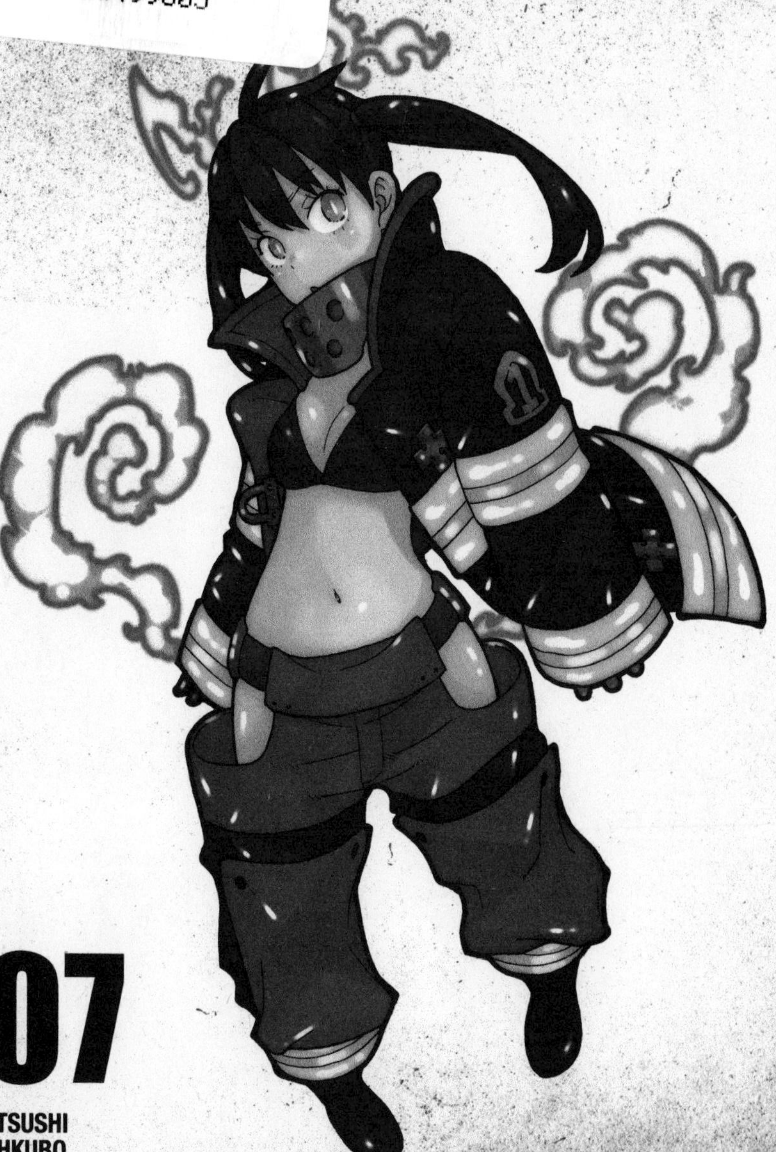

07

ATSUSHI
OHKUBO

you your precious.

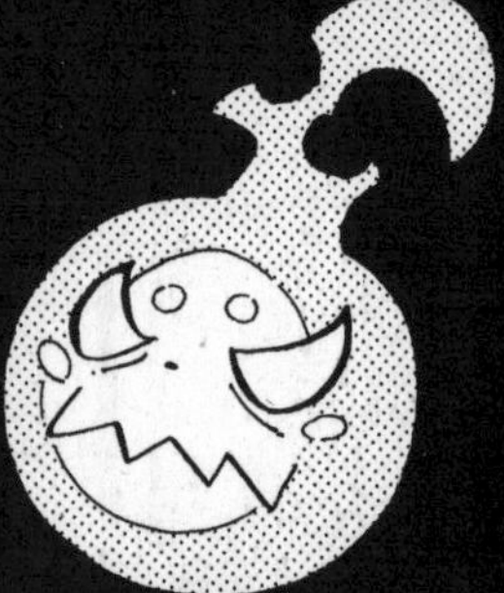

VOL.7

ATSUSHI OHKUBO

The fire connects with

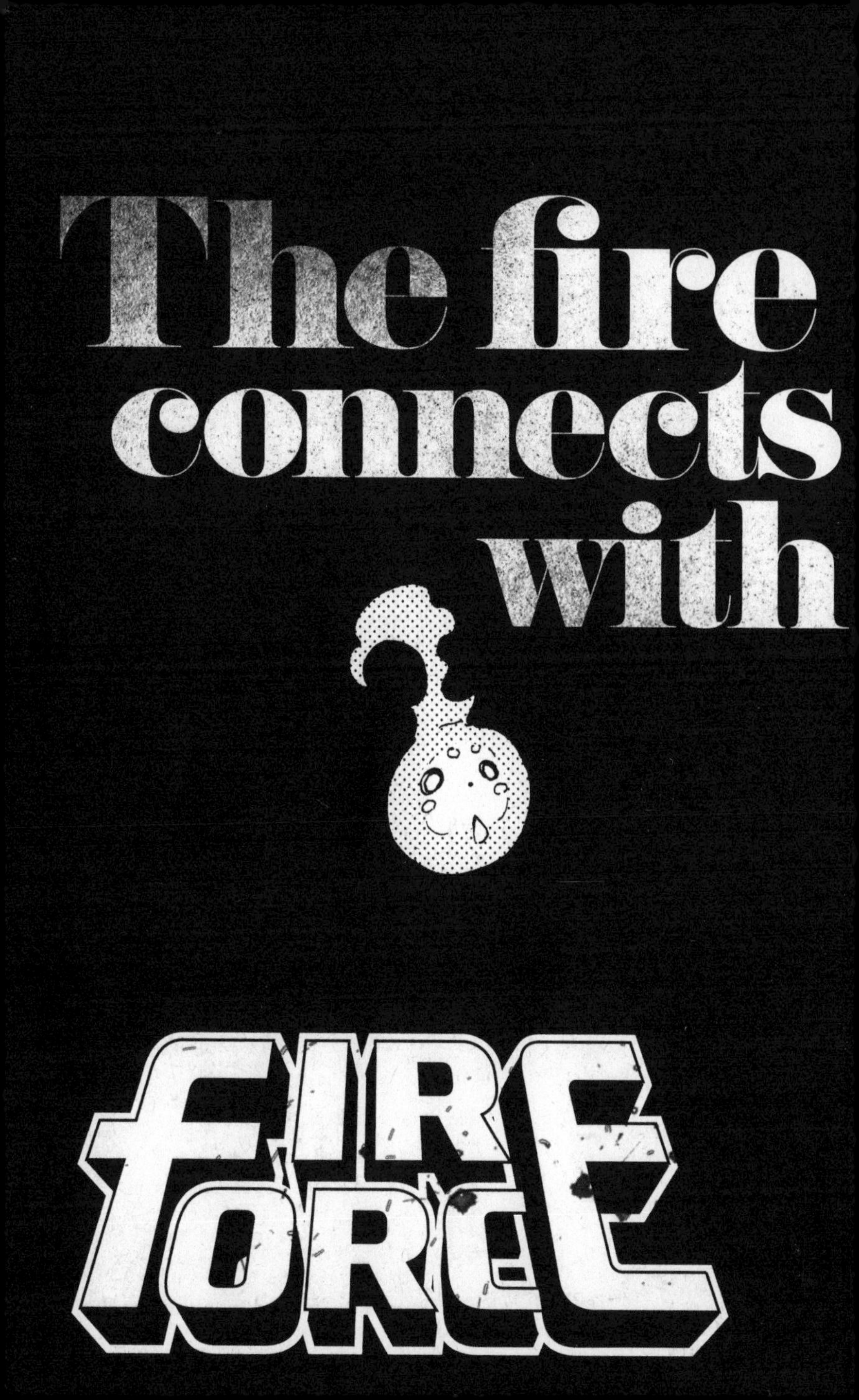

FIRE FORCE

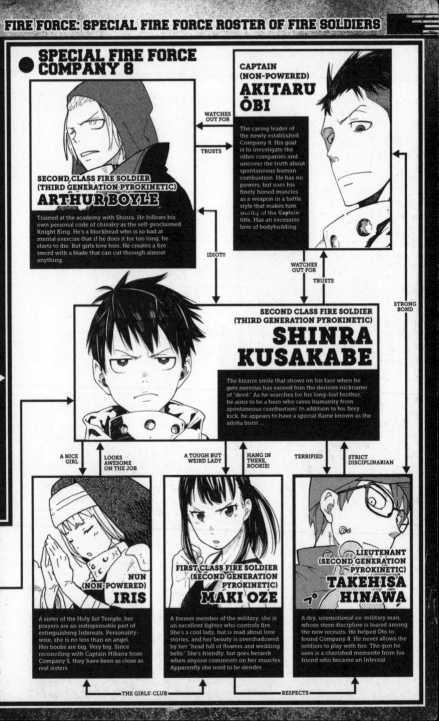

SPECIAL FIRE FORCE COMPANY 8

SECOND CLASS FIRE SOLDIER
(THIRD GENERATION PYROKINETIC)

ARTHUR BOYLE

Trained at the academy with Shinra. He follows his own personal code of chivalry as the self-proclaimed Knight King. He's a blockhead who is so bad at mental exercise that if he does it for too long, he starts to die. But girls love him. He creates a fire sword with a blade that can cut through almost anything.

WATCHES OUT FOR

TRUSTS

CAPTAIN
(NON-POWERED)

AKITARU ŌBI

The caring leader of the newly established Company 8. His goal is to investigate the other companies and uncover the truth about spontaneous human combustion. He has no powers, but uses his finely honed muscles as a weapon in a battle style that makes him worthy of the Captain title. Has an excessive love of bodybuilding.

IDIOT!!

WATCHES OUT FOR

TRUSTS

STRONG BOND

SECOND CLASS FIRE SOLDIER
(THIRD GENERATION PYROKINETIC)

SHINRA KUSAKABE

The bizarre smile that shows on his face when he gets nervous has earned him the derisive nickname of "devil." As he searches for his long-lost brother, he aims to be a hero who saves humanity from spontaneous combustion! In addition to his fiery kick, he appears to have a special flame known as the adolla burst ...

A NICE GIRL

LOOKS AWESOME ON THE JOB

A TOUGH BUT WEIRD LADY

HANG IN THERE, ROOKIE!

TERRIFIED

STRICT DISCIPLINARIAN

NUN
(NON-POWERED)

IRIS

A sister of the Holy Sol Temple, her prayers are an indispensable part of extinguishing Infernals. Personality-wise, she is no less than an angel. Her boobs are big. Very big. Since reconciling with Captain Hibana from Company 5, they have been as close as real sisters.

FIRST CLASS FIRE SOLDIER
(SECOND GENERATION PYROKINETIC)

MAKI OZE

A former member of the military, she is an excellent fighter who controls fire. She's a cool lady, but is mad about love stories, and her beauty is overshadowed by her "head full of flowers and wedding bells." She's friendly, but goes berserk when anyone comments on her muscles. Apparently she used to be slender.

LIEUTENANT
(SECOND GENERATION PYROKINETIC)

TAKEHISA HINAWA

A dry, unemotional ex-military man, whose stern discipline is feared among the new recruits. He helped Ōbi to found Company 8. He never allows the soldiers to play with fire. The gun he uses is a cherished memento from his friend who became an Infernal.

THE GIRLS' CLUB

RESPECTS

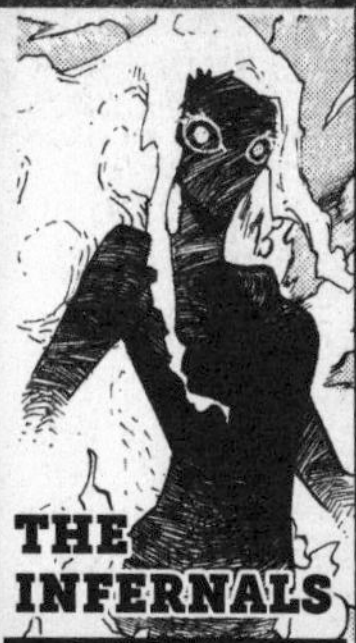

THE INFERNALS

Born from the cryptogenic phenomenon of spontaneous human combustion (SHC), they have no self-awareness, and only wreak havoc until their lives burn out. It would seem, in some cases, they are created artificially by the White Hoods.

● FOLLOWERS OF THE EVANGELIST

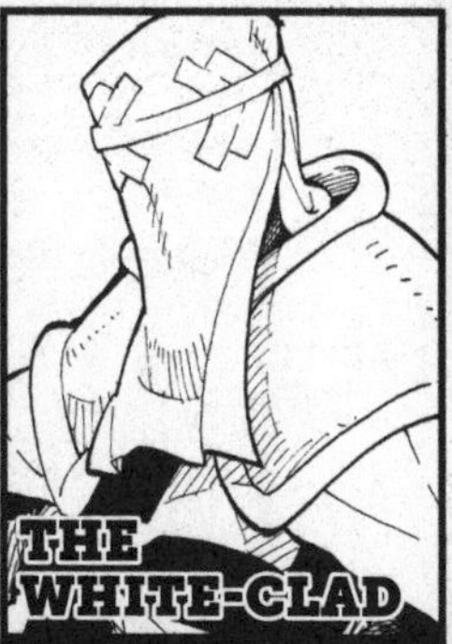

THE WHITE-CLAD

An esoteric group with high-level fighting powers that follows the teachings of the Evangelist. They use bugs to ignite Infernals artificially. They seem to be searching for something, but...?

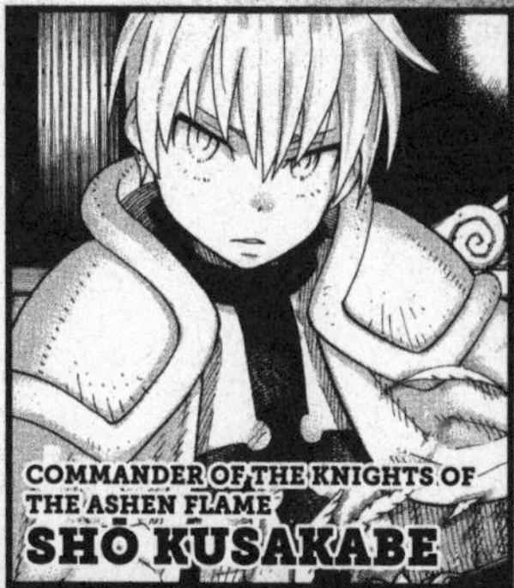

COMMANDER OF THE KNIGHTS OF THE ASHEN FLAME

SHŌ KUSAKABE

A young boy who commands an order of knights organized under the Evangelist. Is he really the brother Shinra thought he lost in the Infernal fire?!

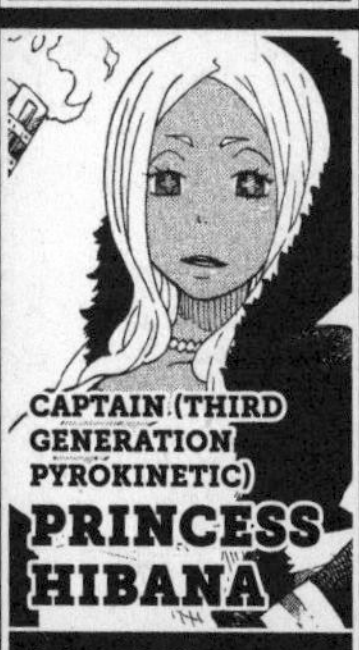

CAPTAIN (THIRD GENERATION PYROKINETIC)

PRINCESS HIBANA

An imperious former woman of the cloth who constantly looks down on others and refers to everyone other than herself as gravel. After a battle with Shinra, she reforms and builds a collaborative relationship with Company 8. Or rather, she developed a crush on Shinra.

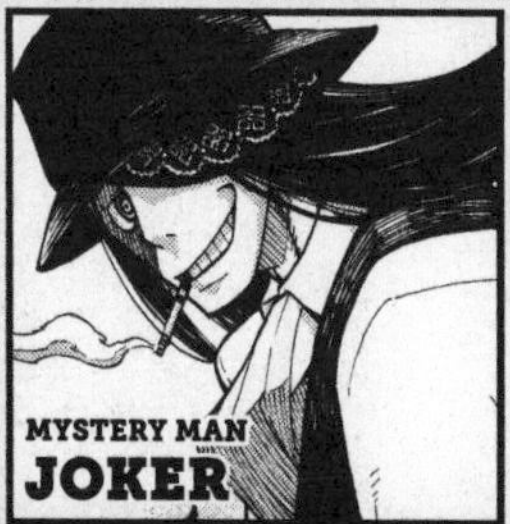

MYSTERY MAN

JOKER

A man who appears when least expected, who once crashed the Fire Force's Rookie Games and attacked fire soldiers. He senses something special about Shinra and tells him that his long-lost brother is alive and with the Evangelist.

↔ CO-CONSPIRATORS?

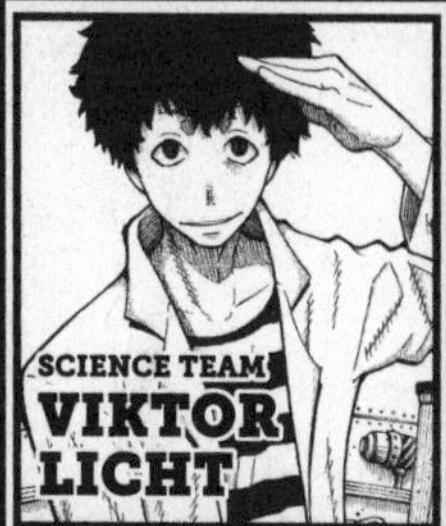

SCIENCE TEAM

VIKTOR LICHT

Abruptly deployed from Haijima Industries to fill the vacancy in Company 8's science department. Even Hibana is suspicious of the sudden assignment—what is his true goal?!

THE NEW SCIENCE TEAM

SUMMARY...

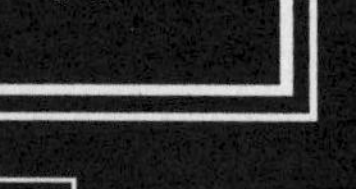

SPUTT
SPUTT

Shinra and Arthur engaged in battle with the white-clad warriors who plunged Asakusa into chaos. One of them ignited himself and became a Demon Infernal, just like the one Shinra saw at the fire that took his family! The demon displayed overwhelming strength, but with Shinra's support and an attack that used all his power, Company 7's Captain Benimaru defeated him! Companies 7 and 8 overcame their differences, and now Company 8 has a strong new ally to aid in their investigations!!

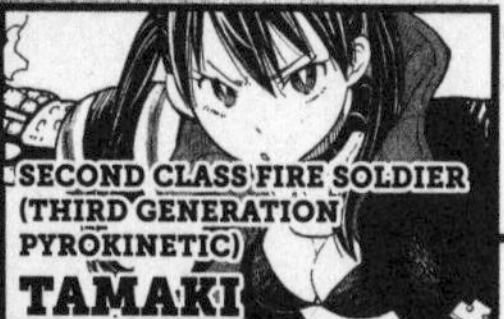

SECOND CLASS FIRE SOLDIER (THIRD GENERATION PYROKINETIC)

TAMAKI KOTATSU

Originally a rookie member of Company 1, she was caught up in the treasonous plot of her superior officer Hoshimiya, and is currently being disciplined under Company 8's watch. A tough girl with an unfortunate "lucky lecher lure" condition, she nevertheless has a pure heart.

HAS HIM ON HER MIND

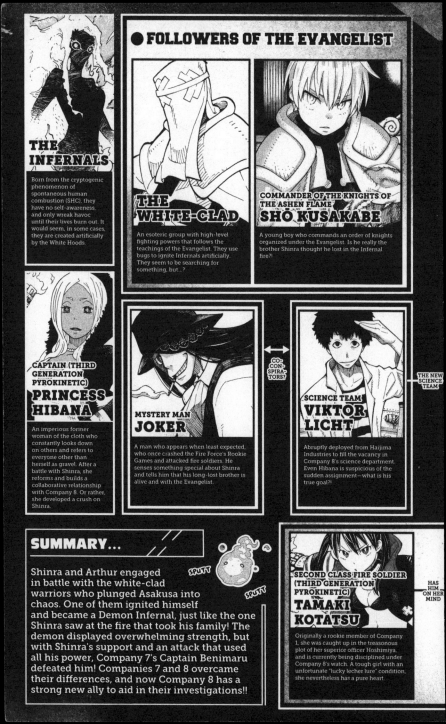

FIRE FORCE 07
CONTENTS

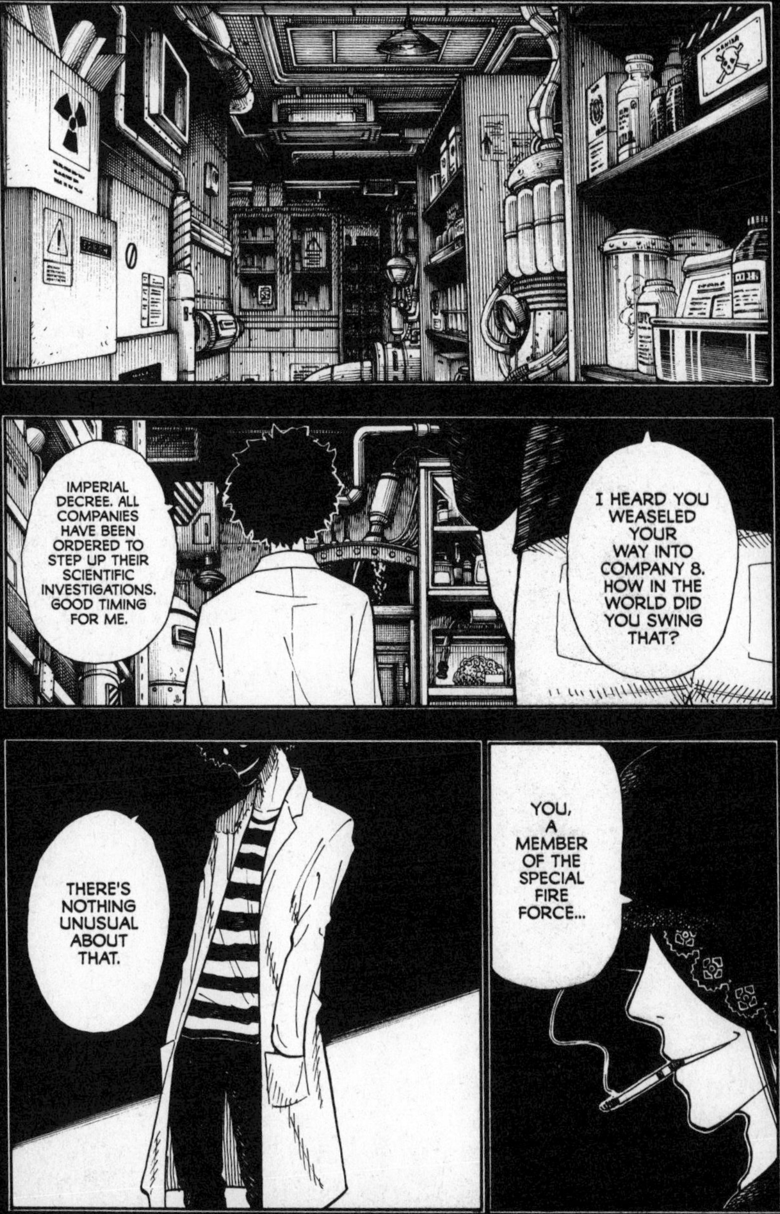
I HEARD YOU WEASELED YOUR WAY INTO COMPANY 8. HOW IN THE WORLD DID YOU SWING THAT?
IMPERIAL DECREE. ALL COMPANIES HAVE BEEN ORDERED TO STEP UP THEIR SCIENTIFIC INVESTIGATIONS. GOOD TIMING FOR ME.
YOU, A MEMBER OF THE SPECIAL FIRE FORCE...
THERE'S NOTHING UNUSUAL ABOUT THAT.

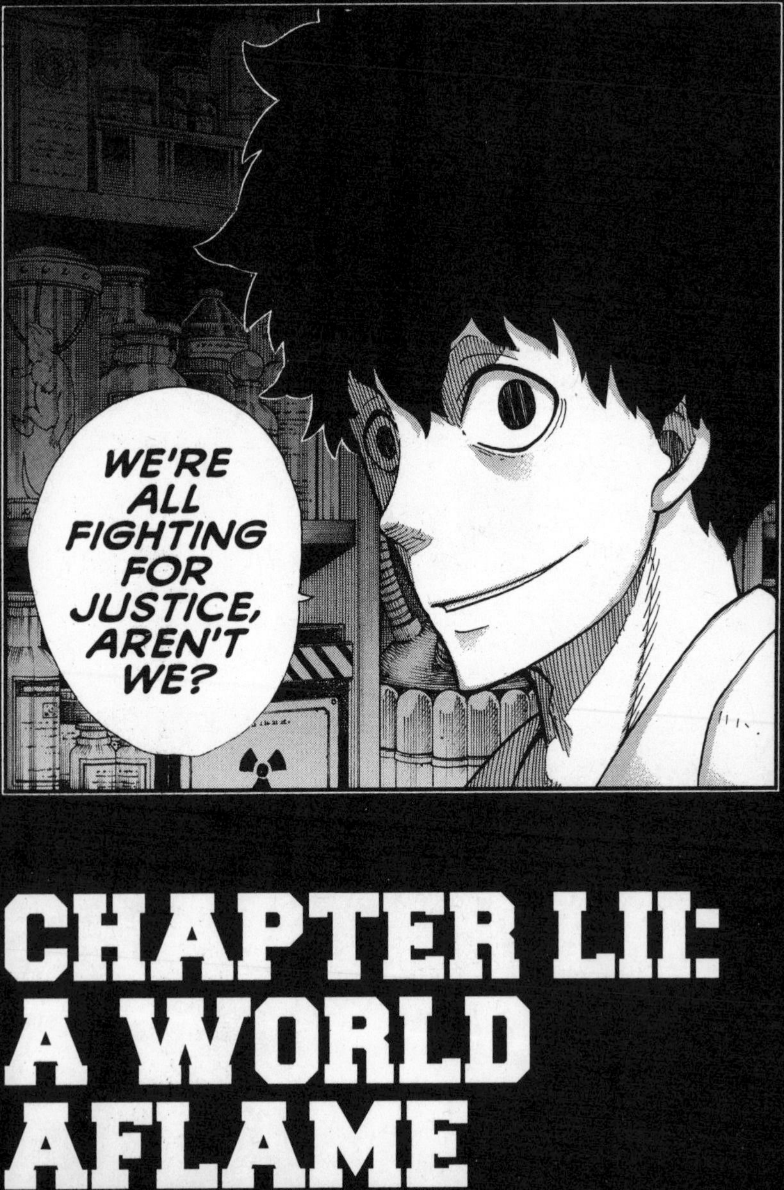
WE'RE ALL FIGHTING FOR JUSTICE, AREN'T WE?

CHAPTER LII: A WORLD AFLAME

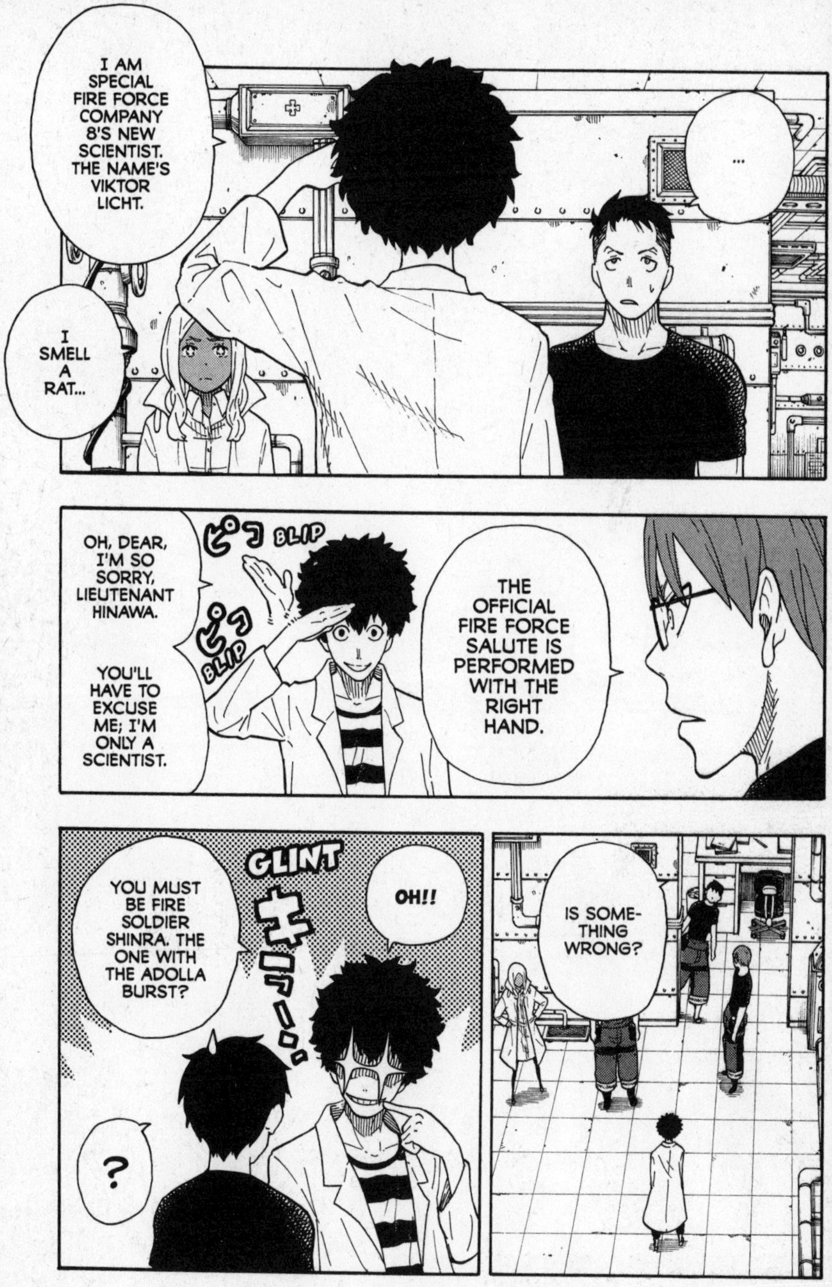
...
I AM SPECIAL FIRE FORCE COMPANY 8'S NEW SCIENTIST. THE NAME'S VIKTOR LICHT.
I SMELL A RAT...
THE OFFICIAL FIRE FORCE SALUTE IS PERFORMED WITH THE RIGHT HAND.
ピコ BLIP
ピコ BLIP
OH, DEAR, I'M SO SORRY, LIEUTENANT HINAWA.
YOU'LL HAVE TO EXCUSE ME; I'M ONLY A SCIENTIST.
IS SOME-THING WRONG?
OH!!
GLINT
キラーン
YOU MUST BE FIRE SOLDIER SHINRA. THE ONE WITH THE ADOLLA BURST?
?

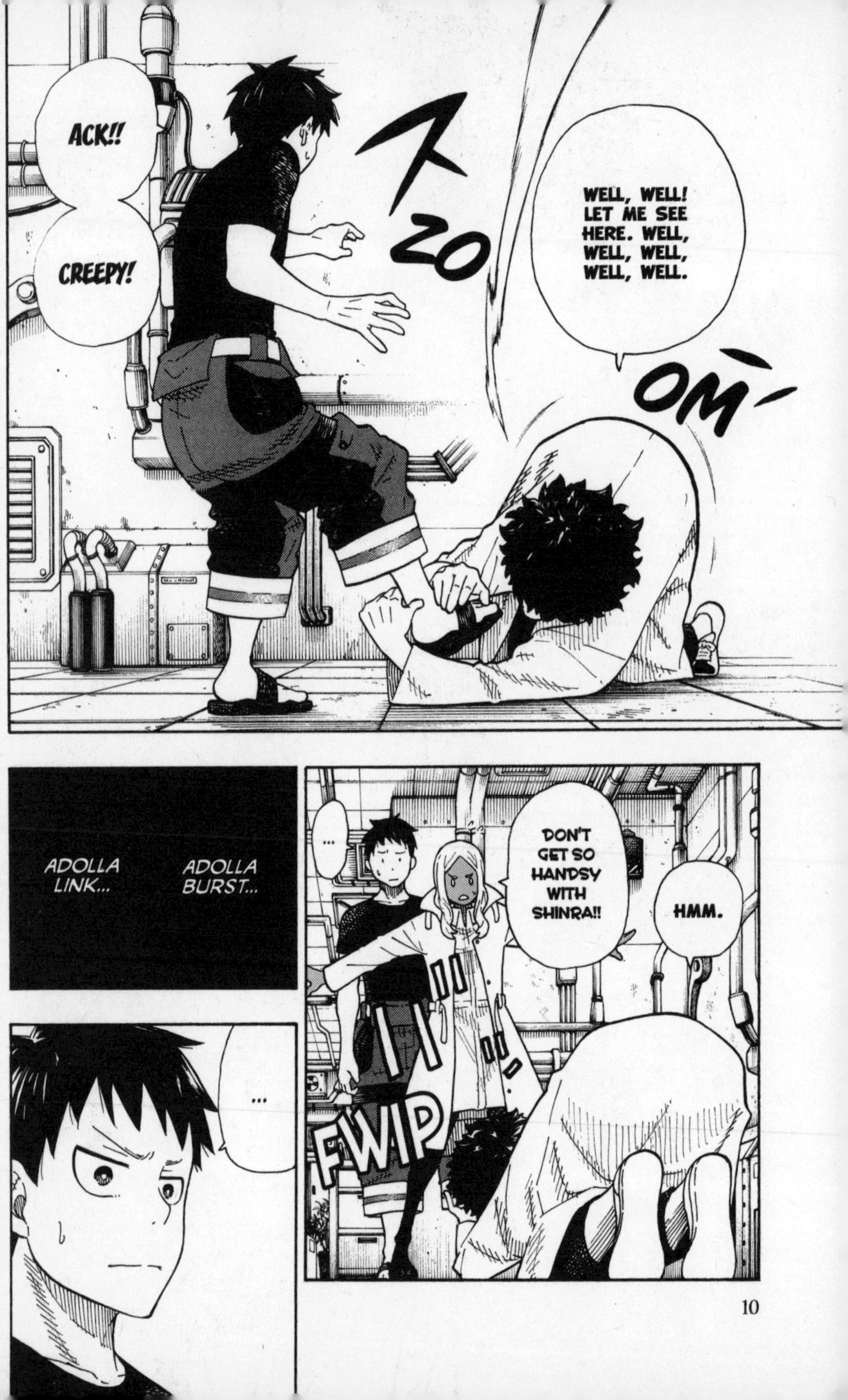

WELL, WELL! LET ME SEE HERE. WELL, WELL, WELL, WELL, WELL.
ZO
OM
ACK!!
CREEPY!
HMM.
DON'T GET SO HANDSY WITH SHINRA!!
...
FWIP
ADOLLA BURST...
ADOLLA LINK...
...

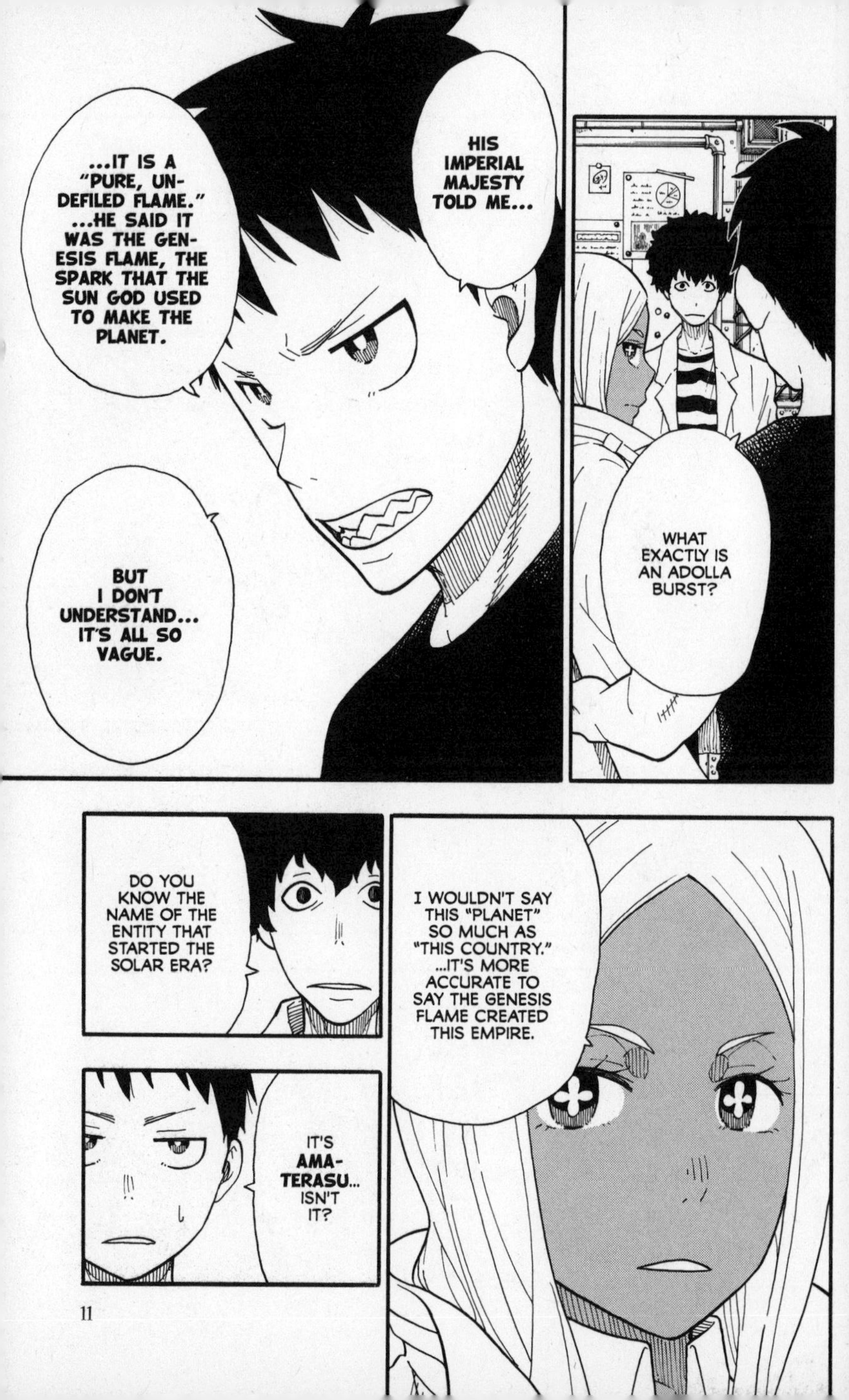
WHAT EXACTLY IS AN ADOLLA BURST?
HIS IMPERIAL MAJESTY TOLD ME...
...IT IS A "PURE, UN-DEFILED FLAME." ...HE SAID IT WAS THE GEN-ESIS FLAME, THE SPARK THAT THE SUN GOD USED TO MAKE THE PLANET.
BUT I DON'T UNDERSTAND... IT'S ALL SO VAGUE.
I WOULDN'T SAY THIS "PLANET" SO MUCH AS "THIS COUNTRY." ...IT'S MORE ACCURATE TO SAY THE GENESIS FLAME CREATED THIS EMPIRE.
DO YOU KNOW THE NAME OF THE ENTITY THAT STARTED THE SOLAR ERA?
IT'S AMA-TERASU... ISN'T IT?

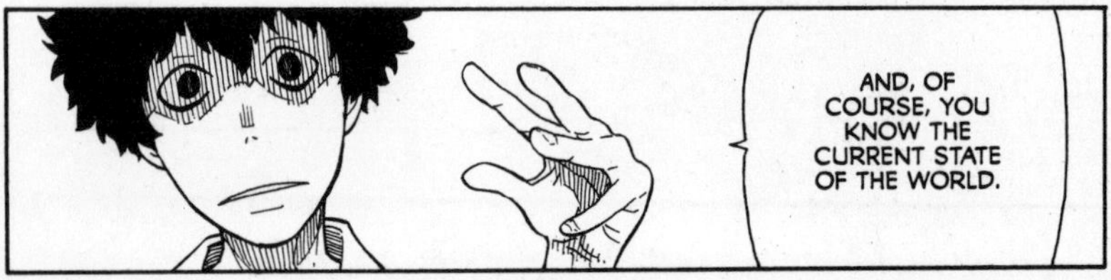
AND, OF COURSE, YOU KNOW THE CURRENT STATE OF THE WORLD.

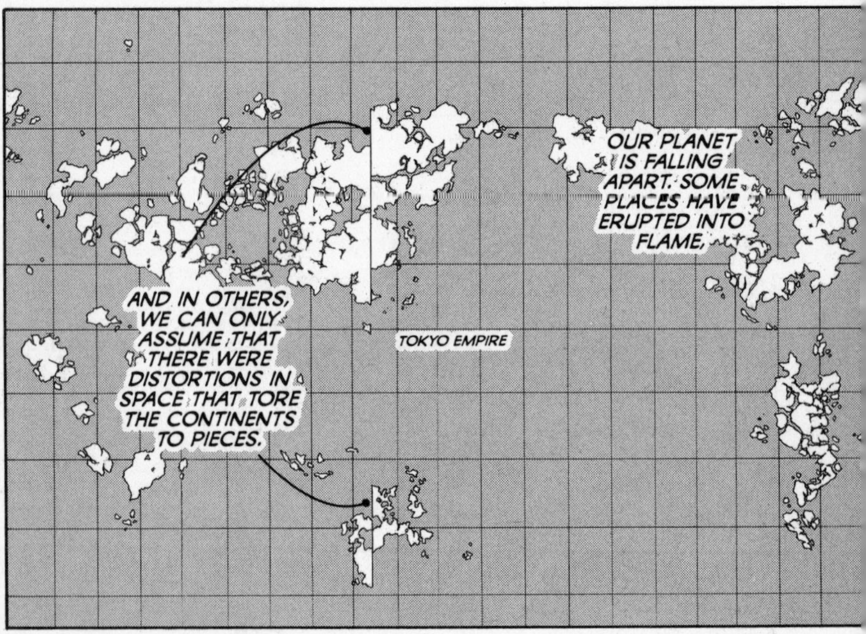
OUR PLANET IS FALLING APART. SOME PLACES HAVE ERUPTED INTO FLAME,
AND IN OTHERS, WE CAN ONLY ASSUME THAT THERE WERE DISTORTIONS IN SPACE THAT TORE THE CONTINENTS TO PIECES.
TOKYO EMPIRE

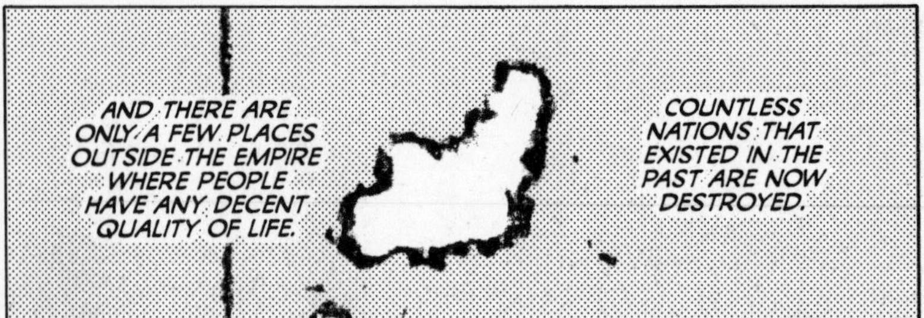
COUNTLESS NATIONS THAT EXISTED IN THE PAST ARE NOW DESTROYED.
AND THERE ARE ONLY A FEW PLACES OUTSIDE THE EMPIRE WHERE PEOPLE HAVE ANY DECENT QUALITY OF LIFE.

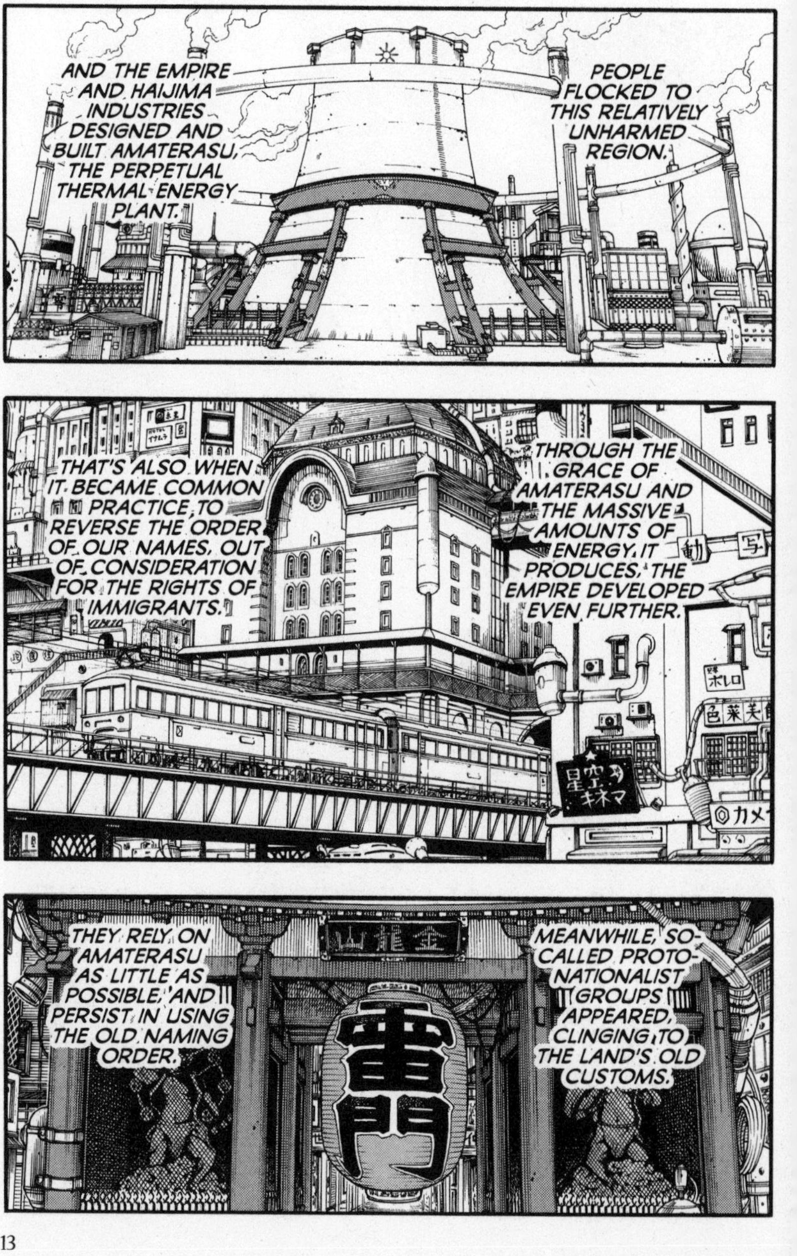
PEOPLE FLOCKED TO THIS RELATIVELY UNHARMED REGION.
AND THE EMPIRE AND HAIJIMA INDUSTRIES DESIGNED AND BUILT AMATERASU, THE PERPETUAL THERMAL ENERGY PLANT.
THROUGH THE GRACE OF AMATERASU AND THE MASSIVE AMOUNTS OF ENERGY IT PRODUCES, THE EMPIRE DEVELOPED EVEN FURTHER.
THAT'S ALSO WHEN IT BECAME COMMON PRACTICE TO REVERSE THE ORDER OF OUR NAMES, OUT OF CONSIDERATION FOR THE RIGHTS OF IMMIGRANTS.
星空キネマ
MEANWHILE, SO-CALLED PROTO-NATIONALIST GROUPS APPEARED, CLINGING TO THE LAND'S OLD CUSTOMS.
THEY RELY ON AMATERASU AS LITTLE AS POSSIBLE, AND PERSIST IN USING THE OLD NAMING ORDER.
雷門

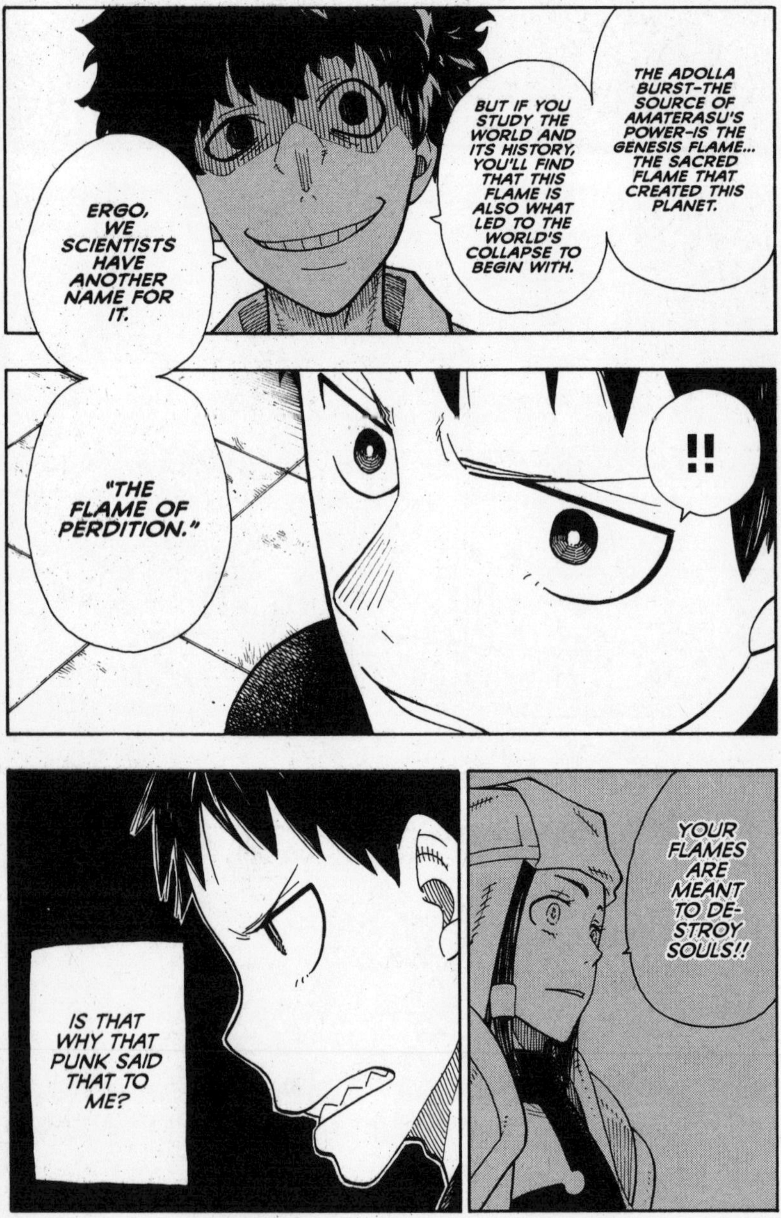
THE ADOLLA BURST–THE SOURCE OF AMATERASU'S POWER–IS THE GENESIS FLAME... THE SACRED FLAME THAT CREATED THIS PLANET.
BUT IF YOU STUDY THE WORLD AND ITS HISTORY, YOU'LL FIND THAT THIS FLAME IS ALSO WHAT LED TO THE WORLD'S COLLAPSE TO BEGIN WITH.
ERGO, WE SCIENTISTS HAVE ANOTHER NAME FOR IT.
"THE FLAME OF PERDITION."
!!
YOUR FLAMES ARE MEANT TO DE-STROY SOULS!!
IS THAT WHY THAT PUNK SAID THAT TO ME?

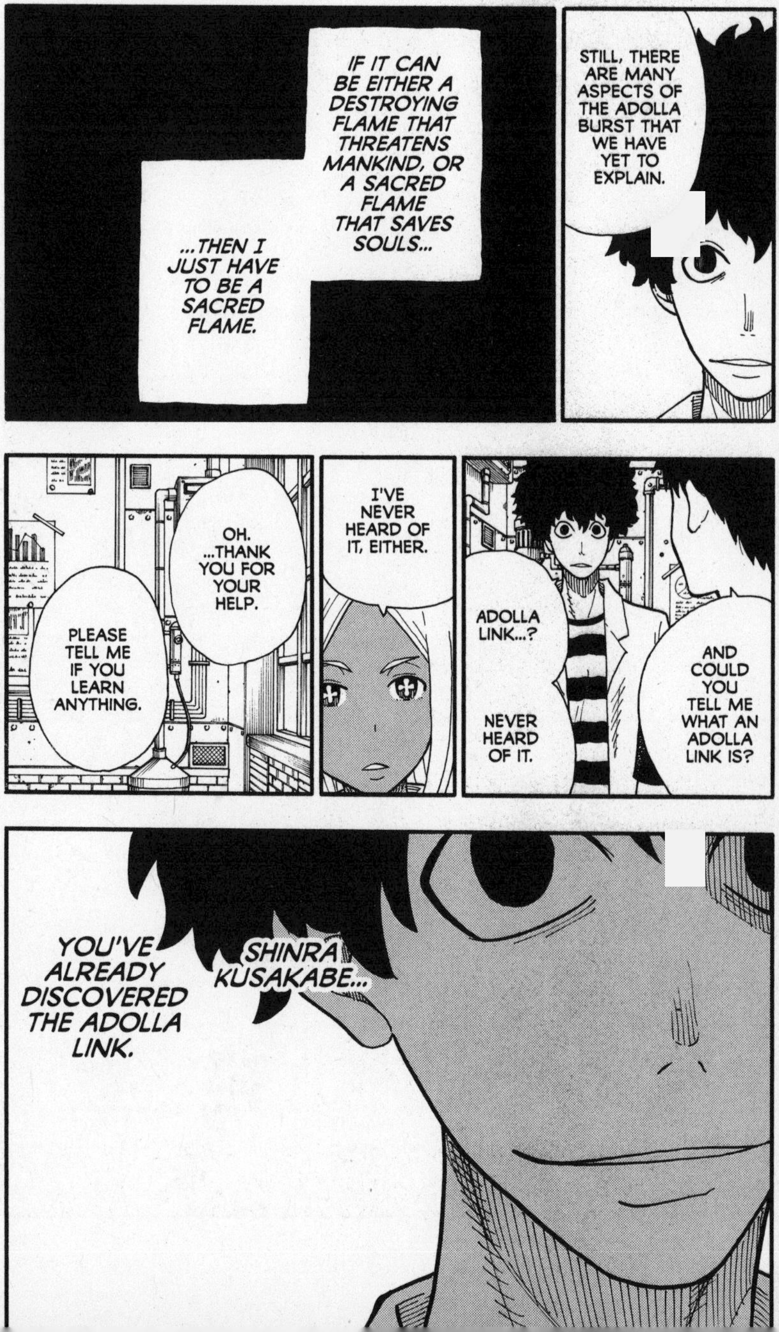
STILL, THERE ARE MANY ASPECTS OF THE ADOLLA BURST THAT WE HAVE YET TO EXPLAIN.
IF IT CAN BE EITHER A DESTROYING FLAME THAT THREATENS MANKIND, OR A SACRED FLAME THAT SAVES SOULS...
...THEN I JUST HAVE TO BE A SACRED FLAME.
AND COULD YOU TELL ME WHAT AN ADOLLA LINK IS?
ADOLLA LINK...?
NEVER HEARD OF IT.
I'VE NEVER HEARD OF IT, EITHER.
OH. ...THANK YOU FOR YOUR HELP.
PLEASE TELL ME IF YOU LEARN ANYTHING.
SHINRA KUSAKABE...
YOU'VE ALREADY DISCOVERED THE ADOLLA LINK.

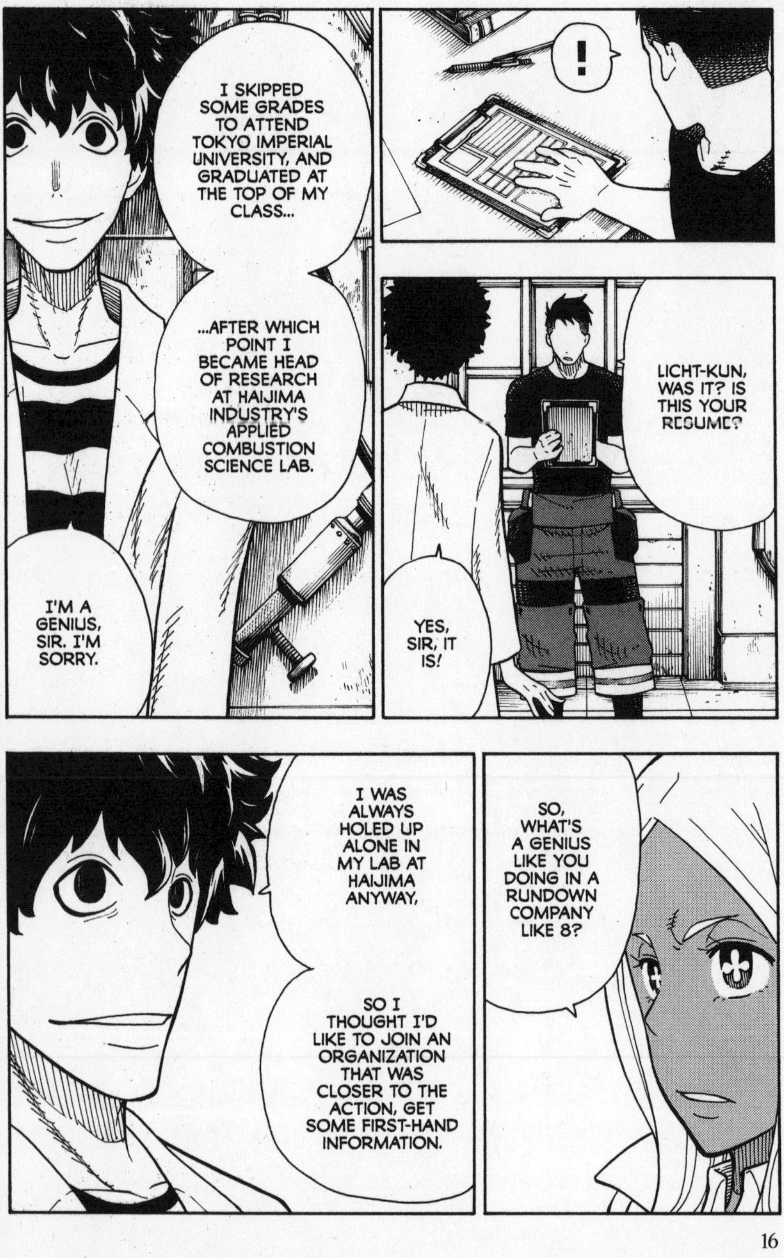
!
LICHT-KUN, WAS IT? IS THIS YOUR RESUME?
YES, SIR, IT IS!
I SKIPPED SOME GRADES TO ATTEND TOKYO IMPERIAL UNIVERSITY, AND GRADUATED AT THE TOP OF MY CLASS...
...AFTER WHICH POINT I BECAME HEAD OF RESEARCH AT HAIJIMA INDUSTRY'S APPLIED COMBUSTION SCIENCE LAB.
I'M A GENIUS, SIR. I'M SORRY.
SO, WHAT'S A GENIUS LIKE YOU DOING IN A RUNDOWN COMPANY LIKE 8?
I WAS ALWAYS HOLED UP ALONE IN MY LAB AT HAIJIMA ANYWAY,
SO I THOUGHT I'D LIKE TO JOIN AN ORGANIZATION THAT WAS CLOSER TO THE ACTION, GET SOME FIRST-HAND INFORMATION.

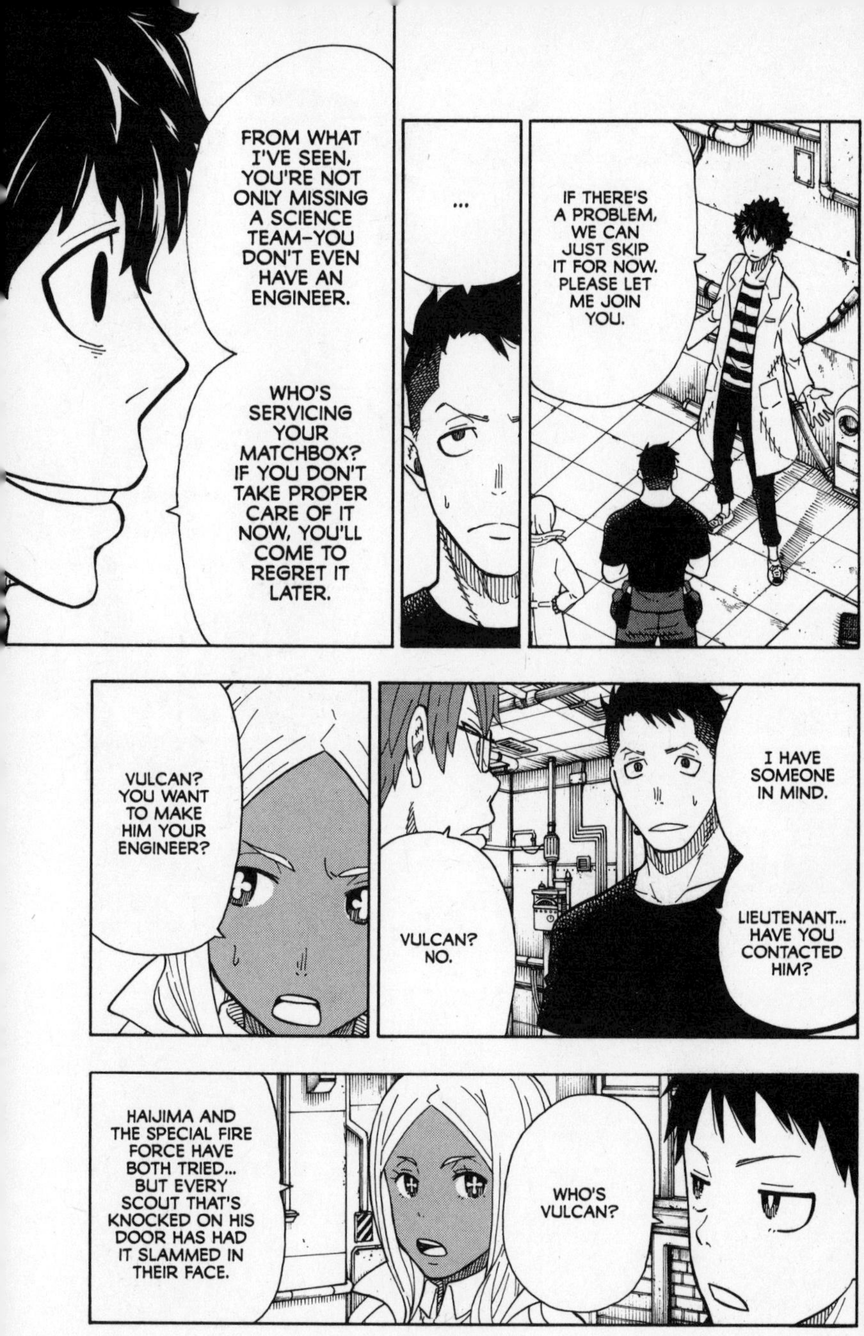
IF THERE'S A PROBLEM, WE CAN JUST SKIP IT FOR NOW. PLEASE LET ME JOIN YOU.
...
FROM WHAT I'VE SEEN, YOU'RE NOT ONLY MISSING A SCIENCE TEAM–YOU DON'T EVEN HAVE AN ENGINEER.
WHO'S SERVICING YOUR MATCHBOX? IF YOU DON'T TAKE PROPER CARE OF IT NOW, YOU'LL COME TO REGRET IT LATER.
I HAVE SOMEONE IN MIND.
LIEUTENANT... HAVE YOU CONTACTED HIM?
VULCAN? NO.
VULCAN? YOU WANT TO MAKE HIM YOUR ENGINEER?
WHO'S VULCAN?
HAIJIMA AND THE SPECIAL FIRE FORCE HAVE BOTH TRIED... BUT EVERY SCOUT THAT'S KNOCKED ON HIS DOOR HAS HAD IT SLAMMED IN THEIR FACE.

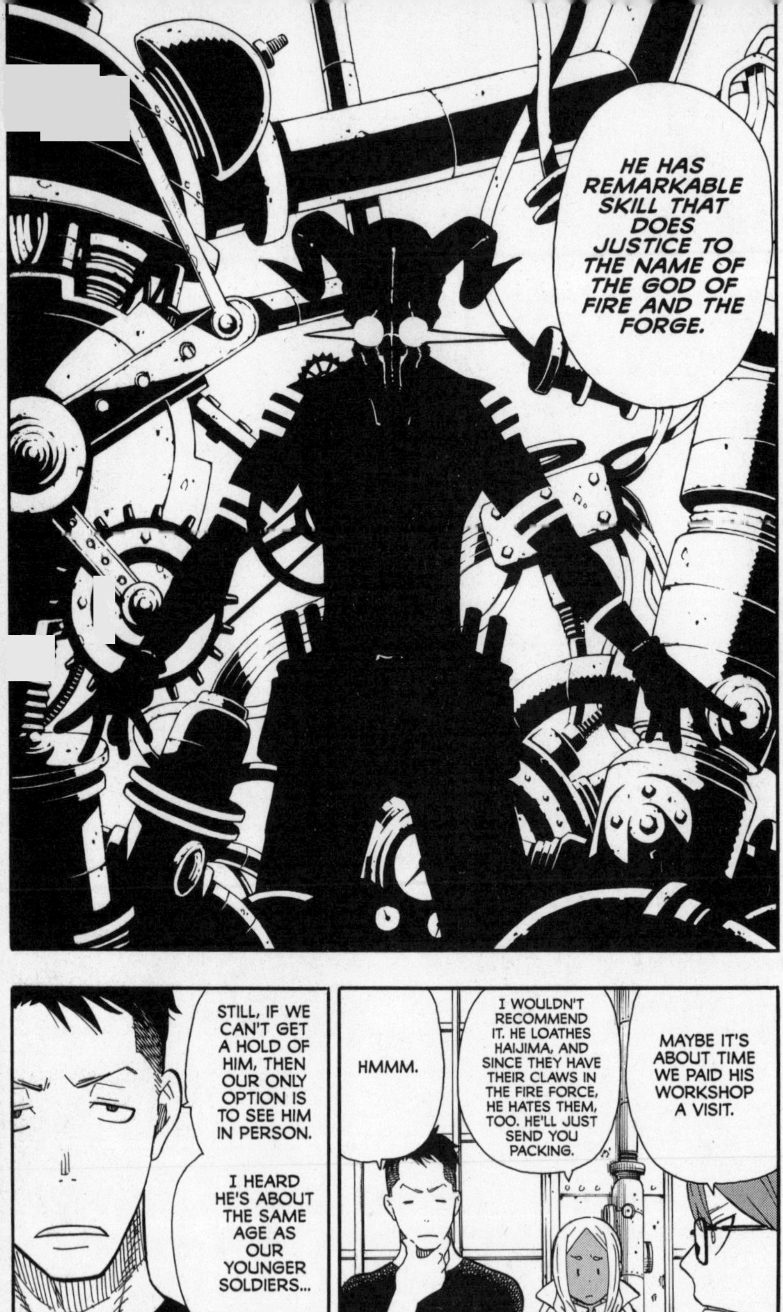
HE HAS REMARKABLE SKILL THAT DOES JUSTICE TO THE NAME OF THE GOD OF FIRE AND THE FORGE.
MAYBE IT'S ABOUT TIME WE PAID HIS WORKSHOP A VISIT.
I WOULDN'T RECOMMEND IT. HE LOATHES HAIJIMA, AND SINCE THEY HAVE THEIR CLAWS IN THE FIRE FORCE, HE HATES THEM, TOO. HE'LL JUST SEND YOU PACKING.
HMMM.
STILL, IF WE CAN'T GET A HOLD OF HIM, THEN OUR ONLY OPTION IS TO SEE HIM IN PERSON.
I HEARD HE'S ABOUT THE SAME AGE AS OUR YOUNGER SOLDIERS...

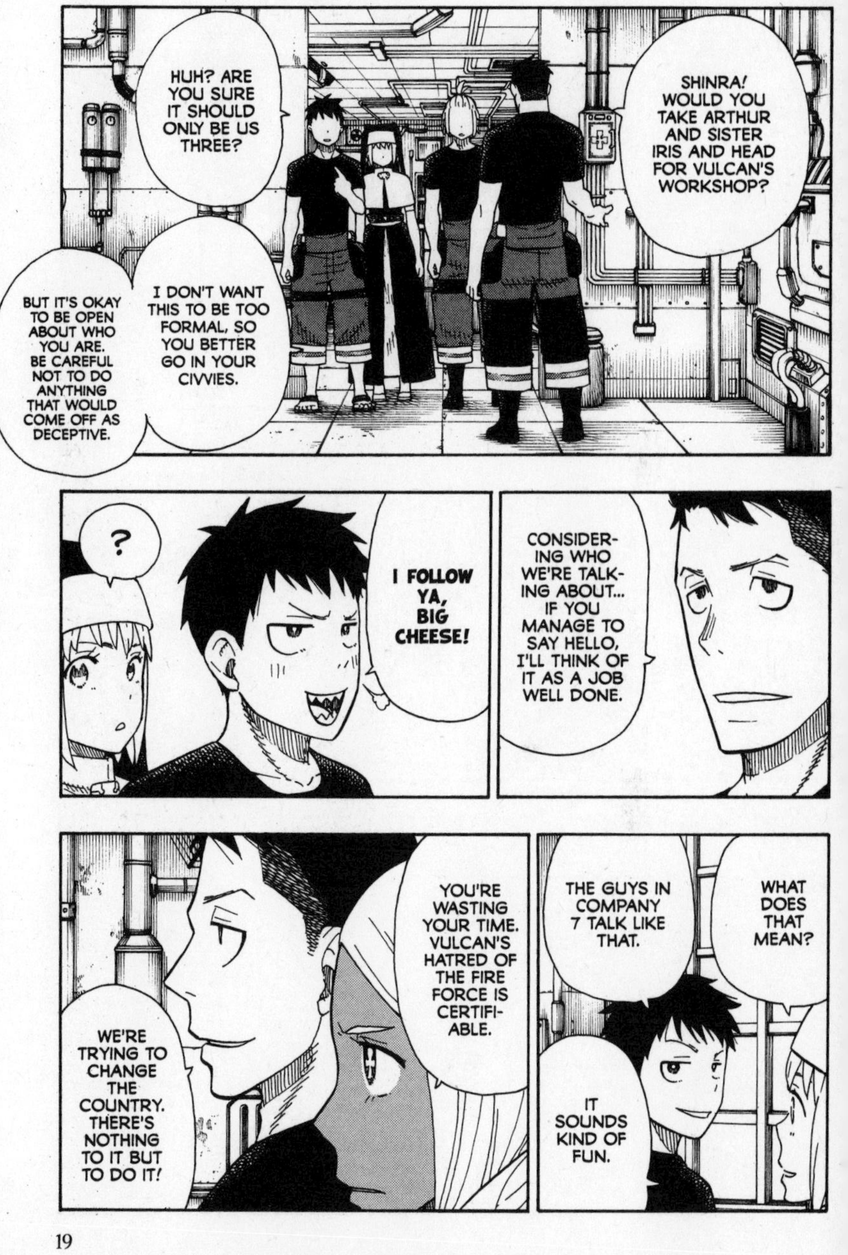
SHINRA! WOULD YOU TAKE ARTHUR AND SISTER IRIS AND HEAD FOR VULCAN'S WORKSHOP?
HUH? ARE YOU SURE IT SHOULD ONLY BE US THREE?
I DON'T WANT THIS TO BE TOO FORMAL, SO YOU BETTER GO IN YOUR CIVVIES.
BUT IT'S OKAY TO BE OPEN ABOUT WHO YOU ARE. BE CAREFUL NOT TO DO ANYTHING THAT WOULD COME OFF AS DECEPTIVE.
CONSIDER-ING WHO WE'RE TALK-ING ABOUT... IF YOU MANAGE TO SAY HELLO, I'LL THINK OF IT AS A JOB WELL DONE.
I FOLLOW YA, BIG CHEESE!
?
WHAT DOES THAT MEAN?
THE GUYS IN COMPANY 7 TALK LIKE THAT.
IT SOUNDS KIND OF FUN.
YOU'RE WASTING YOUR TIME. VULCAN'S HATRED OF THE FIRE FORCE IS CERTIFI-ABLE.
WE'RE TRYING TO CHANGE THE COUNTRY. THERE'S NOTHING TO IT BUT TO DO IT!

WHILE OTHERS TRY TO WIN HIM WITH MONEY AND STATUS, HE TRIES TO CONVINCE HIM USING CHILDREN... COMPANY 8 DOES MOVE IN THE MOST INTERESTING WAYS.

WELL THEN, I GUESS IT'S TIME I SHOWED YOU TO YOUR ROOM. DO YOU HAVE ANY LUGGAGE? IF YOU HAVEN'T PACKED YET, I CAN ARRANGE TO HAVE YOUR THINGS DELIVERED...

WE MADE ALL THE ARRANGEMENTS ON OUR END. HAIJIMA WILL BE SENDING ME ALL THE EQUIPMENT I NEED SHORTLY.

WE'LL SEE IF COMPANY 8 WILL BE USEFUL TO JOKER AND MYSELF...IN ACHIEVING OUR GOAL.

20

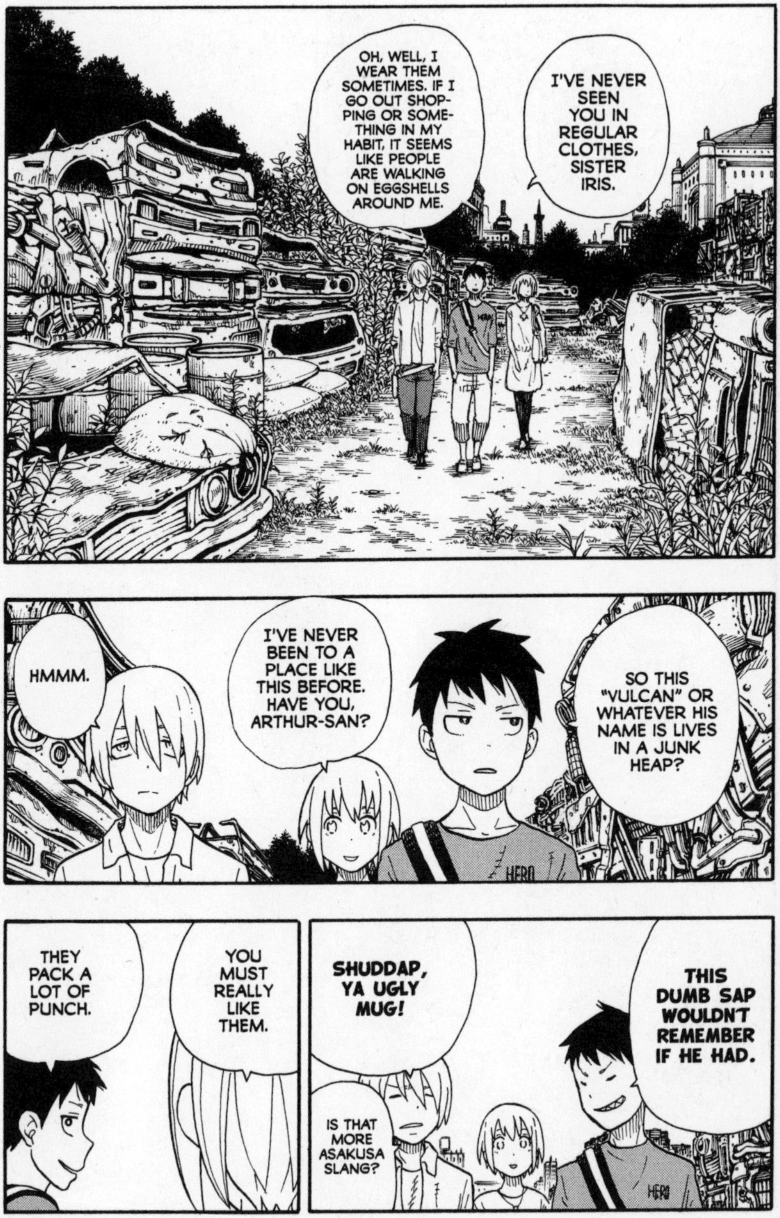
I'VE NEVER SEEN YOU IN REGULAR CLOTHES, SISTER IRIS.
OH, WELL, I WEAR THEM SOMETIMES. IF I GO OUT SHOP-PING OR SOME-THING IN MY HABIT, IT SEEMS LIKE PEOPLE ARE WALKING ON EGGSHELLS AROUND ME.
SO THIS "VULCAN" OR WHATEVER HIS NAME IS LIVES IN A JUNK HEAP?
I'VE NEVER BEEN TO A PLACE LIKE THIS BEFORE. HAVE YOU, ARTHUR-SAN?
HMMM.
THIS DUMB SAP WOULDN'T REMEMBER IF HE HAD.
SHUDDAP, YA UGLY MUG!
IS THAT MORE ASAKUSA SLANG?
YOU MUST REALLY LIKE THEM.
THEY PACK A LOT OF PUNCH.

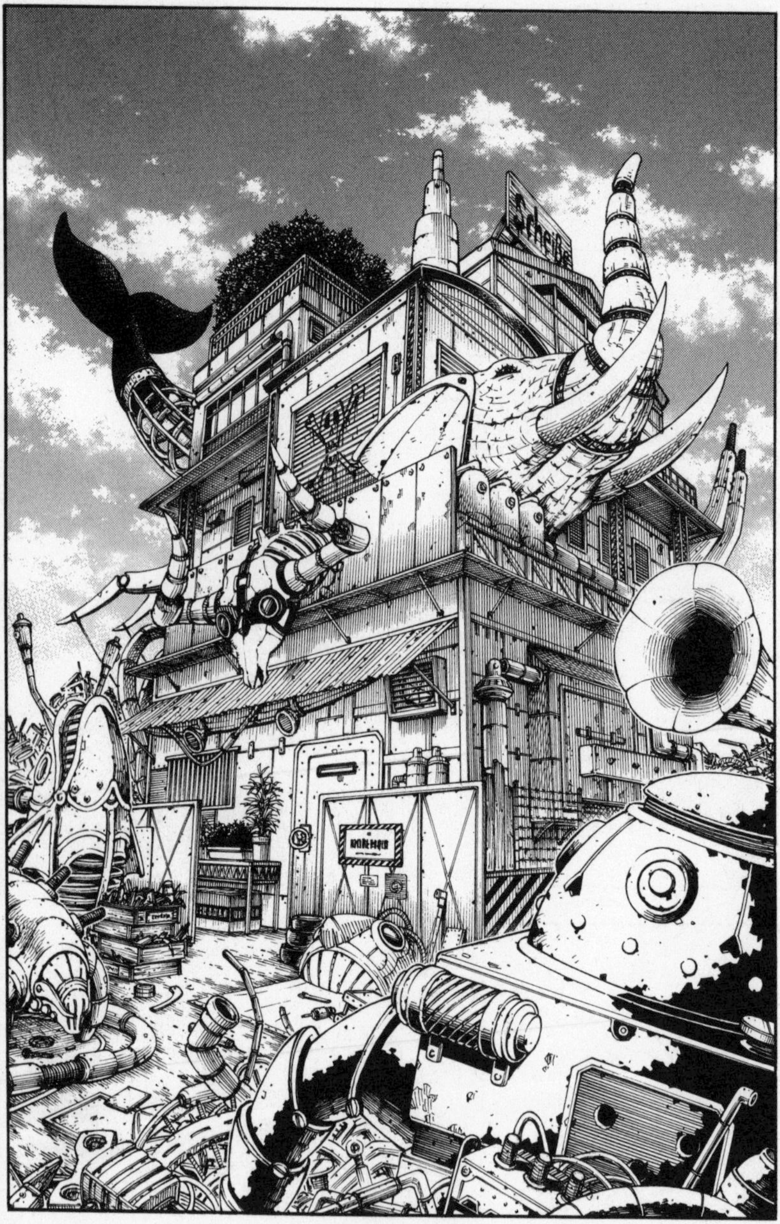
Scheiße

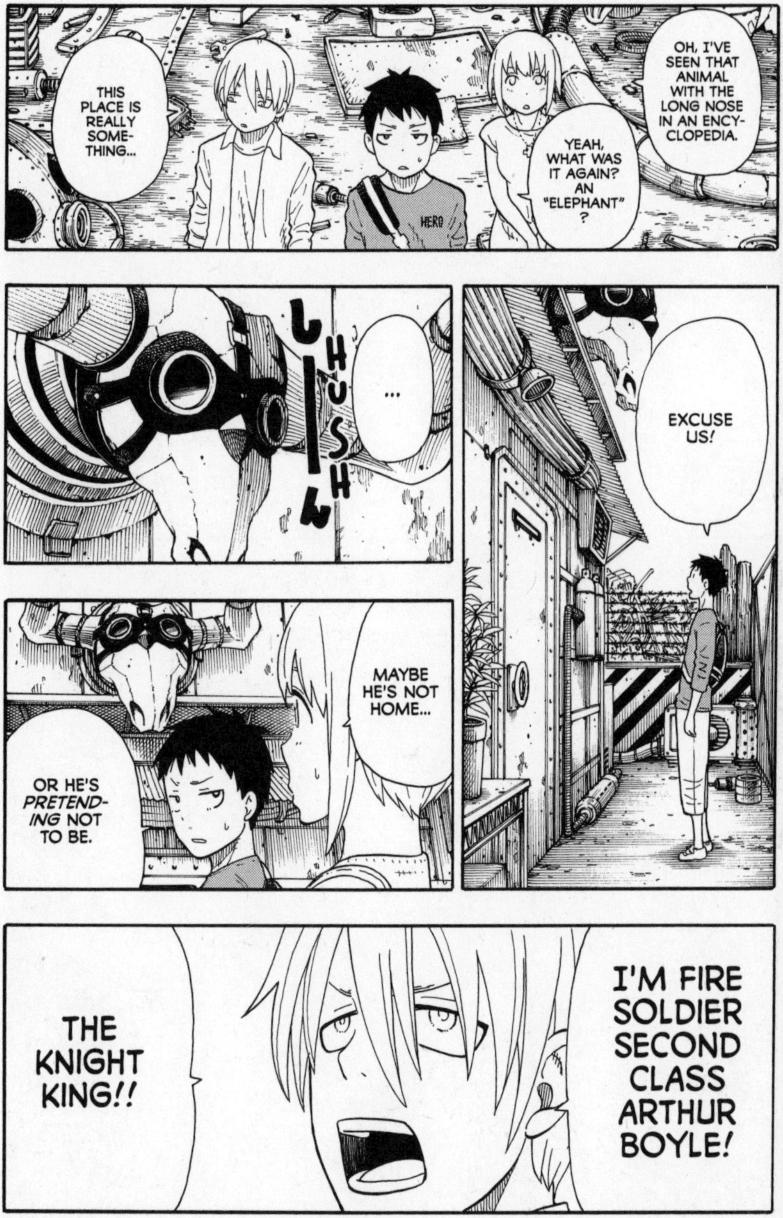
OH, I'VE SEEN THAT ANIMAL WITH THE LONG NOSE IN AN ENCYCLOPEDIA.
YEAH, WHAT WAS IT AGAIN? AN "ELEPHANT"?
THIS PLACE IS REALLY SOMETHING...
EXCUSE US!
...
HUSH
MAYBE HE'S NOT HOME...
OR HE'S *PRETENDING* NOT TO BE.
I'M FIRE SOLDIER SECOND CLASS ARTHUR BOYLE!
THE KNIGHT KING!!

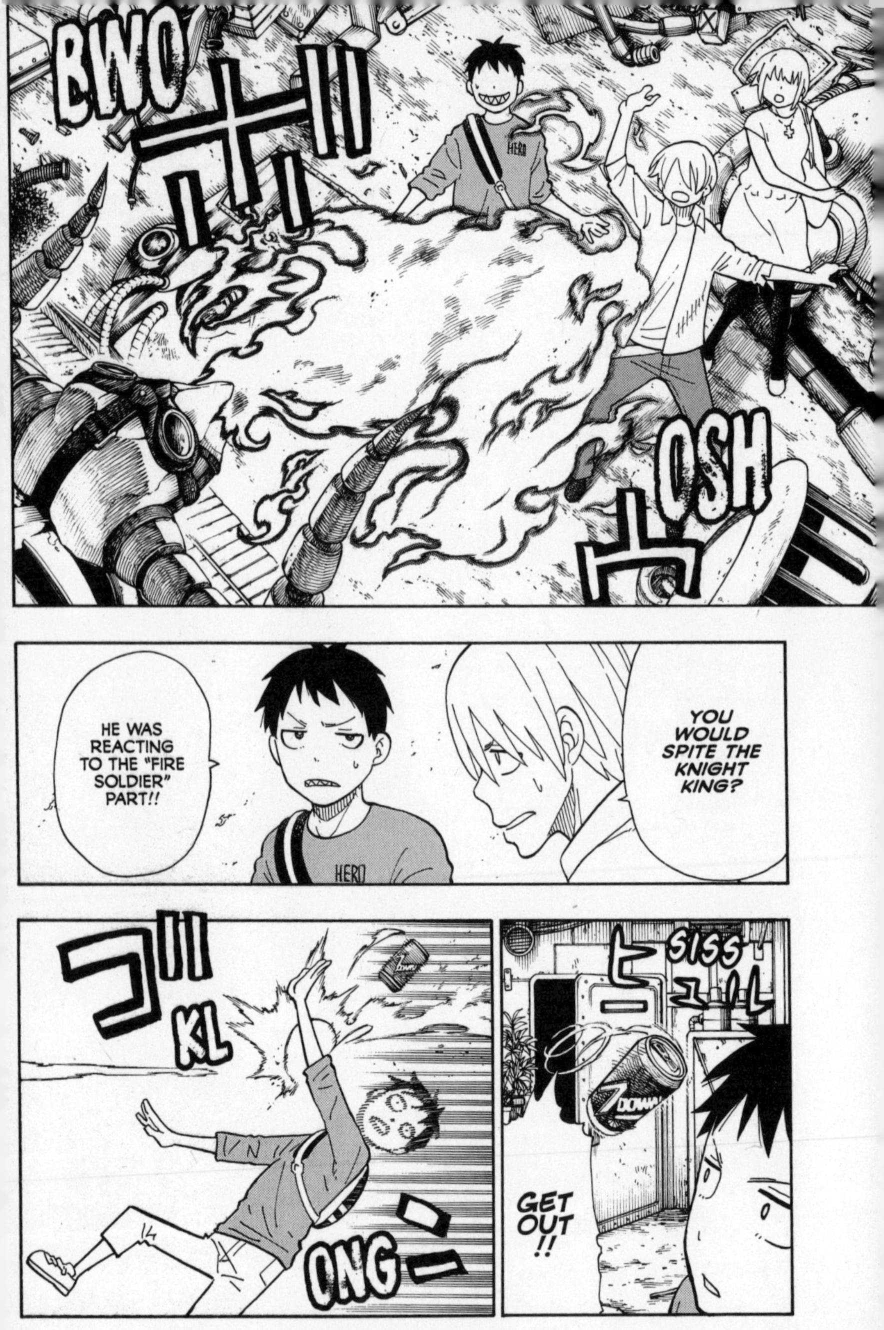
BWO
OSH
YOU WOULD SPITE THE KNIGHT KING?
HE WAS REACTING TO THE "FIRE SOLDIER" PART!!
SISS
GET OUT!!
KL
ONG

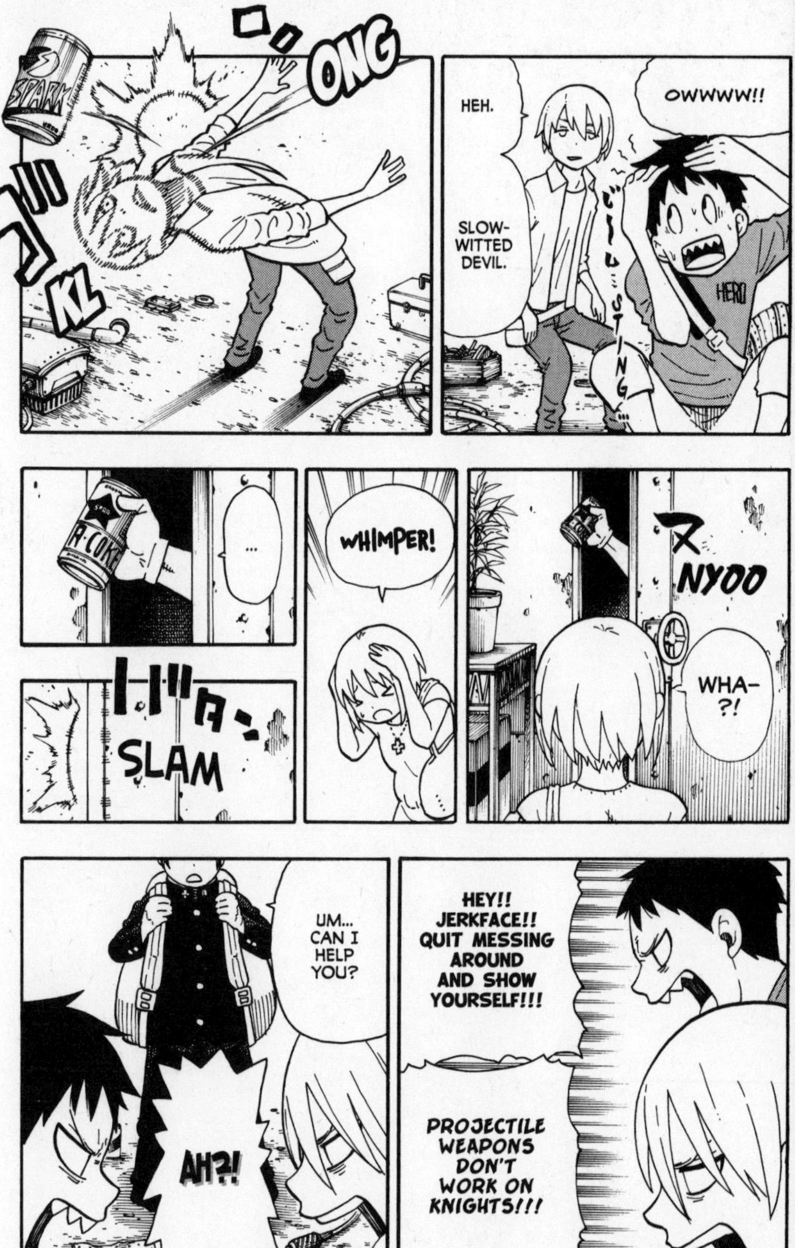
OWWWW!!
STING...
HEH.
SLOW-WITTED DEVIL.
ONG
KL
NYOO
WHA-?!
WHIMPER!
...
SLAM
HEY!! JERKFACE!! QUIT MESSING AROUND AND SHOW YOURSELF!!!
PROJECTILE WEAPONS DON'T WORK ON KNIGHTS!!!
UM... CAN I HELP YOU?
AH?!

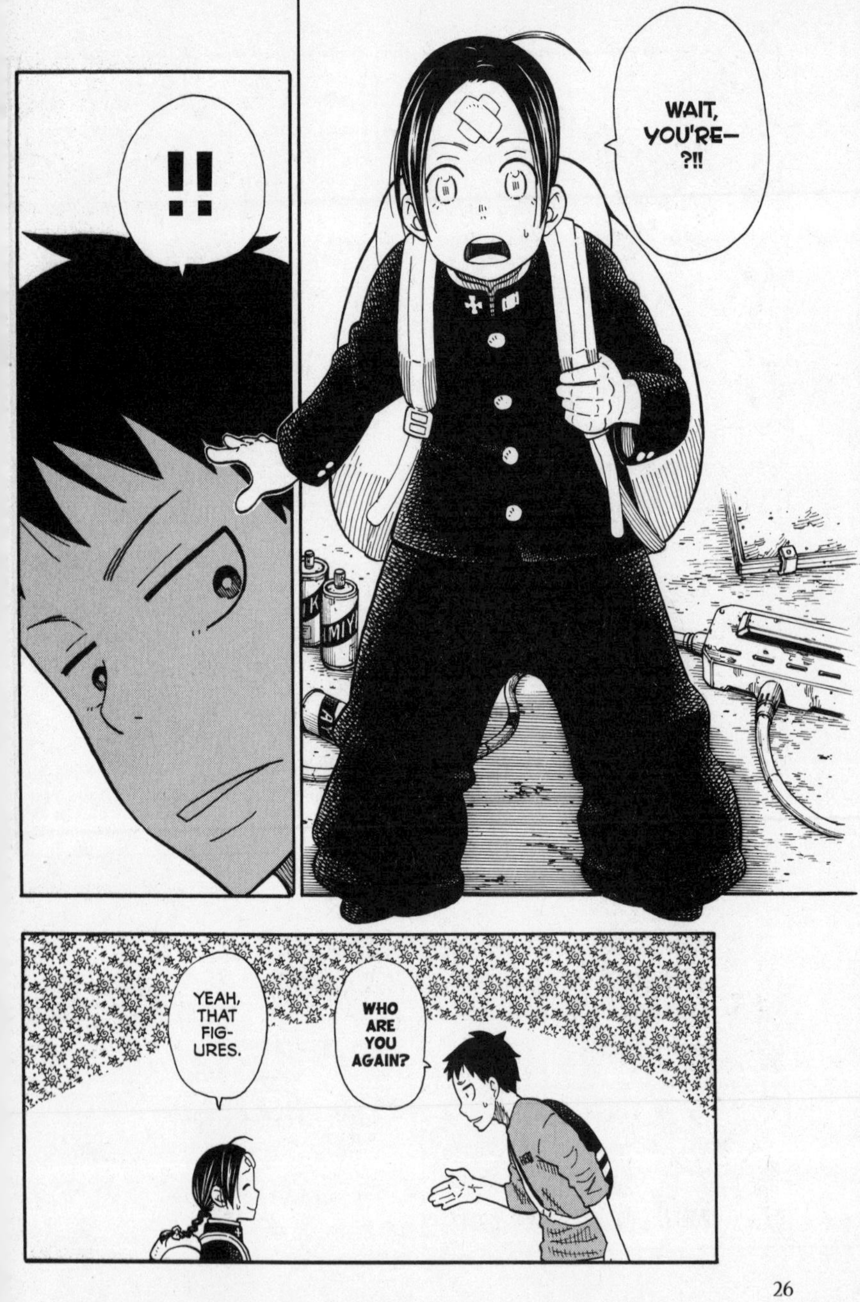
WAIT, YOU'RE—?!!
!!
WHO ARE YOU AGAIN?
YEAH, THAT FIG-URES.

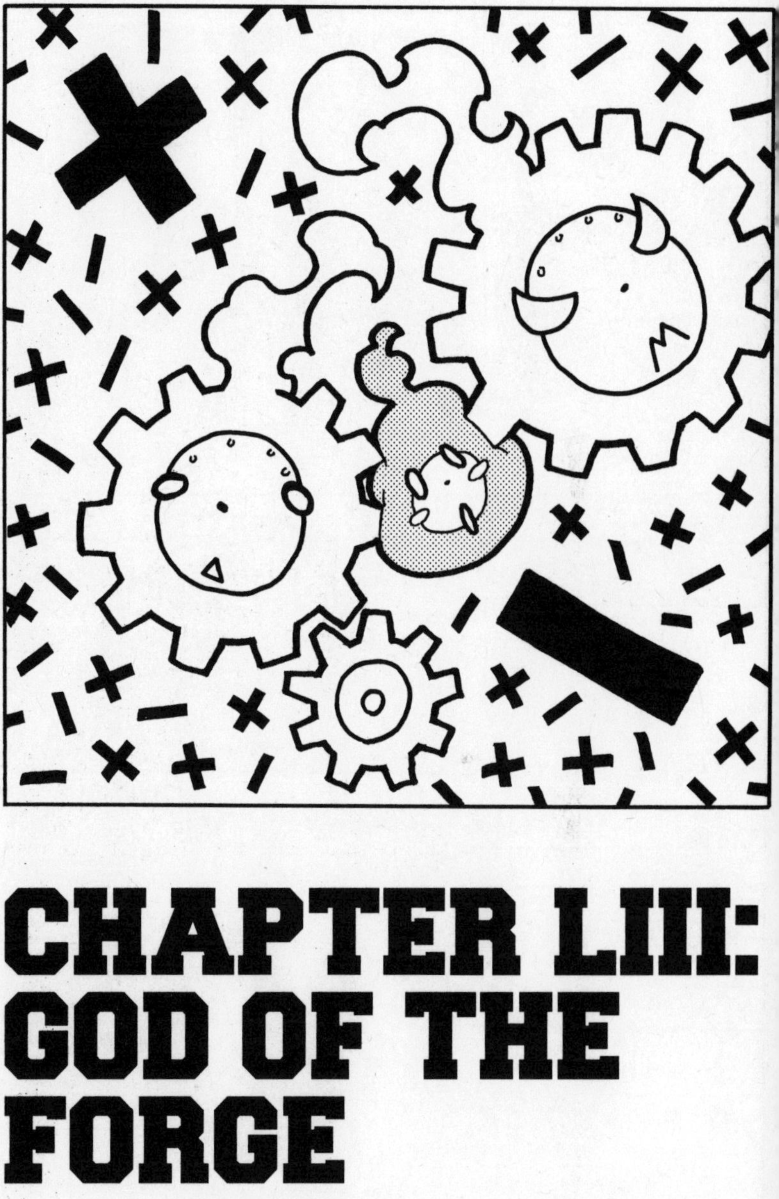

CHAPTER LIII: GOD OF THE FORGE

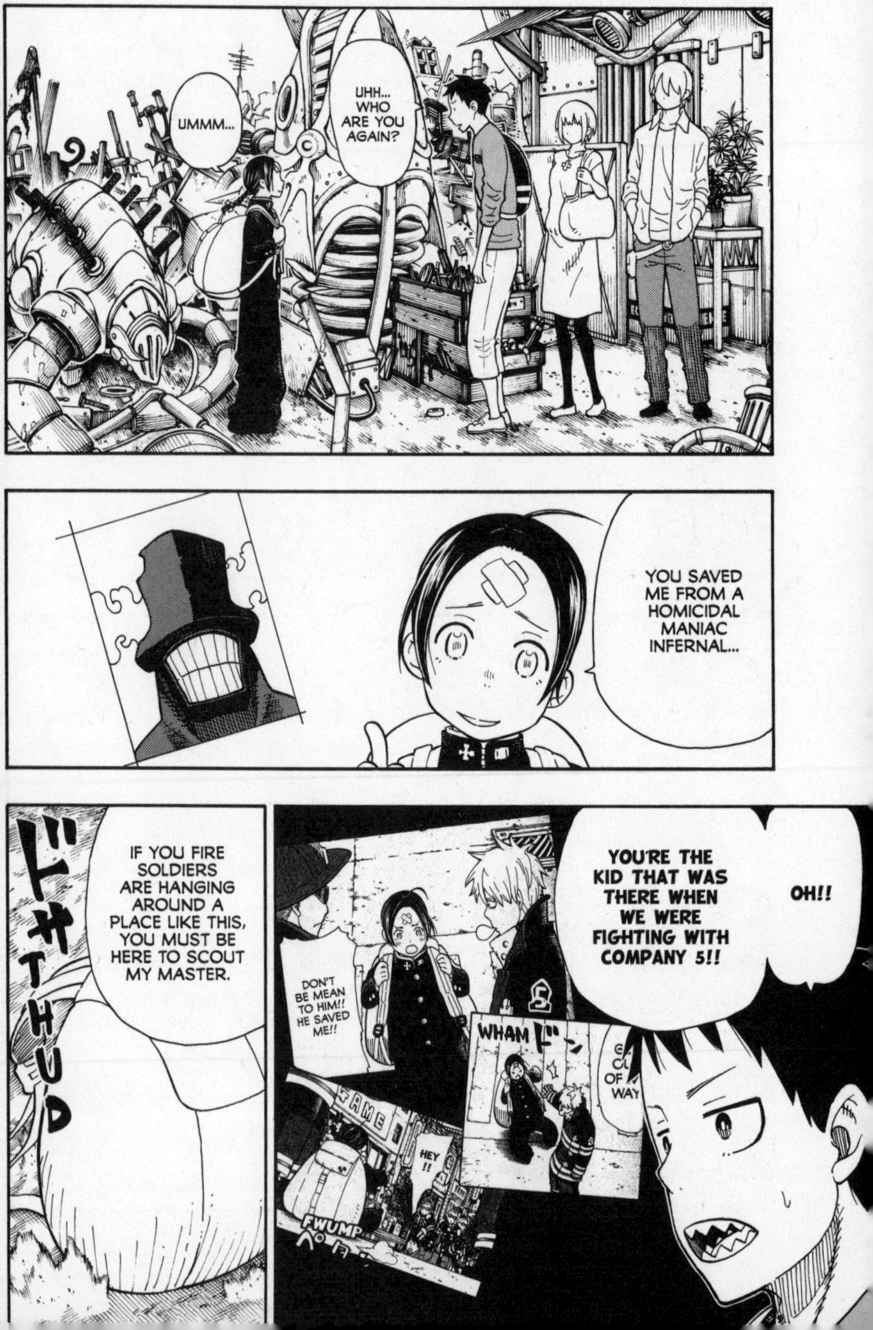
UHH... WHO ARE YOU AGAIN?
UMMM...
YOU SAVED ME FROM A HOMICIDAL MANIAC INFERNAL...
OH!!
YOU'RE THE KID THAT WAS THERE WHEN WE WERE FIGHTING WITH COMPANY 5!!
WHAM
HEY !!
DON'T BE MEAN TO HIM!! HE SAVED ME!!
FWUMP
IF YOU FIRE SOLDIERS ARE HANGING AROUND A PLACE LIKE THIS, YOU MUST BE HERE TO SCOUT MY MASTER.
THUD

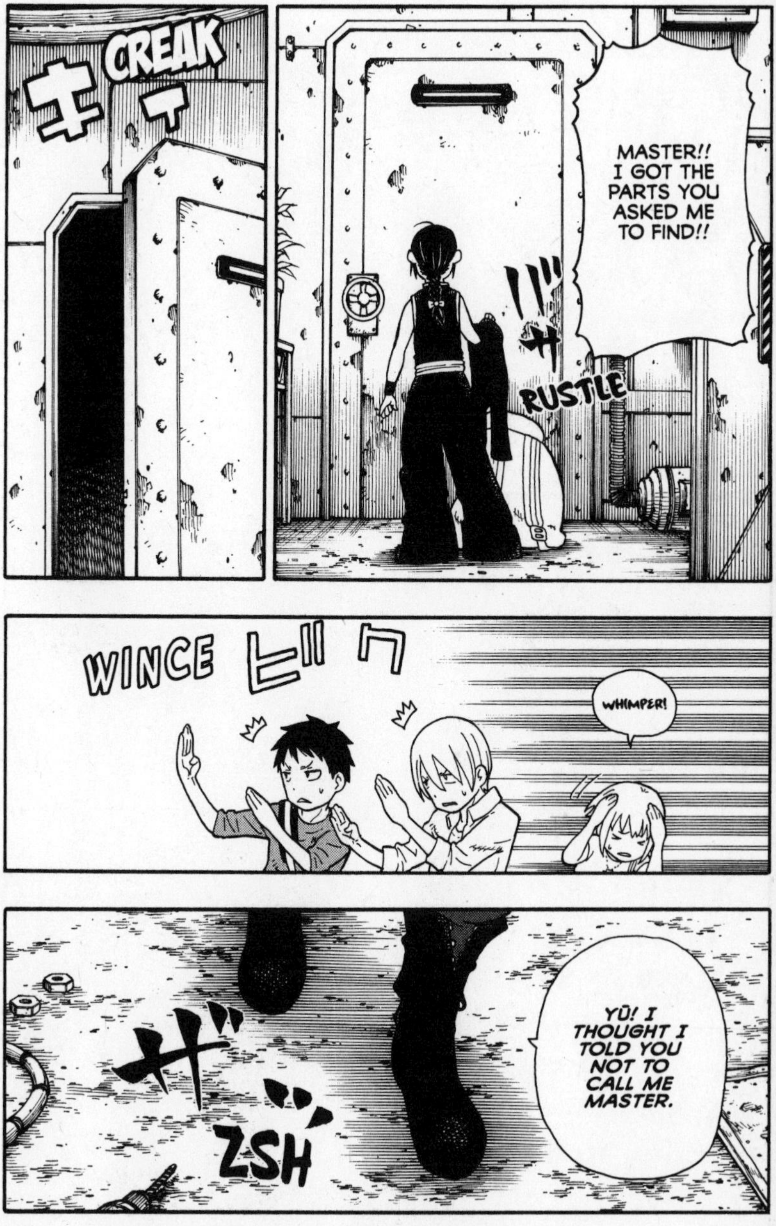
MASTER!! I GOT THE PARTS YOU ASKED ME TO FIND!!
RUSTLE
CREAK
WINCE
WHIMPER!
YŪ! I THOUGHT I TOLD YOU NOT TO CALL ME MASTER.
ZSH

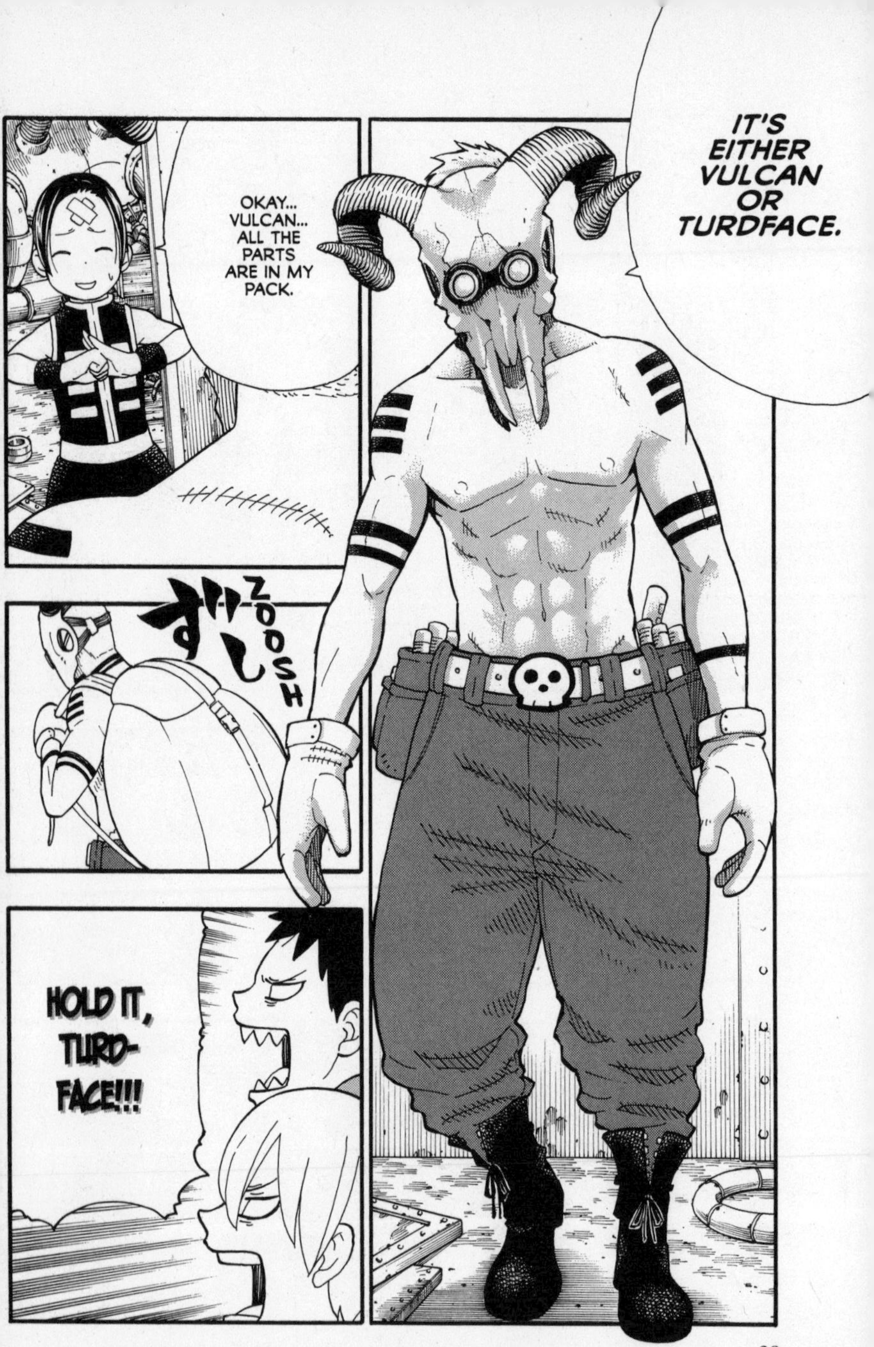
IT'S EITHER VULCAN OR TURDFACE.
OKAY... VULCAN... ALL THE PARTS ARE IN MY PACK.
ZOOSH
HOLD IT, TURD-FACE!!!

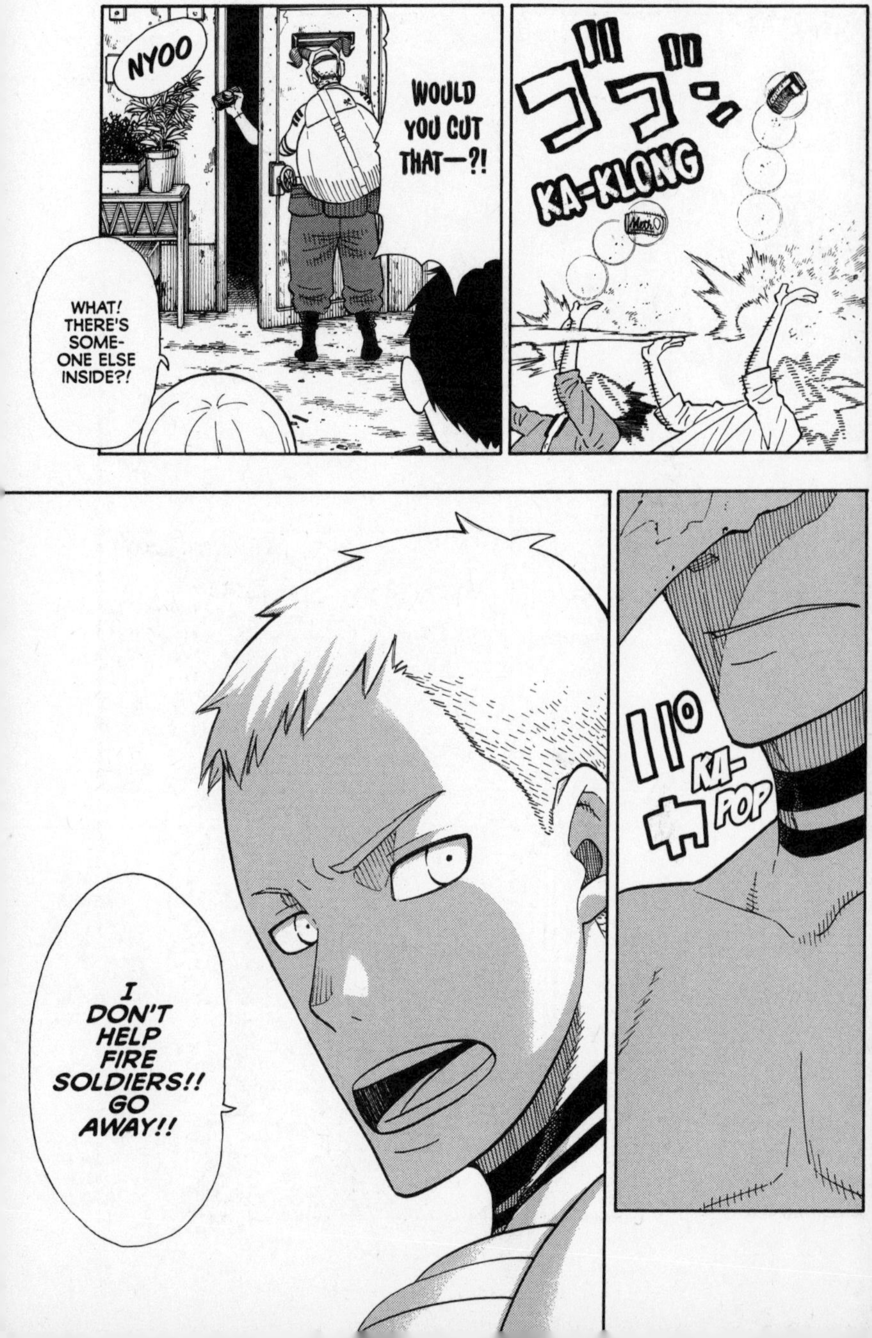
ゴゴッ
KA-KLONG
WOULD YOU CUT THAT—?!
NYOO
WHAT! THERE'S SOME-ONE ELSE INSIDE?!
パカ
KA-POP
I DON'T HELP FIRE SOLDIERS!! GO AWAY!!

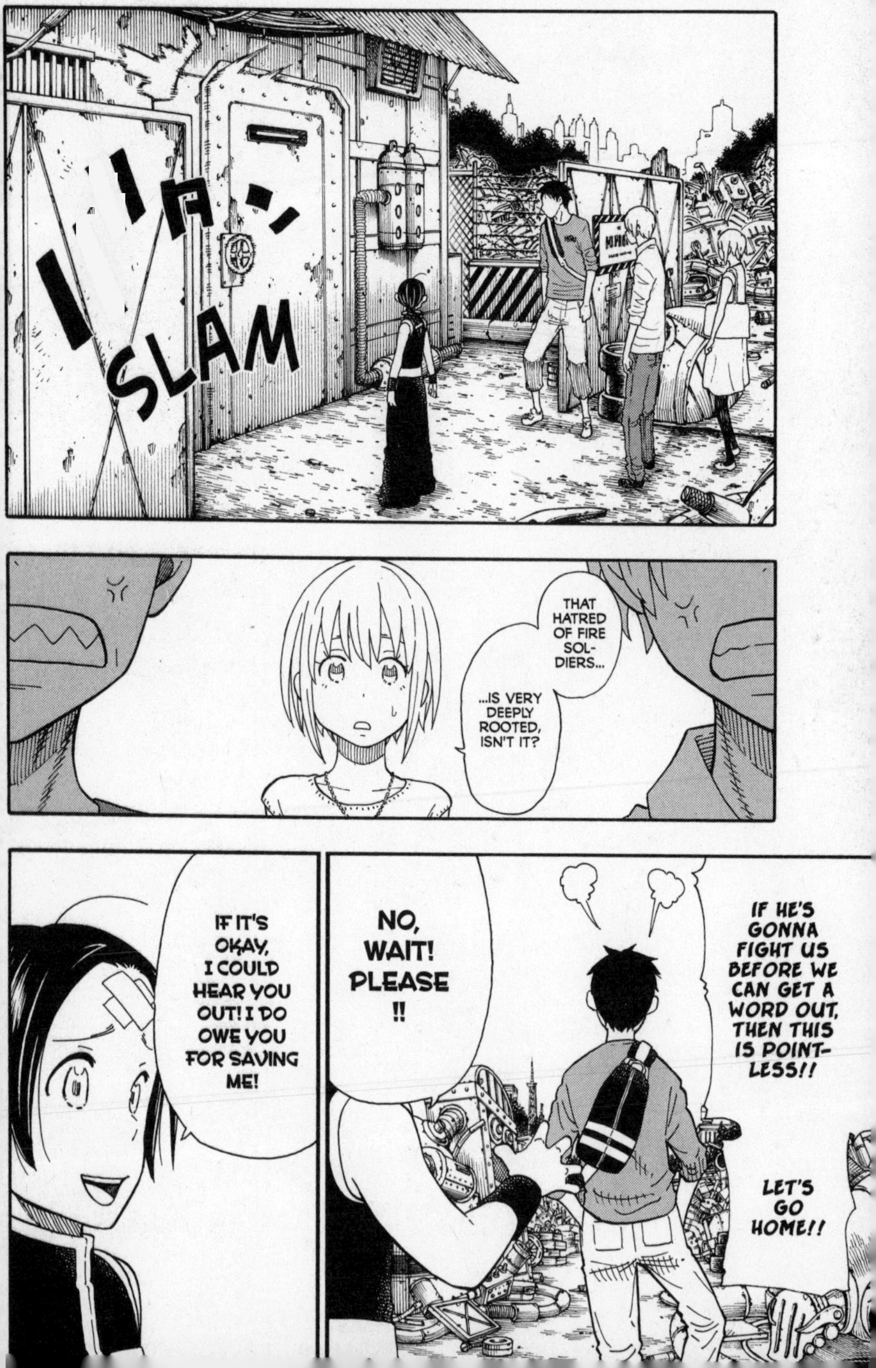
SLAM
THAT HATRED OF FIRE SOL-DIERS...
...IS VERY DEEPLY ROOTED, ISN'T IT?
IF HE'S GONNA FIGHT US BEFORE WE CAN GET A WORD OUT, THEN THIS IS POINT-LESS!!
LET'S GO HOME!!
NO, WAIT! PLEASE!!
IF IT'S OKAY, I COULD HEAR YOU OUT! I DO OWE YOU FOR SAVING ME!

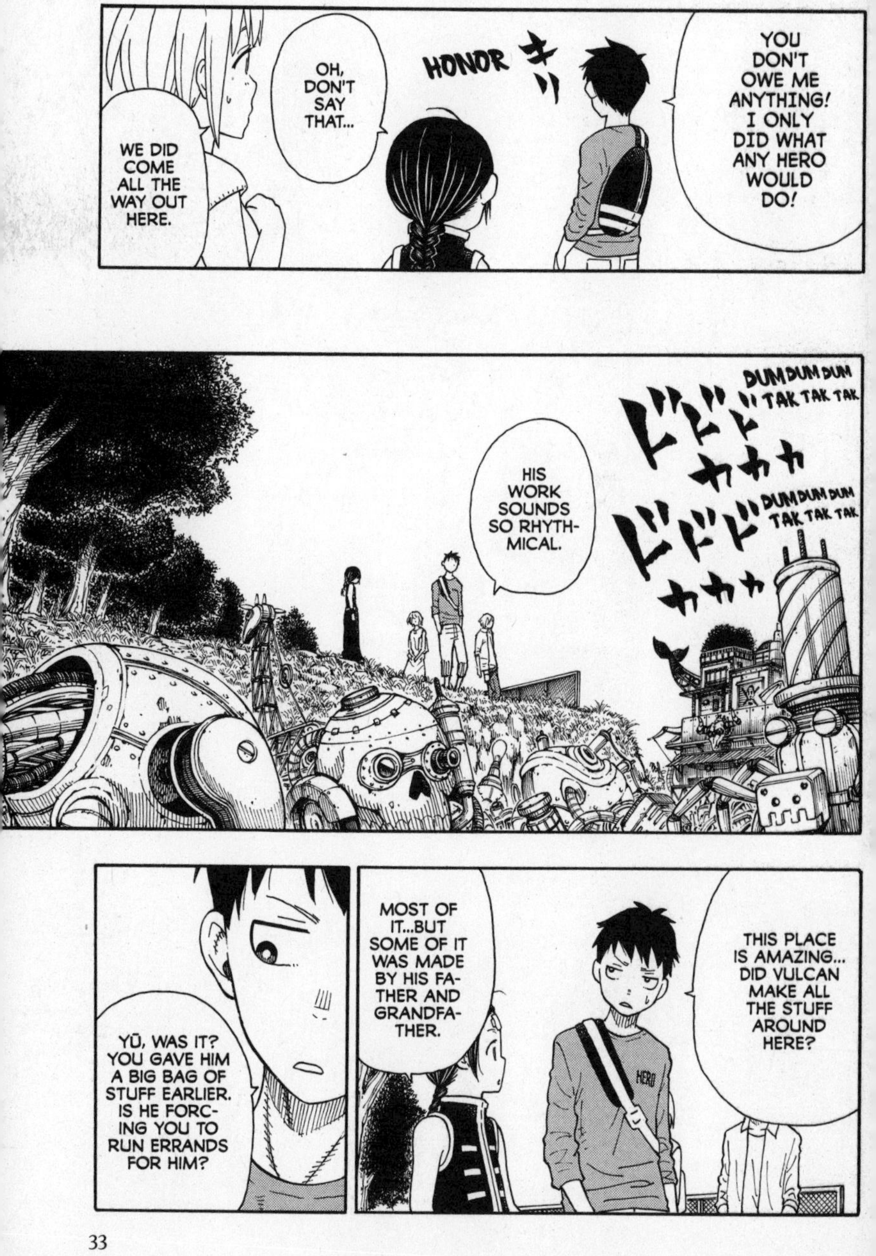
YOU DON'T OWE ME ANYTHING! I ONLY DID WHAT ANY HERO WOULD DO!
HONOR キリ
OH, DON'T SAY THAT...
WE DID COME ALL THE WAY OUT HERE.
ドドドカカカ DUM DUM DUM TAK TAK TAK
ドドドカカカ DUM DUM DUM TAK TAK TAK
HIS WORK SOUNDS SO RHYTHM-ICAL.
THIS PLACE IS AMAZING... DID VULCAN MAKE ALL THE STUFF AROUND HERE?
MOST OF IT...BUT SOME OF IT WAS MADE BY HIS FA-THER AND GRANDFA-THER.
YŪ, WAS IT? YOU GAVE HIM A BIG BAG OF STUFF EARLIER. IS HE FORC-ING YOU TO RUN ERRANDS FOR HIM?

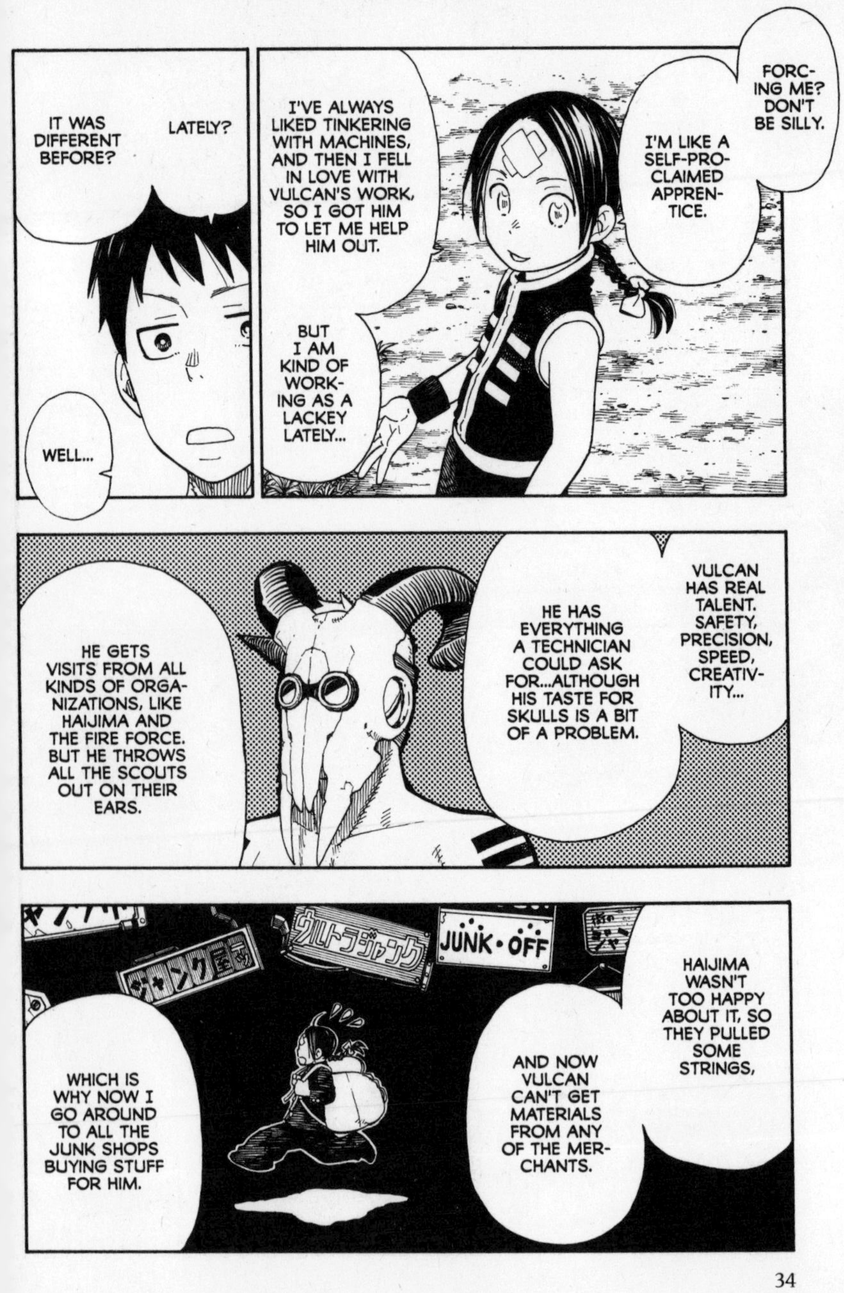
FORCING ME? DON'T BE SILLY.
I'M LIKE A SELF-PROCLAIMED APPRENTICE.
I'VE ALWAYS LIKED TINKERING WITH MACHINES, AND THEN I FELL IN LOVE WITH VULCAN'S WORK, SO I GOT HIM TO LET ME HELP HIM OUT.
BUT I AM KIND OF WORKING AS A LACKEY LATELY...
LATELY?
IT WAS DIFFERENT BEFORE?
WELL...
VULCAN HAS REAL TALENT. SAFETY, PRECISION, SPEED, CREATIVITY...
HE HAS EVERYTHING A TECHNICIAN COULD ASK FOR...ALTHOUGH HIS TASTE FOR SKULLS IS A BIT OF A PROBLEM.
HE GETS VISITS FROM ALL KINDS OF ORGANIZATIONS, LIKE HAIJIMA AND THE FIRE FORCE. BUT HE THROWS ALL THE SCOUTS OUT ON THEIR EARS.
JUNK・OFF
ウルトラジャンク
HAIJIMA WASN'T TOO HAPPY ABOUT IT, SO THEY PULLED SOME STRINGS,
AND NOW VULCAN CAN'T GET MATERIALS FROM ANY OF THE MERCHANTS.
WHICH IS WHY NOW I GO AROUND TO ALL THE JUNK SHOPS BUYING STUFF FOR HIM.

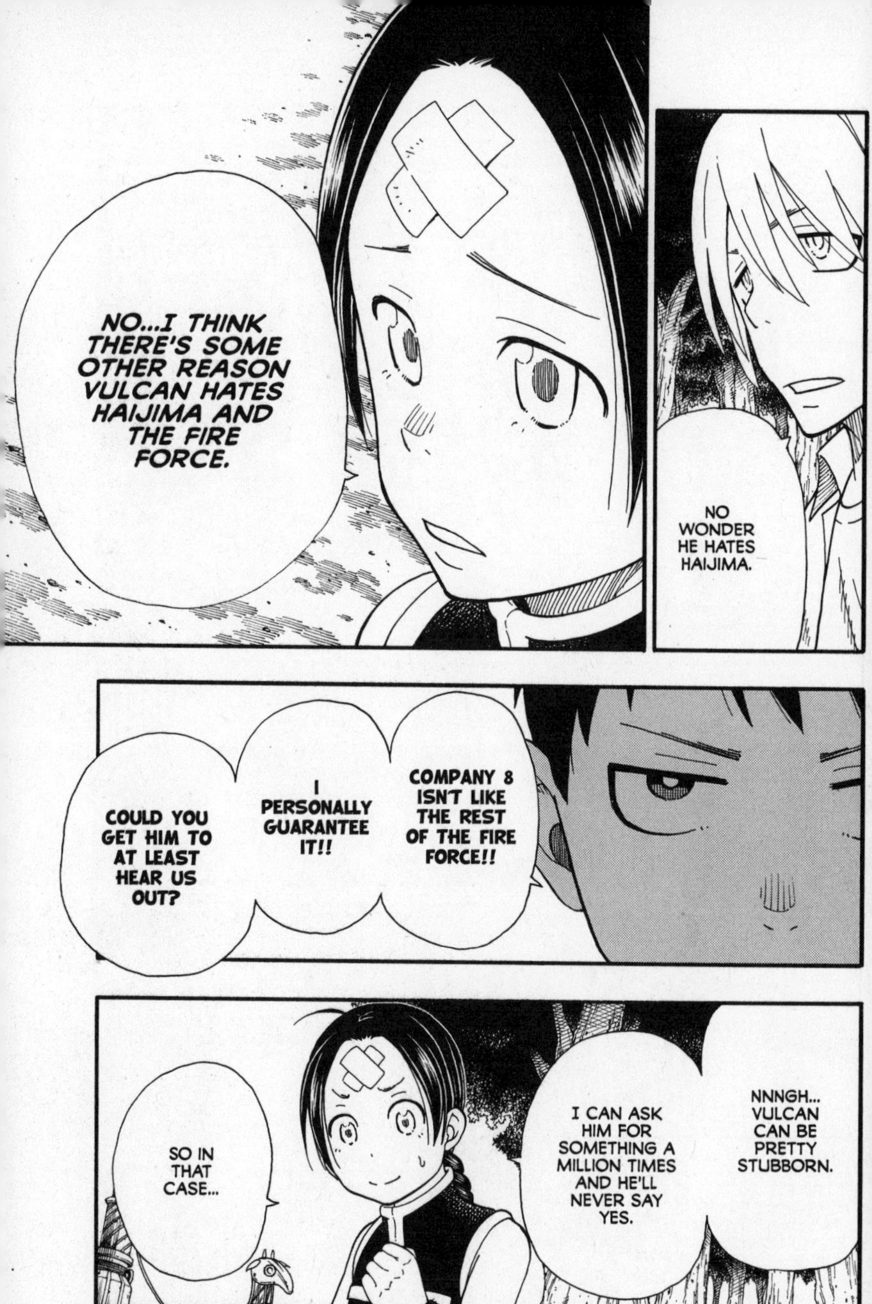
NO WONDER HE HATES HAIJIMA.
NO...I THINK THERE'S SOME OTHER REASON VULCAN HATES HAIJIMA AND THE FIRE FORCE.
COMPANY 8 ISN'T LIKE THE REST OF THE FIRE FORCE!!
I PERSONALLY GUARANTEE IT!!
COULD YOU GET HIM TO AT LEAST HEAR US OUT?
NNNGH... VULCAN CAN BE PRETTY STUBBORN.
I CAN ASK HIM FOR SOMETHING A MILLION TIMES AND HE'LL NEVER SAY YES.
SO IN THAT CASE...

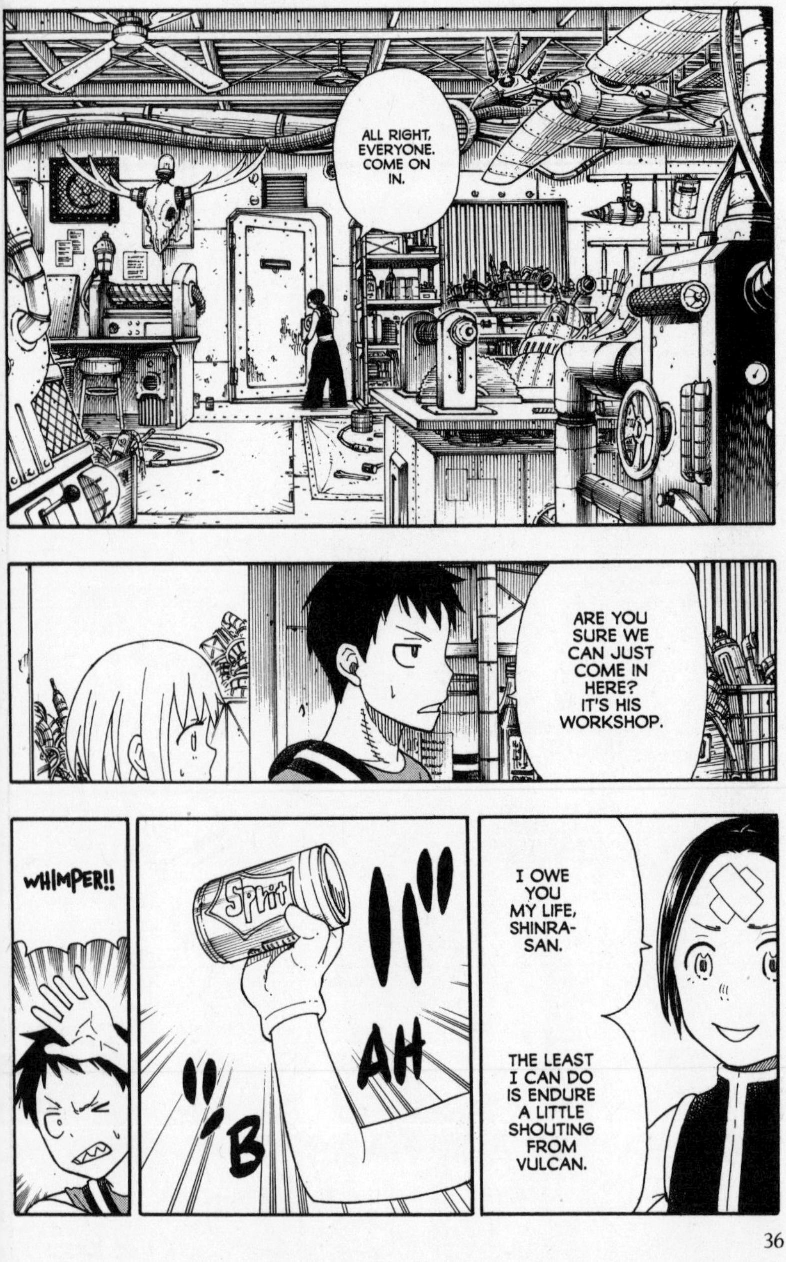
ALL RIGHT, EVERYONE. COME ON IN.
ARE YOU SURE WE CAN JUST COME IN HERE? IT'S HIS WORKSHOP.
I OWE YOU MY LIFE, SHINRA-SAN.
THE LEAST I CAN DO IS ENDURE A LITTLE SHOUTING FROM VULCAN.
Sprit
AH
B
WHIMPER!!

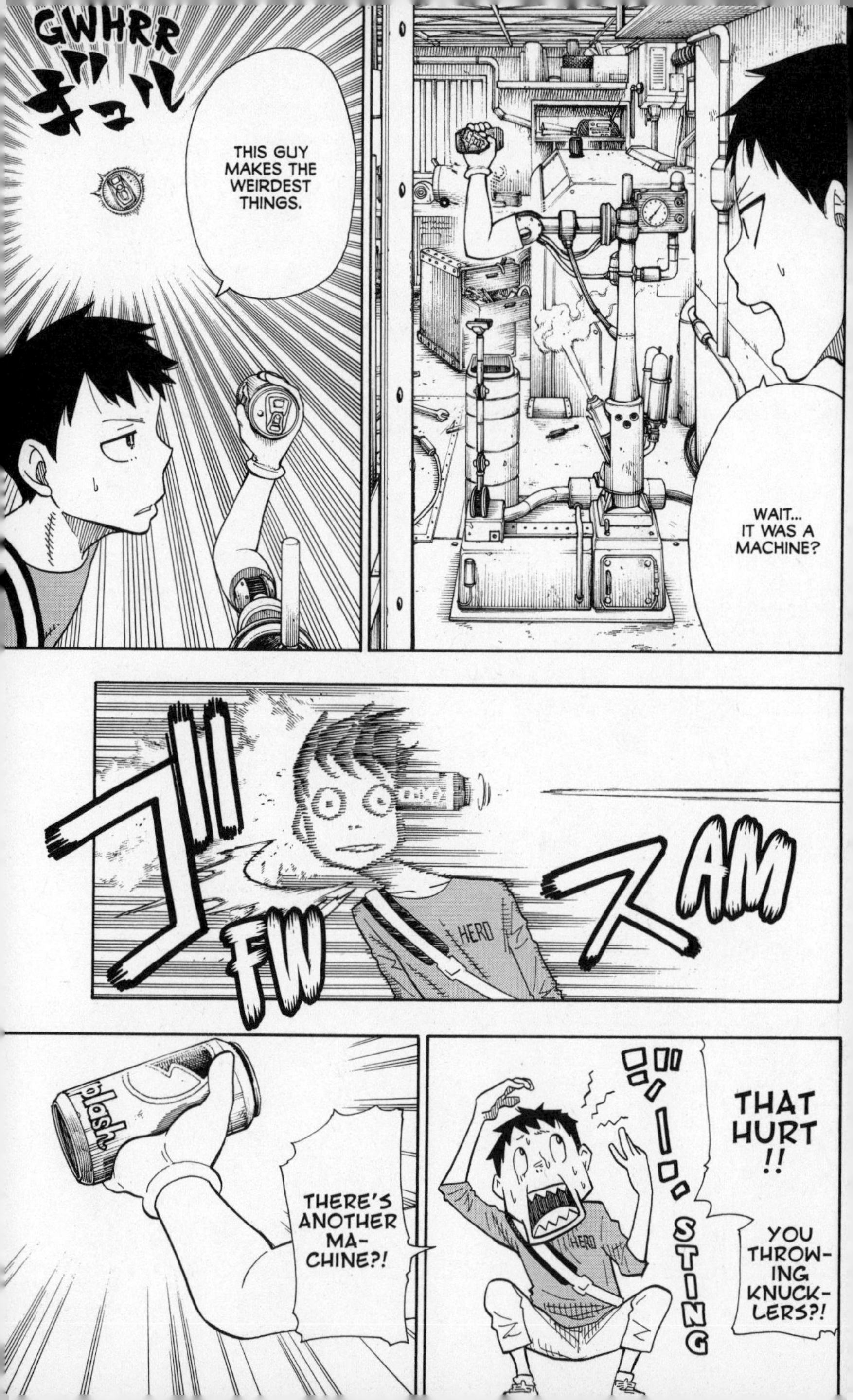
WAIT... IT WAS A MACHINE?
GWHRR
THIS GUY MAKES THE WEIRDEST THINGS.
AM
FW
HERO
STING
THAT HURT!!
YOU THROWING KNUCKLERS?!
HERO
THERE'S ANOTHER MACHINE?!
splash

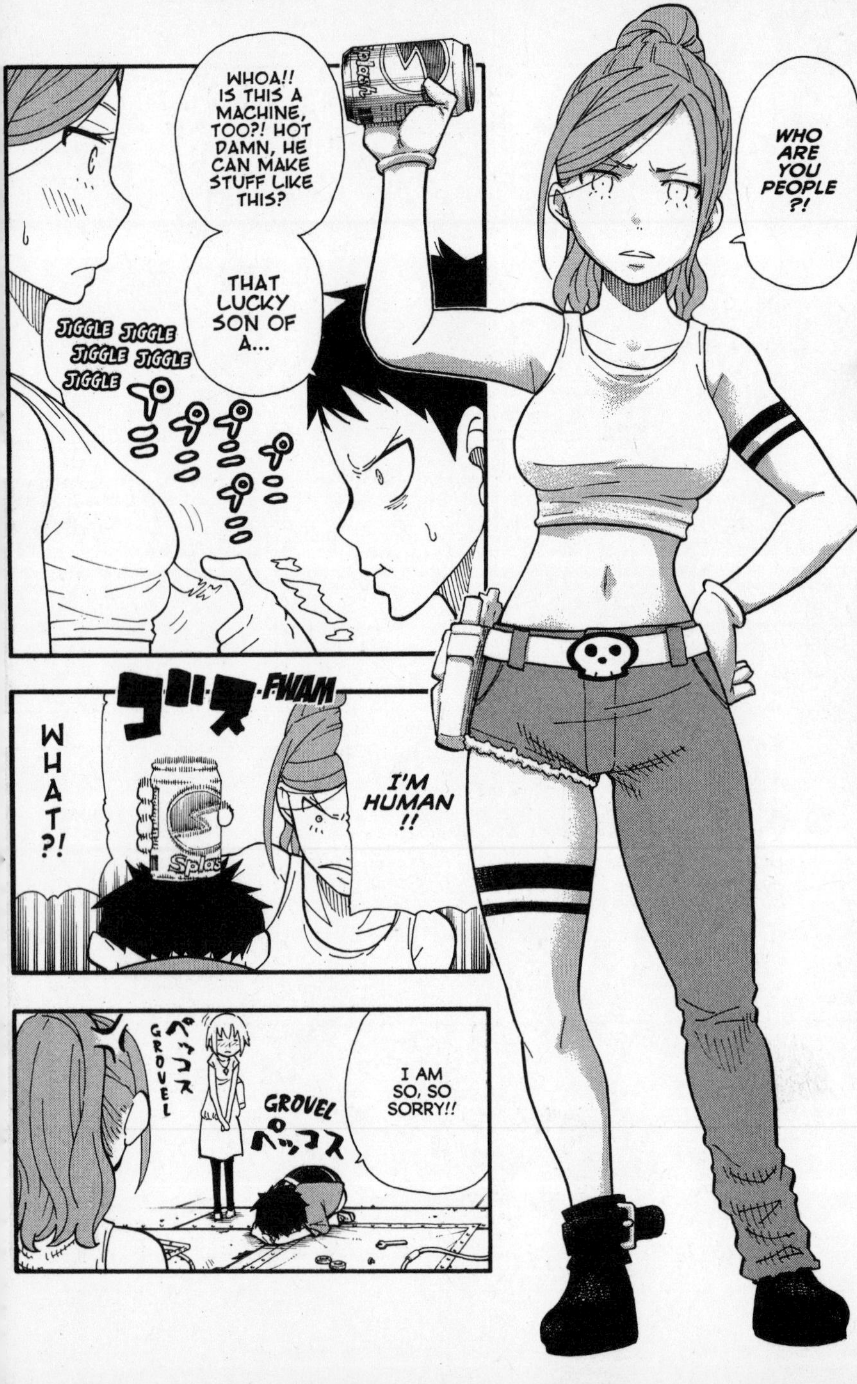

WHO ARE YOU PEOPLE?!
WHOA!! IS THIS A MACHINE, TOO?! HOT DAMN, HE CAN MAKE STUFF LIKE THIS?
THAT LUCKY SON OF A...
JIGGLE JIGGLE JIGGLE JIGGLE JIGGLE
FWAM
I'M HUMAN!!
WHAT?!
I AM SO, SO SORRY!!
GROVEL
GROVEL

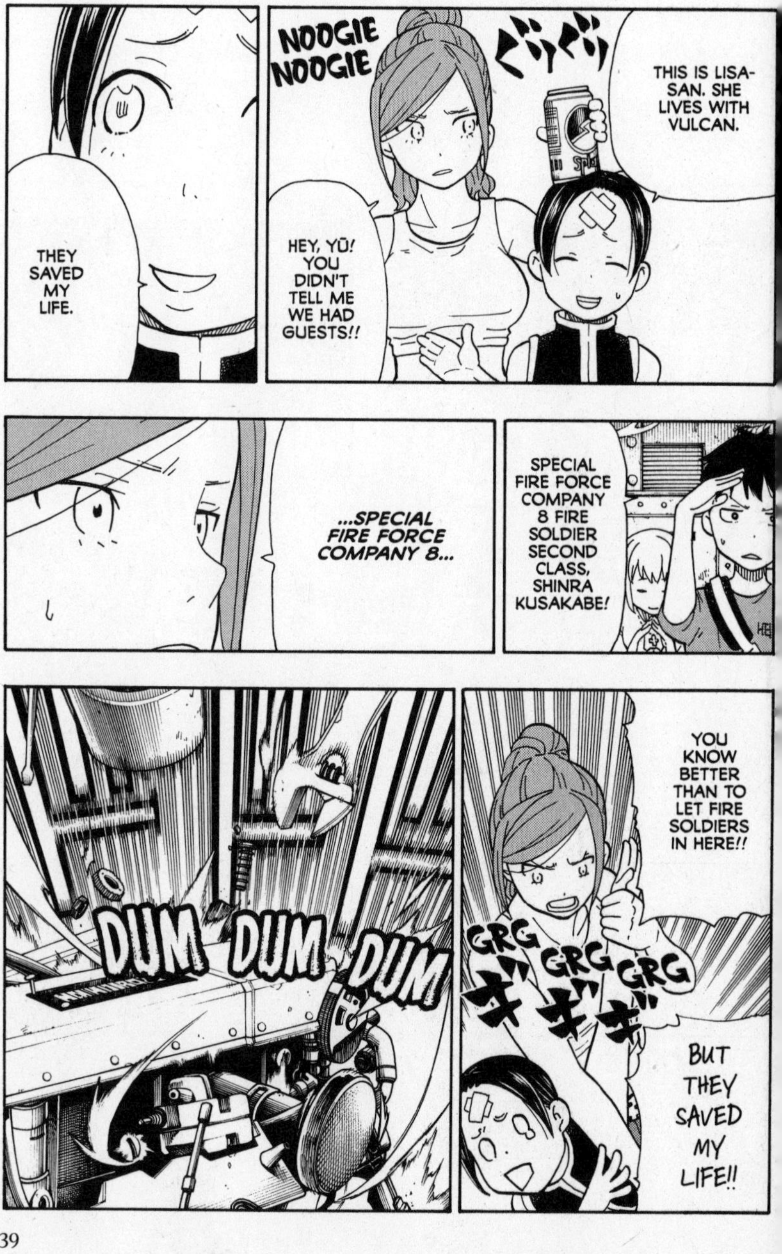
NOOGIE NOOGIE
THIS IS LISA-SAN. SHE LIVES WITH VULCAN.
HEY, YŪ! YOU DIDN'T TELL ME WE HAD GUESTS!!
THEY SAVED MY LIFE.
SPECIAL FIRE FORCE COMPANY 8 FIRE SOLDIER SECOND CLASS, SHINRA KUSAKABE!
...SPECIAL FIRE FORCE COMPANY 8...
YOU KNOW BETTER THAN TO LET FIRE SOLDIERS IN HERE!!
GRG GRG GRG
BUT THEY SAVED MY LIFE!!
DUM DUM DUM

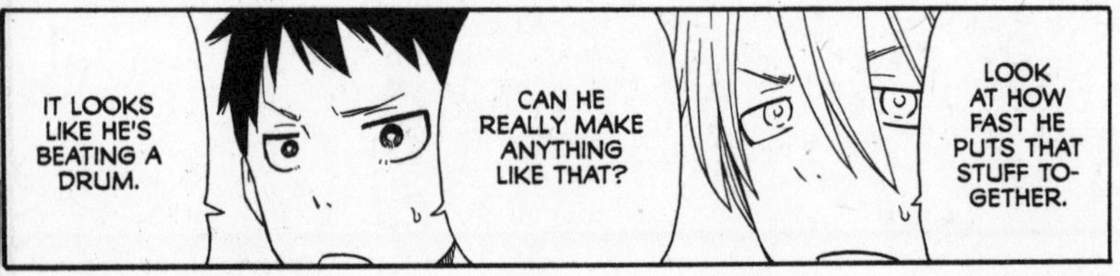
LOOK AT HOW FAST HE PUTS THAT STUFF TO-GETHER.
CAN HE REALLY MAKE ANYTHING LIKE THAT?
IT LOOKS LIKE HE'S BEATING A DRUM.

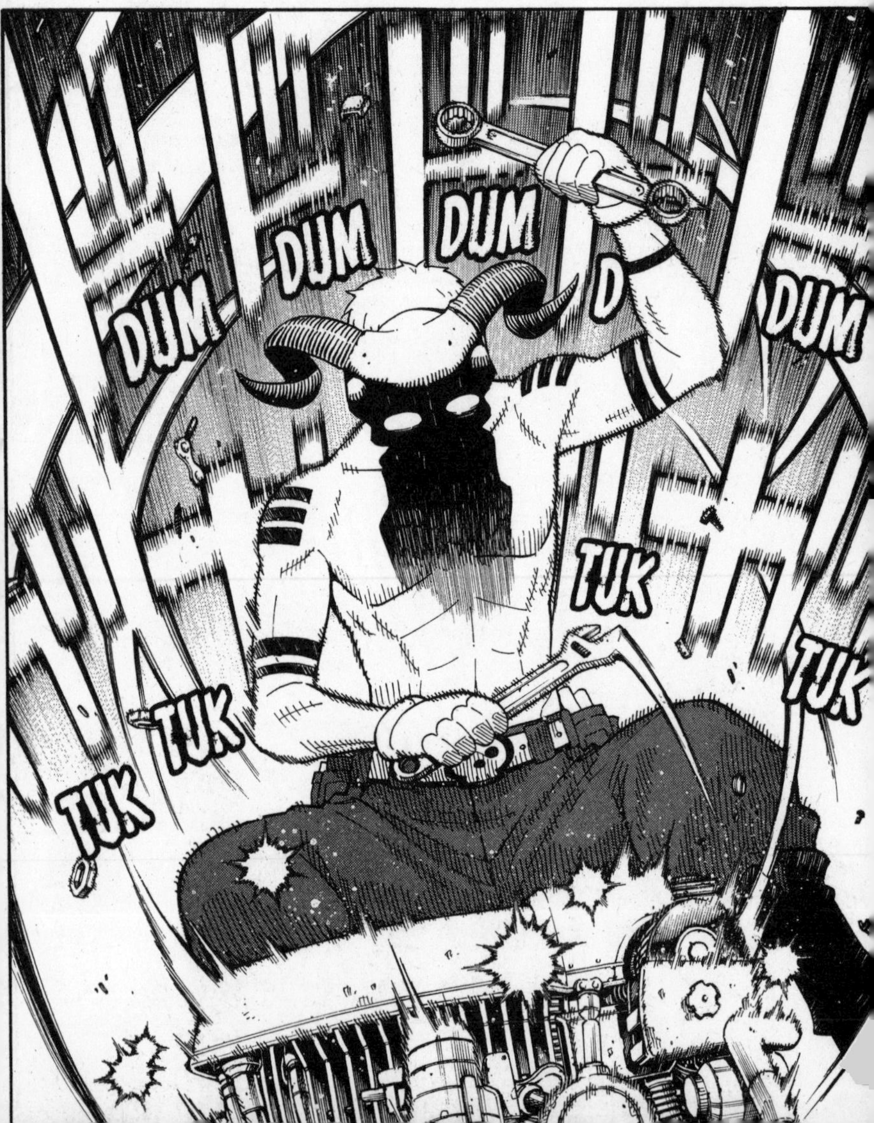
DUM
D
DUM
DUM
DUM
TUK
TUK
TUK
TUK

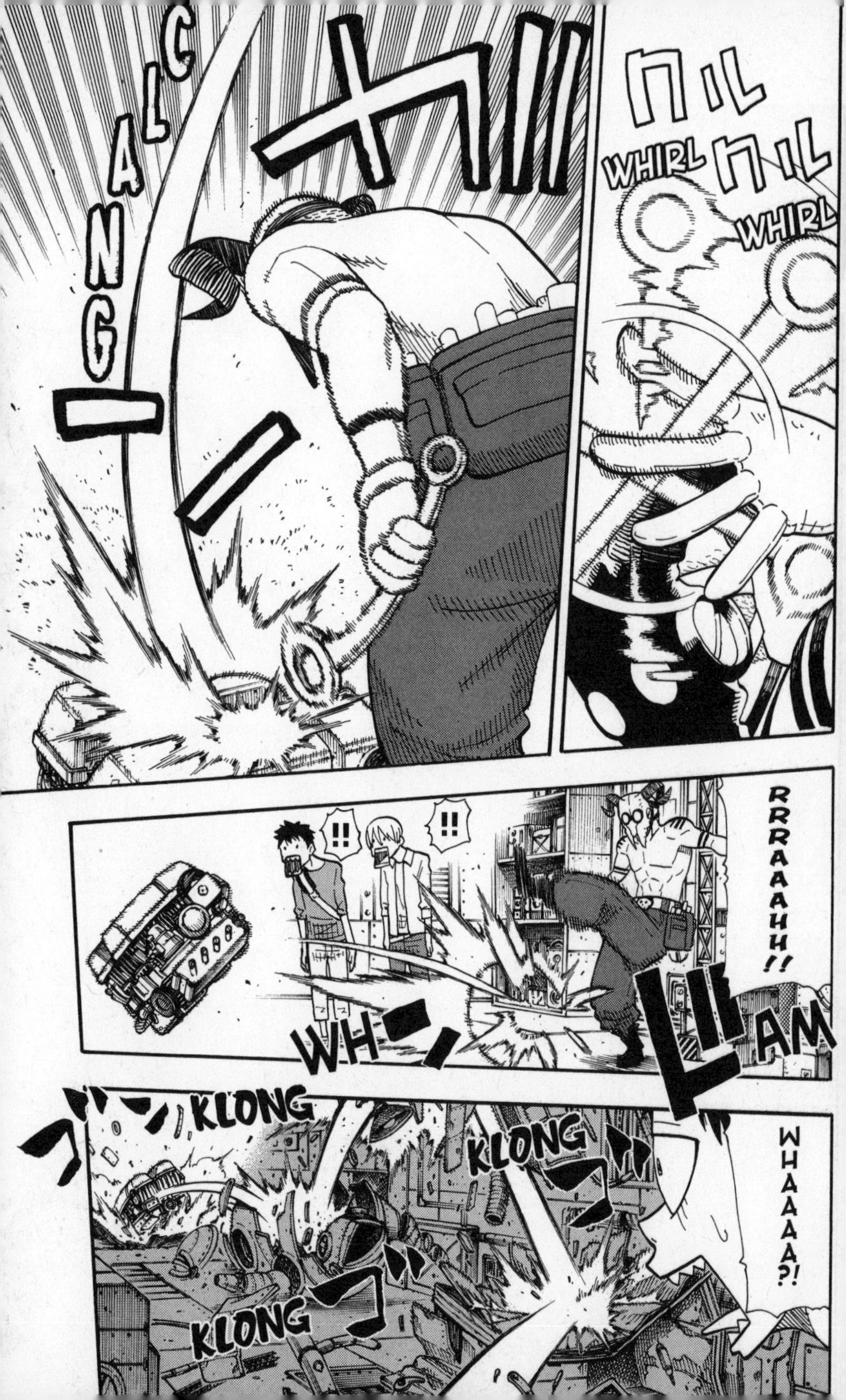

WHIRL
WHIRL
CLANG
RRRAAAAHH!!
!!
!!
WHAM
WHAAAAA?!
KLONG
KLONG
KLONG

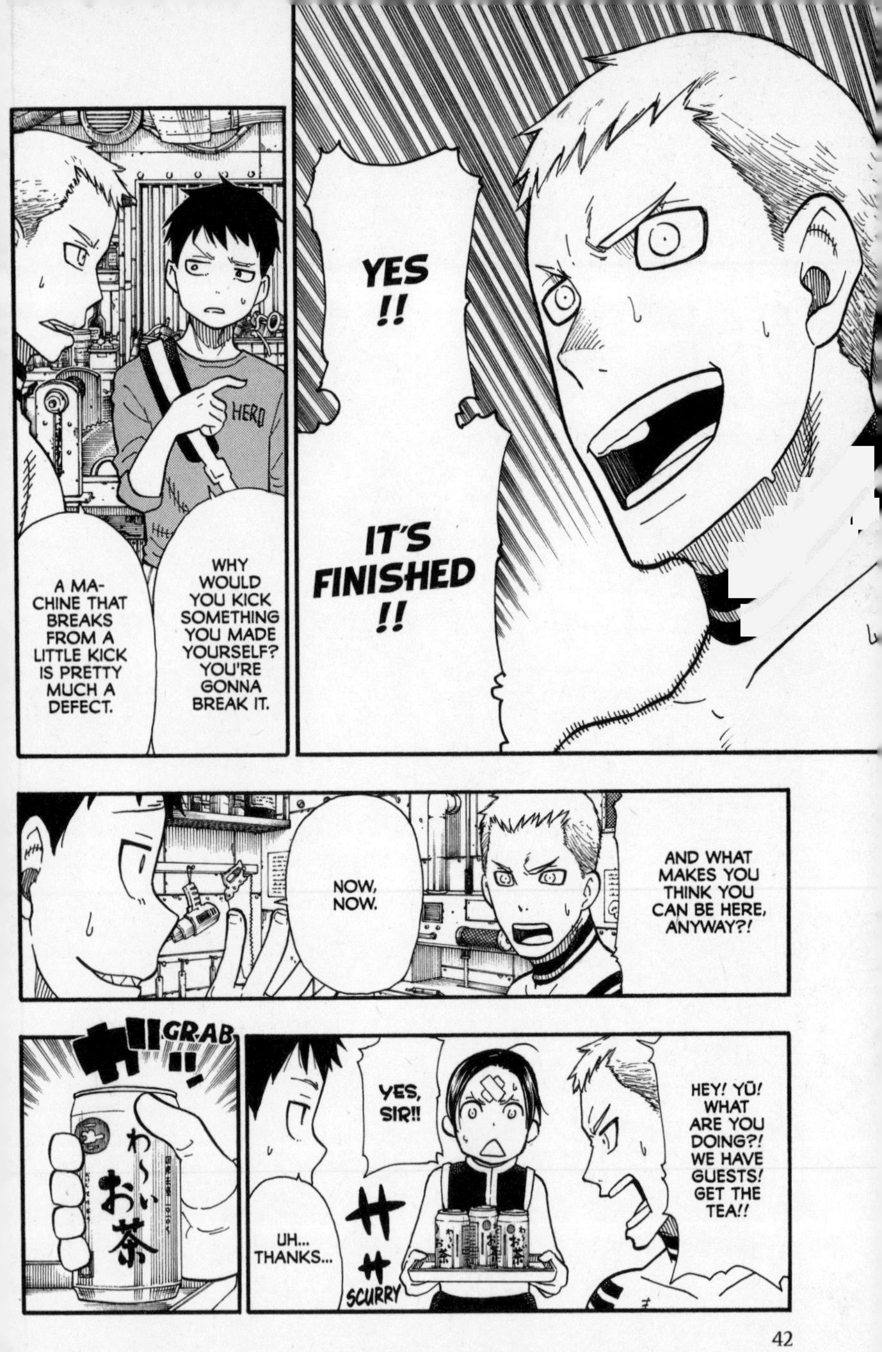
YES!!
IT'S FINISHED!!
WHY WOULD YOU KICK SOMETHING YOU MADE YOURSELF? YOU'RE GONNA BREAK IT.
A MA-CHINE THAT BREAKS FROM A LITTLE KICK IS PRETTY MUCH A DEFECT.
AND WHAT MAKES YOU THINK YOU CAN BE HERE, ANYWAY?!
NOW, NOW.
HEY! YŪ! WHAT ARE YOU DOING?! WE HAVE GUESTS! GET THE TEA!!
YES, SIR!!
SCURRY
UH... THANKS...
GRAB

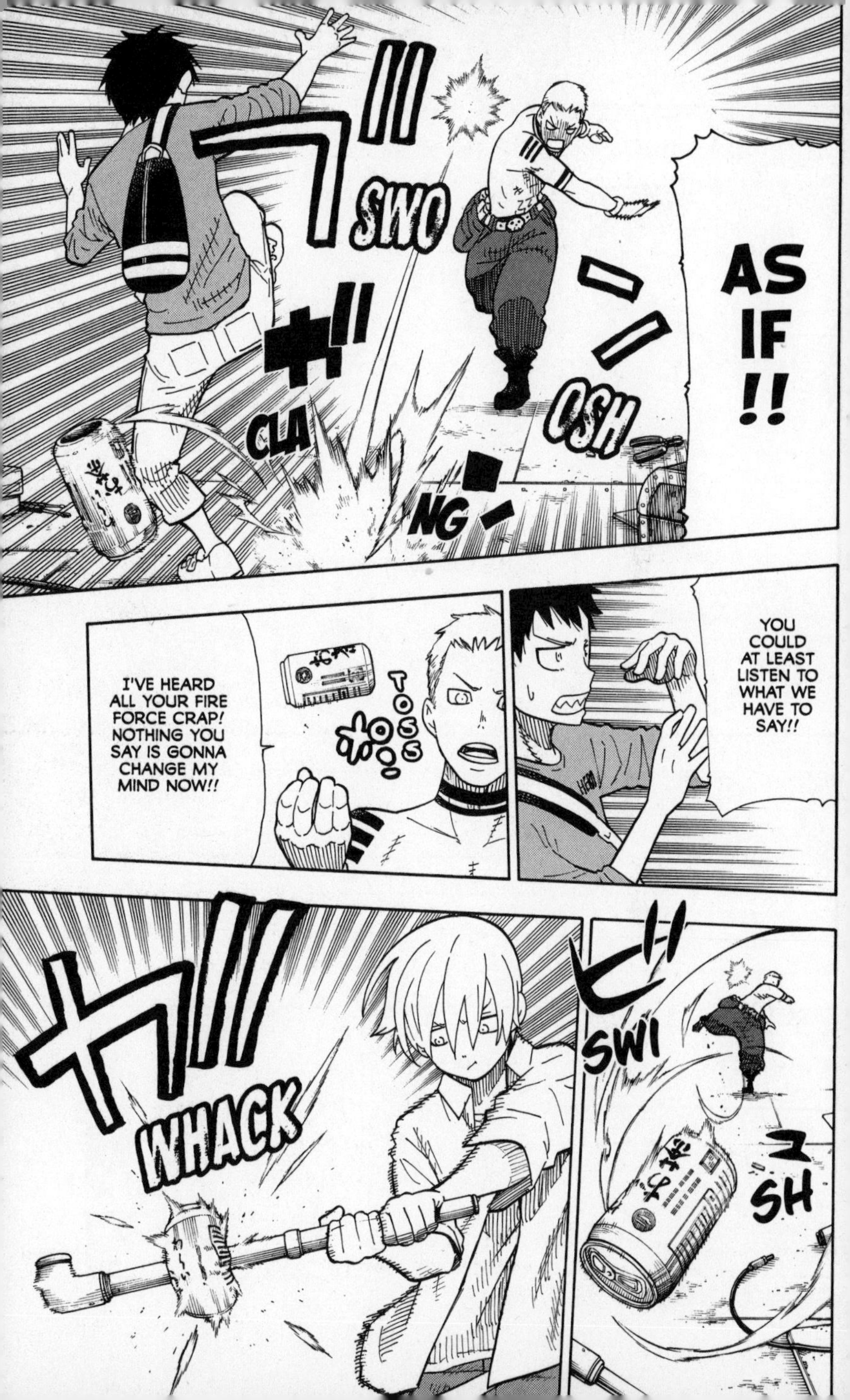
AS IF!!
SWO
OSH
CLA
NG
YOU COULD AT LEAST LISTEN TO WHAT WE HAVE TO SAY!!
TOSS
I'VE HEARD ALL YOUR FIRE FORCE CRAP! NOTHING YOU SAY IS GONNA CHANGE MY MIND NOW!!
SWI
SH
WHACK

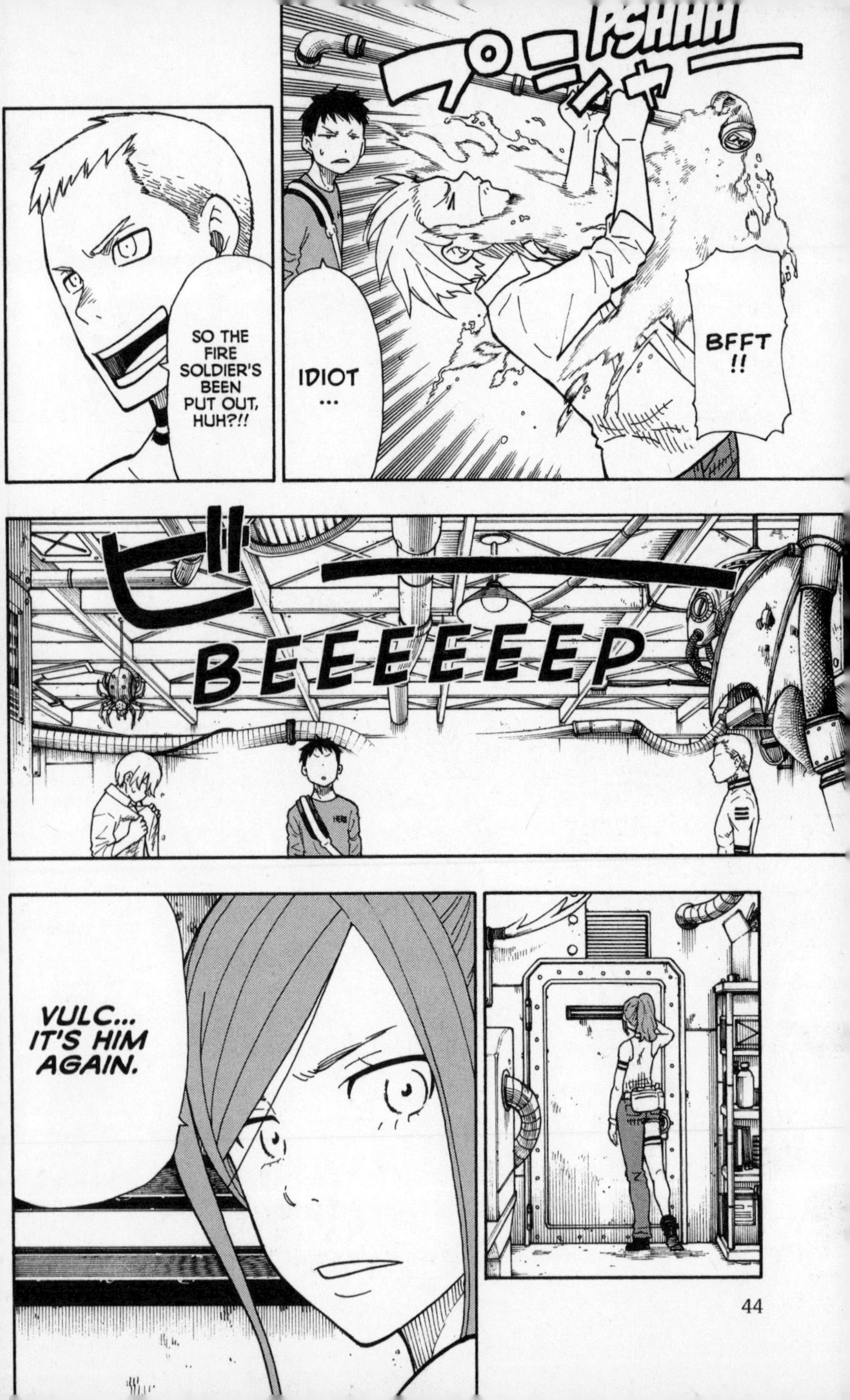
PSHHH
BFFT !!
IDIOT ...
SO THE FIRE SOLDIER'S BEEN PUT OUT, HUH?!!
ビー
BEEEEEEP
VULC... IT'S HIM AGAIN.

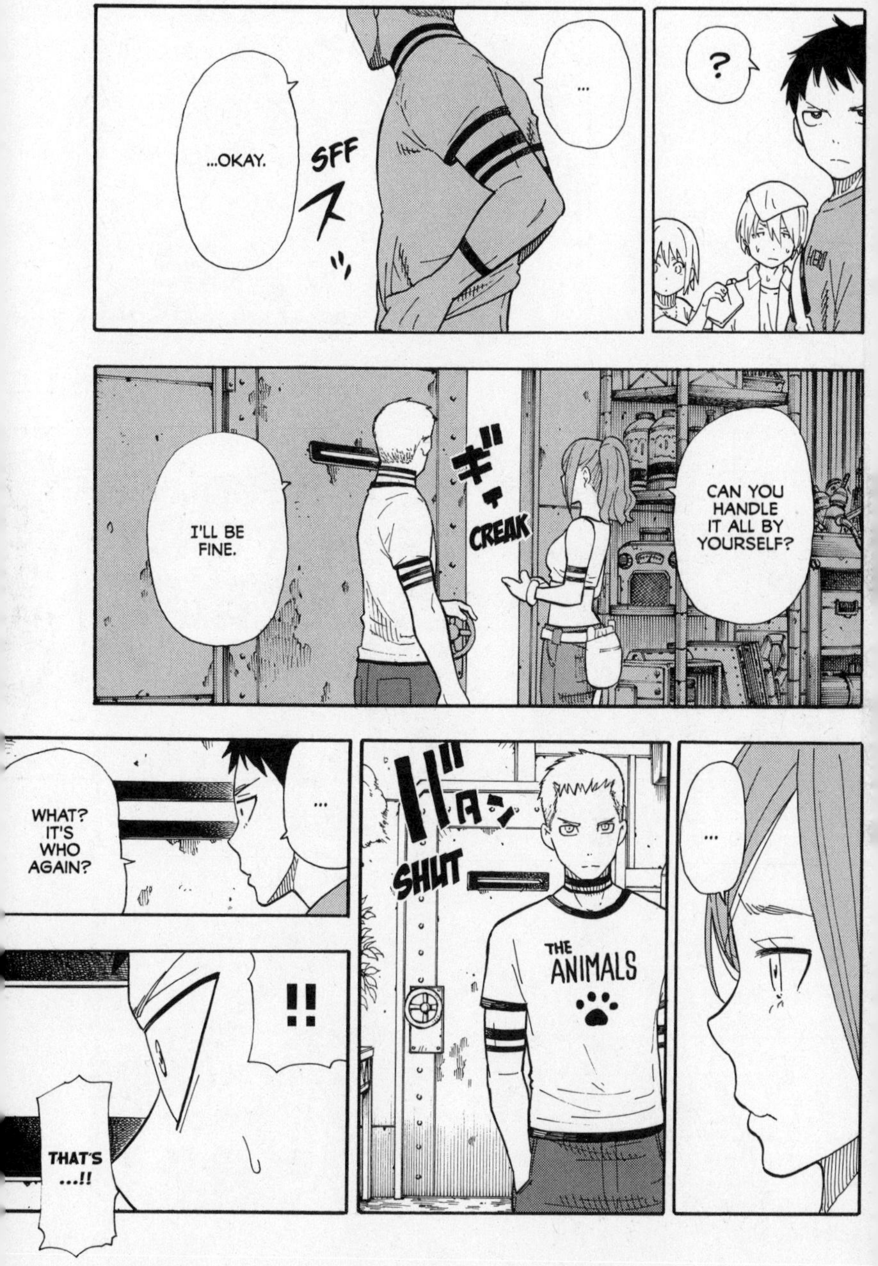
?
...
...OKAY.
SFF
CAN YOU HANDLE IT ALL BY YOURSELF?
CREAK
I'LL BE FINE.
...
SHUT
THE ANIMALS
...
WHAT? IT'S WHO AGAIN?
!!
THAT'S ...!!

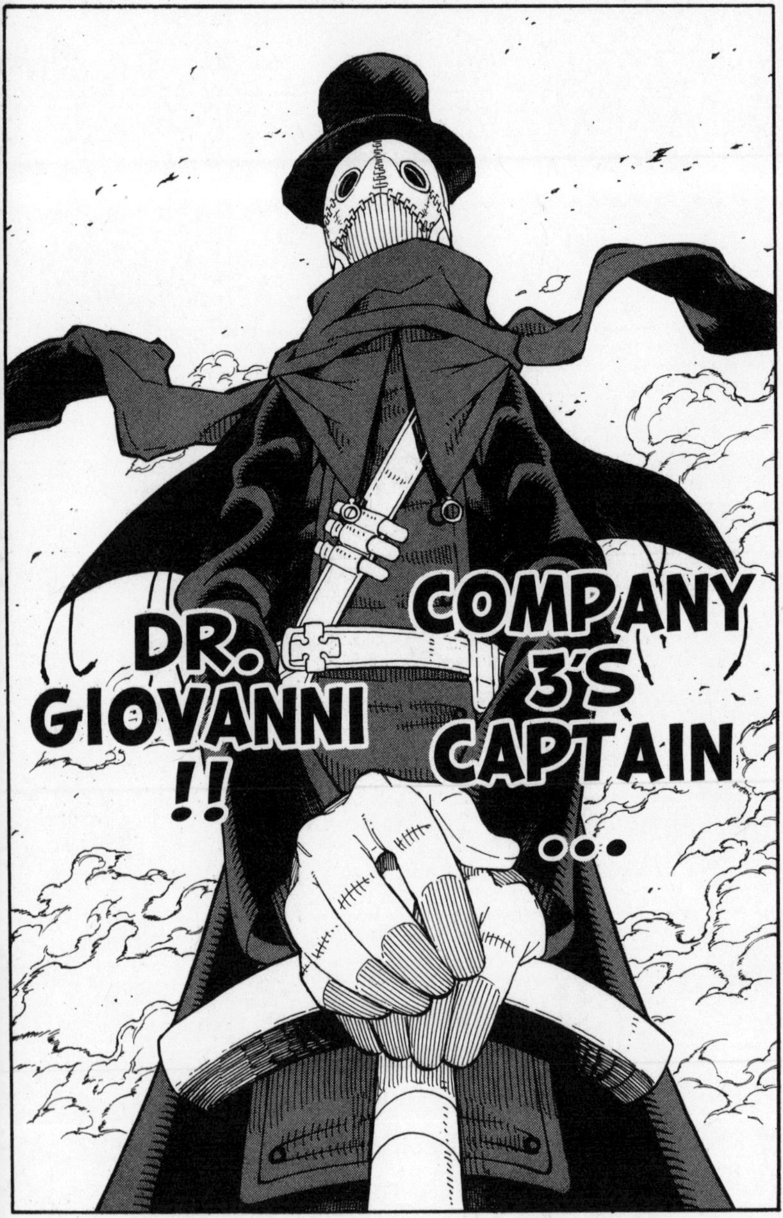
COMPANY 3'S CAPTAIN...
DR. GIOVANNI!!

FIRE FORCE

FIRE FORCE

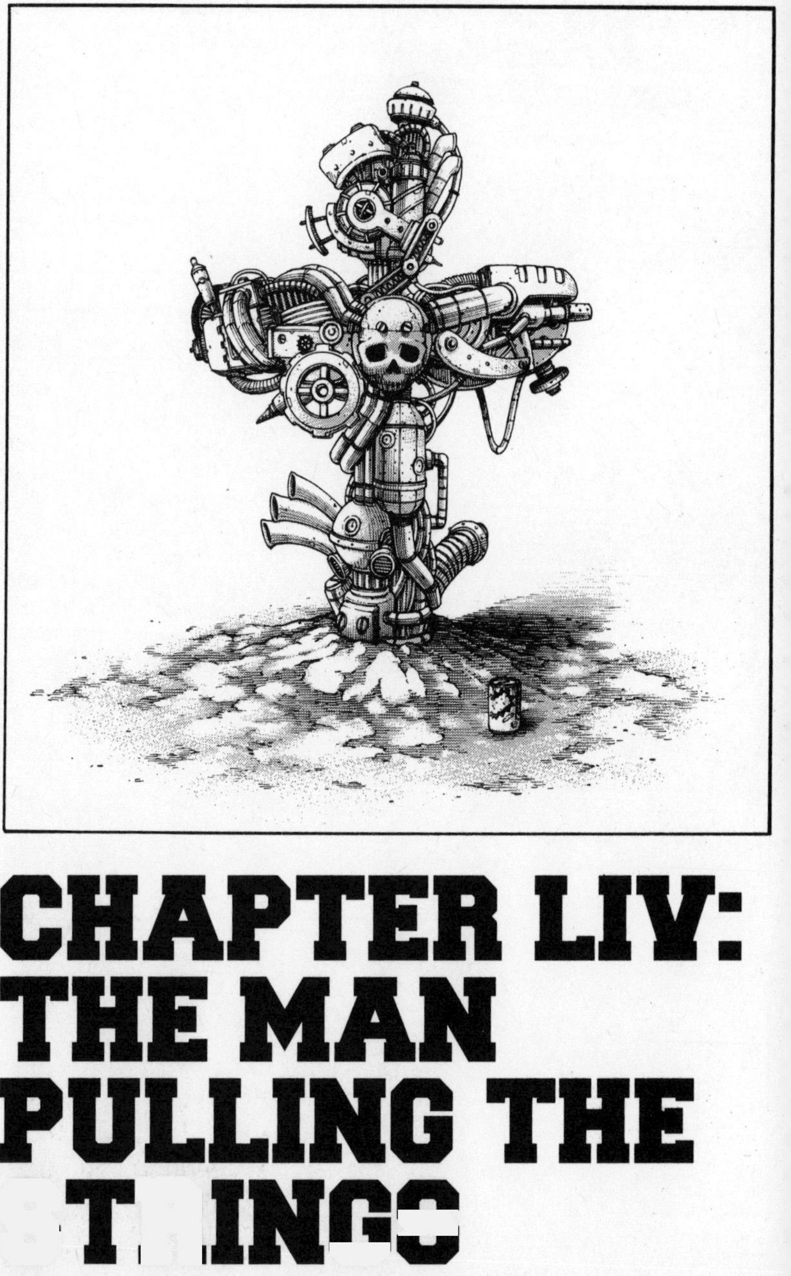

CHAPTER LIV: THE MAN PULLING THE STRINGS

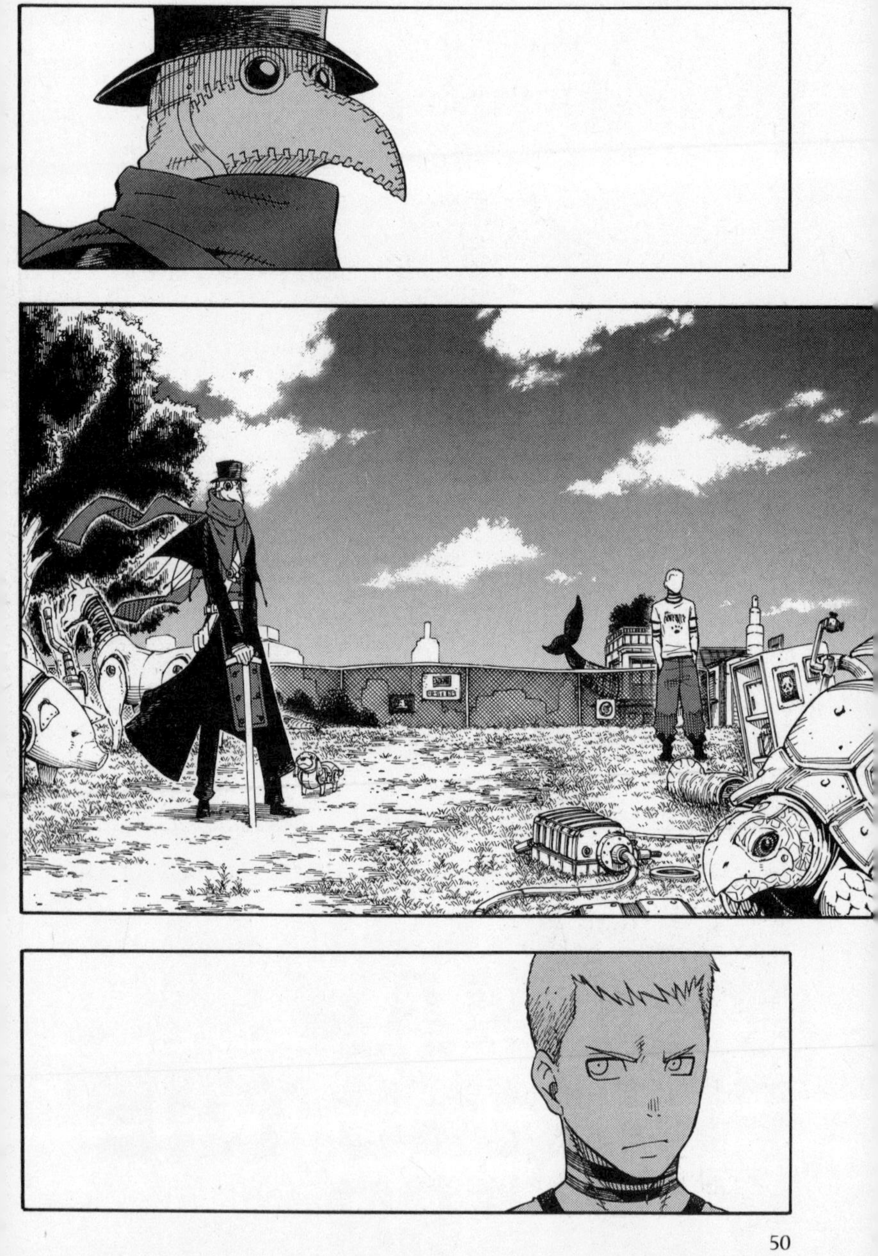

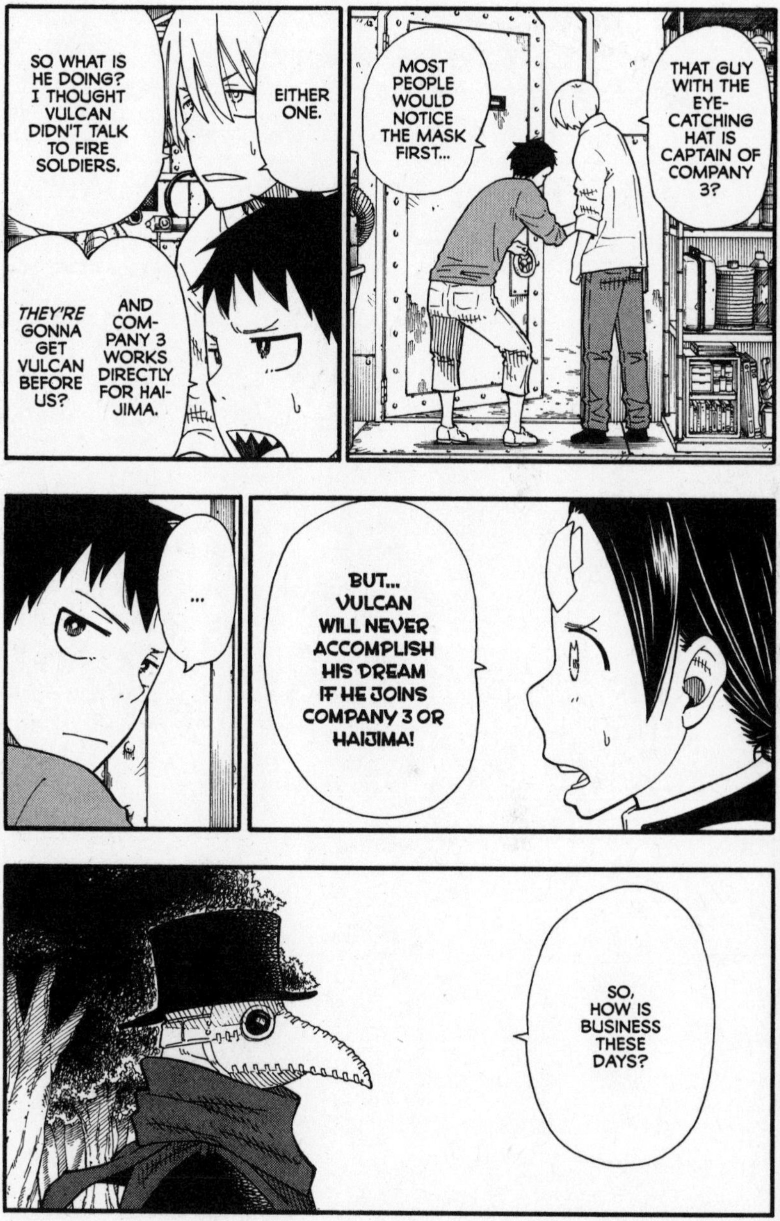
THAT GUY WITH THE EYE-CATCHING HAT IS CAPTAIN OF COMPANY 3?
MOST PEOPLE WOULD NOTICE THE MASK FIRST...
EITHER ONE.
SO WHAT IS HE DOING? I THOUGHT VULCAN DIDN'T TALK TO FIRE SOLDIERS.
AND COMPANY 3 WORKS DIRECTLY FOR HAIJIMA.
THEY'RE GONNA GET VULCAN BEFORE US?
BUT... VULCAN WILL NEVER ACCOMPLISH HIS DREAM IF HE JOINS COMPANY 3 OR HAIJIMA!
...
SO, HOW IS BUSINESS THESE DAYS?

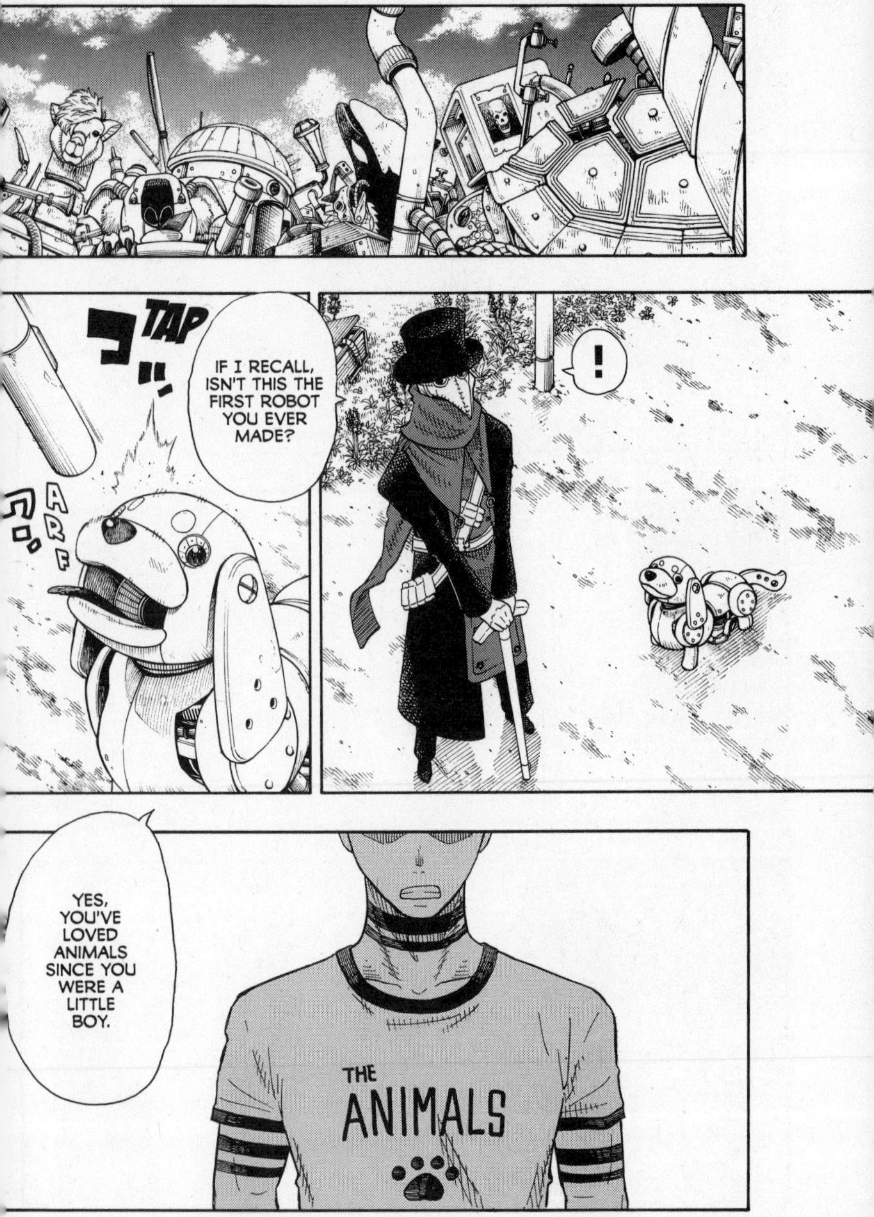
!
TAP
IF I RECALL, ISN'T THIS THE FIRST ROBOT YOU EVER MADE?
ARF
YES, YOU'VE LOVED ANIMALS SINCE YOU WERE A LITTLE BOY.
THE ANIMALS

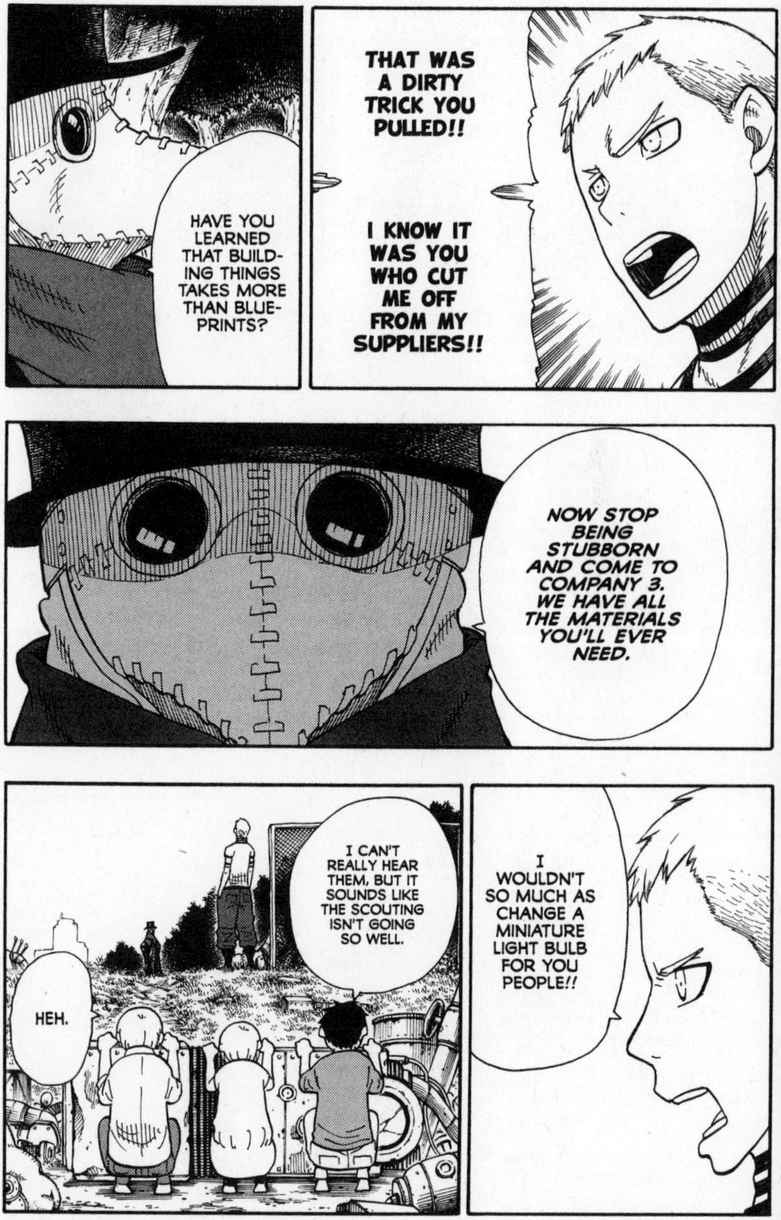
THAT WAS A DIRTY TRICK YOU PULLED!!
I KNOW IT WAS YOU WHO CUT ME OFF FROM MY SUPPLIERS!!
HAVE YOU LEARNED THAT BUILDING THINGS TAKES MORE THAN BLUEPRINTS?
NOW STOP BEING STUBBORN AND COME TO COMPANY 3. WE HAVE ALL THE MATERIALS YOU'LL EVER NEED.
I WOULDN'T SO MUCH AS CHANGE A MINIATURE LIGHT BULB FOR YOU PEOPLE!!
I CAN'T REALLY HEAR THEM, BUT IT SOUNDS LIKE THE SCOUTING ISN'T GOING SO WELL.
HEH.

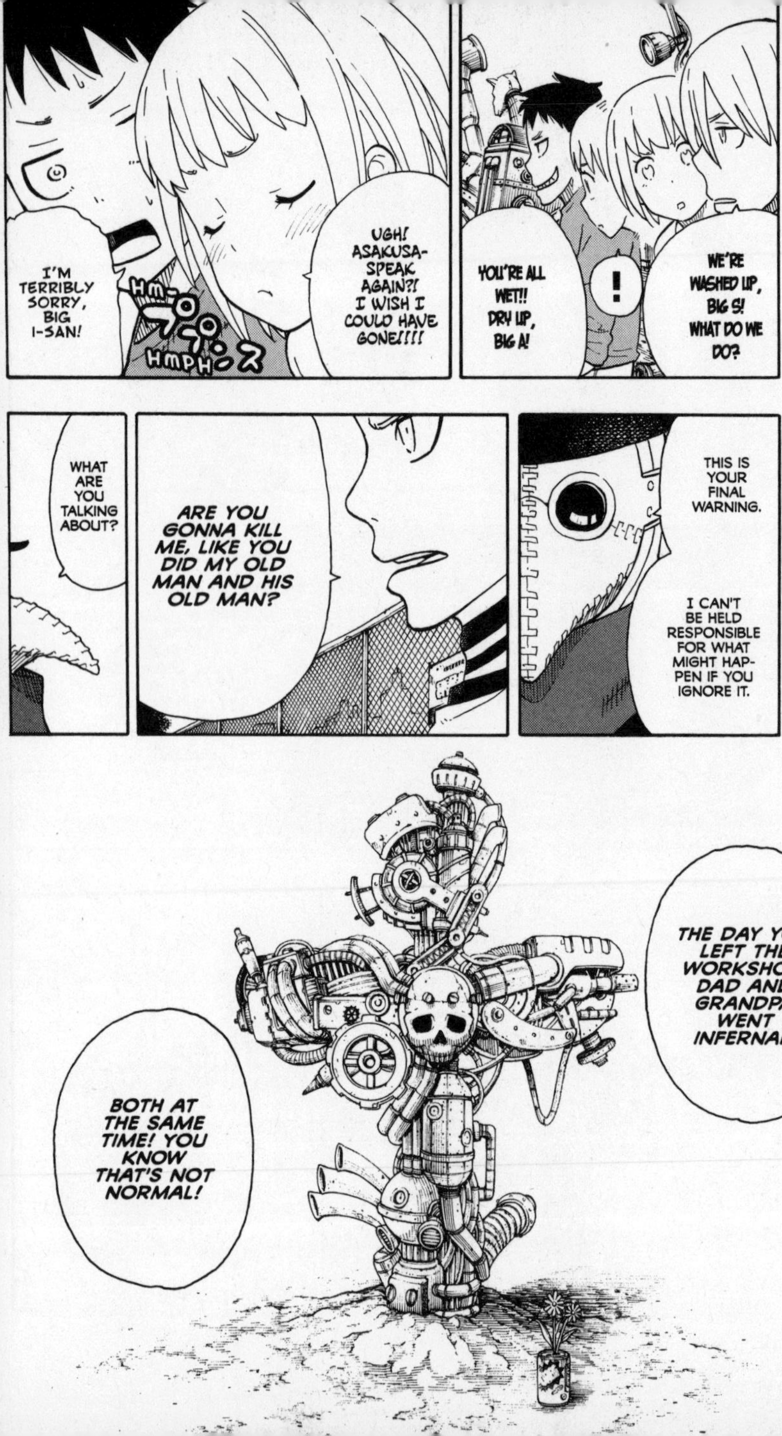

WE'RE WASHED UP, BIG S! WHAT DO WE DO?
!
YOU'RE ALL WET!! DRY UP, BIG A!
UGH! ASAKUSA-SPEAK AGAIN?! I WISH I COULD HAVE GONE!!!!
Hm-
HMPH
I'M TERRIBLY SORRY, BIG I-SAN!
THIS IS YOUR FINAL WARNING.
I CAN'T BE HELD RESPONSIBLE FOR WHAT MIGHT HAP-PEN IF YOU IGNORE IT.
ARE YOU GONNA KILL ME, LIKE YOU DID MY OLD MAN AND HIS OLD MAN?
WHAT ARE YOU TALKING ABOUT?
THE DAY YOU LEFT THE WORKSHOP, DAD AND GRANDPA WENT INFERNAL.
BOTH AT THE SAME TIME! YOU KNOW THAT'S NOT NORMAL!

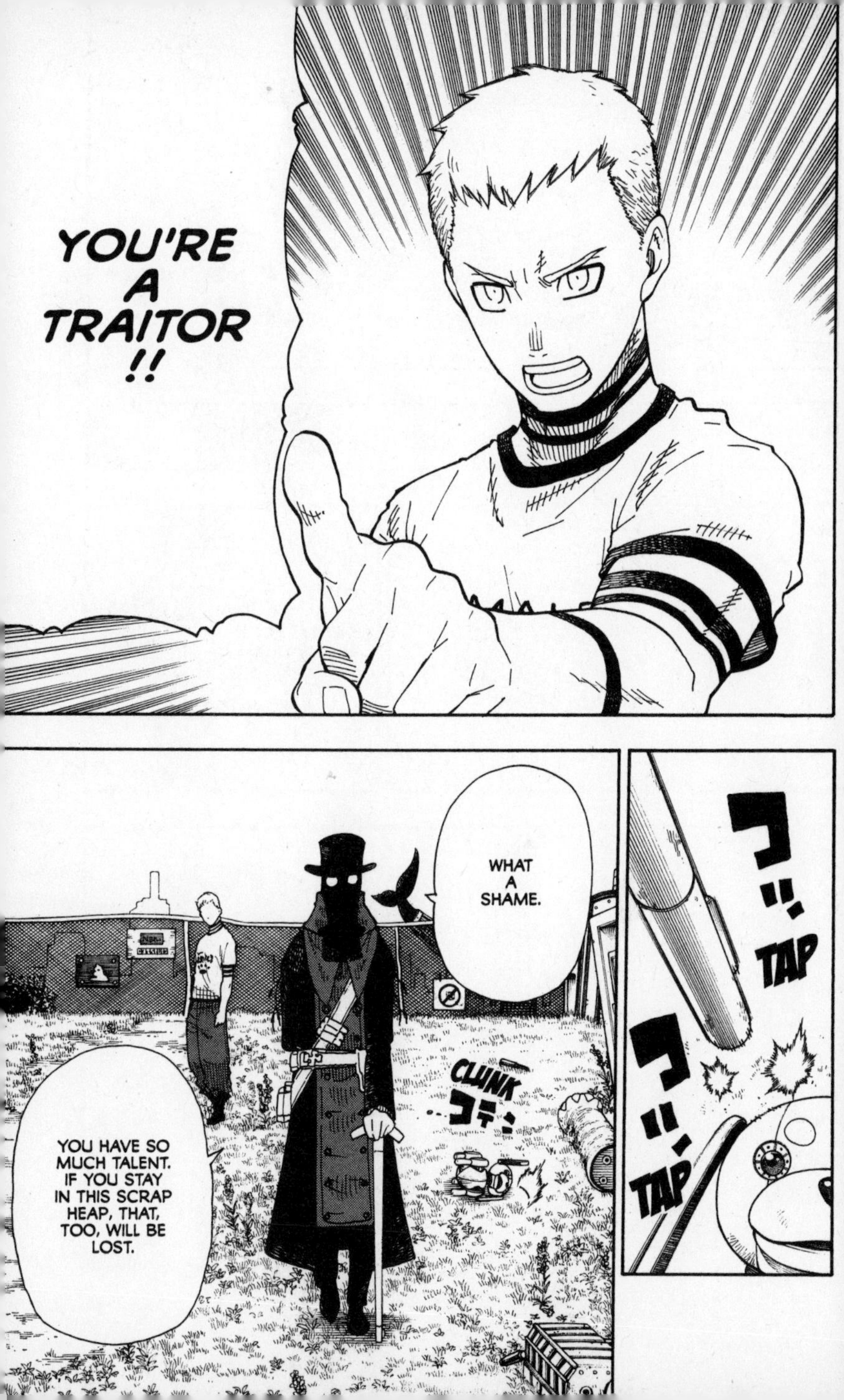
YOU'RE A TRAITOR!!
TAP
TAP
WHAT A SHAME.
CLUNK
YOU HAVE SO MUCH TALENT. IF YOU STAY IN THIS SCRAP HEAP, THAT, TOO, WILL BE LOST.

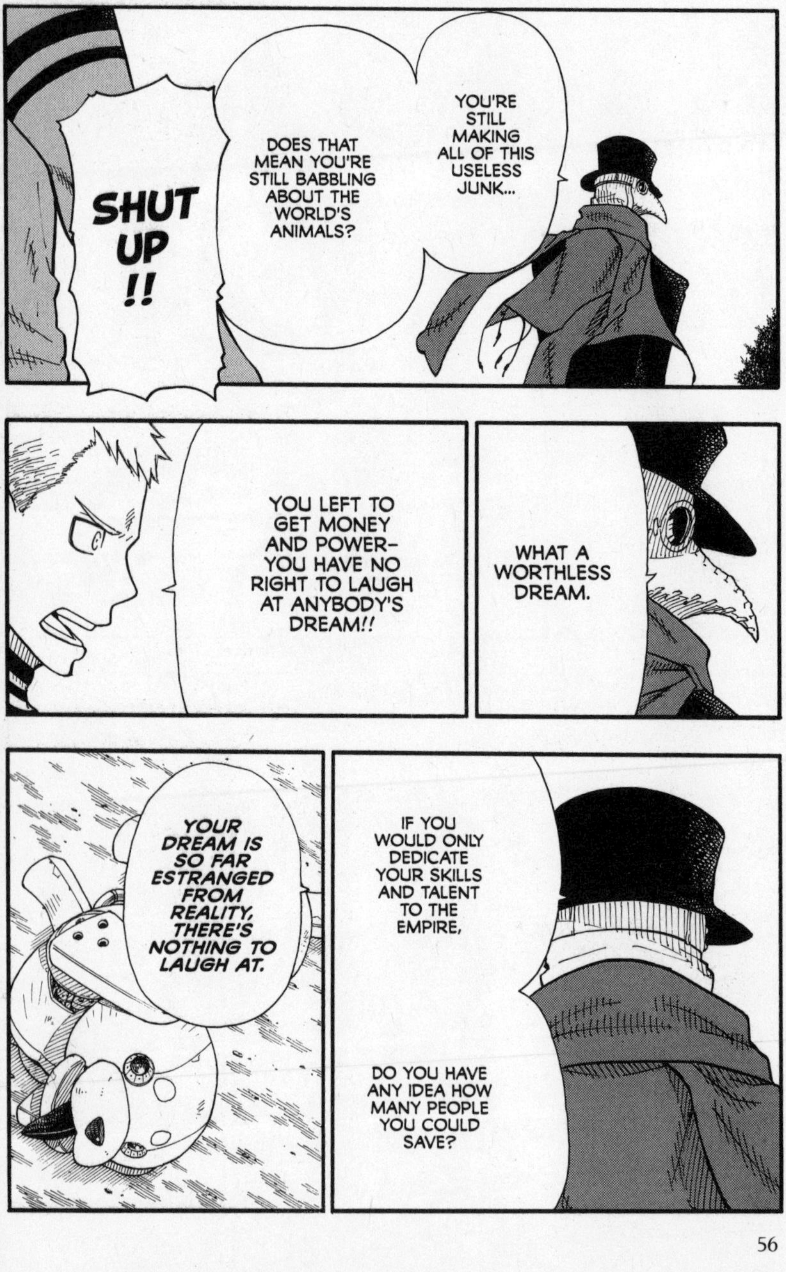
YOU'RE STILL MAKING ALL OF THIS USELESS JUNK...
DOES THAT MEAN YOU'RE STILL BABBLING ABOUT THE WORLD'S ANIMALS?
SHUT UP!!
WHAT A WORTHLESS DREAM.
YOU LEFT TO GET MONEY AND POWER–YOU HAVE NO RIGHT TO LAUGH AT ANYBODY'S DREAM!!
IF YOU WOULD ONLY DEDICATE YOUR SKILLS AND TALENT TO THE EMPIRE,
DO YOU HAVE ANY IDEA HOW MANY PEOPLE YOU COULD SAVE?
YOUR DREAM IS SO FAR ESTRANGED FROM REALITY, THERE'S NOTHING TO LAUGH AT.

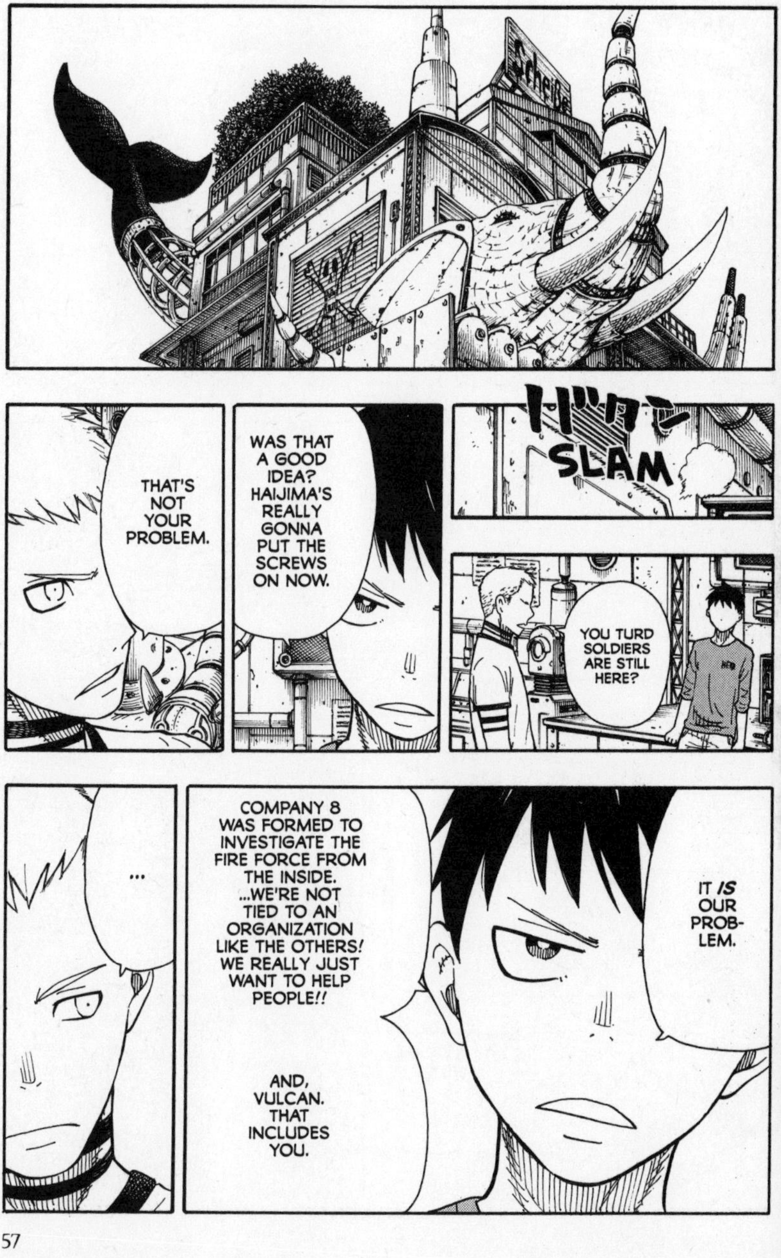
Scheiße
SLAM
YOU TURD SOLDIERS ARE STILL HERE?
WAS THAT A GOOD IDEA? HAIJIMA'S REALLY GONNA PUT THE SCREWS ON NOW.
THAT'S NOT YOUR PROBLEM.
IT *IS* OUR PROB-LEM.
COMPANY 8 WAS FORMED TO INVESTIGATE THE FIRE FORCE FROM THE INSIDE. ...WE'RE NOT TIED TO AN ORGANIZATION LIKE THE OTHERS! WE REALLY JUST WANT TO HELP PEOPLE!!
AND, VULCAN. THAT INCLUDES YOU.
...

WHOA!

ピ

SN

AP

ニャ

WHERE DID THAT COME FROM?!

NO!! WHATEVER YOU DO, DON'T PUSH THAT!!

WHAT'S THIS?

うず ITCH
うず ITCH

WHY?!

ポチ PUSH

OOOOH

WELL, DON'T TOUCH IT SOMEWHERE WEIRD. WE'RE HAVING A SERIOUS DISCUSSION HERE.

SORRY. I TOUCHED IT SOMEWHERE WEIRD AND IT WENT ALL WEIRD.

WHIZZN
ちょばばば

58

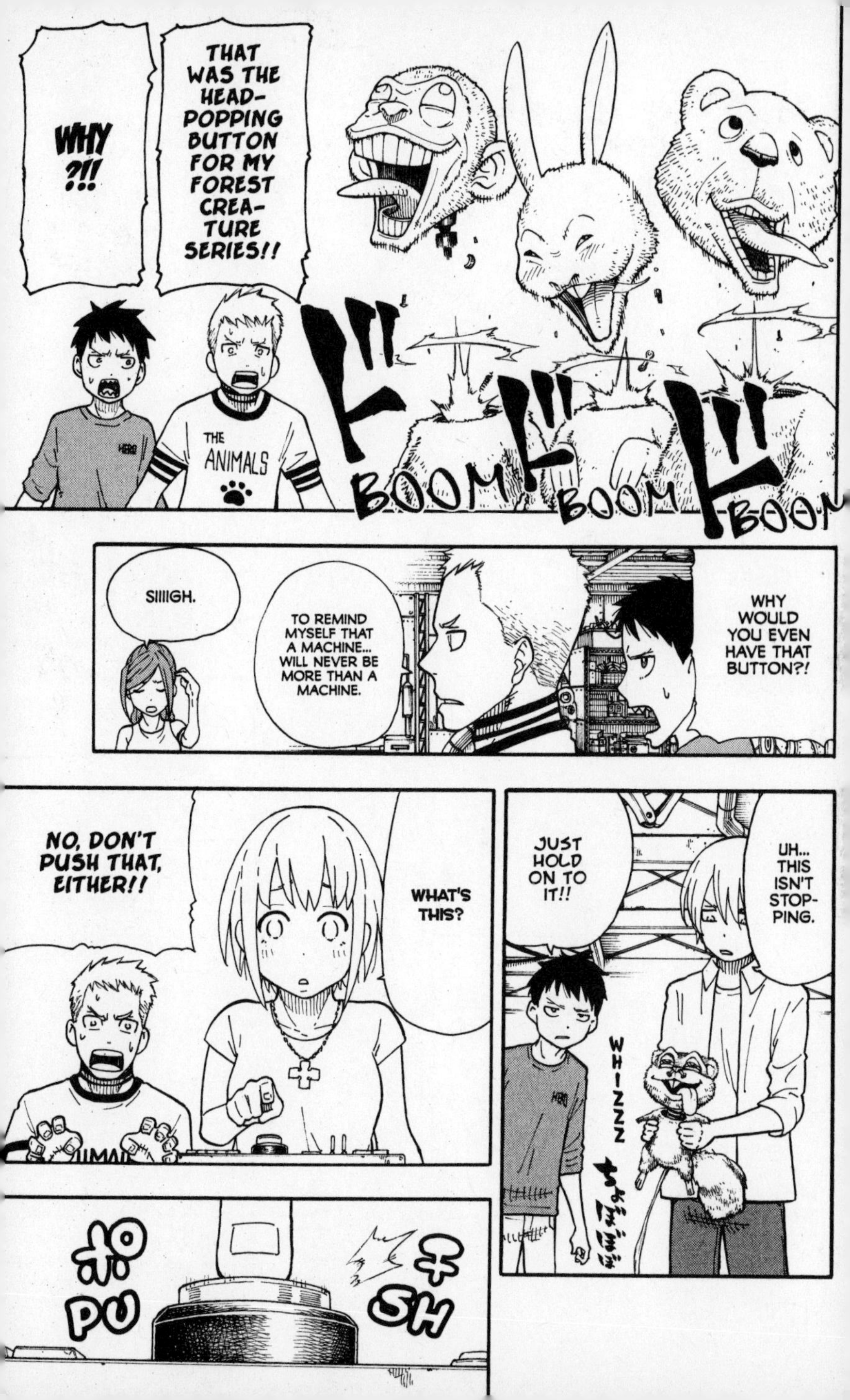
THAT WAS THE HEAD-POPPING BUTTON FOR MY FOREST CREA-TURE SERIES!!
WHY ?!!
BOOM
BOOM
BOOM
WHY WOULD YOU EVEN HAVE THAT BUTTON?!
TO REMIND MYSELF THAT A MACHINE... WILL NEVER BE MORE THAN A MACHINE.
SIIIGH.
UH... THIS ISN'T STOP-PING.
JUST HOLD ON TO IT!!
WHIZZZ
WHAT'S THIS?
NO, DON'T PUSH THAT, EITHER!!
PU
SH

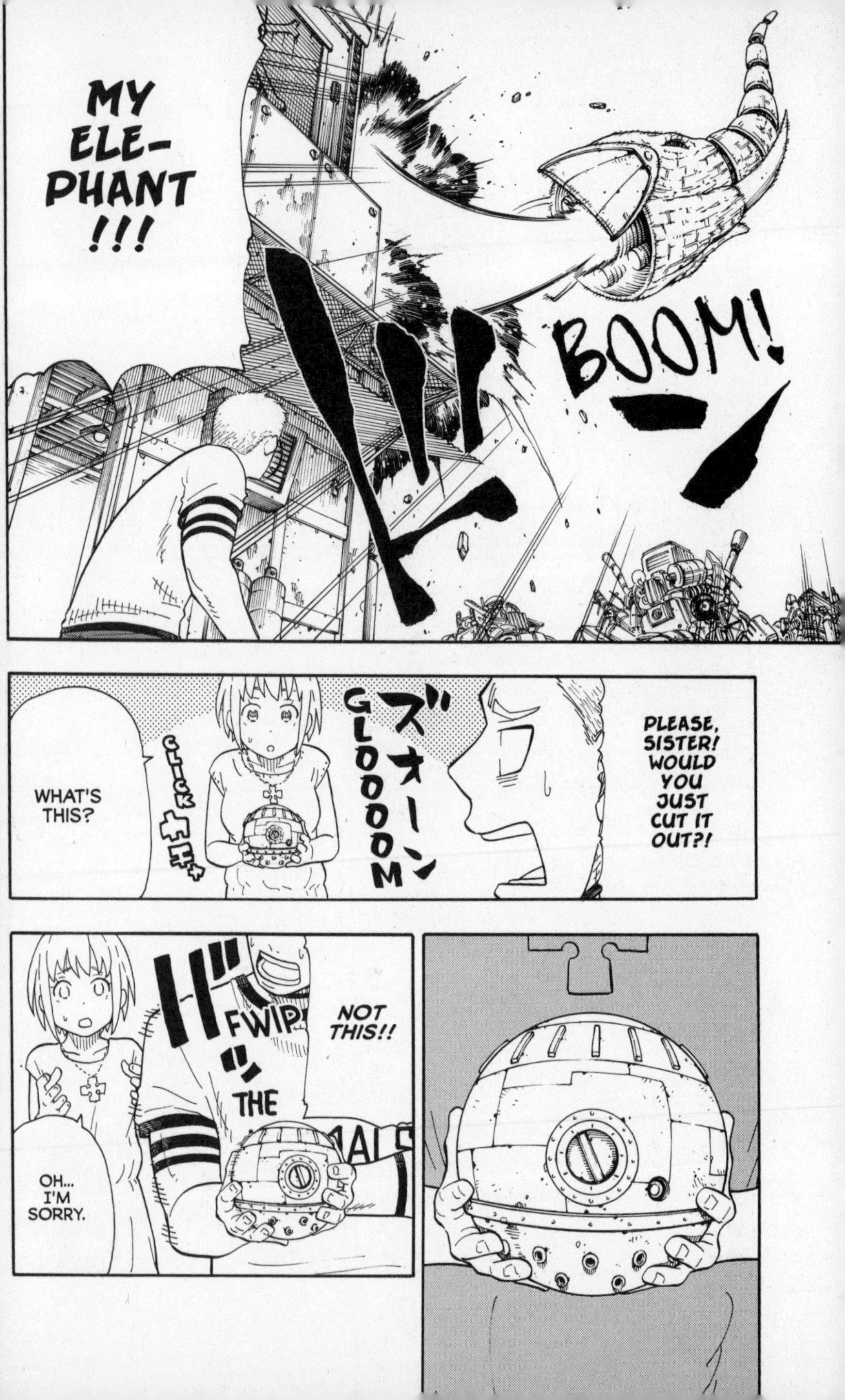
MY ELE-PHANT!!!
BOOM!
PLEASE, SISTER! WOULD YOU JUST CUT IT OUT?!
GLOOOOOM
CLICK
WHAT'S THIS?
NOT THIS!!
FWIP!
THE
OH... I'M SORRY.

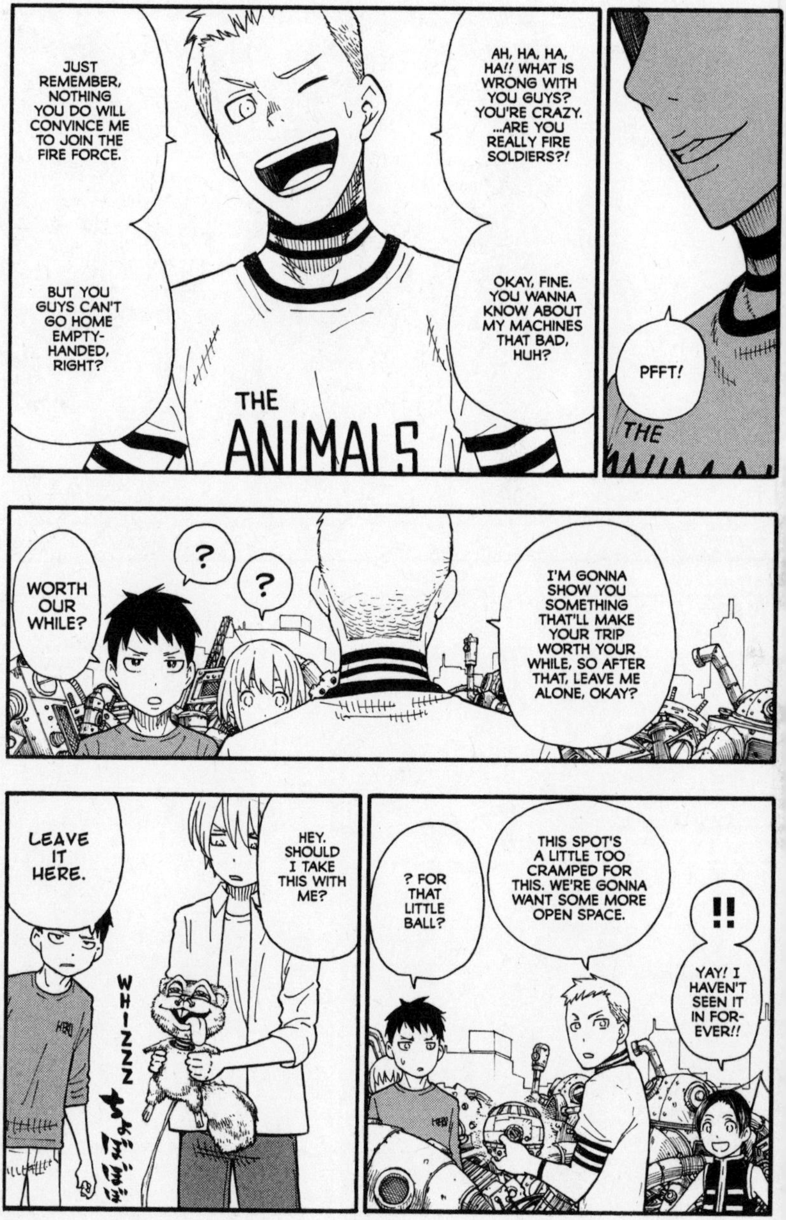
PFFT!
THE
AH, HA, HA, HA!! WHAT IS WRONG WITH YOU GUYS? YOU'RE CRAZY. ...ARE YOU REALLY FIRE SOLDIERS?!
OKAY, FINE. YOU WANNA KNOW ABOUT MY MACHINES THAT BAD, HUH?
JUST REMEMBER, NOTHING YOU DO WILL CONVINCE ME TO JOIN THE FIRE FORCE.
BUT YOU GUYS CAN'T GO HOME EMPTY-HANDED, RIGHT?
THE ANIMALS
I'M GONNA SHOW YOU SOMETHING THAT'LL MAKE YOUR TRIP WORTH YOUR WHILE, SO AFTER THAT, LEAVE ME ALONE, OKAY?
?
?
WORTH OUR WHILE?
!!
YAY! I HAVEN'T SEEN IT IN FOR-EVER!!
THIS SPOT'S A LITTLE TOO CRAMPED FOR THIS. WE'RE GONNA WANT SOME MORE OPEN SPACE.
? FOR THAT LITTLE BALL?
HEY. SHOULD I TAKE THIS WITH ME?
WHIZZZ
LEAVE IT HERE.

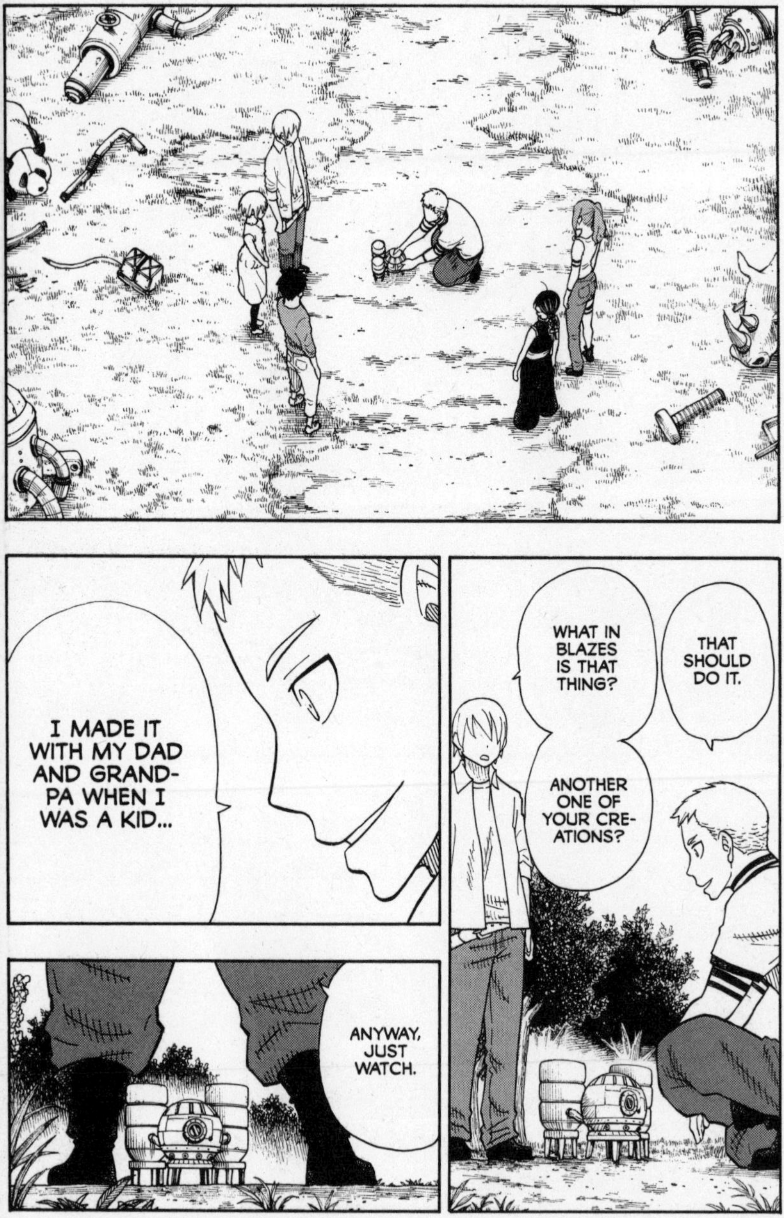
THAT SHOULD DO IT.
WHAT IN BLAZES IS THAT THING?
ANOTHER ONE OF YOUR CRE-ATIONS?
I MADE IT WITH MY DAD AND GRAND-PA WHEN I WAS A KID...
ANYWAY, JUST WATCH.

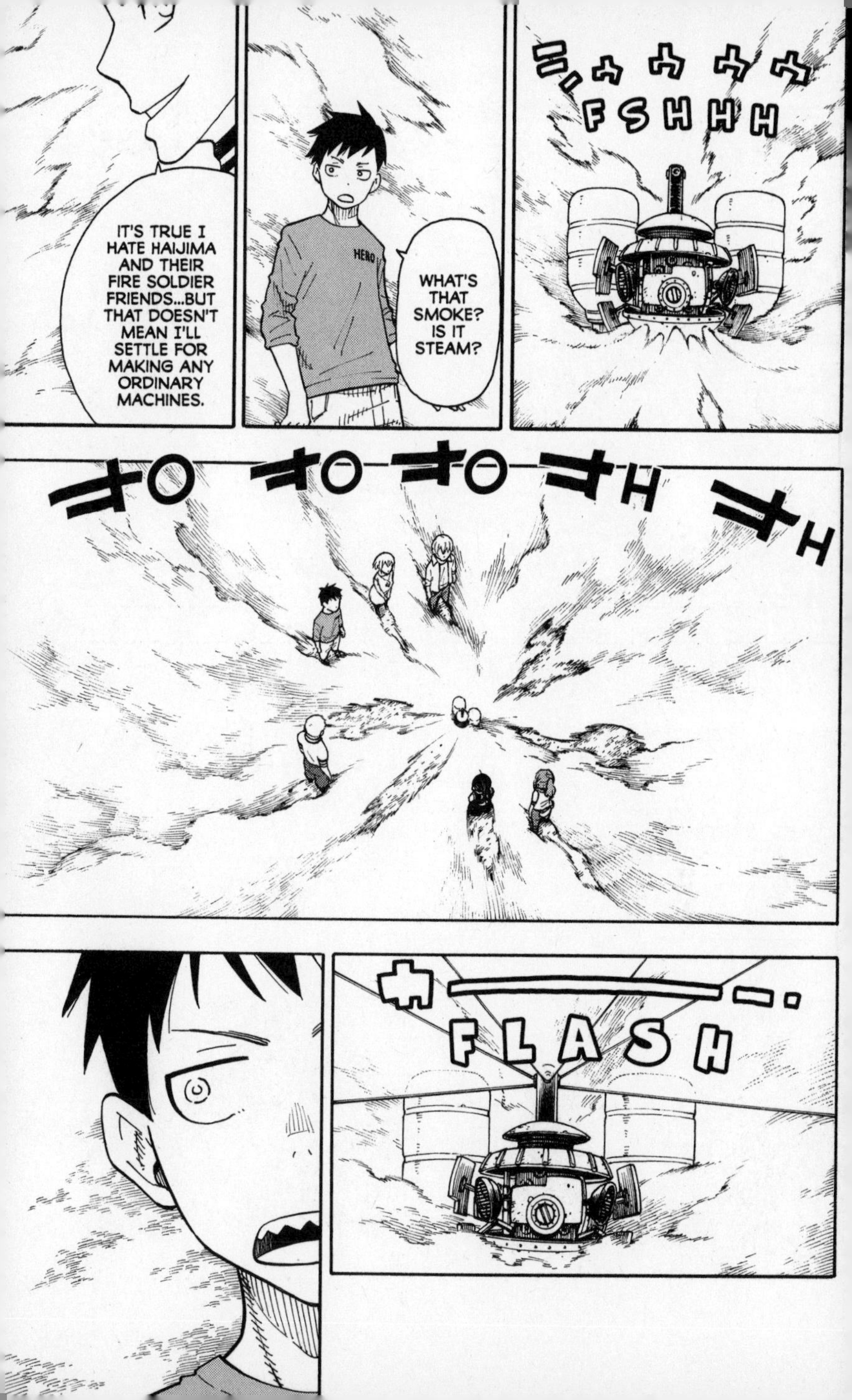
FSHHHH
WHAT'S THAT SMOKE? IS IT STEAM?
IT'S TRUE I HATE HAIJIMA AND THEIR FIRE SOLDIER FRIENDS...BUT THAT DOESN'T MEAN I'LL SETTLE FOR MAKING ANY ORDINARY MACHINES.
FLASH

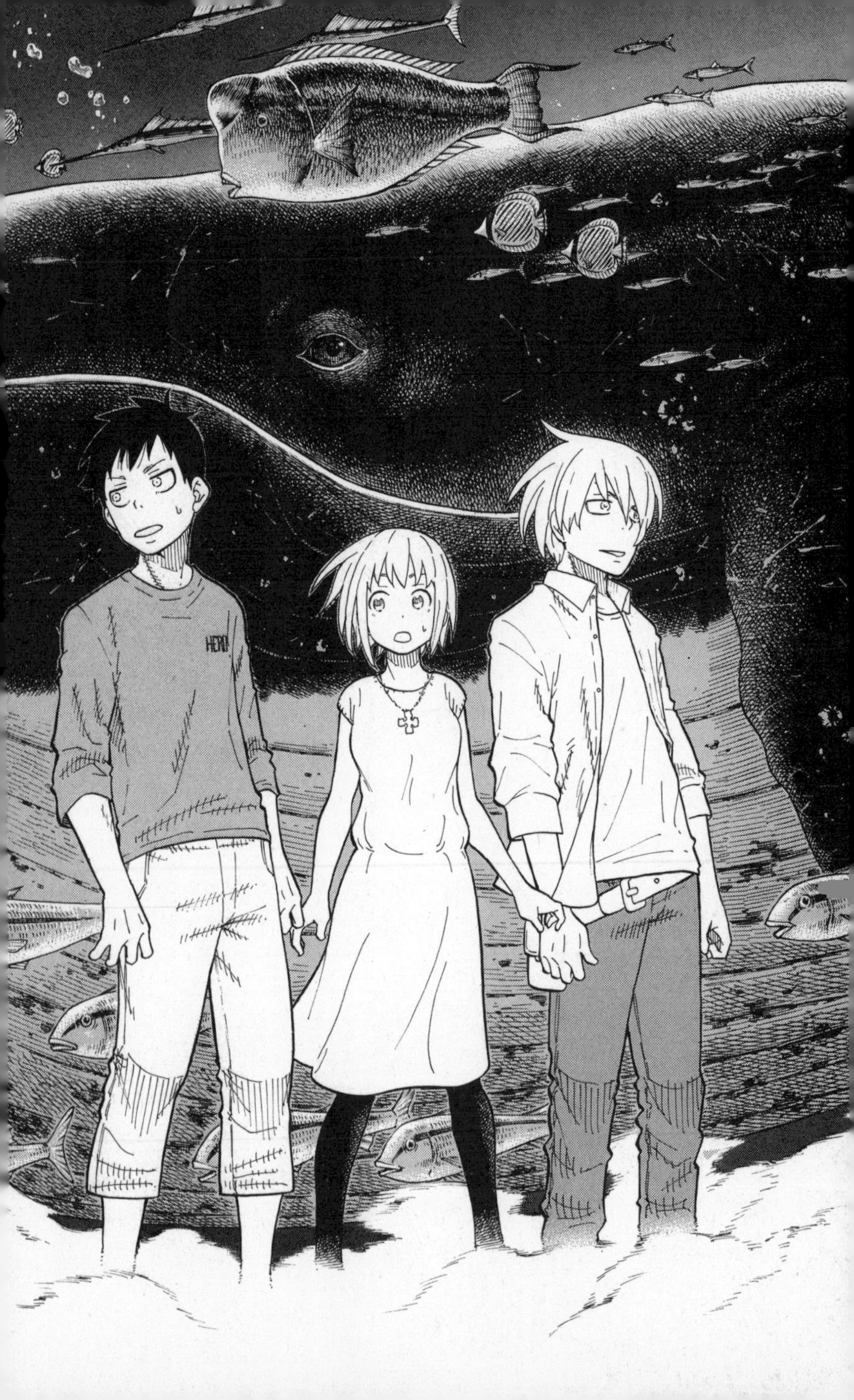
HERO

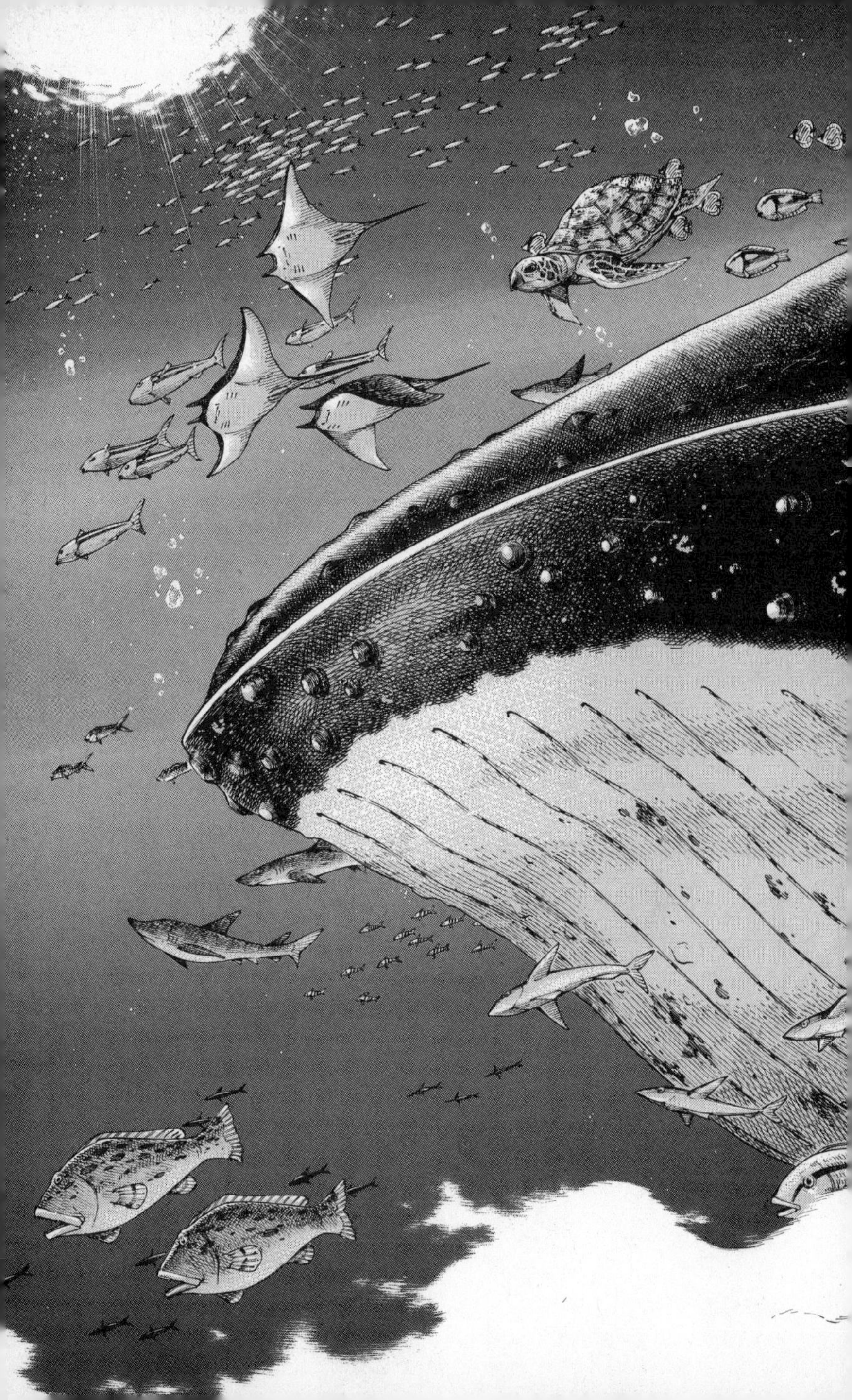

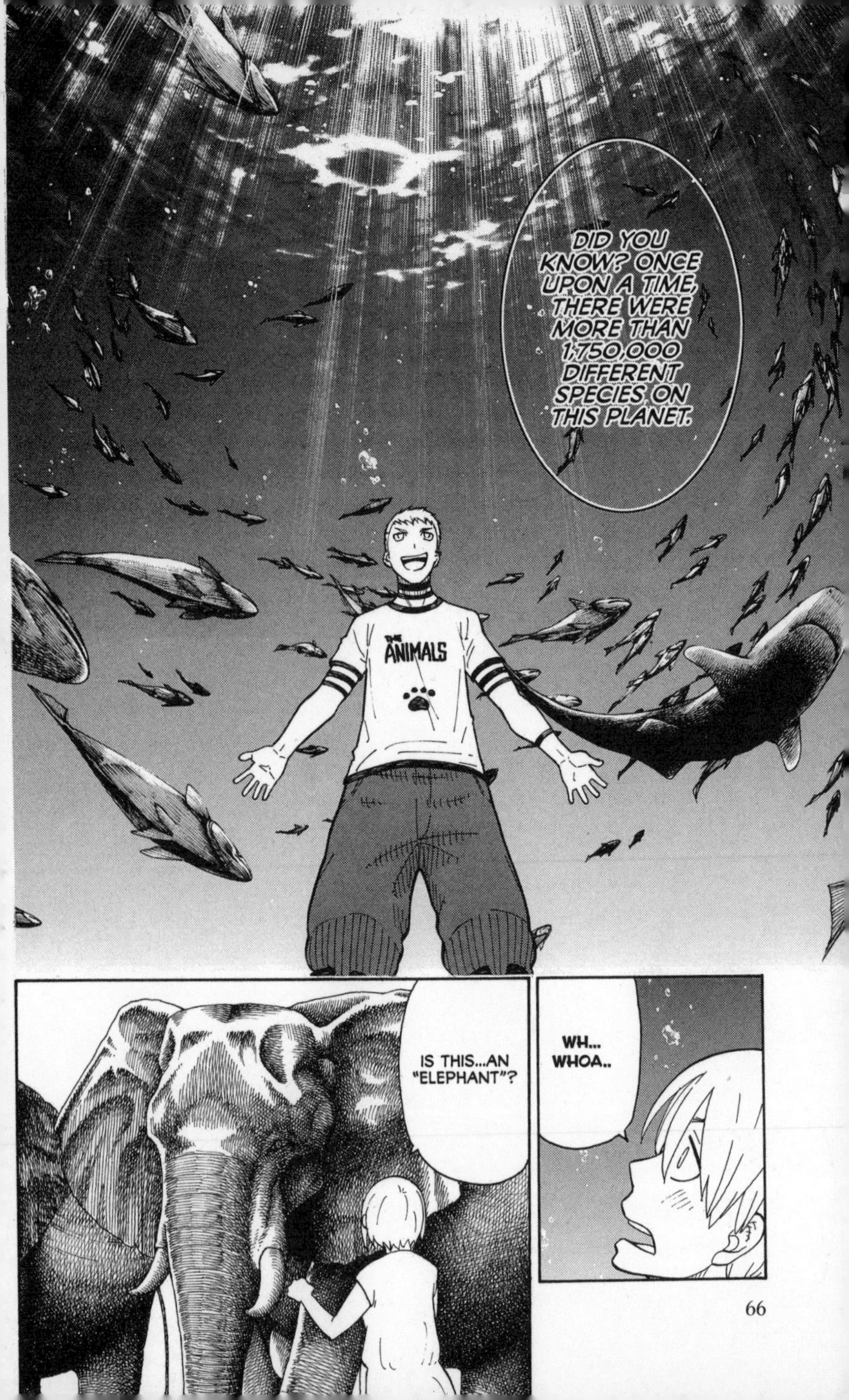
DID YOU KNOW? ONCE UPON A TIME, THERE WERE MORE THAN 1,750,000 DIFFERENT SPECIES ON THIS PLANET.
THE ANIMALS
WH... WHOA..
IS THIS...AN "ELEPHANT"?

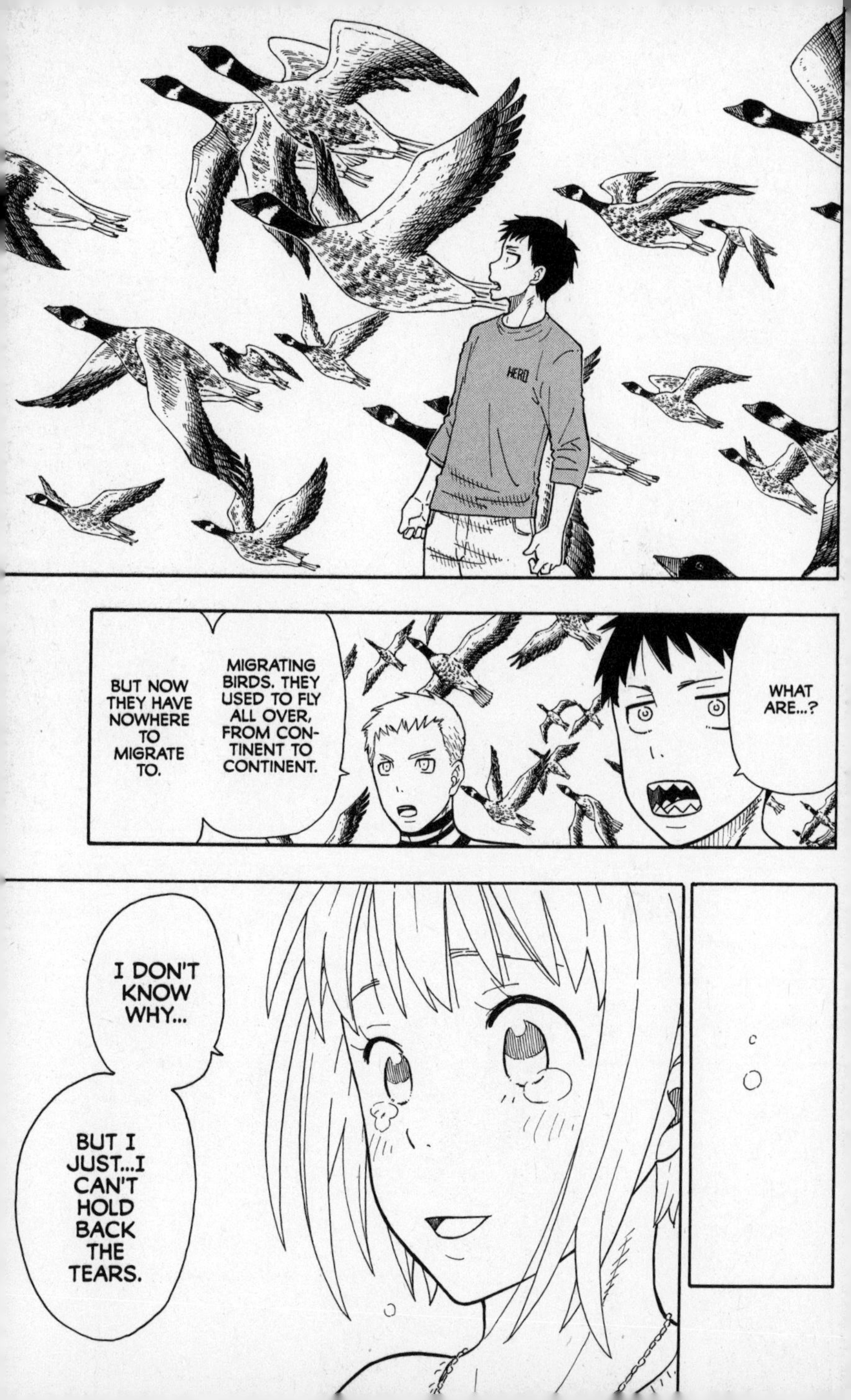
WHAT ARE...?
MIGRATING BIRDS. THEY USED TO FLY ALL OVER, FROM CONTINENT TO CONTINENT.
BUT NOW THEY HAVE NOWHERE TO MIGRATE TO.
I DON'T KNOW WHY...
BUT I JUST...I CAN'T HOLD BACK THE TEARS.

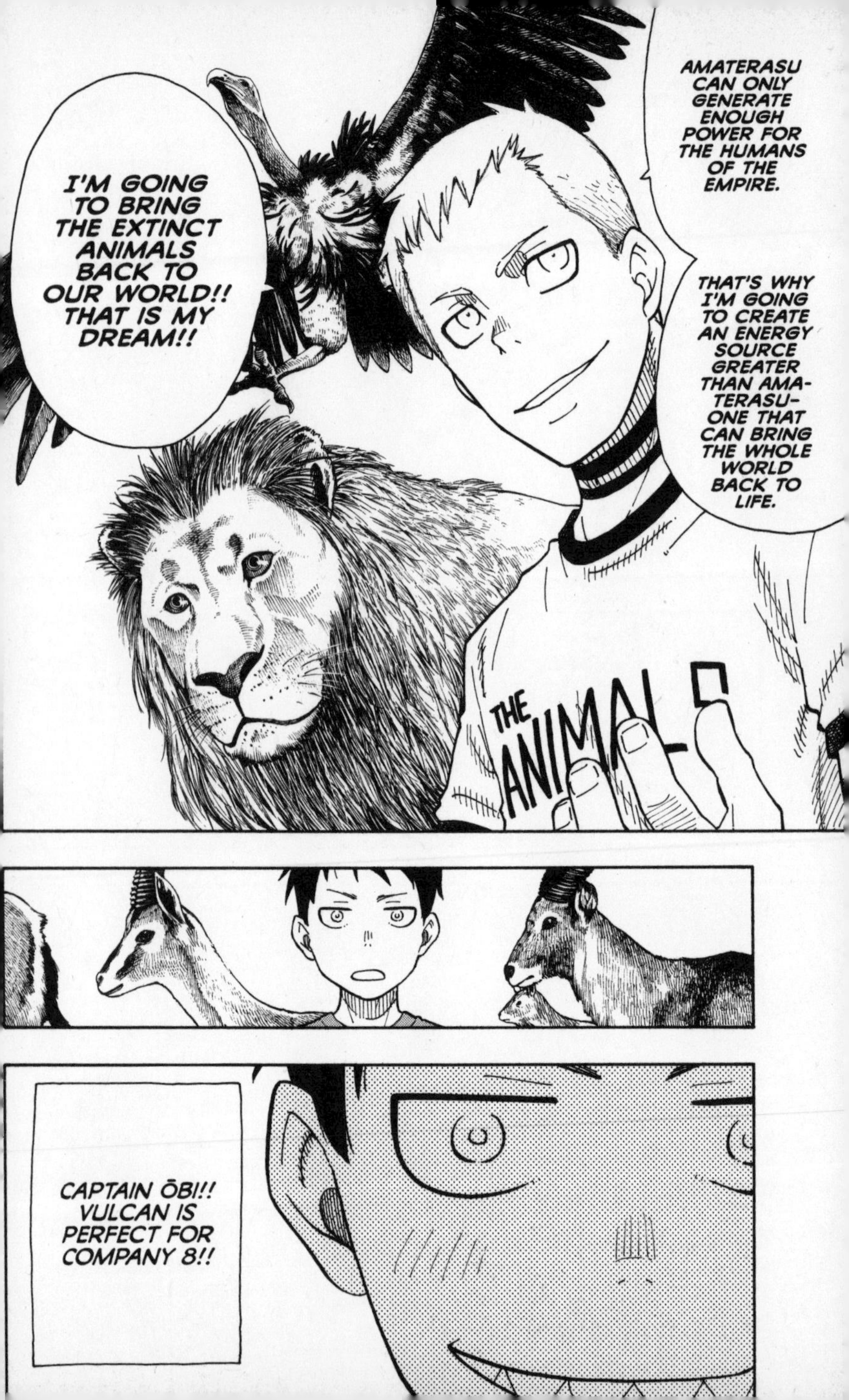
AMATERASU CAN ONLY GENERATE ENOUGH POWER FOR THE HUMANS OF THE EMPIRE.
THAT'S WHY I'M GOING TO CREATE AN ENERGY SOURCE GREATER THAN AMATERASU-ONE THAT CAN BRING THE WHOLE WORLD BACK TO LIFE.
I'M GOING TO BRING THE EXTINCT ANIMALS BACK TO OUR WORLD!! THAT IS MY DREAM!!
CAPTAIN ŌBI!! VULCAN IS PERFECT FOR COMPANY 8!!

FIRE FORCE

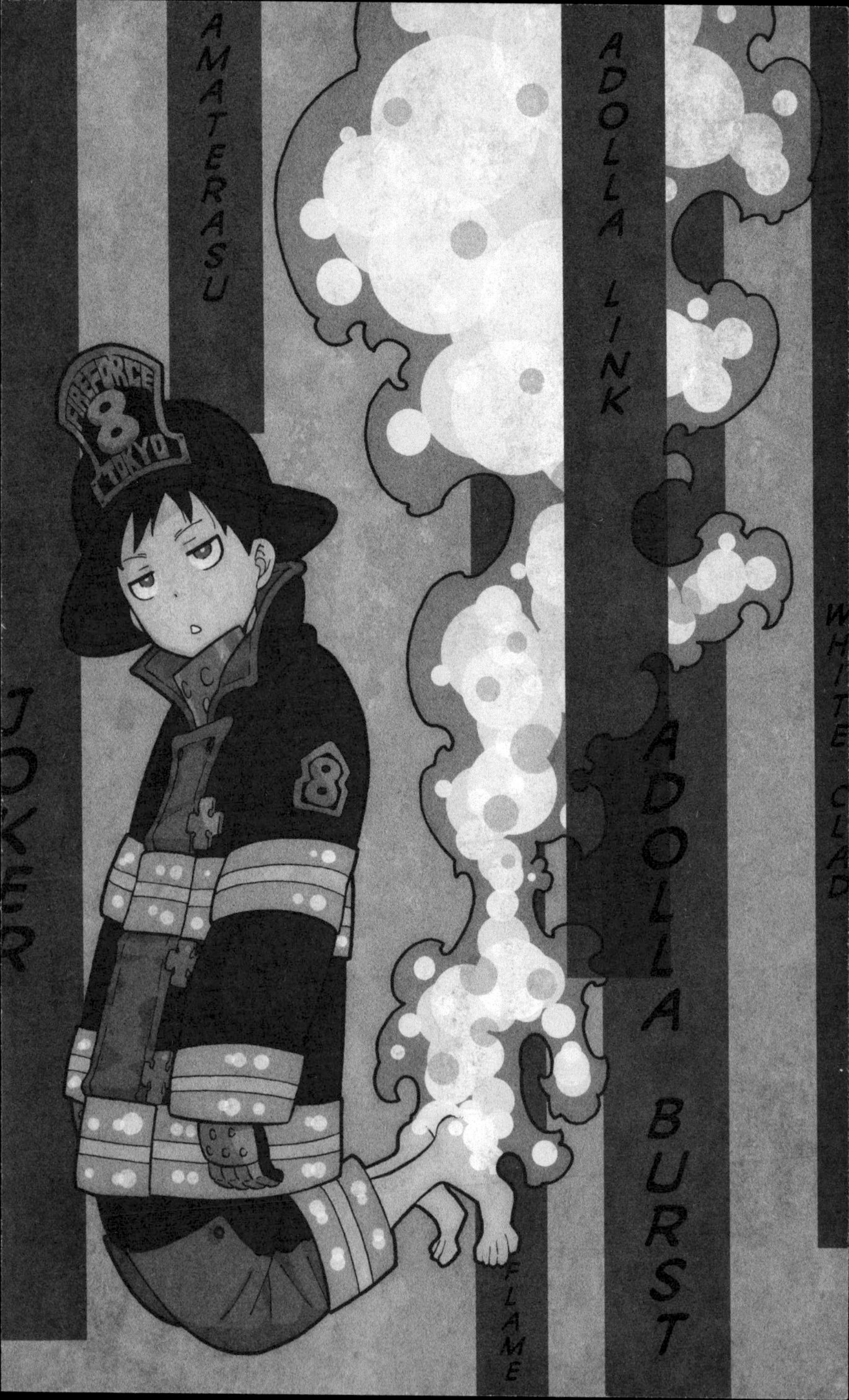
WHITE CLAD
ADOLLA BURST
ADOLLA LINK
FLAME
AMATERASU
FIREFORCE
8
TOKYO
8
JOKER

CHAPTER LV: THE BLACKSMITH'S DREAM

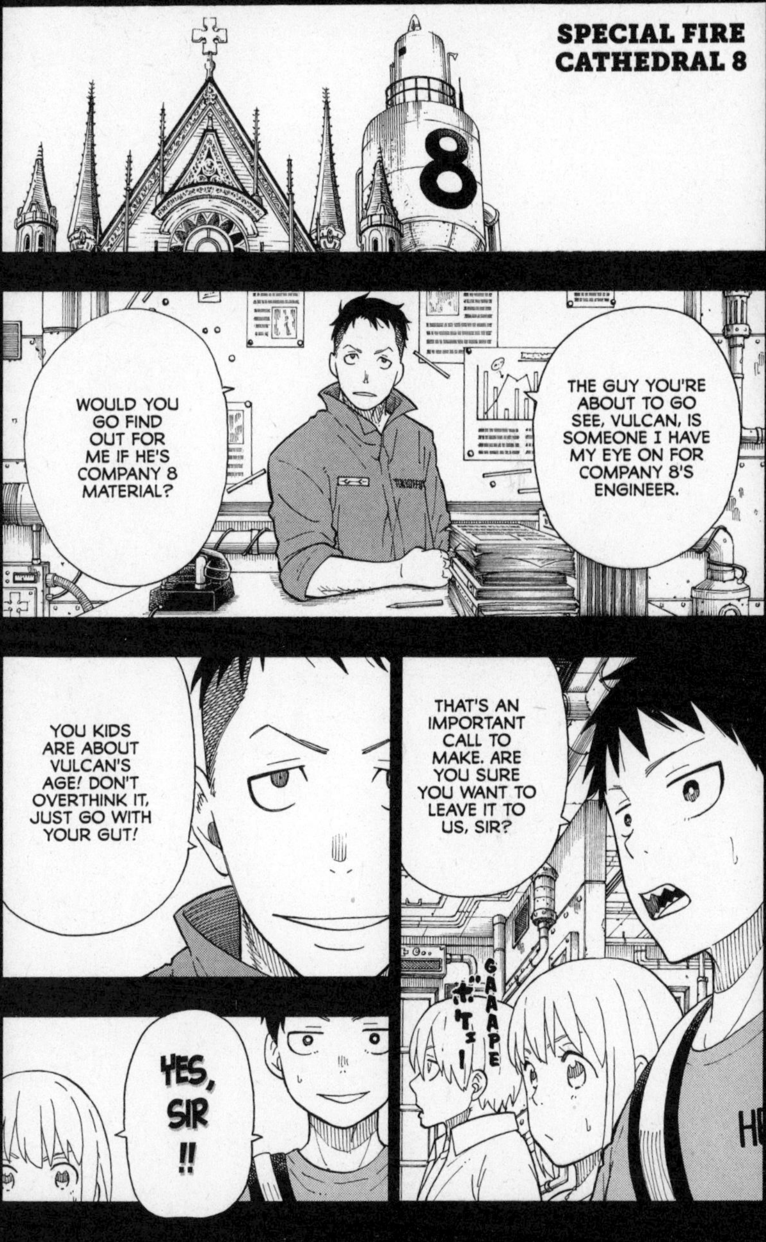
SPECIAL FIRE CATHEDRAL 8
THE GUY YOU'RE ABOUT TO GO SEE, VULCAN, IS SOMEONE I HAVE MY EYE ON FOR COMPANY 8'S ENGINEER.
WOULD YOU GO FIND OUT FOR ME IF HE'S COMPANY 8 MATERIAL?
THAT'S AN IMPORTANT CALL TO MAKE. ARE YOU SURE YOU WANT TO LEAVE IT TO US, SIR?
GAAAPE
YOU KIDS ARE ABOUT VULCAN'S AGE! DON'T OVERTHINK IT, JUST GO WITH YOUR GUT!
YES, SIR!!

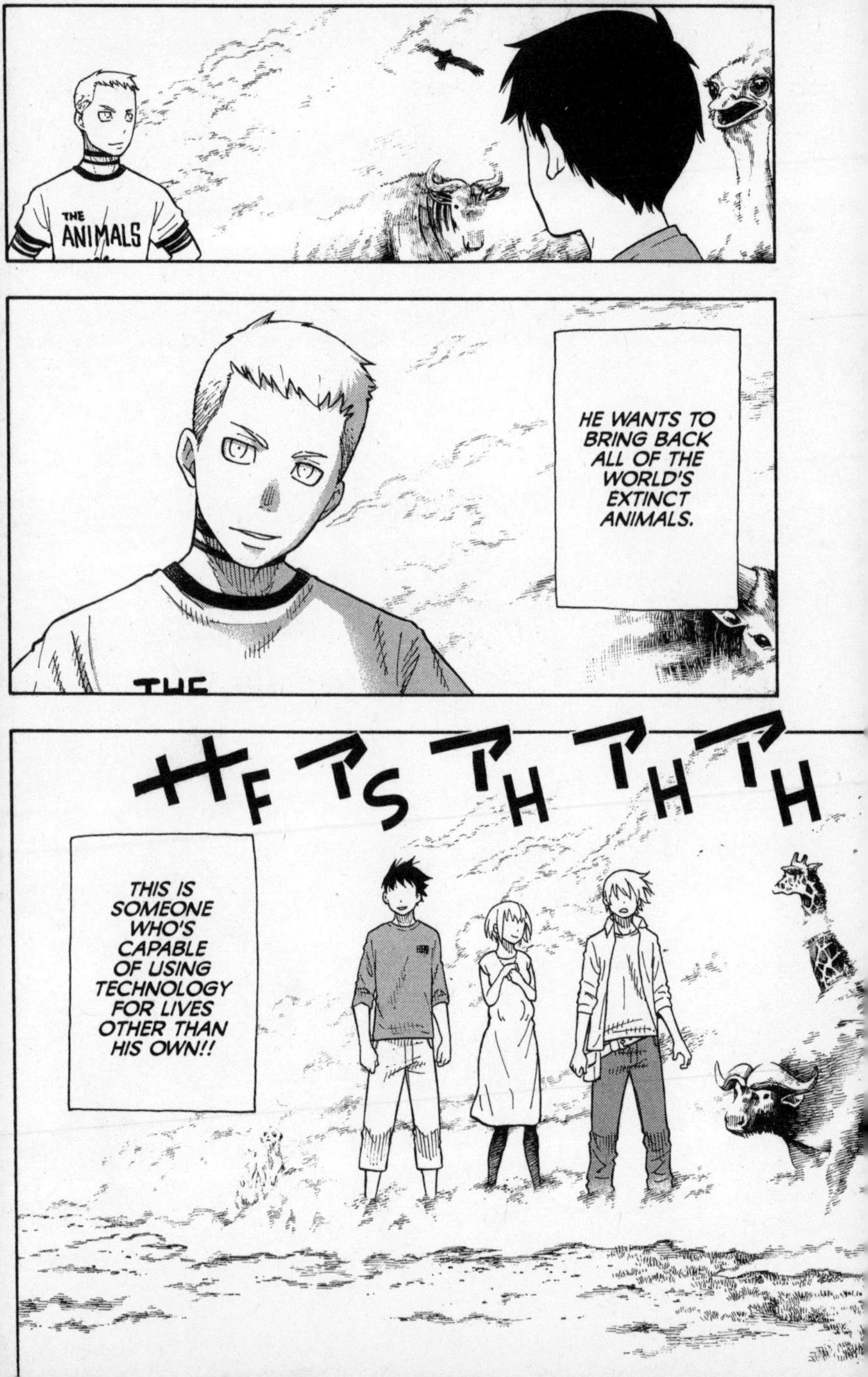
THE ANIMALS
HE WANTS TO BRING BACK ALL OF THE WORLD'S EXTINCT ANIMALS.
THE
FSHHH
THIS IS SOMEONE WHO'S CAPABLE OF USING TECHNOLOGY FOR LIVES OTHER THAN HIS OWN!!

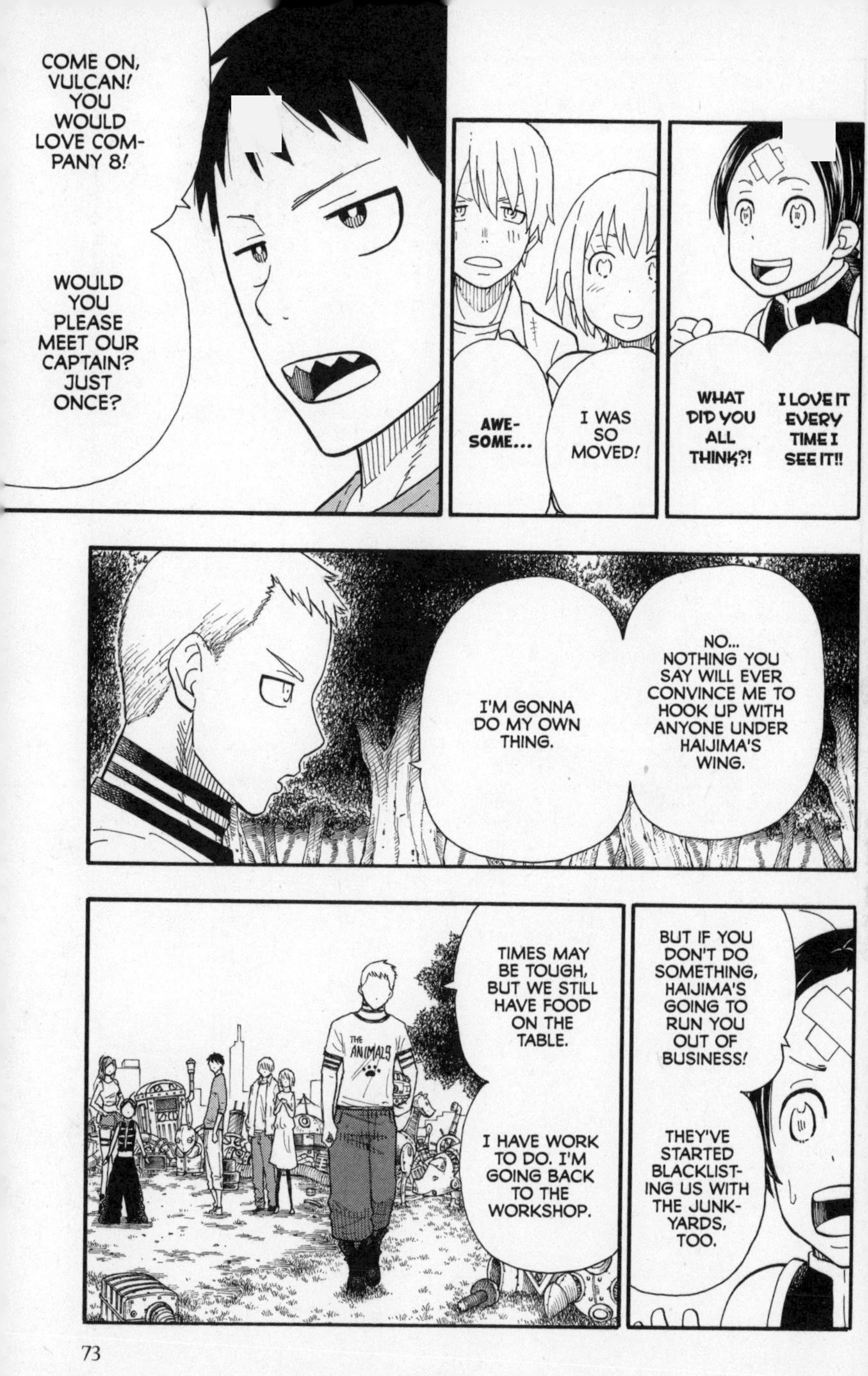
I LOVE IT EVERY TIME I SEE IT!!
WHAT DID YOU ALL THINK?!
I WAS SO MOVED!
AWE-SOME...
COME ON, VULCAN! YOU WOULD LOVE COM-PANY 8!
WOULD YOU PLEASE MEET OUR CAPTAIN? JUST ONCE?
NO... NOTHING YOU SAY WILL EVER CONVINCE ME TO HOOK UP WITH ANYONE UNDER HAIJIMA'S WING.
I'M GONNA DO MY OWN THING.
BUT IF YOU DON'T DO SOMETHING, HAIJIMA'S GOING TO RUN YOU OUT OF BUSINESS!
THEY'VE STARTED BLACKLIST-ING US WITH THE JUNK-YARDS, TOO.
TIMES MAY BE TOUGH, BUT WE STILL HAVE FOOD ON THE TABLE.
I HAVE WORK TO DO. I'M GOING BACK TO THE WORKSHOP.
THE ANIMALS

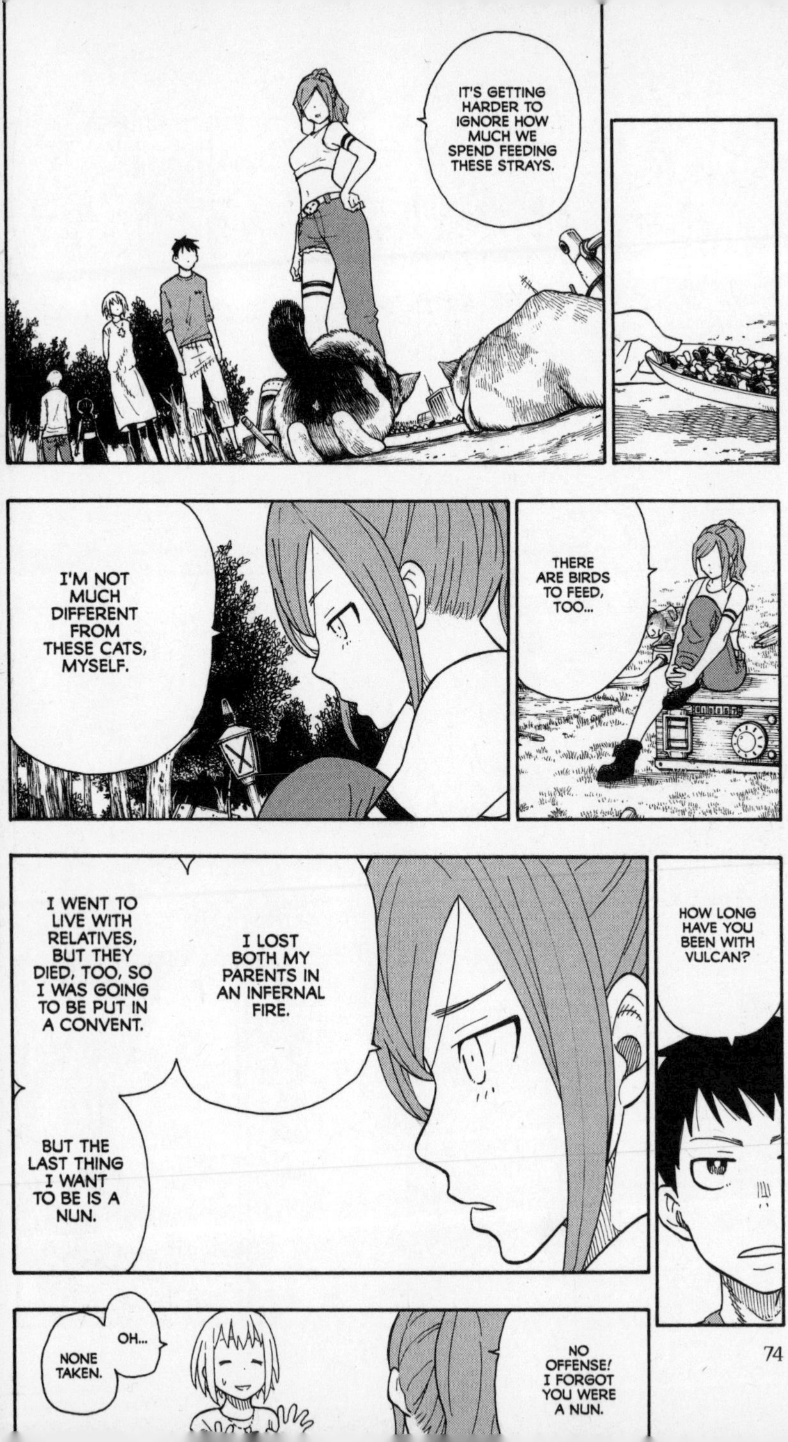
IT'S GETTING HARDER TO IGNORE HOW MUCH WE SPEND FEEDING THESE STRAYS.
THERE ARE BIRDS TO FEED, TOO...
I'M NOT MUCH DIFFERENT FROM THESE CATS, MYSELF.
HOW LONG HAVE YOU BEEN WITH VULCAN?
I LOST BOTH MY PARENTS IN AN INFERNAL FIRE.
I WENT TO LIVE WITH RELATIVES, BUT THEY DIED, TOO, SO I WAS GOING TO BE PUT IN A CONVENT.
BUT THE LAST THING I WANT TO BE IS A NUN.
NO OFFENSE! I FORGOT YOU WERE A NUN.
OH... NONE TAKEN.

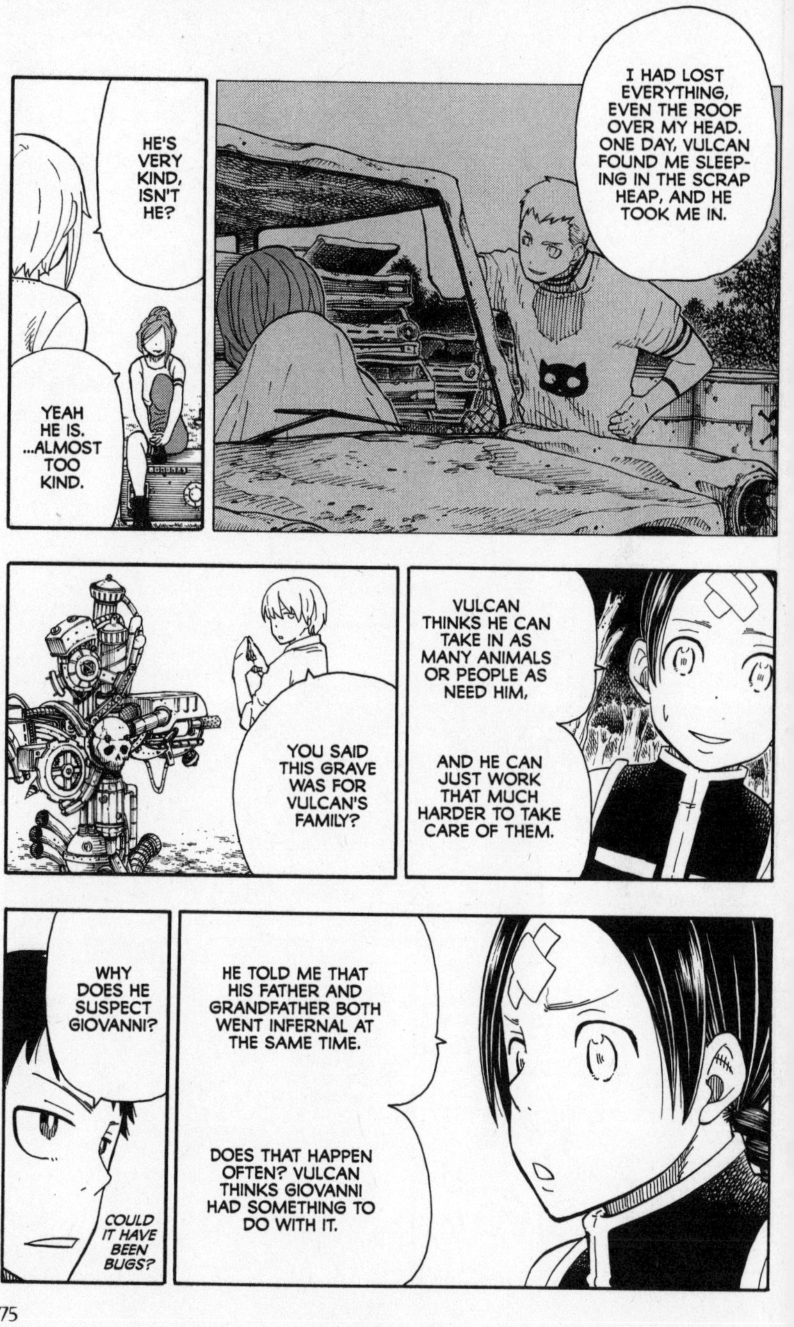
I HAD LOST EVERYTHING, EVEN THE ROOF OVER MY HEAD. ONE DAY, VULCAN FOUND ME SLEEPING IN THE SCRAP HEAP, AND HE TOOK ME IN.
HE'S VERY KIND, ISN'T HE?
YEAH HE IS. ...ALMOST TOO KIND.
VULCAN THINKS HE CAN TAKE IN AS MANY ANIMALS OR PEOPLE AS NEED HIM,
AND HE CAN JUST WORK THAT MUCH HARDER TO TAKE CARE OF THEM.
YOU SAID THIS GRAVE WAS FOR VULCAN'S FAMILY?
HE TOLD ME THAT HIS FATHER AND GRANDFATHER BOTH WENT INFERNAL AT THE SAME TIME.
DOES THAT HAPPEN OFTEN? VULCAN THINKS GIOVANNI HAD SOMETHING TO DO WITH IT.
WHY DOES HE SUSPECT GIOVANNI?
COULD IT HAVE BEEN BUGS?

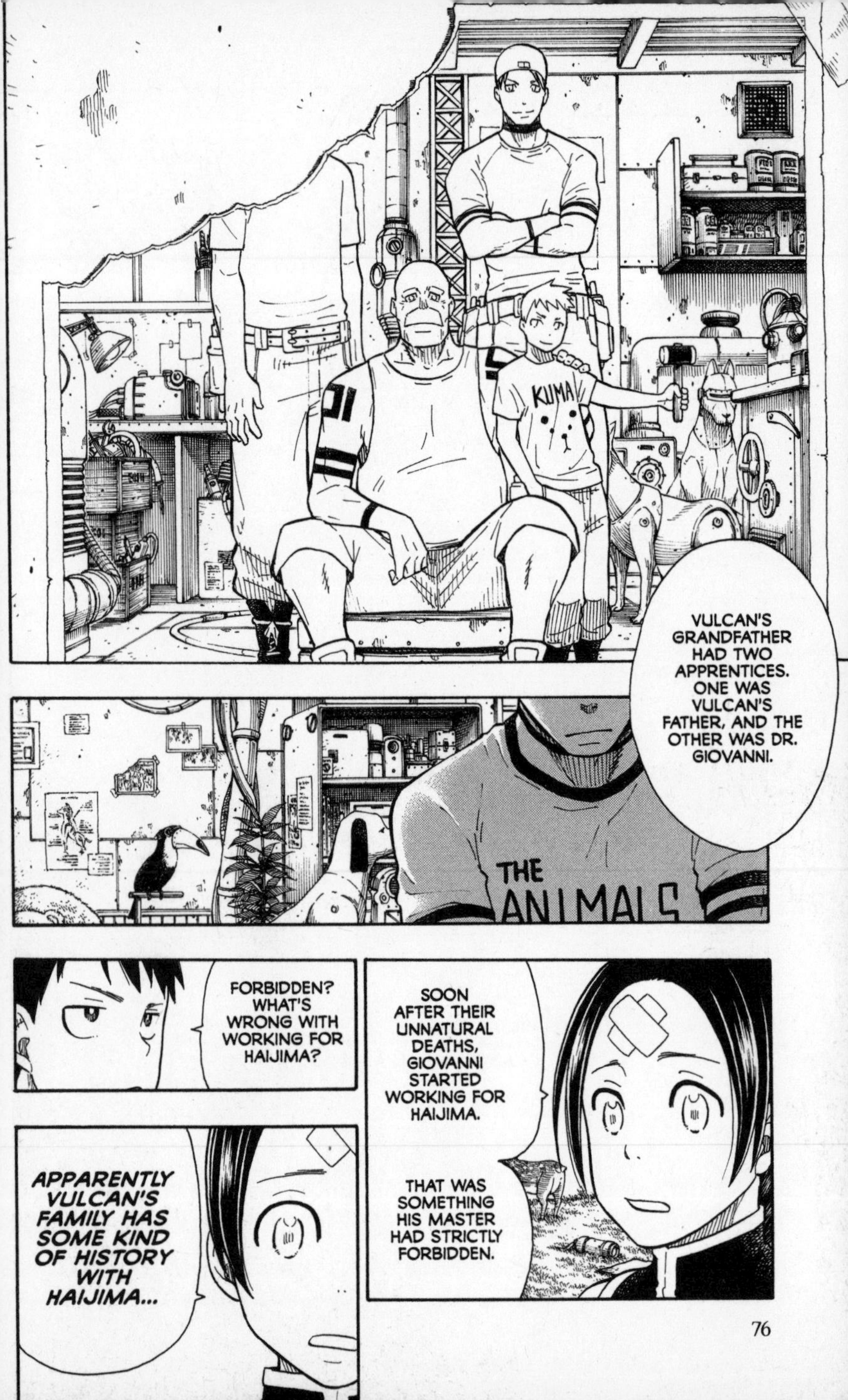
KUMA
VULCAN'S GRANDFATHER HAD TWO APPRENTICES. ONE WAS VULCAN'S FATHER, AND THE OTHER WAS DR. GIOVANNI.
THE ANIMALS
SOON AFTER THEIR UNNATURAL DEATHS, GIOVANNI STARTED WORKING FOR HAIJIMA.
THAT WAS SOMETHING HIS MASTER HAD STRICTLY FORBIDDEN.
FORBIDDEN? WHAT'S WRONG WITH WORKING FOR HAIJIMA?
APPARENTLY VULCAN'S FAMILY HAS SOME KIND OF HISTORY WITH HAIJIMA...

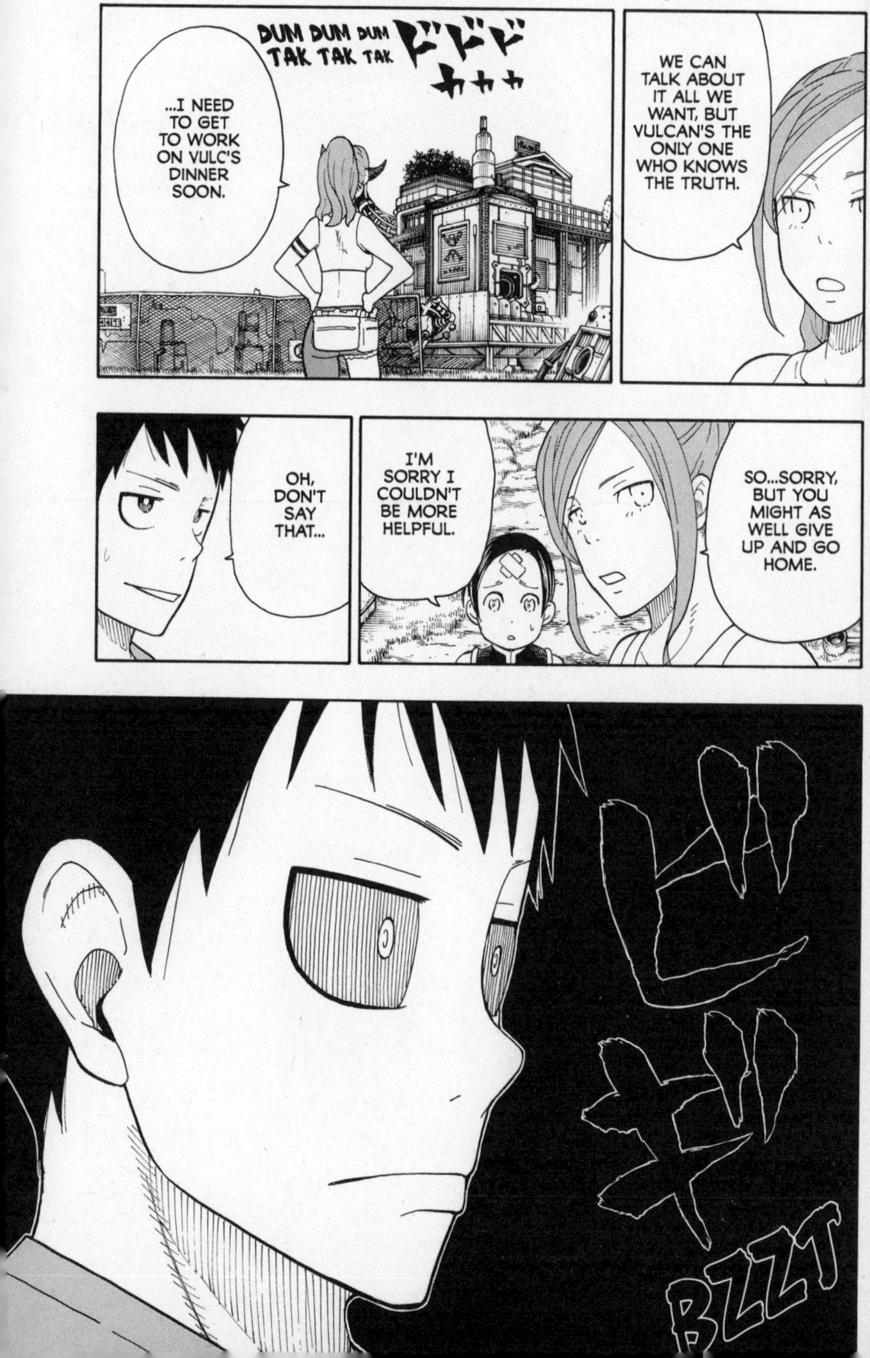
WE CAN TALK ABOUT IT ALL WE WANT, BUT VULCAN'S THE ONLY ONE WHO KNOWS THE TRUTH.
DUM DUM DUM TAK TAK TAK
...I NEED TO GET TO WORK ON VULC'S DINNER SOON.
SO...SORRY, BUT YOU MIGHT AS WELL GIVE UP AND GO HOME.
I'M SORRY I COULDN'T BE MORE HELPFUL.
OH, DON'T SAY THAT...
BZZT

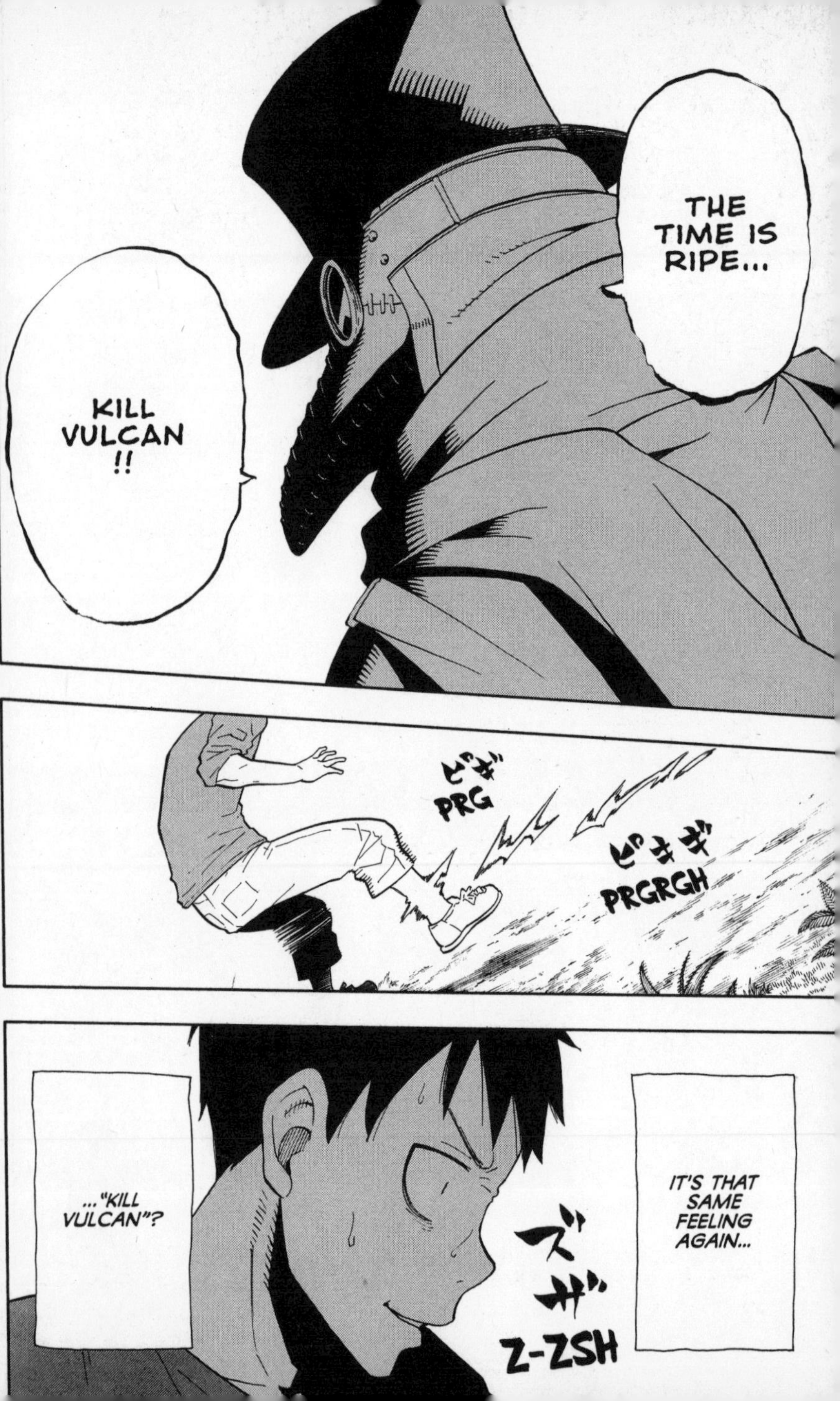
THE TIME IS RIPE...
KILL VULCAN !!
PRG
PRGRGH
IT'S THAT SAME FEELING AGAIN...
Z-ZSH
..."KILL VULCAN"?

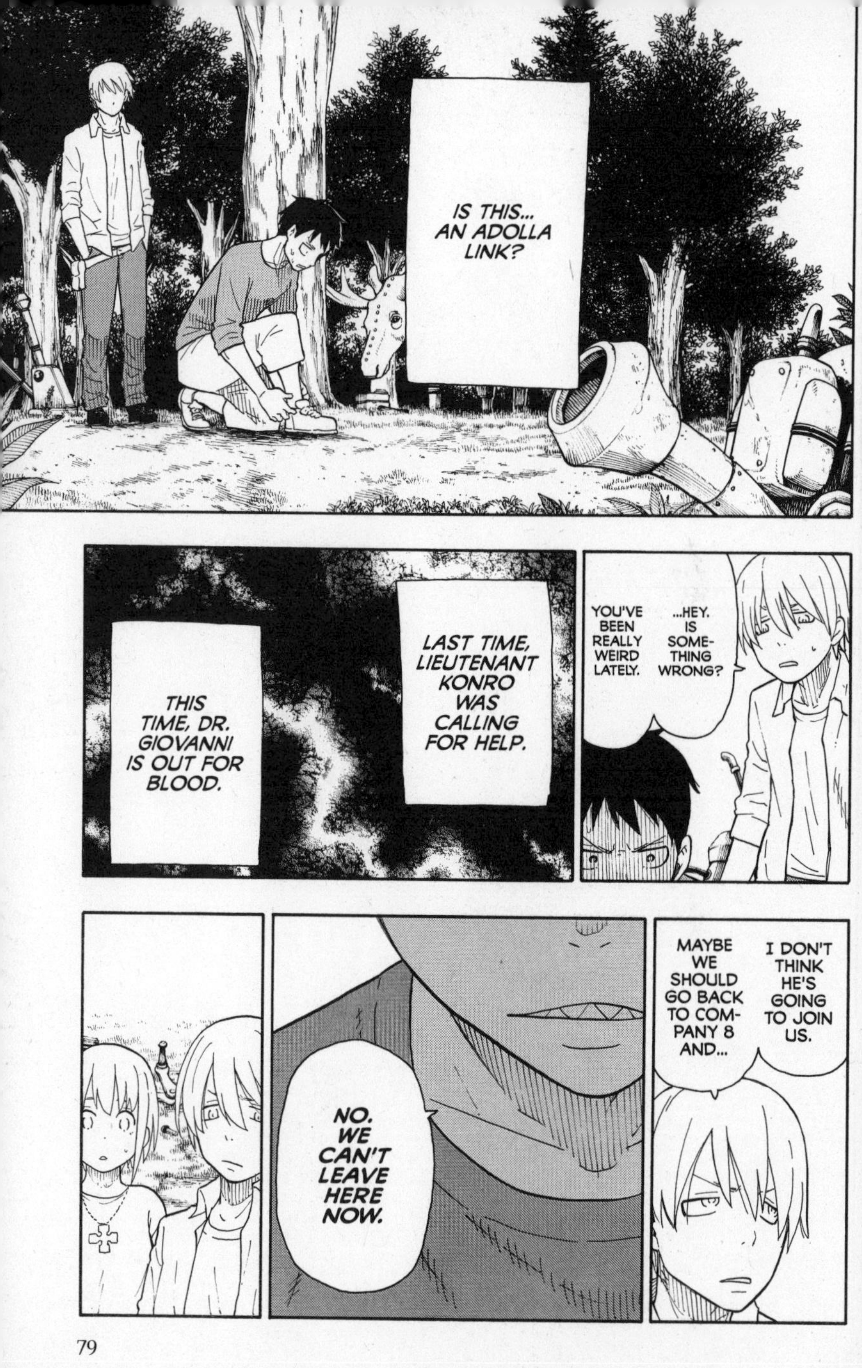
IS THIS... AN ADOLLA LINK?
...HEY. IS SOMETHING WRONG?
YOU'VE BEEN REALLY WEIRD LATELY.
LAST TIME, LIEUTENANT KONRO WAS CALLING FOR HELP.
THIS TIME, DR. GIOVANNI IS OUT FOR BLOOD.
I DON'T THINK HE'S GOING TO JOIN US.
MAYBE WE SHOULD GO BACK TO COMPANY 8 AND...
NO. WE CAN'T LEAVE HERE NOW.

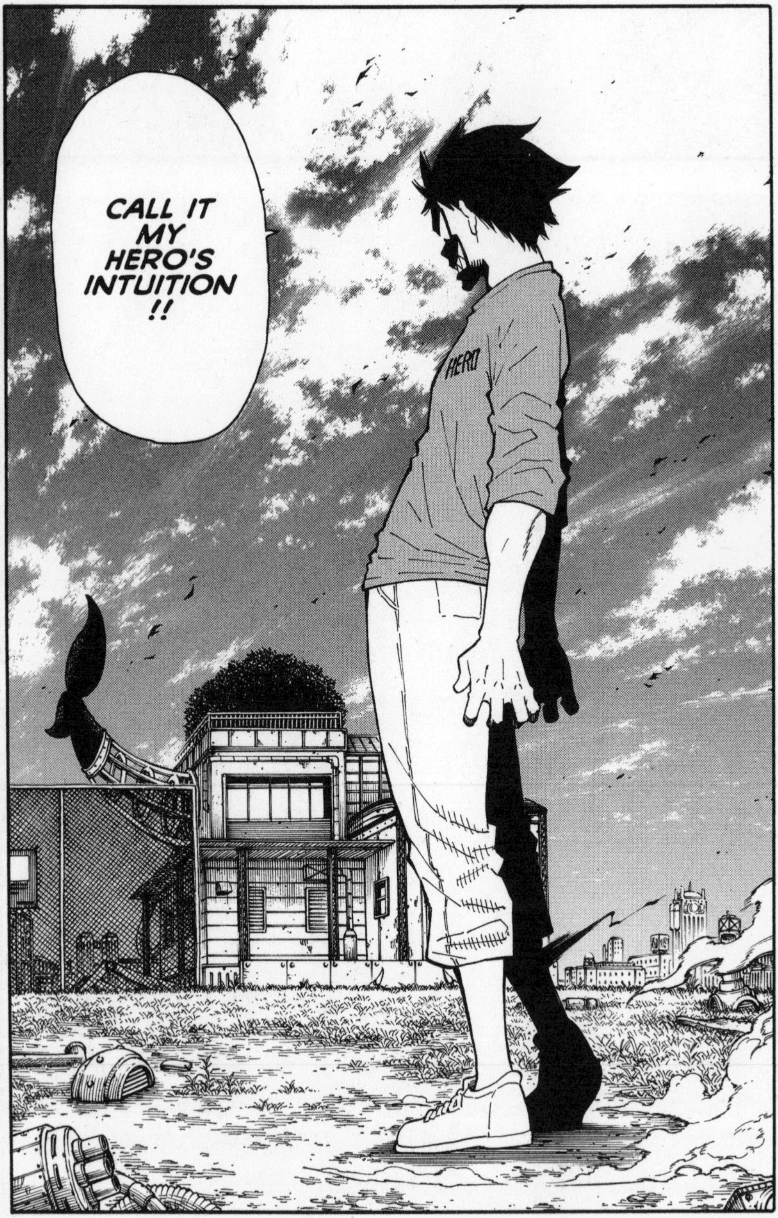
CALL IT MY HERO'S INTUITION !!
HERO

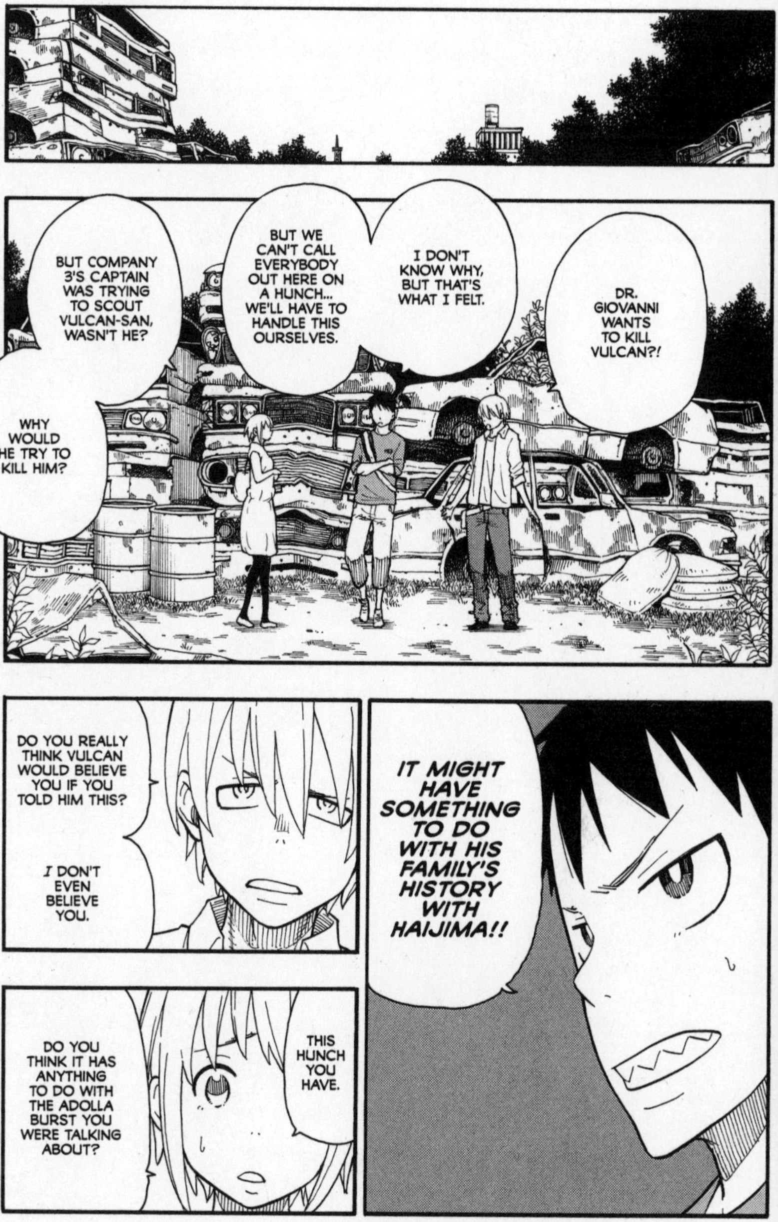
DR. GIOVANNI WANTS TO KILL VULCAN?!
I DON'T KNOW WHY, BUT THAT'S WHAT I FELT.
BUT WE CAN'T CALL EVERYBODY OUT HERE ON A HUNCH... WE'LL HAVE TO HANDLE THIS OURSELVES.
BUT COMPANY 3'S CAPTAIN WAS TRYING TO SCOUT VULCAN-SAN, WASN'T HE?
WHY WOULD HE TRY TO KILL HIM?
IT MIGHT HAVE SOMETHING TO DO WITH HIS FAMILY'S HISTORY WITH HAIJIMA!!
DO YOU REALLY THINK VULCAN WOULD BELIEVE YOU IF YOU TOLD HIM THIS?
I DON'T EVEN BELIEVE YOU.
THIS HUNCH YOU HAVE.
DO YOU THINK IT HAS ANYTHING TO DO WITH THE ADOLLA BURST YOU WERE TALKING ABOUT?

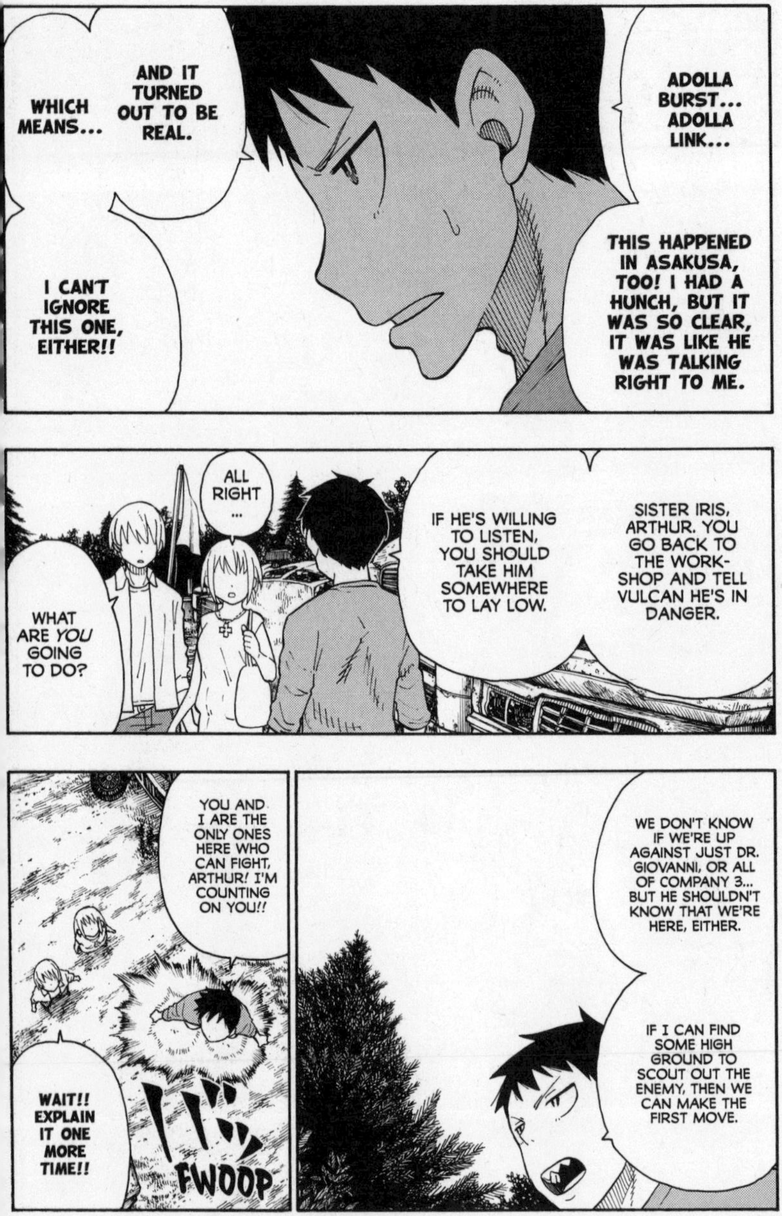
ADOLLA BURST... ADOLLA LINK...
THIS HAPPENED IN ASAKUSA, TOO! I HAD A HUNCH, BUT IT WAS SO CLEAR, IT WAS LIKE HE WAS TALKING RIGHT TO ME.
AND IT TURNED OUT TO BE REAL.
WHICH MEANS...
I CAN'T IGNORE THIS ONE, EITHER!!
SISTER IRIS, ARTHUR. YOU GO BACK TO THE WORK-SHOP AND TELL VULCAN HE'S IN DANGER.
IF HE'S WILLING TO LISTEN, YOU SHOULD TAKE HIM SOMEWHERE TO LAY LOW.
ALL RIGHT ...
WHAT ARE *YOU* GOING TO DO?
WE DON'T KNOW IF WE'RE UP AGAINST JUST DR. GIOVANNI, OR ALL OF COMPANY 3... BUT HE SHOULDN'T KNOW THAT WE'RE HERE, EITHER.
IF I CAN FIND SOME HIGH GROUND TO SCOUT OUT THE ENEMY, THEN WE CAN MAKE THE FIRST MOVE.
YOU AND I ARE THE ONLY ONES HERE WHO CAN FIGHT, ARTHUR! I'M COUNTING ON YOU!!
WAIT!! EXPLAIN IT ONE MORE TIME!!
FWOOP

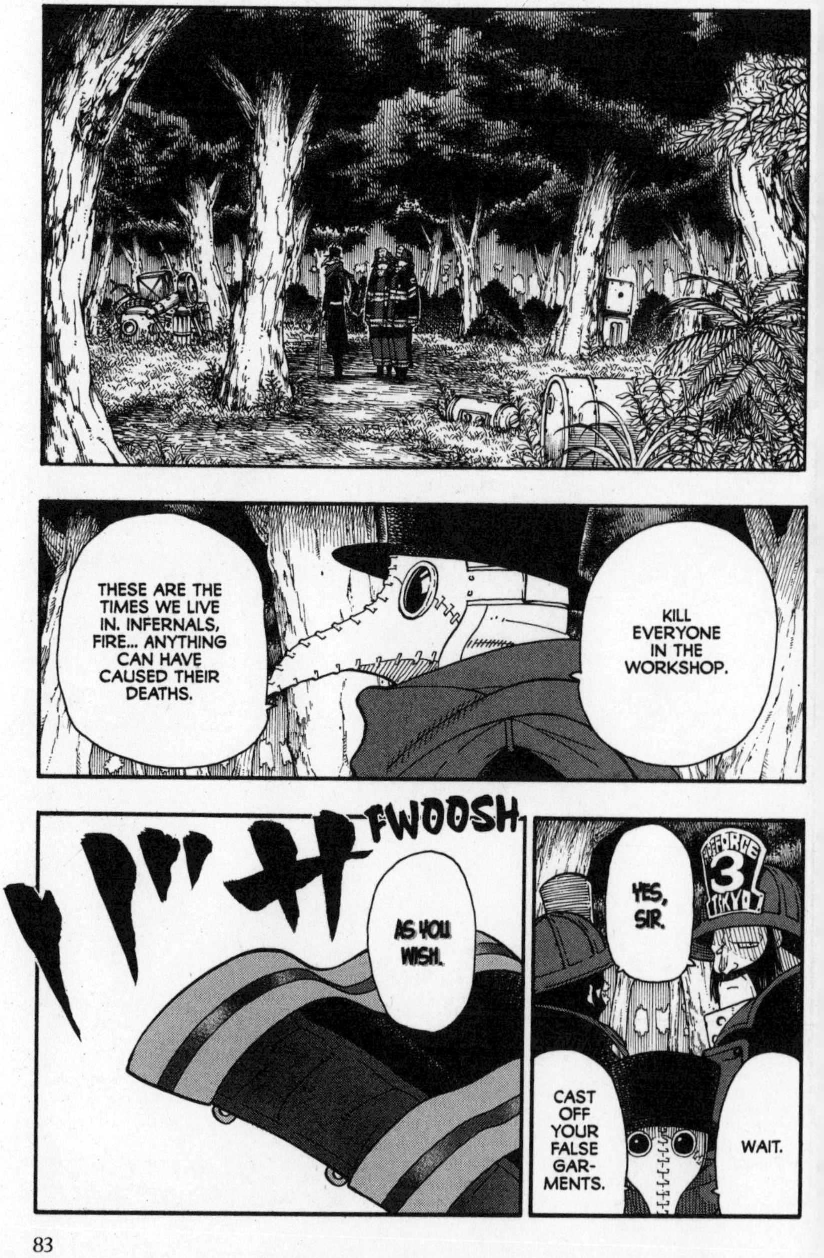
KILL EVERYONE IN THE WORKSHOP.
THESE ARE THE TIMES WE LIVE IN. INFERNALS, FIRE... ANYTHING CAN HAVE CAUSED THEIR DEATHS.
YES, SIR.
WAIT.
CAST OFF YOUR FALSE GAR-MENTS.
FWOOSH
AS YOU WISH.

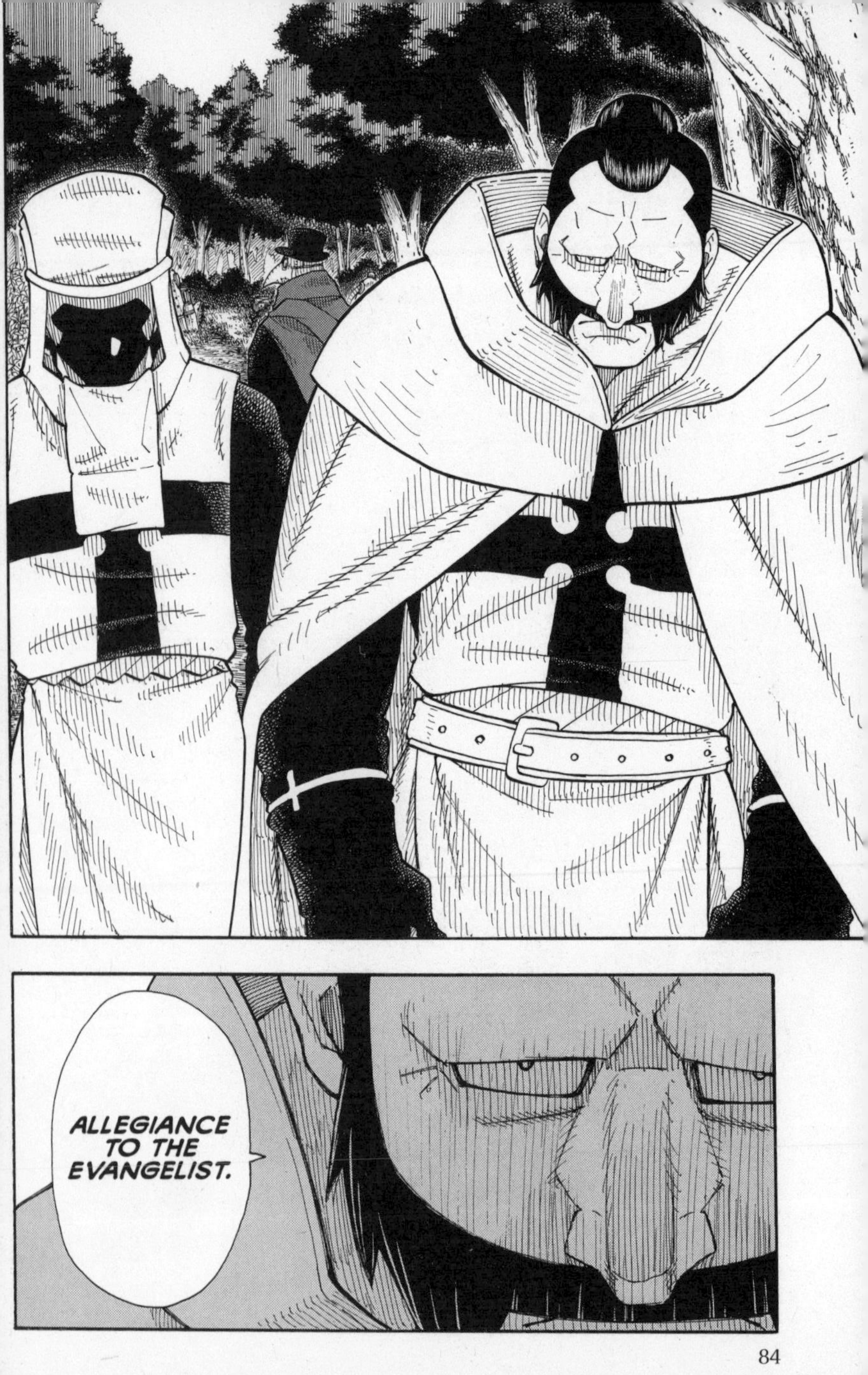
ALLEGIANCE TO THE EVANGELIST.

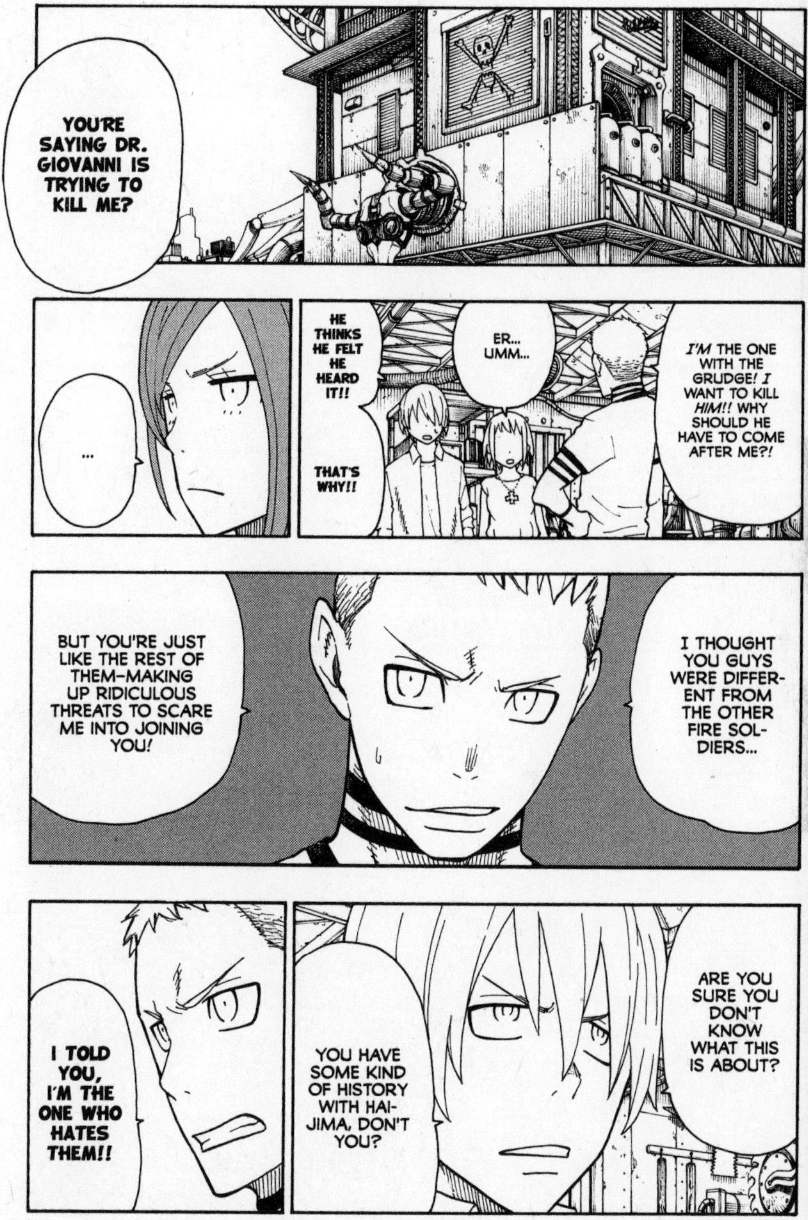
YOU'RE SAYING DR. GIOVANNI IS TRYING TO KILL ME?
I'M THE ONE WITH THE GRUDGE! *I* WANT TO KILL *HIM*!! WHY SHOULD HE HAVE TO COME AFTER ME?!
ER... UMM...
HE THINKS HE FELT HE HEARD IT!!
THAT'S WHY!!
...
I THOUGHT YOU GUYS WERE DIFFER-ENT FROM THE OTHER FIRE SOL-DIERS...
BUT YOU'RE JUST LIKE THE REST OF THEM–MAKING UP RIDICULOUS THREATS TO SCARE ME INTO JOINING YOU!
ARE YOU SURE YOU DON'T KNOW WHAT THIS IS ABOUT?
YOU HAVE SOME KIND OF HISTORY WITH HAI-JIMA, DON'T YOU?
I TOLD YOU, I'M THE ONE WHO HATES THEM!!

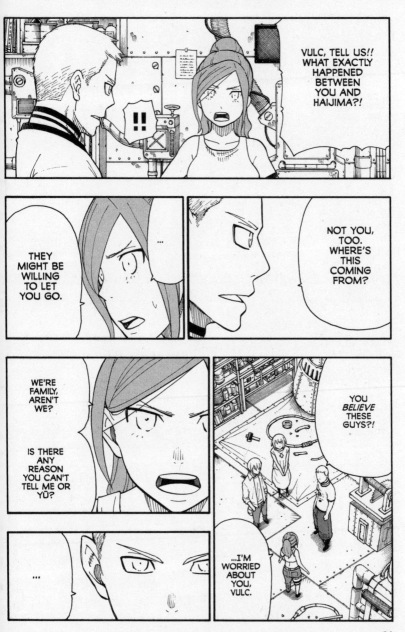

VULC, TELL US!! WHAT EXACTLY HAPPENED BETWEEN YOU AND HAIJIMA?!
!!
NOT YOU, TOO. WHERE'S THIS COMING FROM?
...
THEY MIGHT BE WILLING TO LET YOU GO.
YOU *BELIEVE* THESE GUYS?!
...I'M WORRIED ABOUT YOU, VULC.
WE'RE FAMILY, AREN'T WE?
IS THERE ANY REASON YOU CAN'T TELL ME OR YŪ?
...

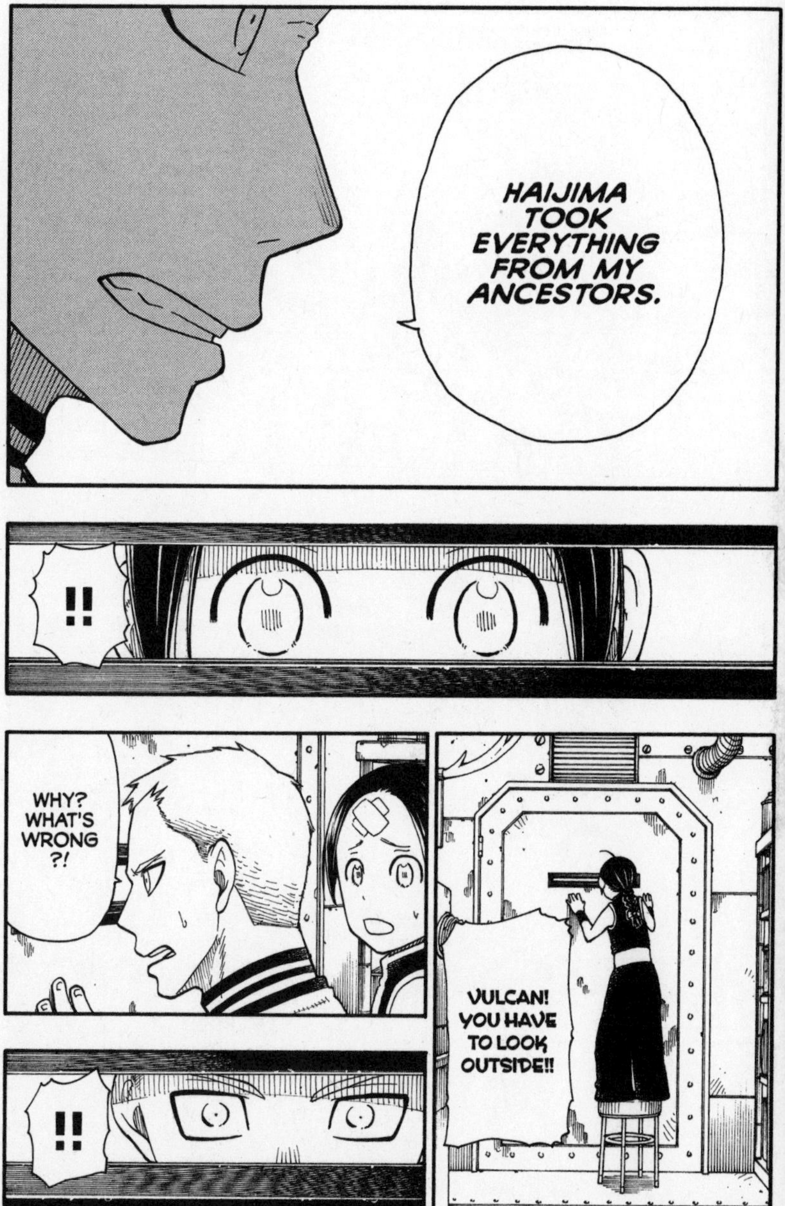
HAIJIMA TOOK EVERYTHING FROM MY ANCESTORS.
!!
VULCAN! YOU HAVE TO LOOK OUTSIDE!!
WHY? WHAT'S WRONG ?!
!!

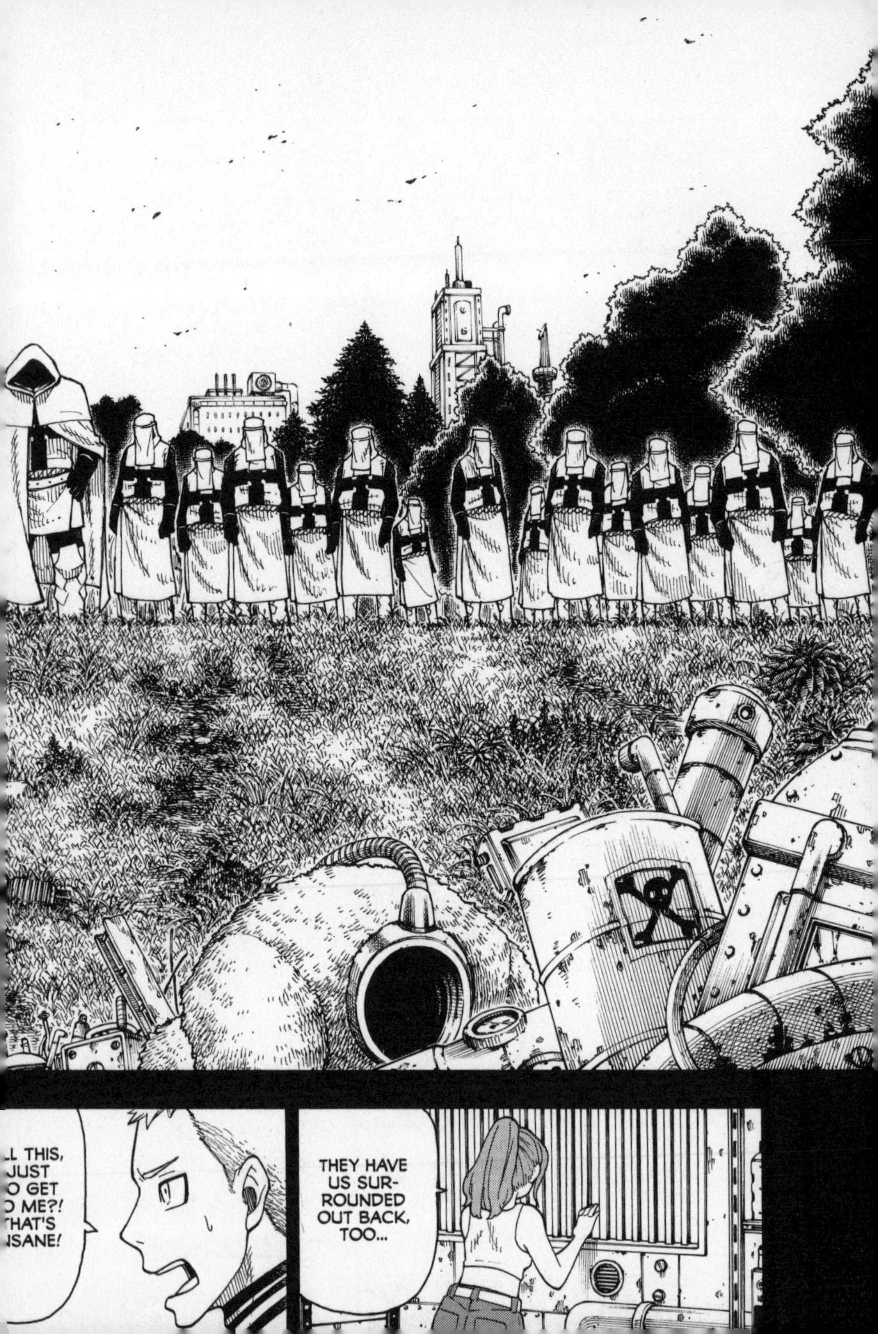
THEY HAVE US SUR-ROUNDED OUT BACK, TOO...
L THIS, JUST O GET O ME?! THAT'S ISANE!

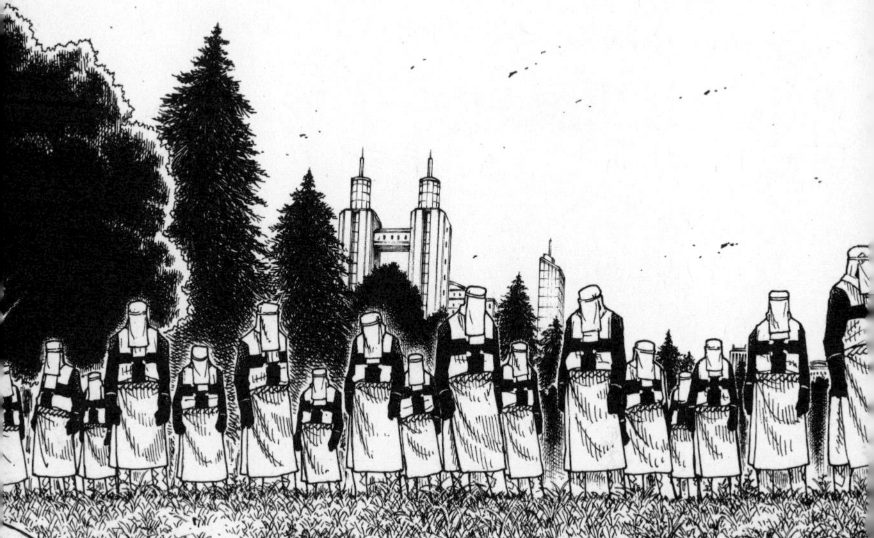

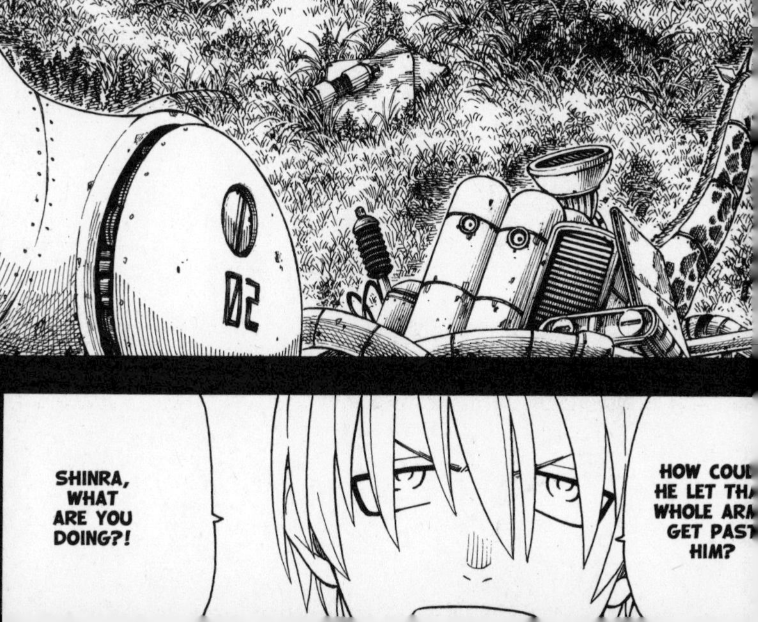
HOW COUL HE LET THA WHOLE AR GET PAST HIM?
SHINRA, WHAT ARE YOU DOING?!

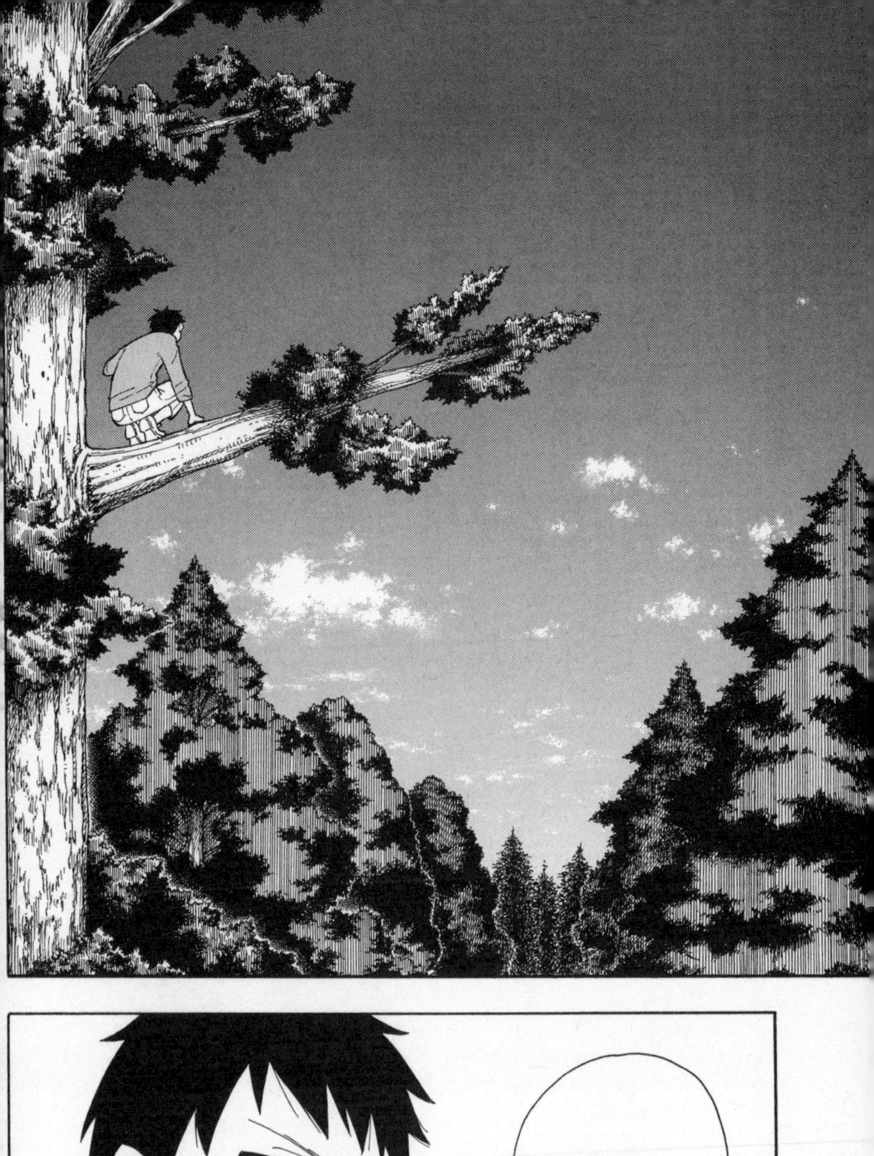

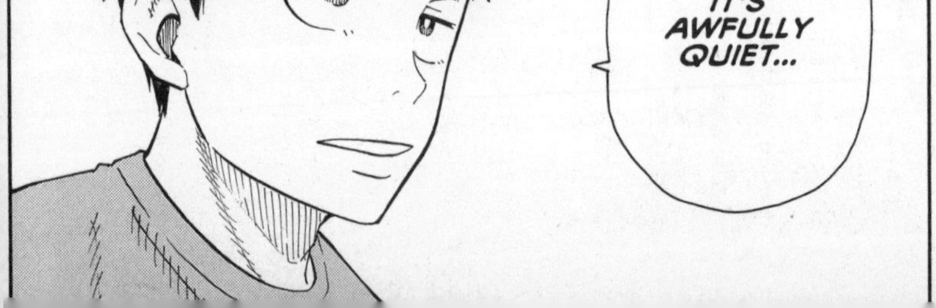
IT'S AWFULLY QUIET...

FIRE FORCE

FIRE FORCE

CHAPTER LVI: THE KNIGHT KING ATOP HIS STEED

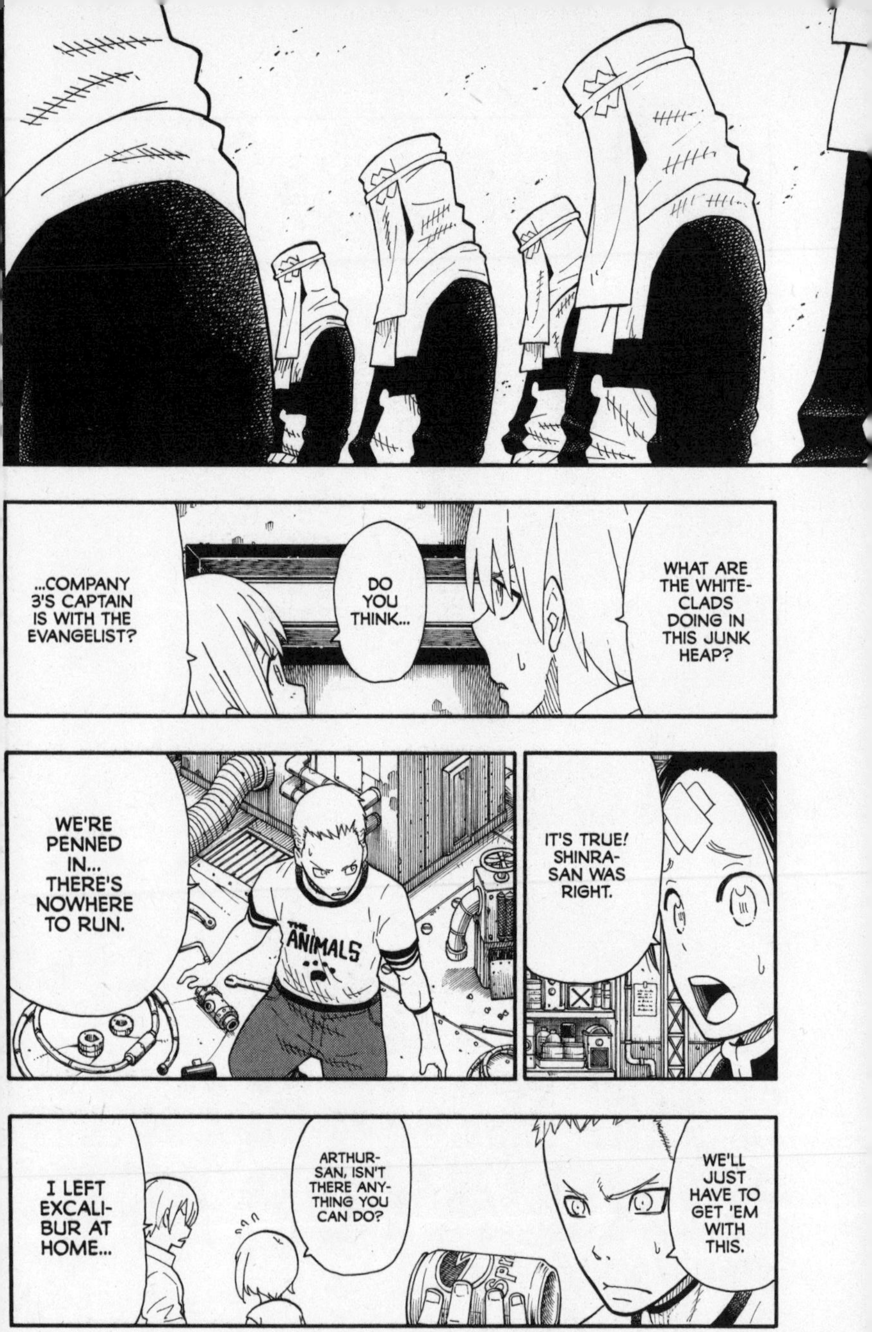
WHAT ARE THE WHITE-CLADS DOING IN THIS JUNK HEAP?
DO YOU THINK...
...COMPANY 3'S CAPTAIN IS WITH THE EVANGELIST?
IT'S TRUE! SHINRA-SAN WAS RIGHT.
WE'RE PENNED IN... THERE'S NOWHERE TO RUN.
WE'LL JUST HAVE TO GET 'EM WITH THIS.
ARTHUR-SAN, ISN'T THERE ANYTHING YOU CAN DO?
I LEFT EXCALIBUR AT HOME...

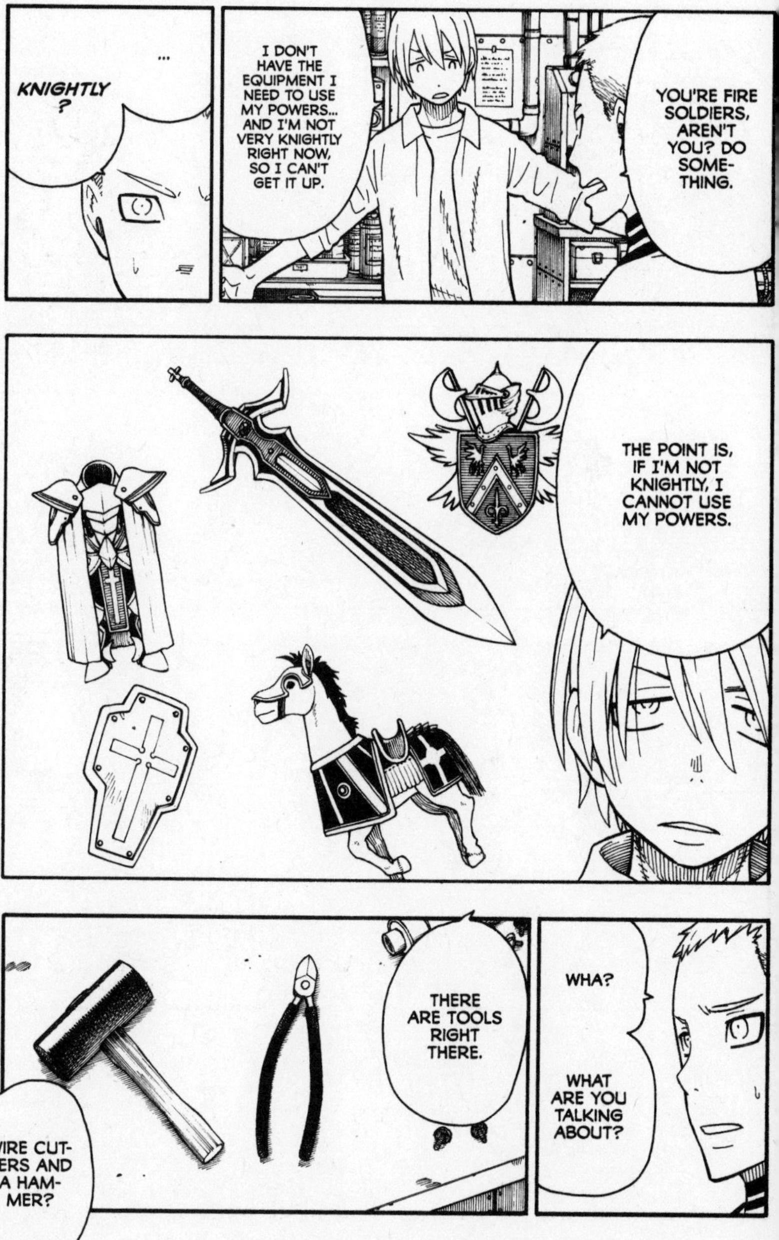
YOU'RE FIRE SOLDIERS, AREN'T YOU? DO SOME-THING.
I DON'T HAVE THE EQUIPMENT I NEED TO USE MY POWERS... AND I'M NOT VERY KNIGHTLY RIGHT NOW, SO I CAN'T GET IT UP.
...
KNIGHTLY?
THE POINT IS, IF I'M NOT KNIGHTLY, I CANNOT USE MY POWERS.
WHA?
WHAT ARE YOU TALKING ABOUT?
THERE ARE TOOLS RIGHT THERE.
WIRE CUT-TERS AND A HAM-MER?

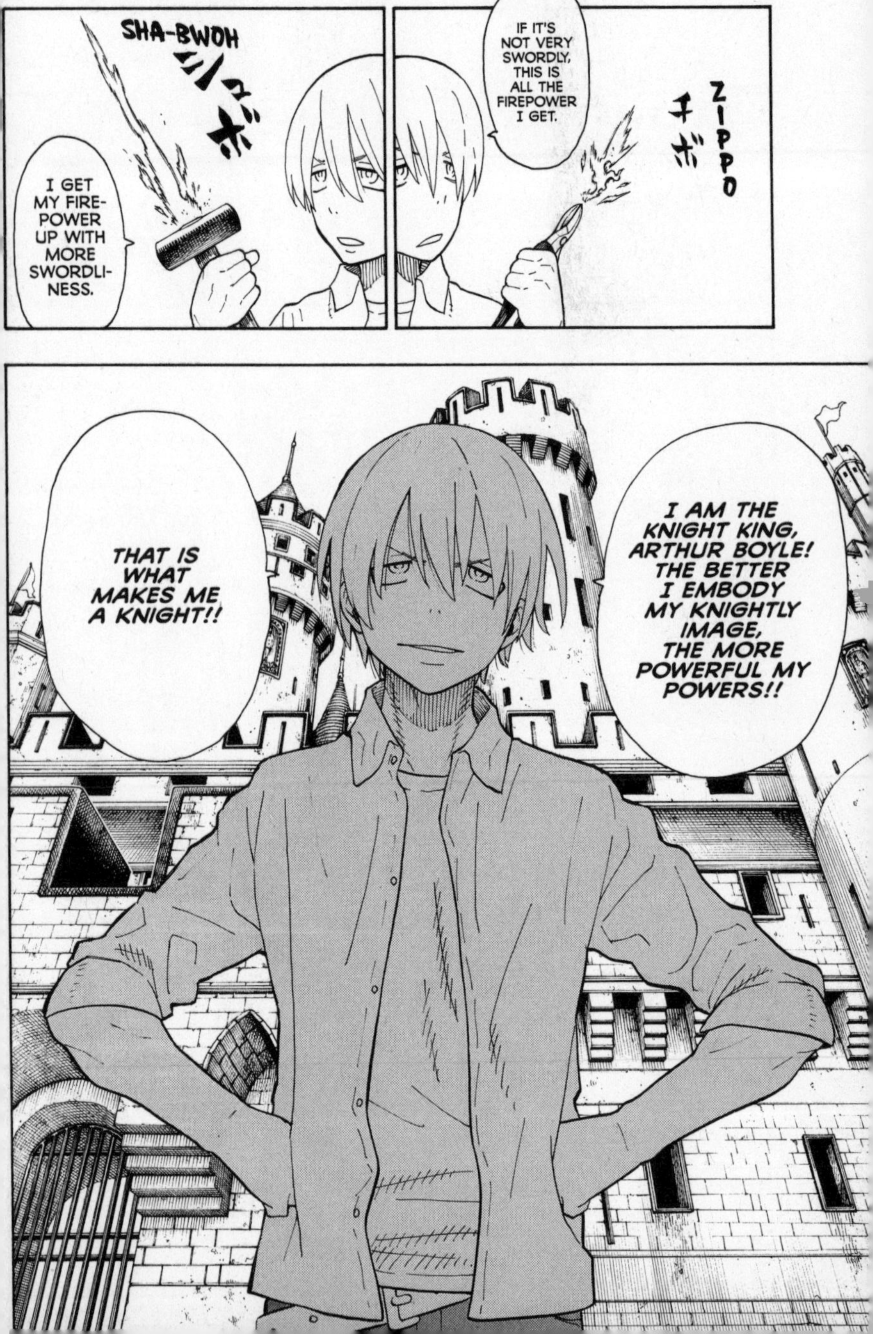
IF IT'S NOT VERY SWORDLY, THIS IS ALL THE FIREPOWER I GET.
ZIPPO
チボ
SHA-BWOH
シュボ
I GET MY FIRE-POWER UP WITH MORE SWORDLI-NESS.
I AM THE KNIGHT KING, ARTHUR BOYLE! THE BETTER I EMBODY MY KNIGHTLY IMAGE, THE MORE POWERFUL MY POWERS!!
THAT IS WHAT MAKES ME A KNIGHT!!

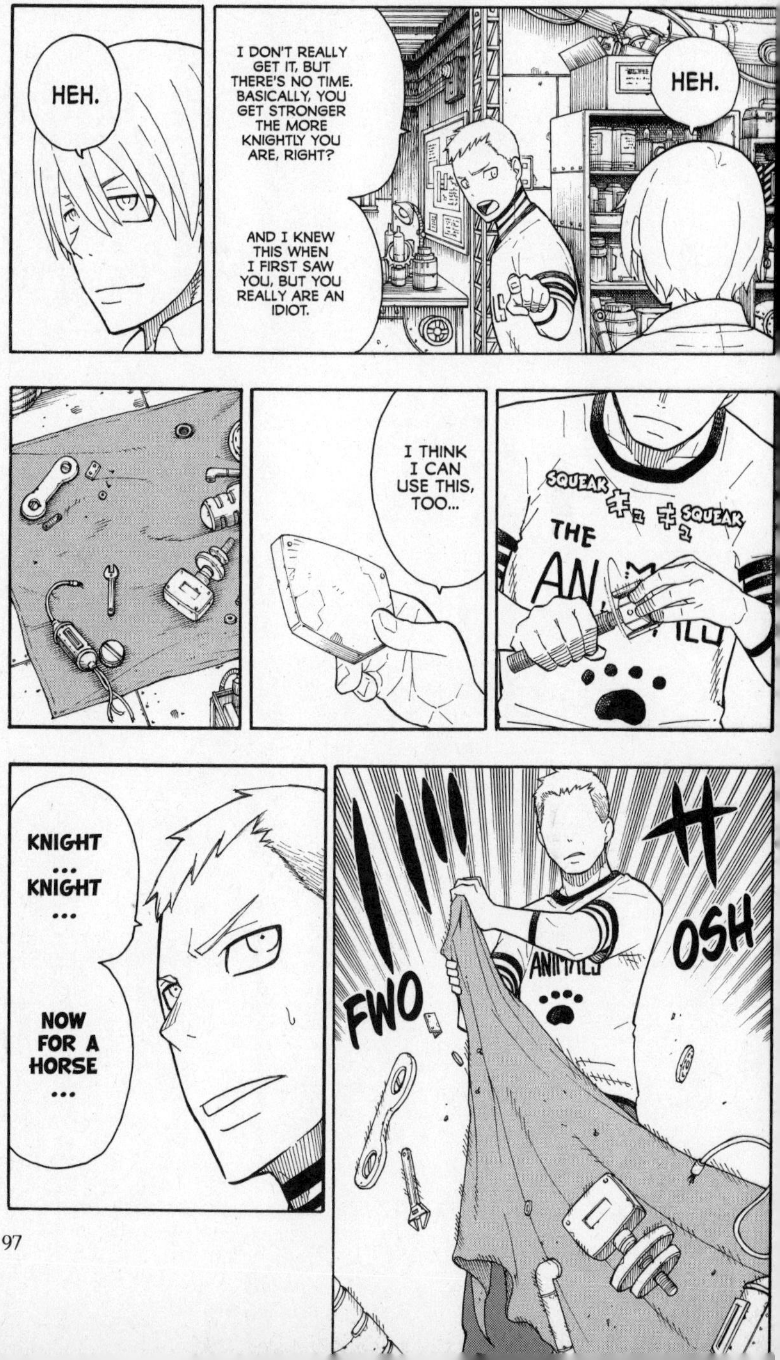
HEH.
I DON'T REALLY GET IT, BUT THERE'S NO TIME. BASICALLY, YOU GET STRONGER THE MORE KNIGHTLY YOU ARE, RIGHT?
AND I KNEW THIS WHEN I FIRST SAW YOU, BUT YOU REALLY ARE AN IDIOT.
HEH.
SQUEAK キュ キュ SQUEAK
I THINK I CAN USE THIS, TOO...
FWO OSH
KNIGHT ... KNIGHT ...
NOW FOR A HORSE ...

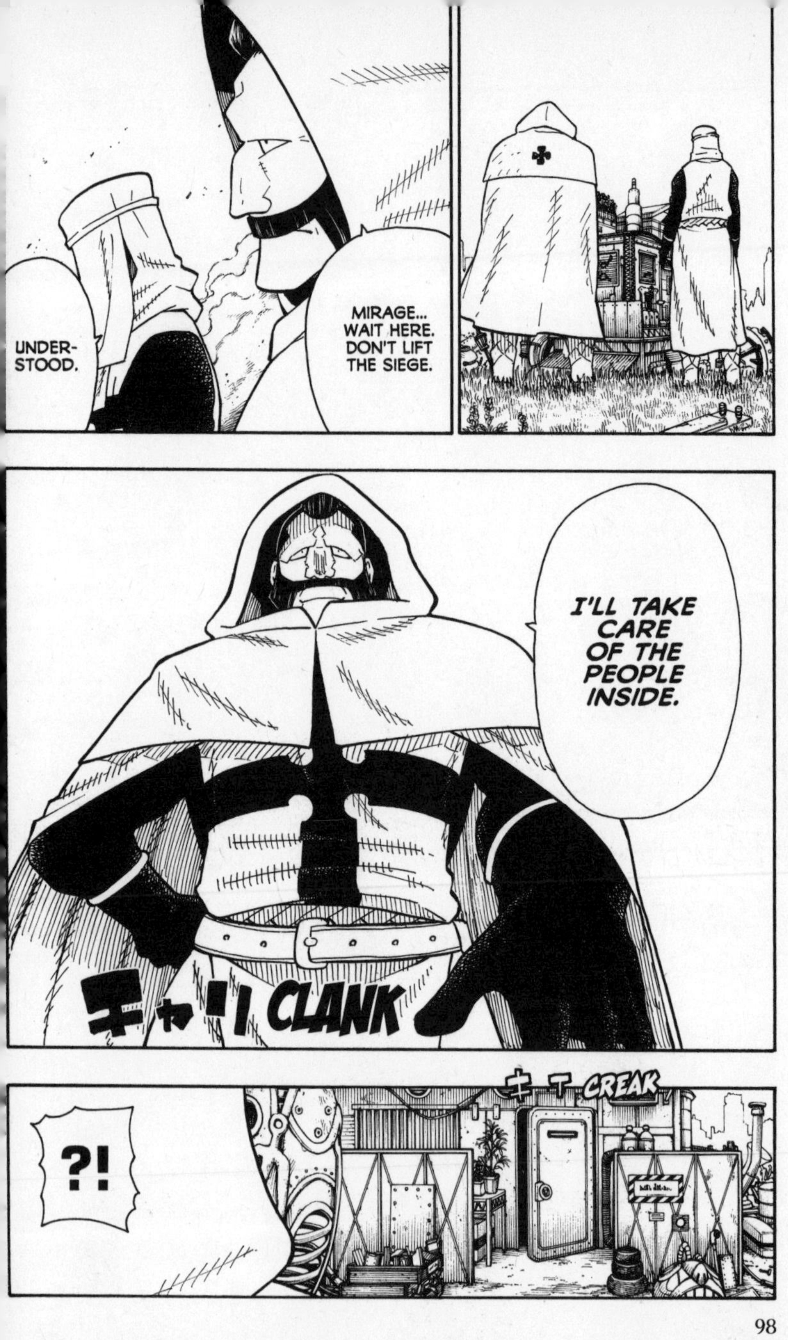
MIRAGE... WAIT HERE. DON'T LIFT THE SIEGE.
UNDER-STOOD.
I'LL TAKE CARE OF THE PEOPLE INSIDE.
CLANK
CREAK
?!

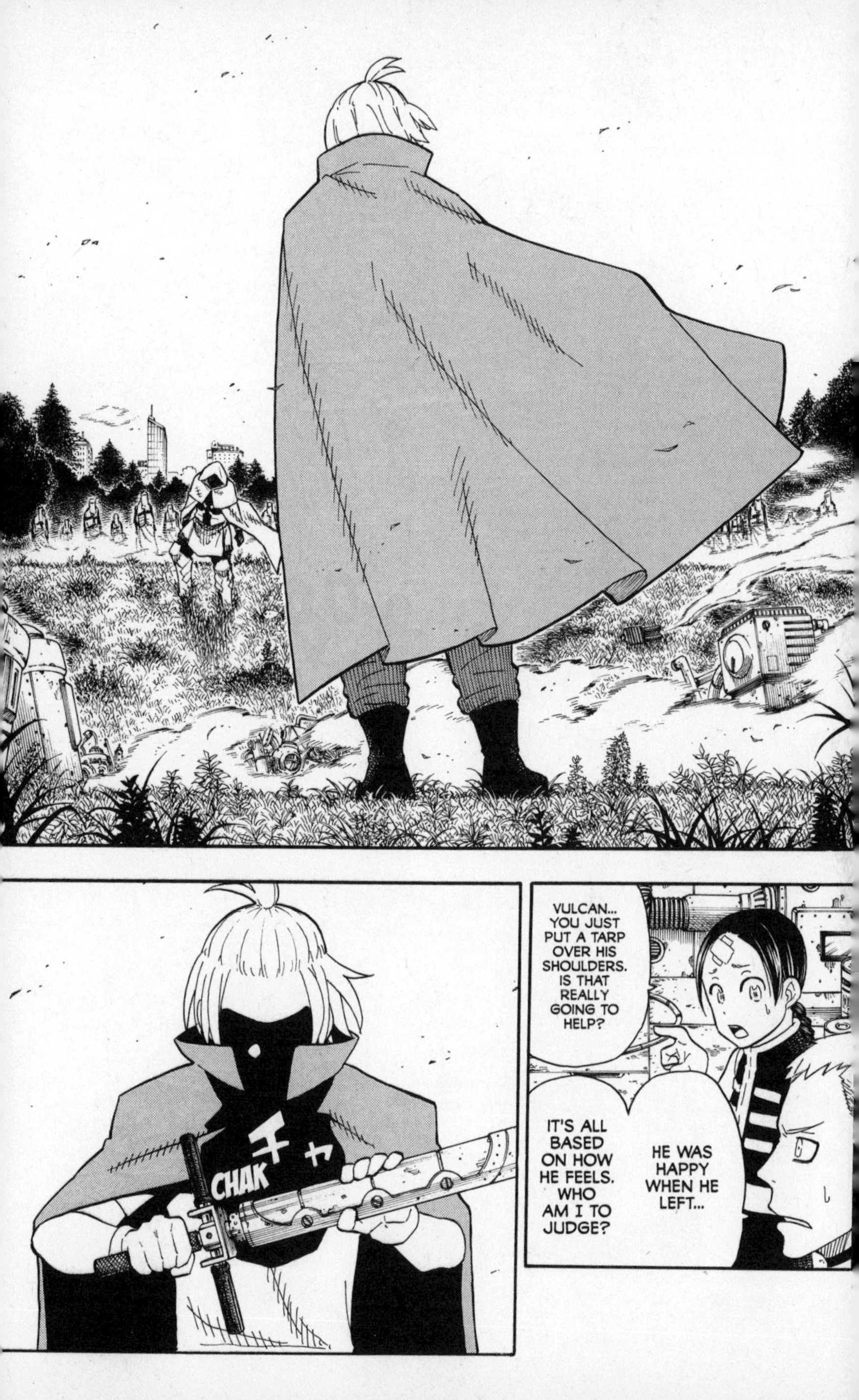
VULCAN... YOU JUST PUT A TARP OVER HIS SHOULDERS. IS THAT REALLY GOING TO HELP?
HE WAS HAPPY WHEN HE LEFT...
IT'S ALL BASED ON HOW HE FEELS. WHO AM I TO JUDGE?
チャ
CHAK

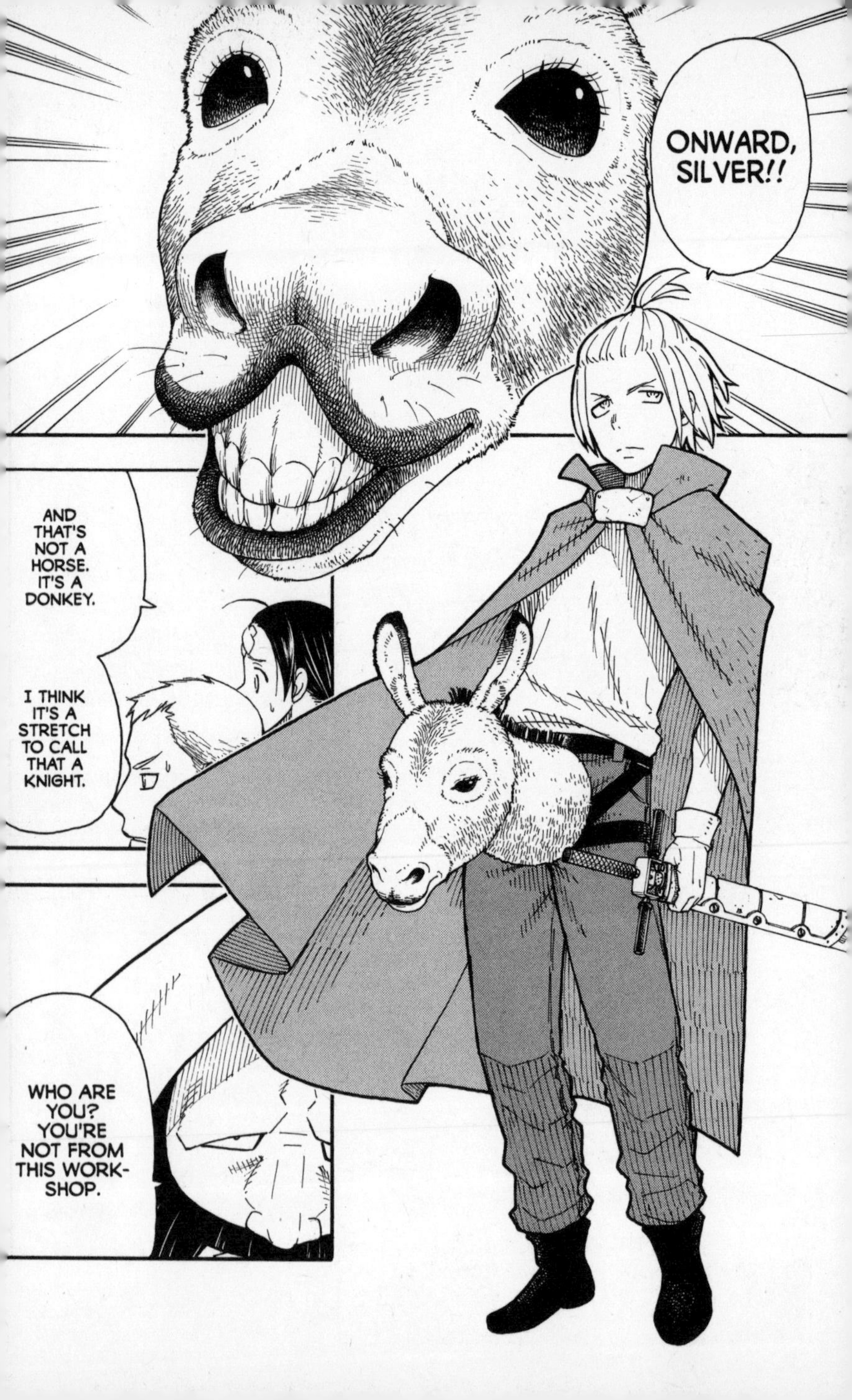
ONWARD, SILVER!!
AND THAT'S NOT A HORSE. IT'S A DONKEY.
I THINK IT'S A STRETCH TO CALL THAT A KNIGHT.
WHO ARE YOU? YOU'RE NOT FROM THIS WORK-SHOP.

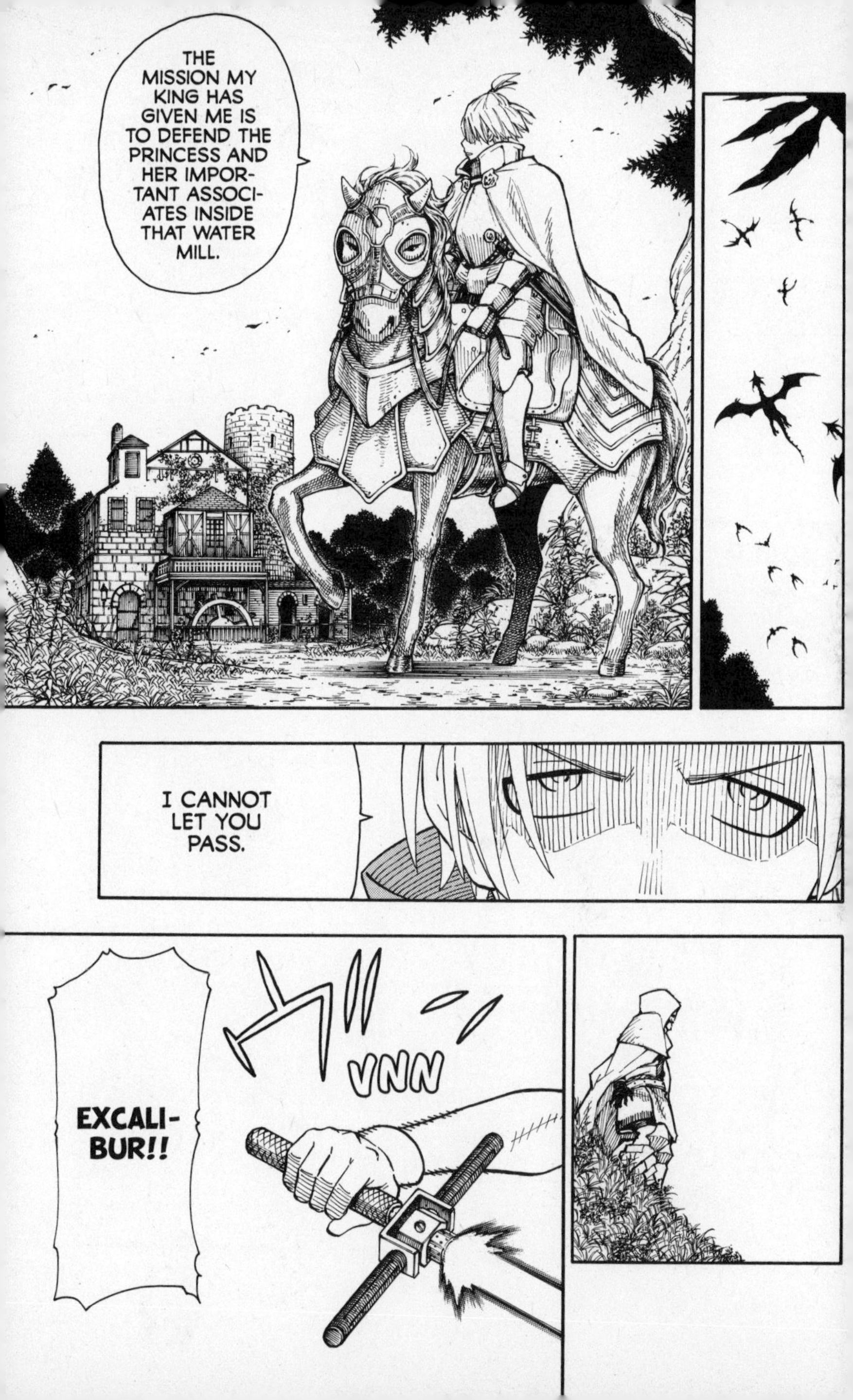
THE MISSION MY KING HAS GIVEN ME IS TO DEFEND THE PRINCESS AND HER IMPORTANT ASSOCIATES INSIDE THAT WATER MILL.
I CANNOT LET YOU PASS.
VNN
EXCALIBUR!!

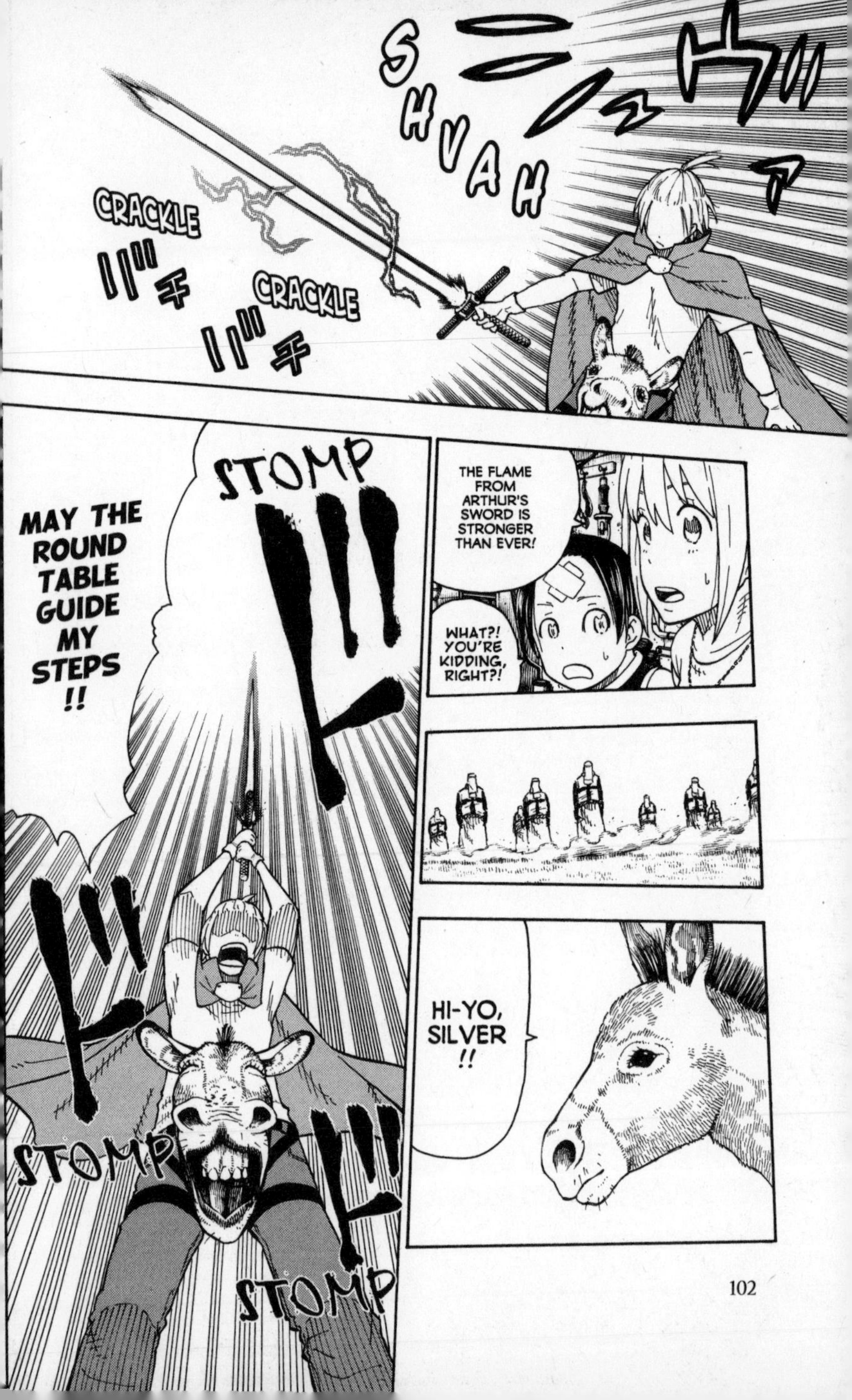
SHVAH
CRACKLE
CRACKLE
THE FLAME FROM ARTHUR'S SWORD IS STRONGER THAN EVER!
WHAT?! YOU'RE KIDDING, RIGHT?!
HI-YO, SILVER !!
MAY THE ROUND TABLE GUIDE MY STEPS !!
STOMP
STOMP
STOMP

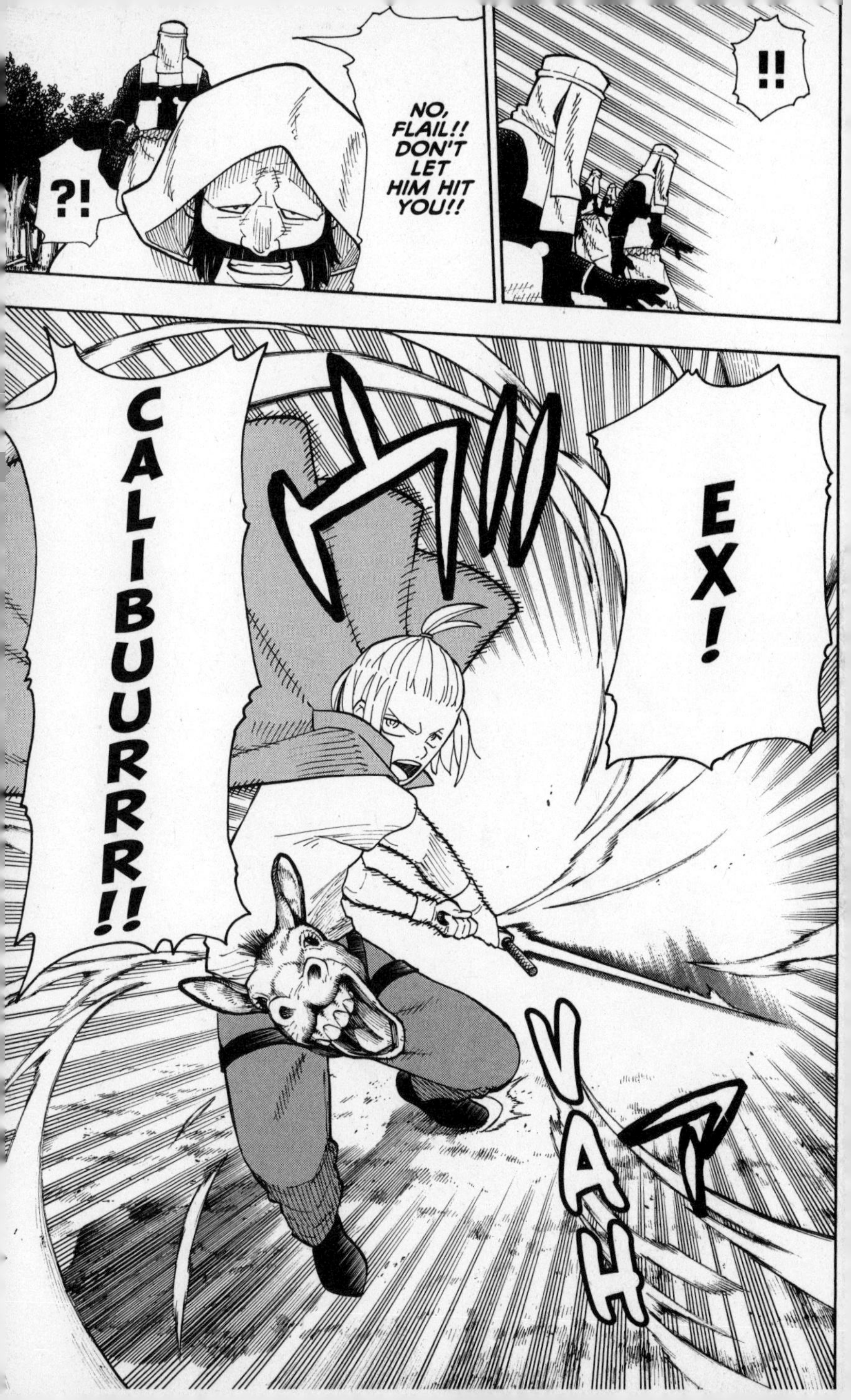
!!
NO, FLAIL!! DON'T LET HIM HIT YOU!!
?!
EX!
CALIBUURRRR!!
VAH

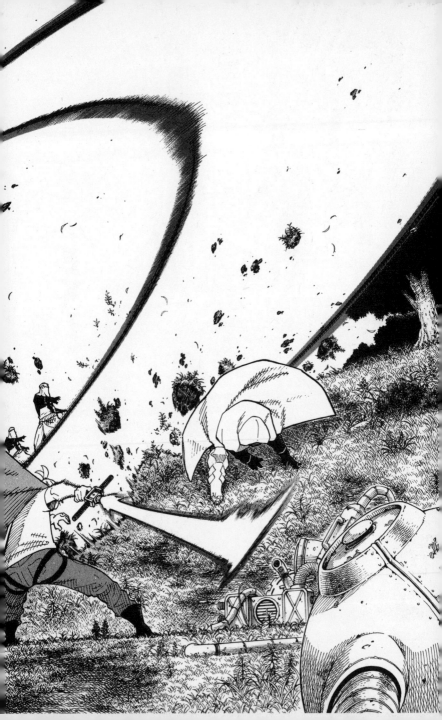

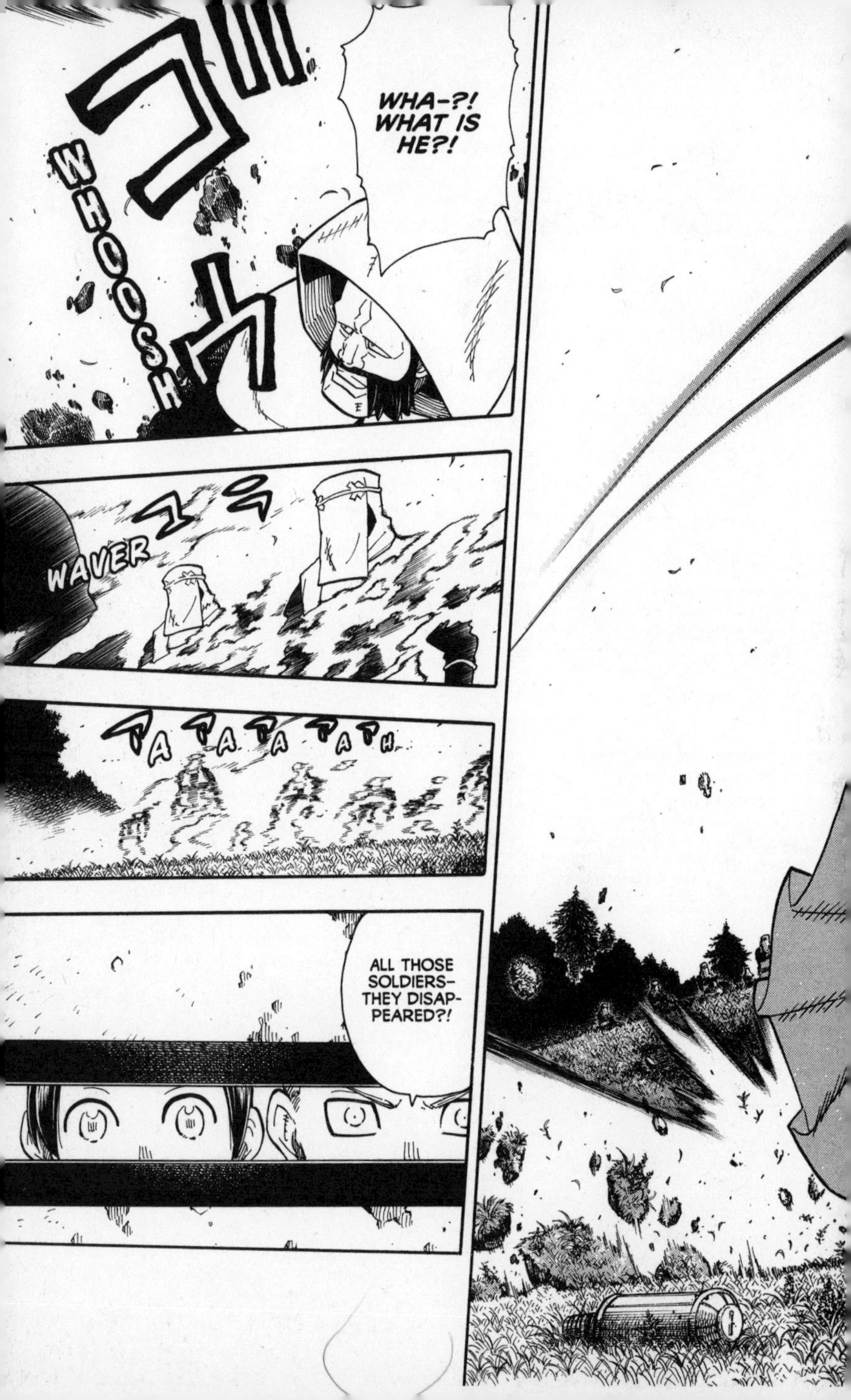
WHA-?! WHAT IS HE?!
WHOOSH
WAVER
TA TA TA TATH
ALL THOSE SOLDIERS- THEY DISAP-PEARED?!

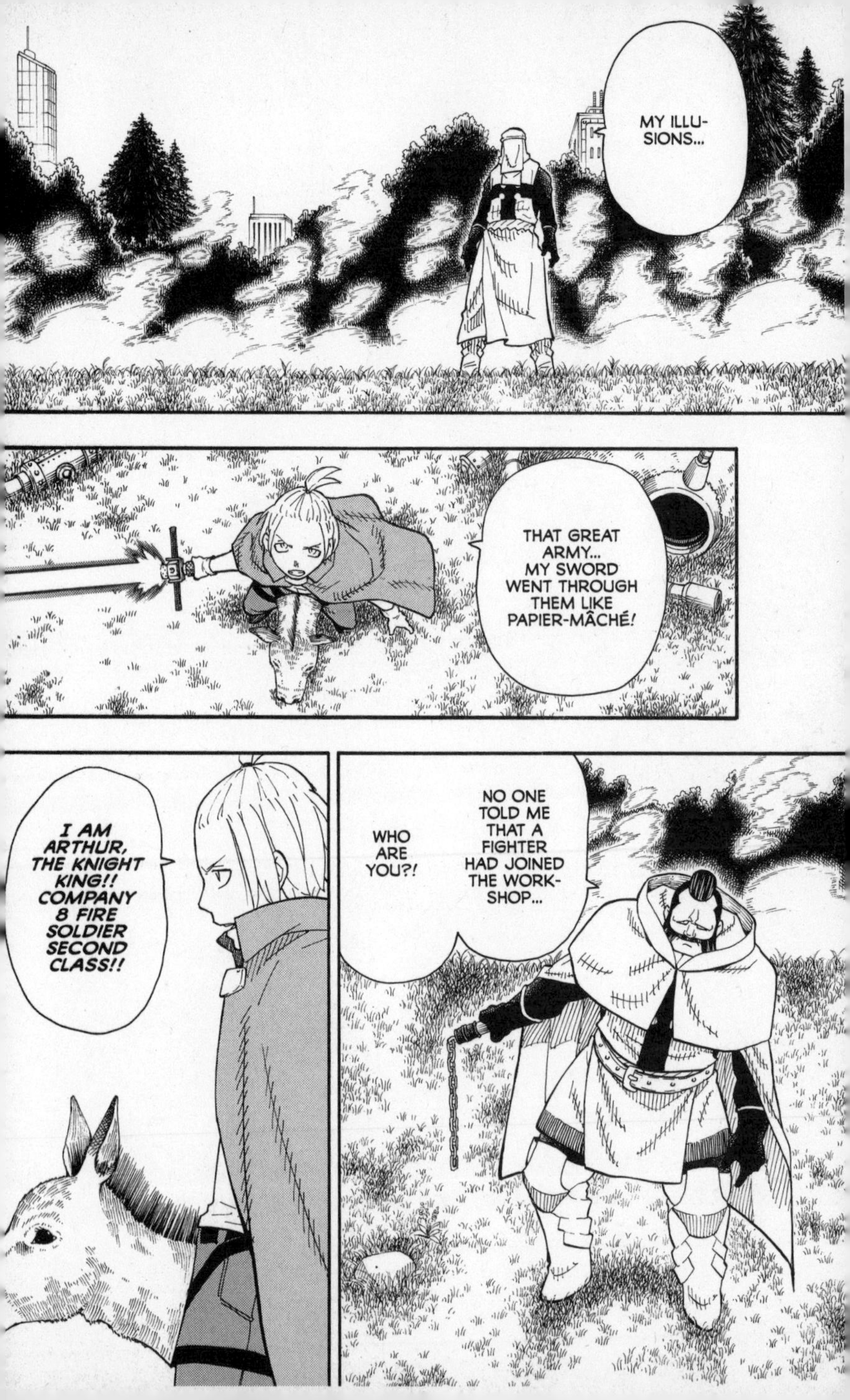
MY ILLUSIONS...
THAT GREAT ARMY... MY SWORD WENT THROUGH THEM LIKE PAPIER-MÂCHÉ!
NO ONE TOLD ME THAT A FIGHTER HAD JOINED THE WORKSHOP...
WHO ARE YOU?!
I AM ARTHUR, THE KNIGHT KING!! COMPANY 8 FIRE SOLDIER SECOND CLASS!!

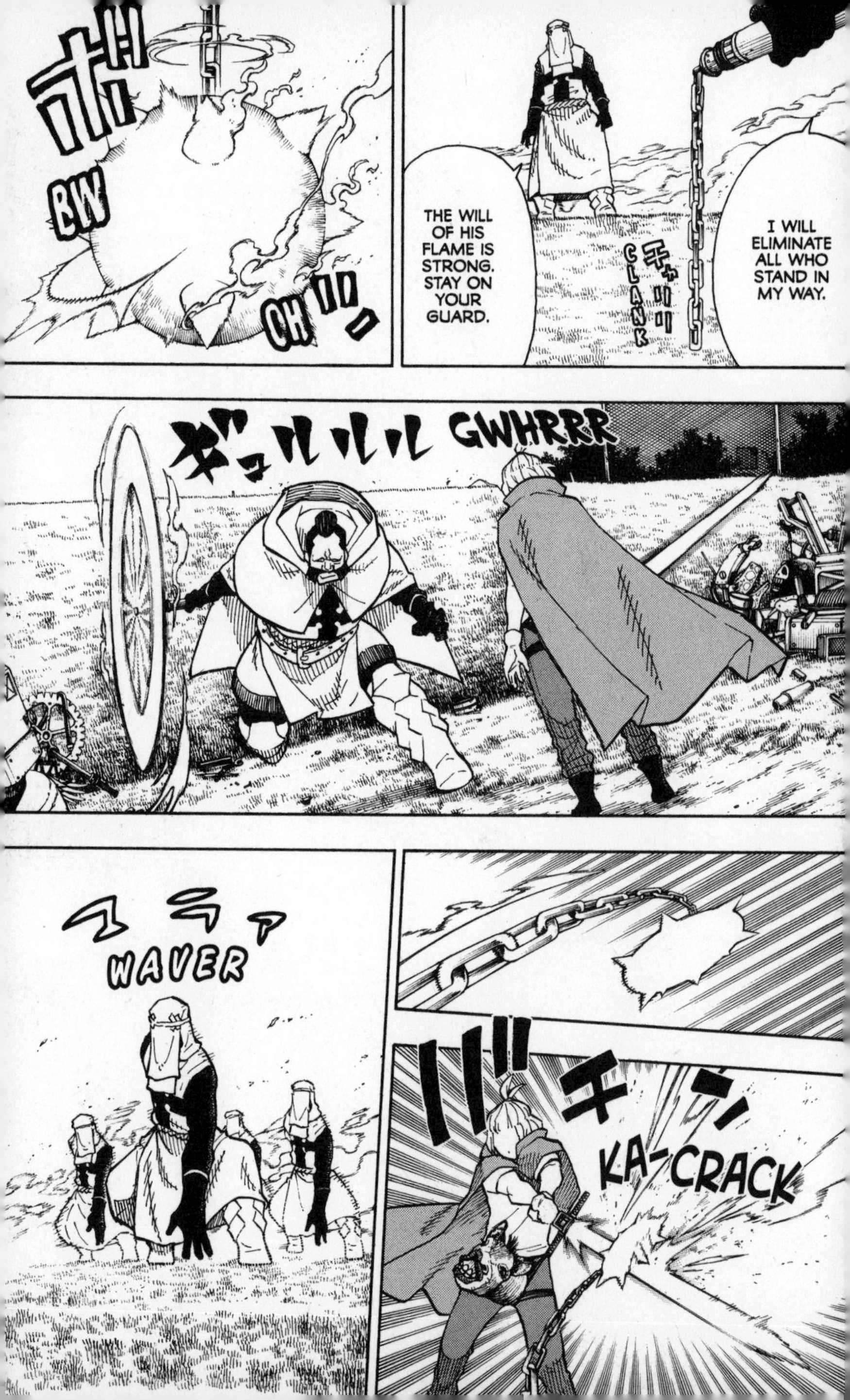
I WILL ELIMINATE ALL WHO STAND IN MY WAY.
CLANK
THE WILL OF HIS FLAME IS STRONG. STAY ON YOUR GUARD.
BW
OH
GWHRRR
KA-CRACK
WAVER

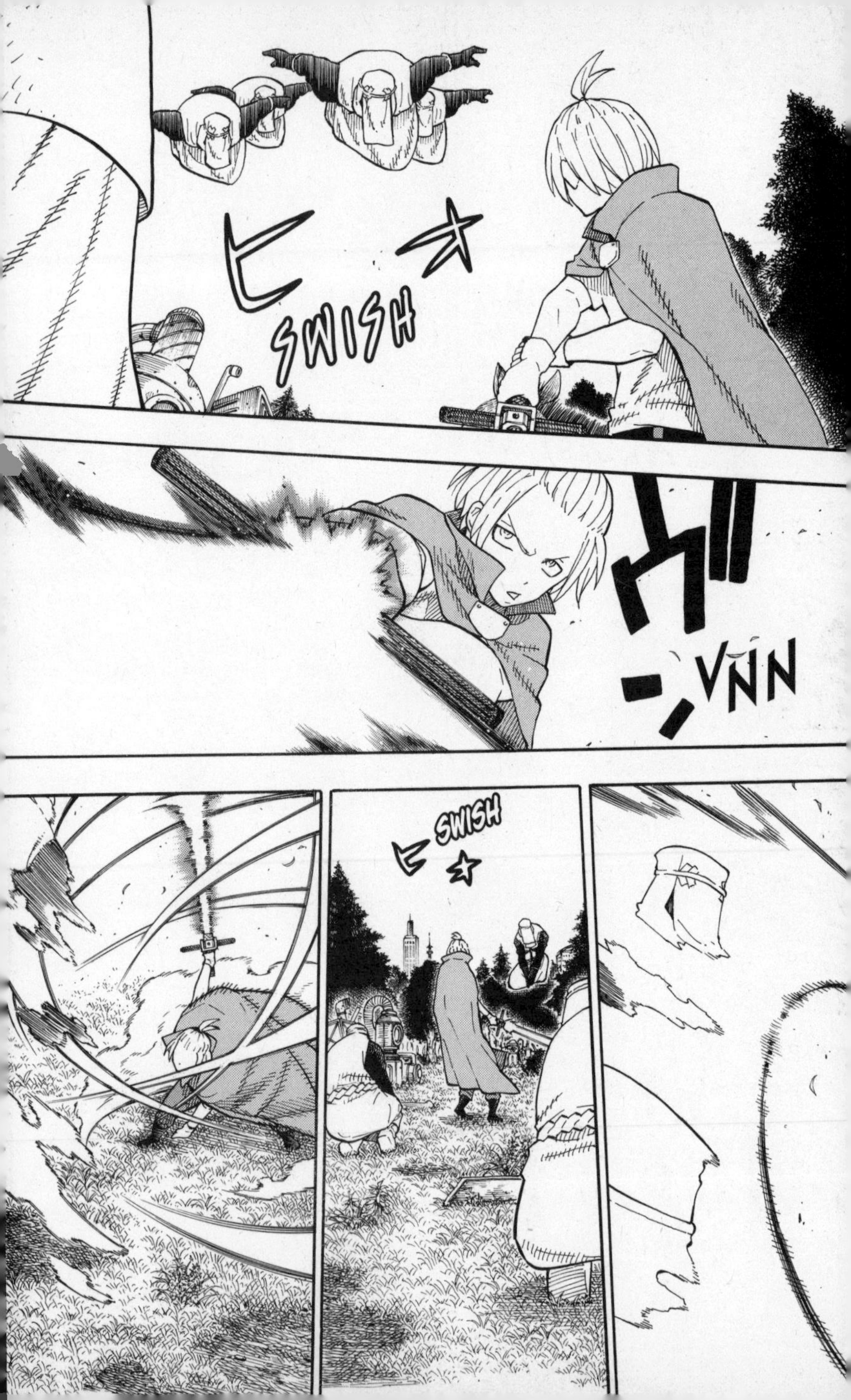
SWISH
VNN
SWISH

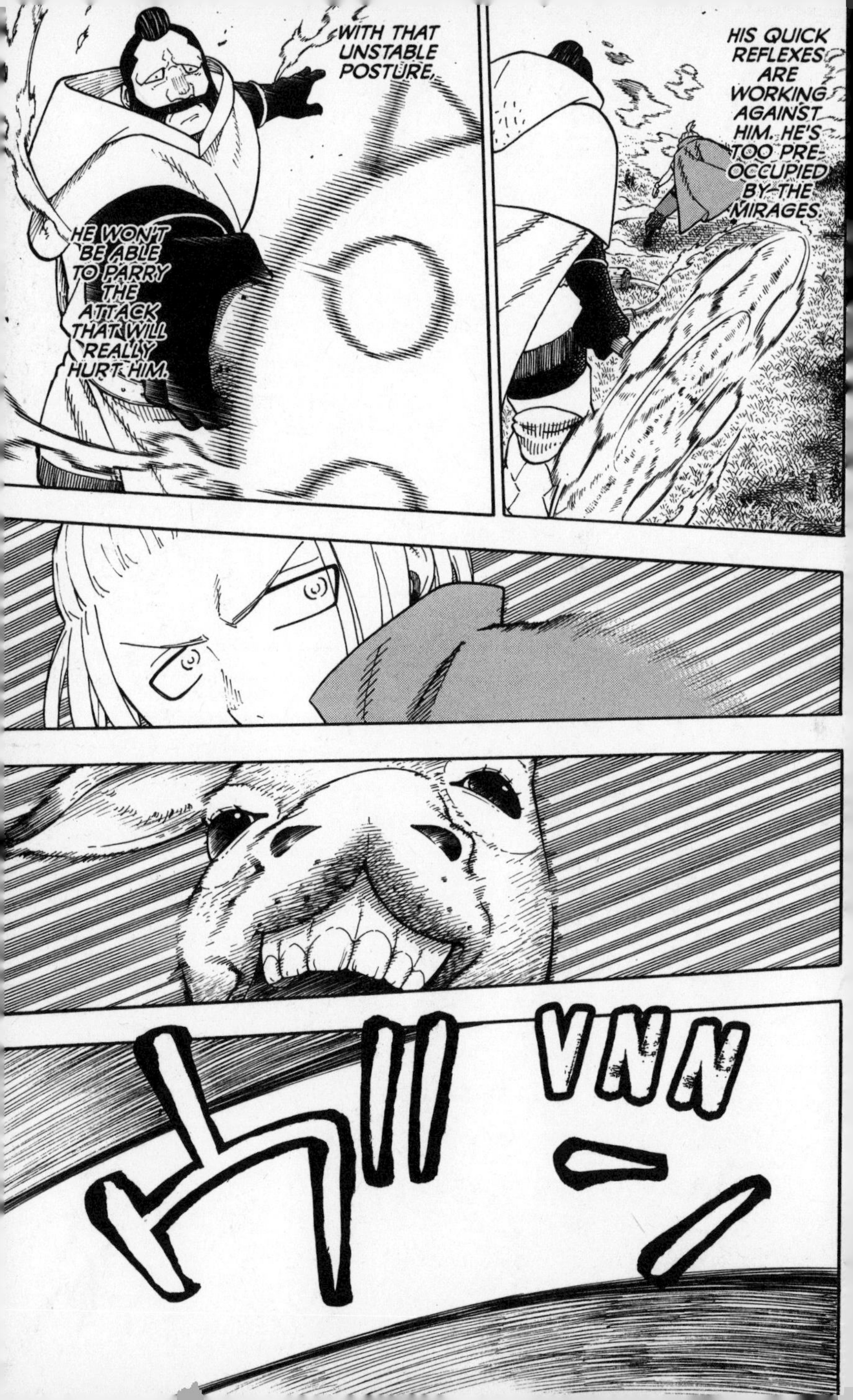
HIS QUICK REFLEXES ARE WORKING AGAINST HIM. HE'S TOO PRE-OCCUPIED BY THE MIRAGES.
WITH THAT UNSTABLE POSTURE,
HE WON'T BE ABLE TO PARRY THE ATTACK THAT WILL REALLY HURT HIM.
VNN

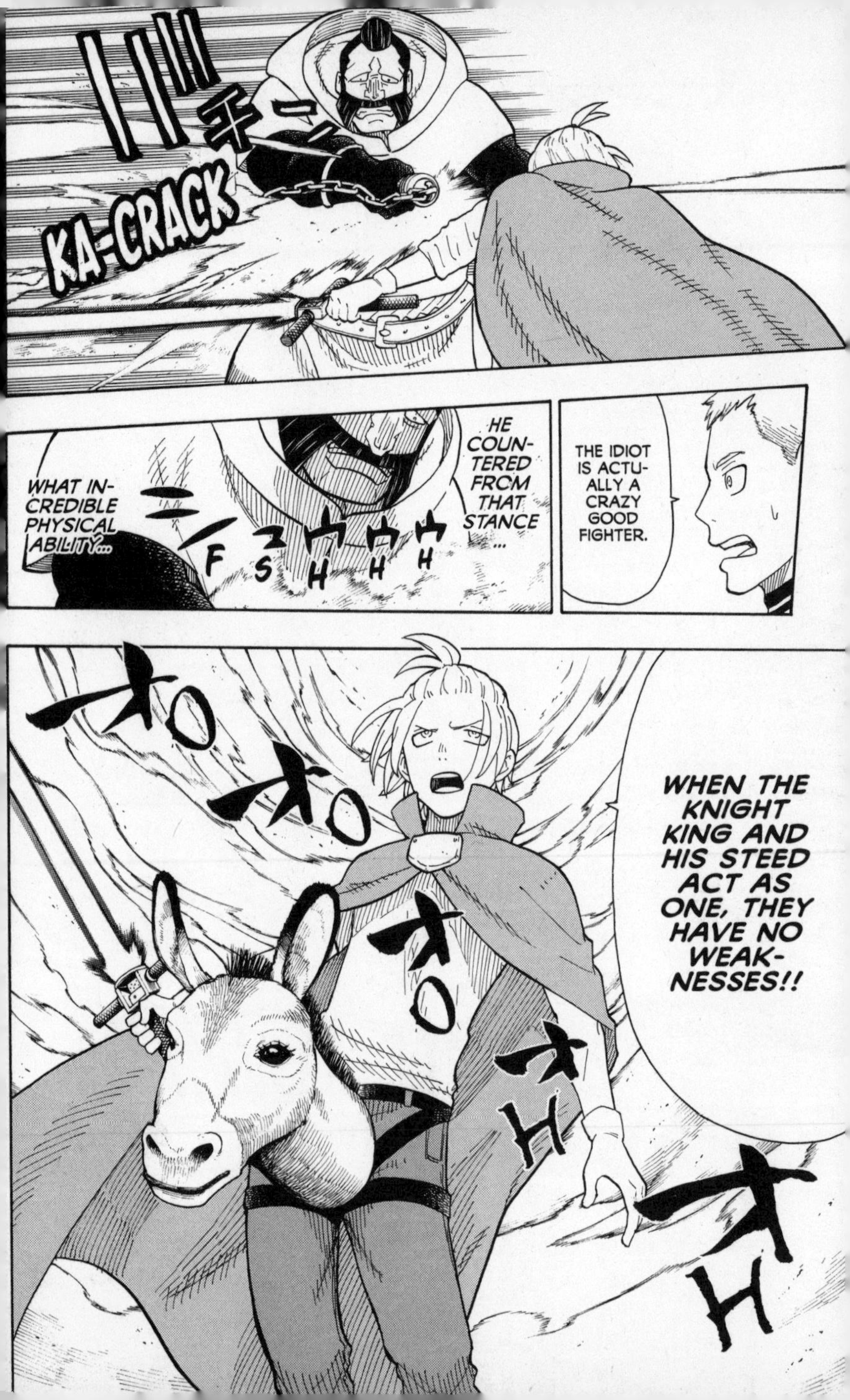
KA-CRACK
THE IDIOT IS ACTU-ALLY A CRAZY GOOD FIGHTER.
HE COUN-TERED FROM THAT STANCE ...
WHAT IN-CREDIBLE PHYSICAL ABILITY...
F S H H H
WHEN THE KNIGHT KING AND HIS STEED ACT AS ONE, THEY HAVE NO WEAK-NESSES!!
H
H

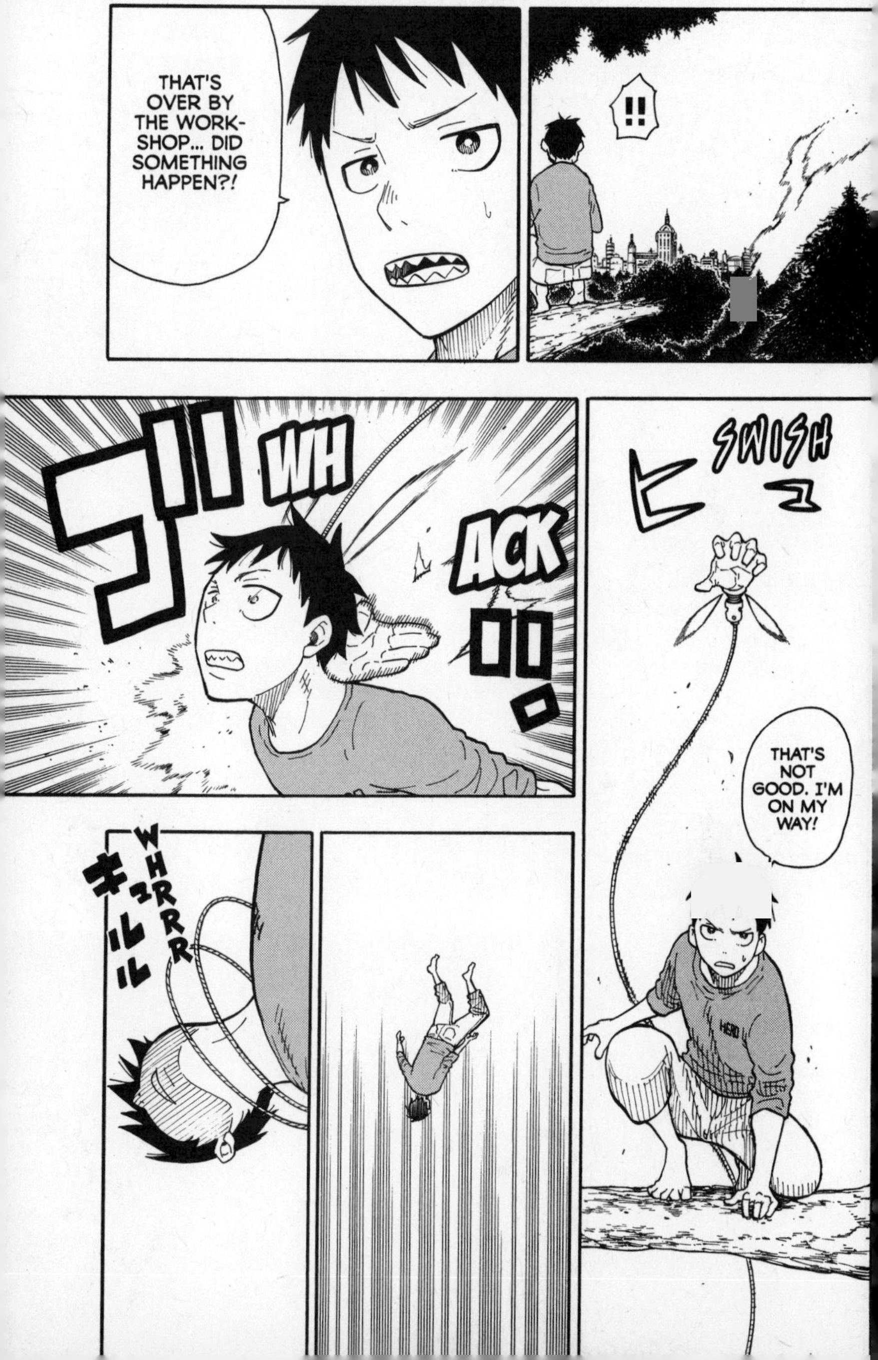
!!
THAT'S OVER BY THE WORK-SHOP... DID SOMETHING HAPPEN?!
SWISH
THAT'S NOT GOOD. I'M ON MY WAY!
WH
ACK
WHRRR

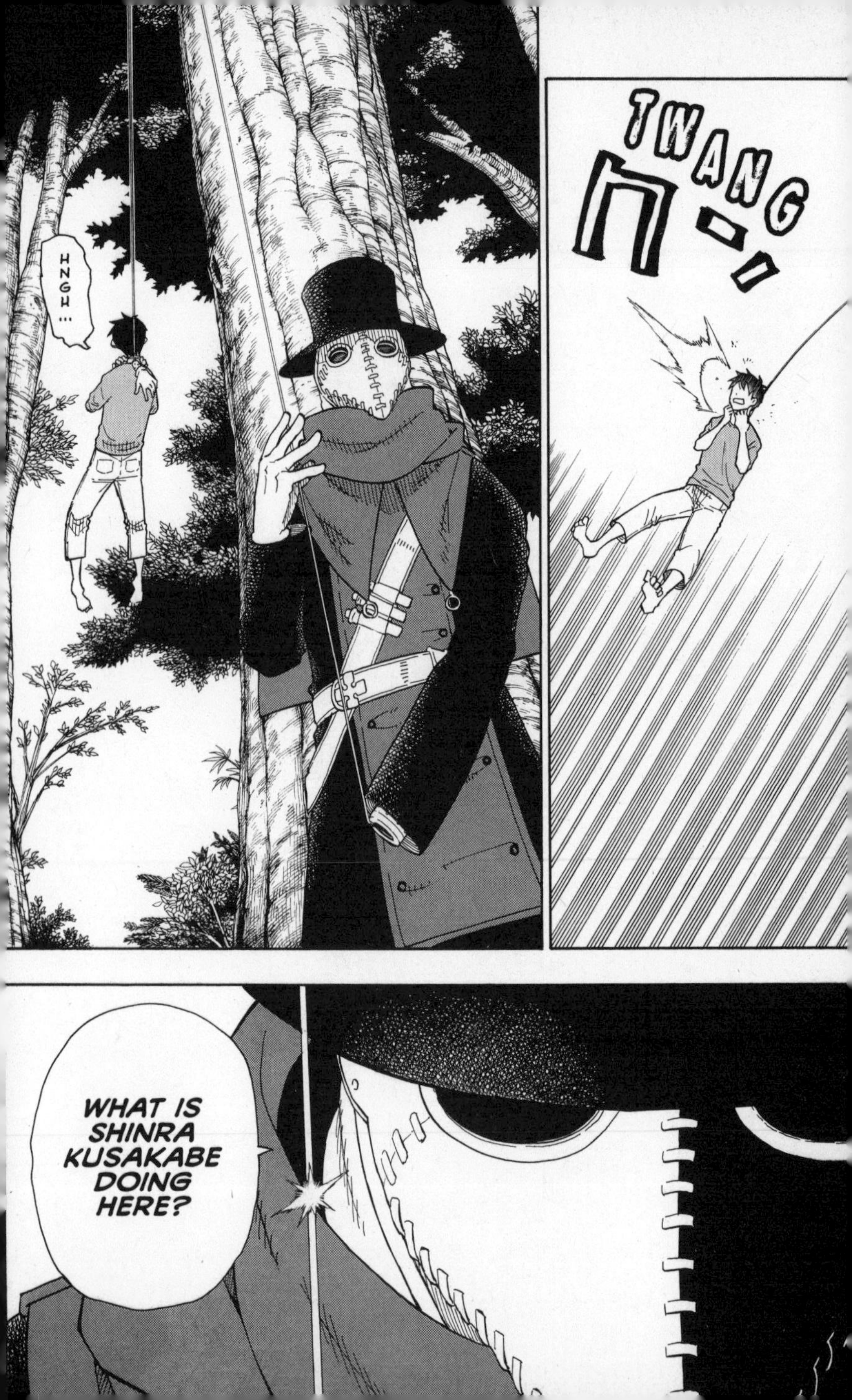
TWANG
HNGH...
WHAT IS SHINRA KUSAKABE DOING HERE?

FIRE FORCE

FIRE FORCE

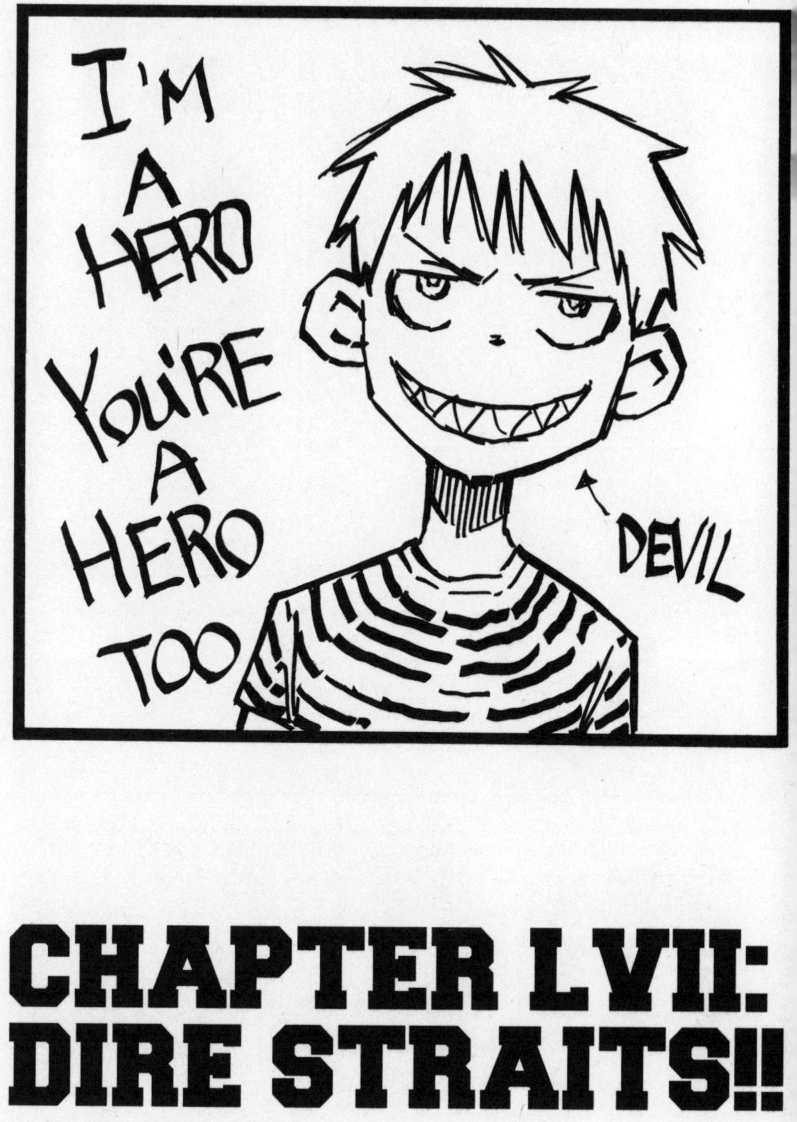
I'M A HERO
YOU'RE A HERO TOO
DEVIL

CHAPTER LVII: DIRE STRAITS!!

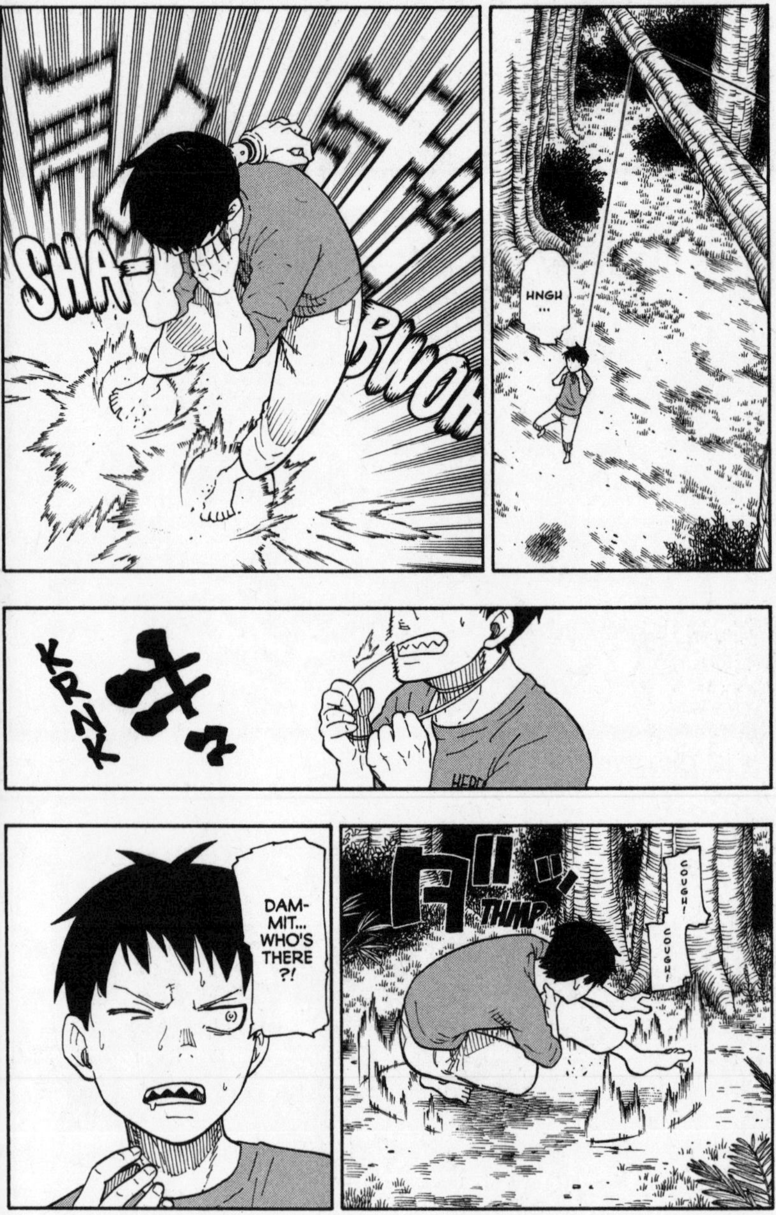
HNGH ...
SHA-
BWOH
KRNK
THMP
COUGH! COUGH!
DAM-MIT... WHO'S THERE ?!

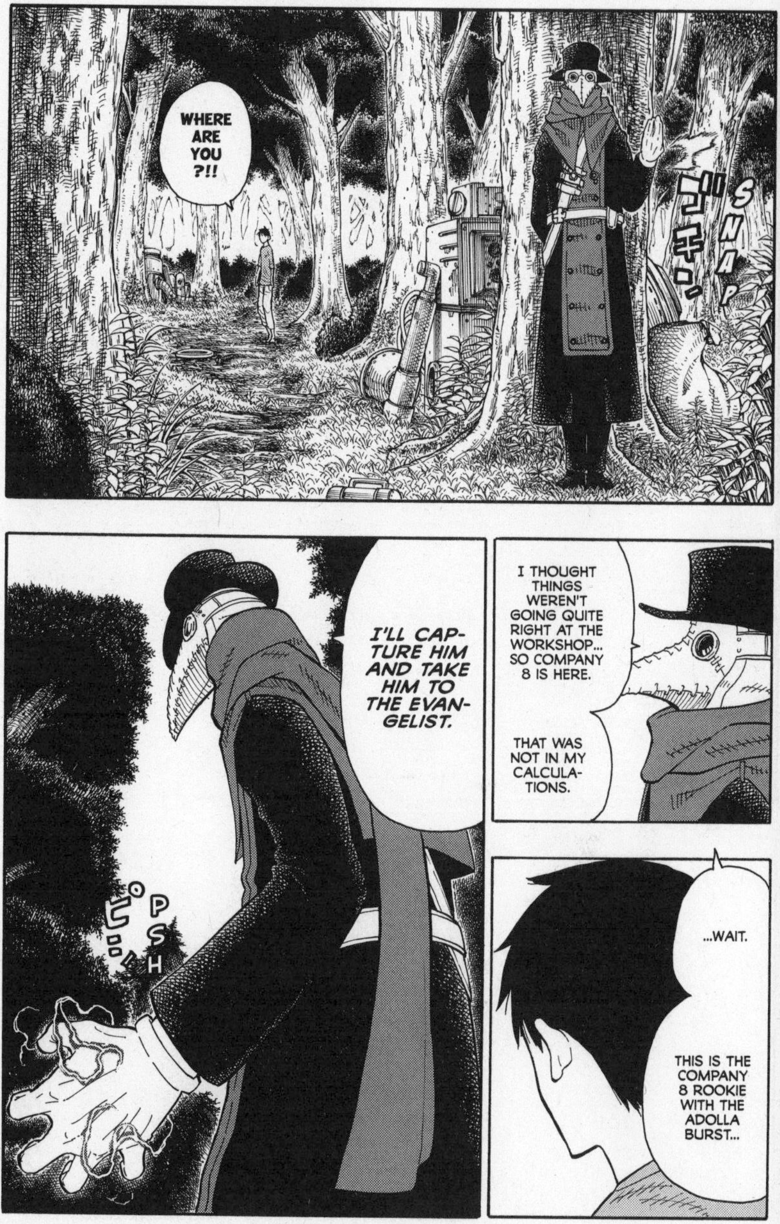
WHERE ARE YOU ?!!
SNAP
I THOUGHT THINGS WEREN'T GOING QUITE RIGHT AT THE WORKSHOP... SO COMPANY 8 IS HERE.
THAT WAS NOT IN MY CALCULATIONS.
...WAIT.
THIS IS THE COMPANY 8 ROOKIE WITH THE ADOLLA BURST...
I'LL CAPTURE HIM AND TAKE HIM TO THE EVANGELIST.
PSH

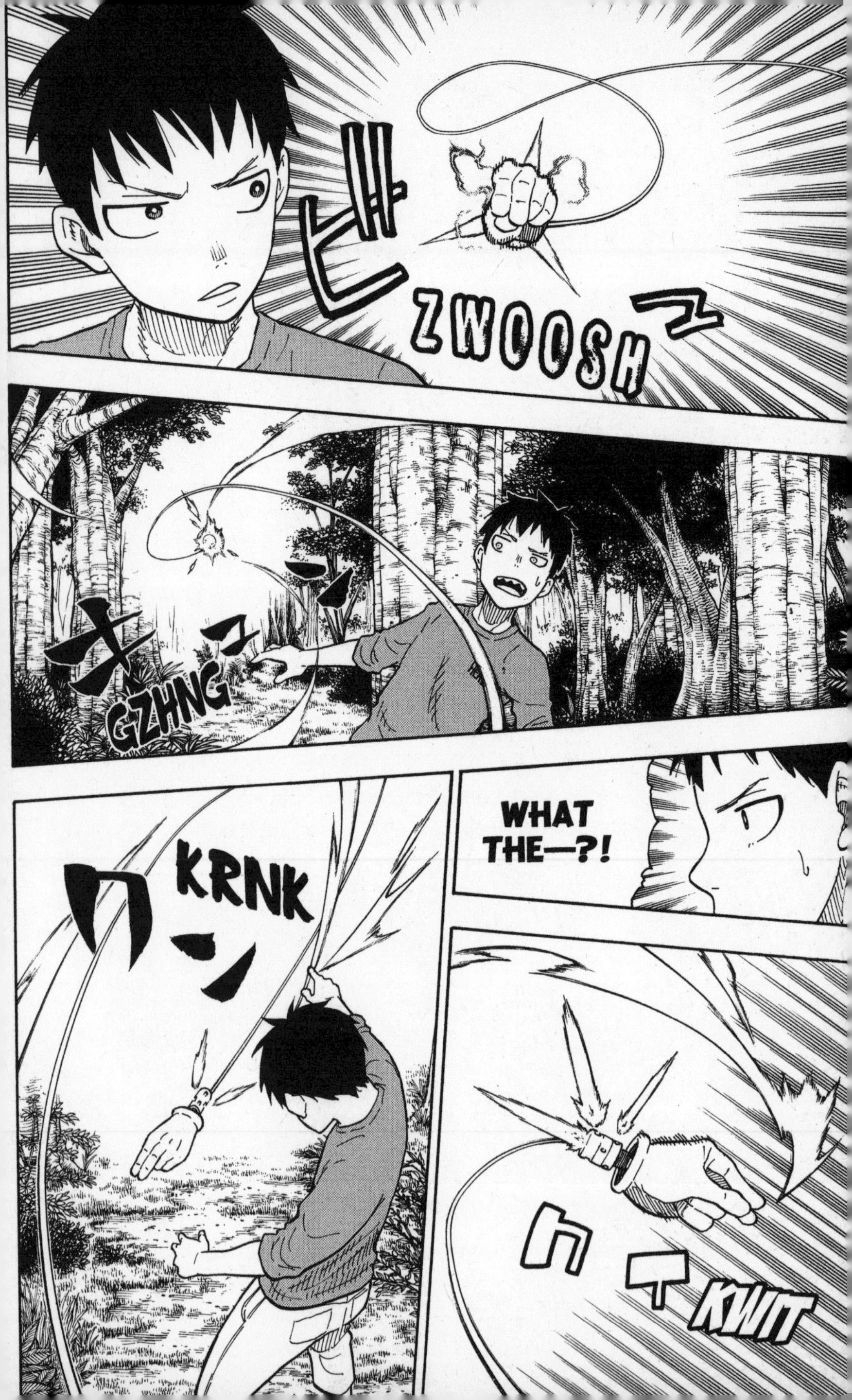
ZWOOSH
GZHNG
WHAT THE—?!
KWIT
KRNK

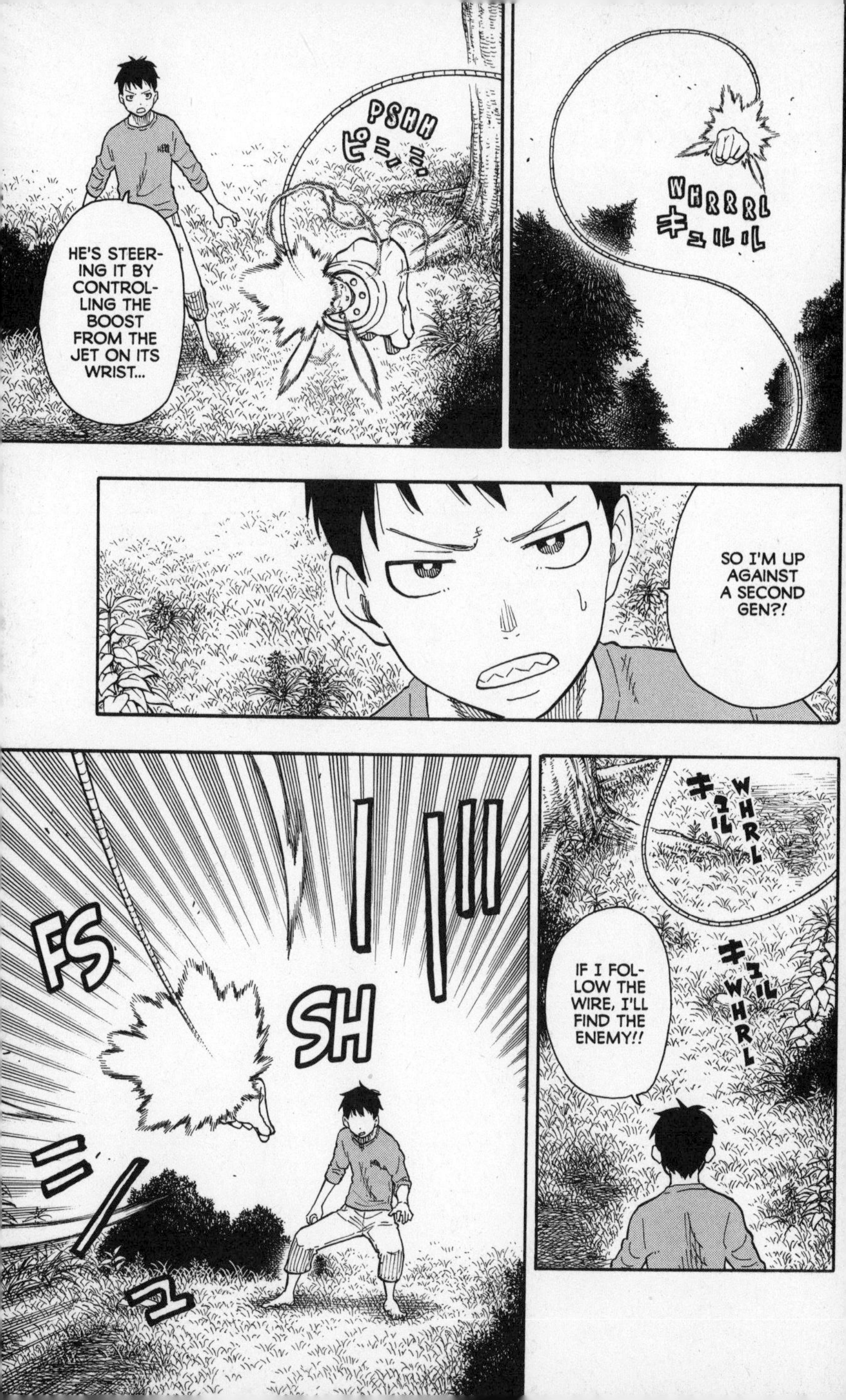
WHRRRL
キュルル
PSHH
HE'S STEERING IT BY CONTROLLING THE BOOST FROM THE JET ON ITS WRIST...
SO I'M UP AGAINST A SECOND GEN?!
WHRL
キュル
IF I FOLLOW THE WIRE, I'LL FIND THE ENEMY!!
キュル
WHRL
FS
SH

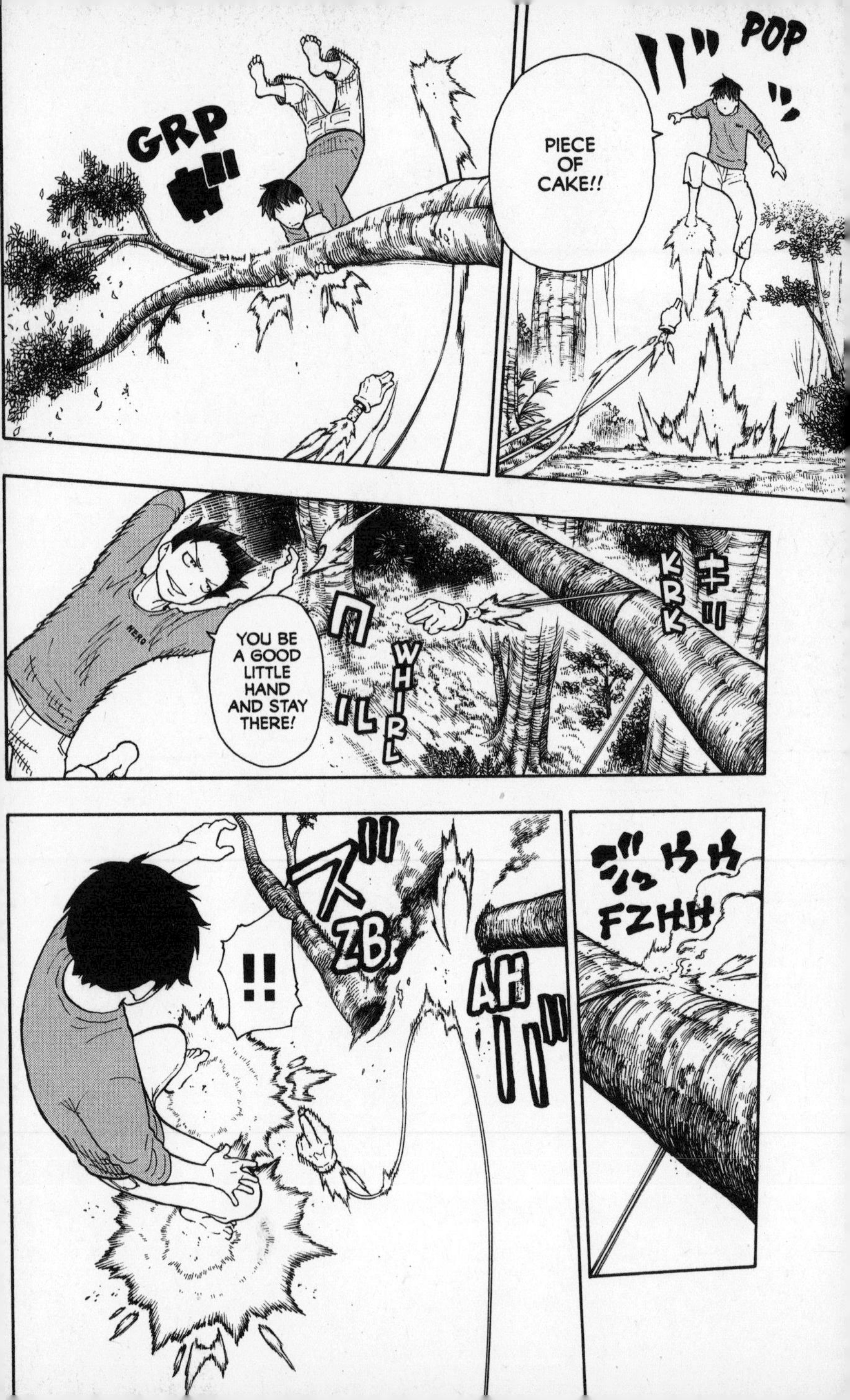
POP
PIECE OF CAKE!!
GRP
KRK
YOU BE A GOOD LITTLE HAND AND STAY THERE!
WHIRL
FZHH
ZB
!!
AH

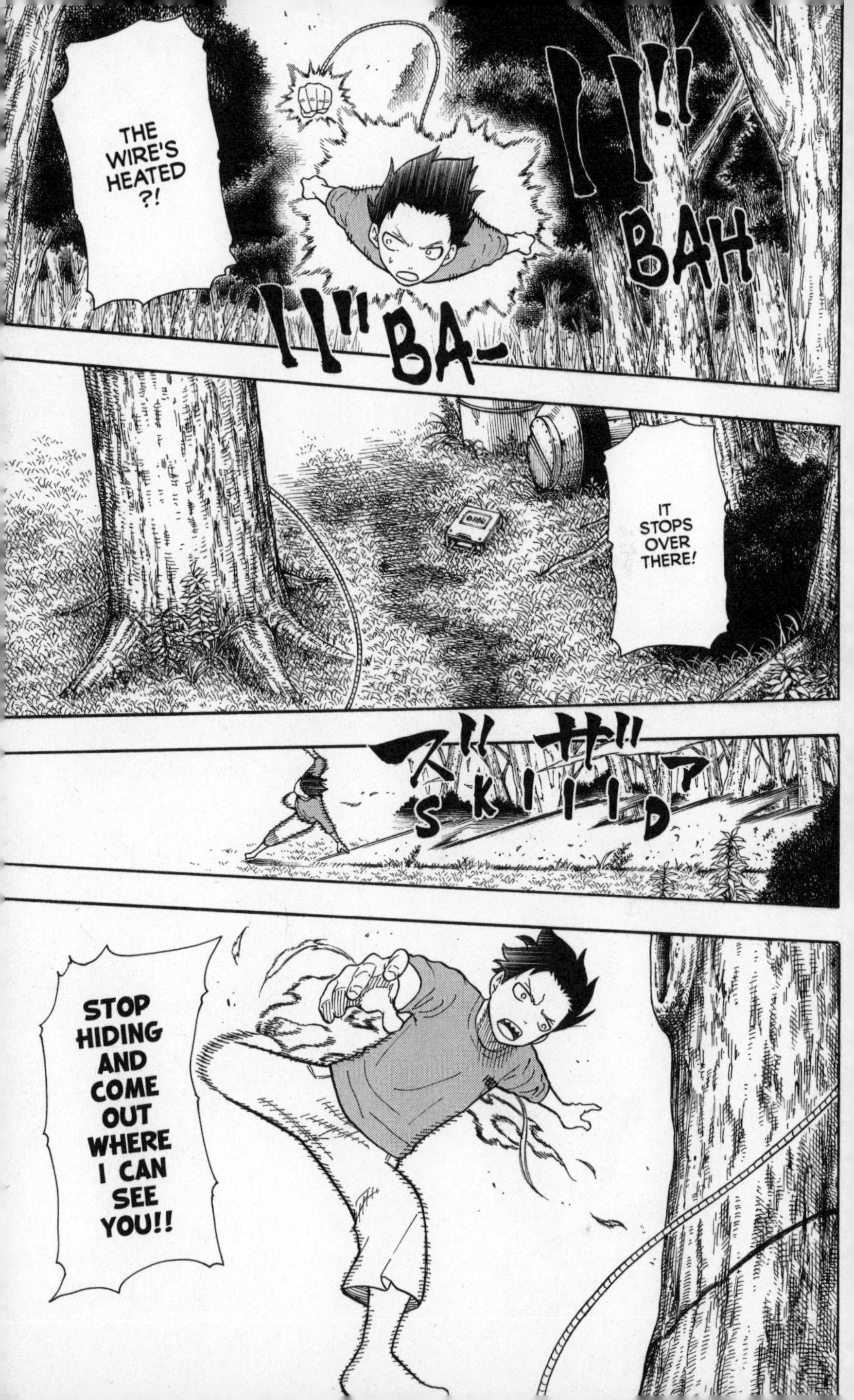
THE WIRE'S HEATED ?!
BA-BAH
IT STOPS OVER THERE!
SKIIID
STOP HIDING AND COME OUT WHERE I CAN SEE YOU!!

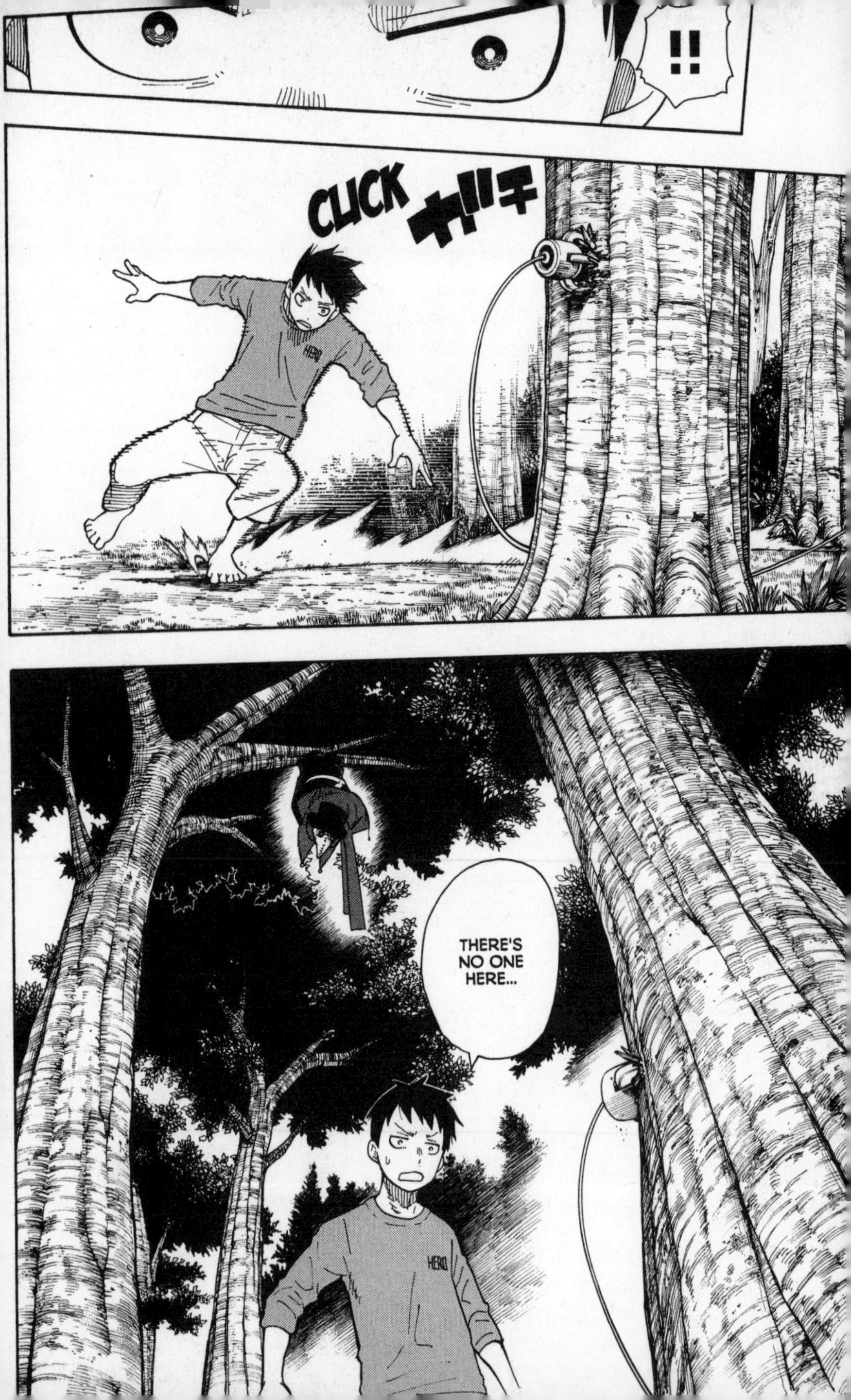
!!
CLICK
カチ
THERE'S NO ONE HERE...

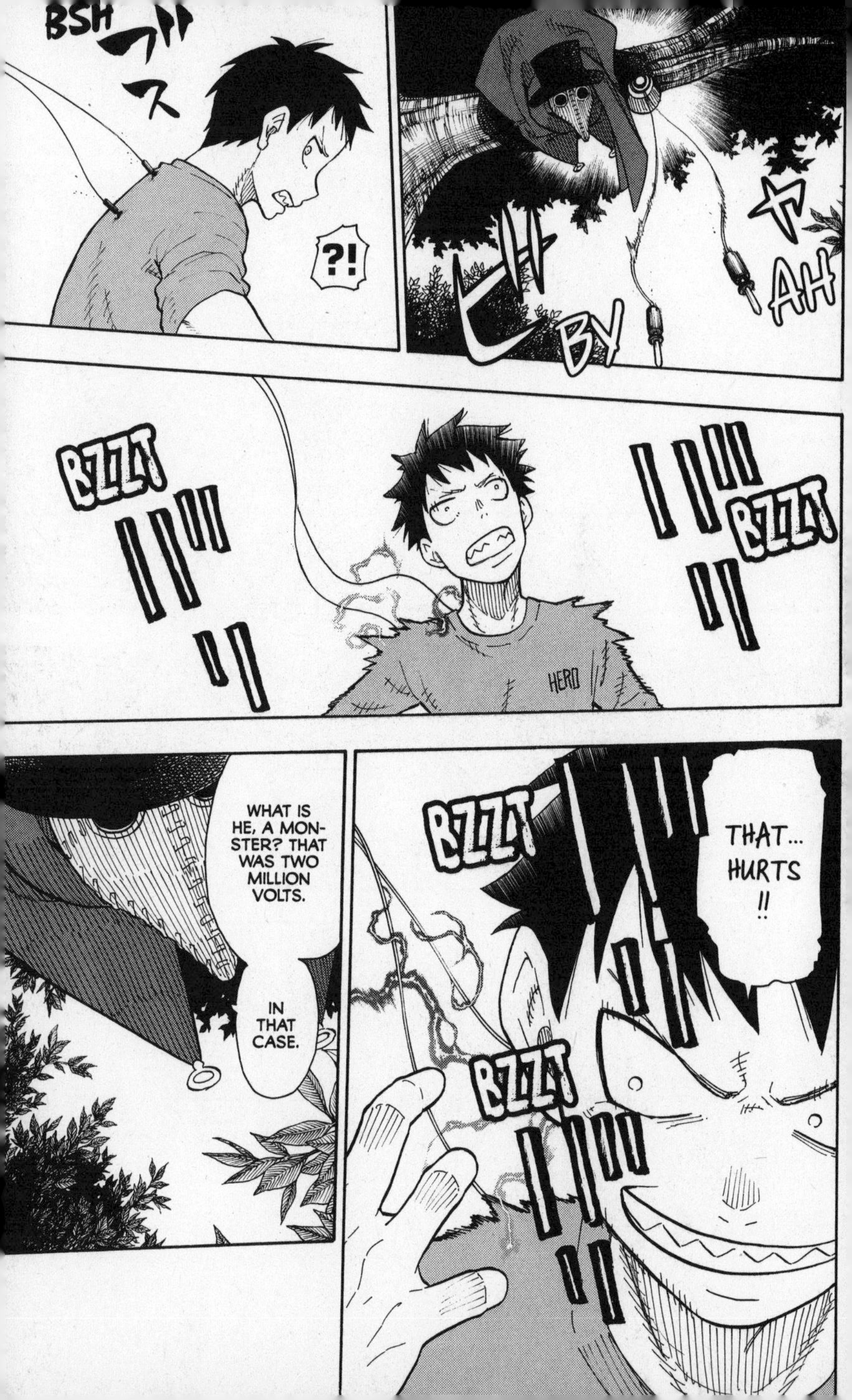
BY
AH
BSH
?!
BZZZT
BZZZT
BZZZT
THAT... HURTS !!
BZZZT
WHAT IS HE, A MONSTER? THAT WAS TWO MILLION VOLTS.
IN THAT CASE.

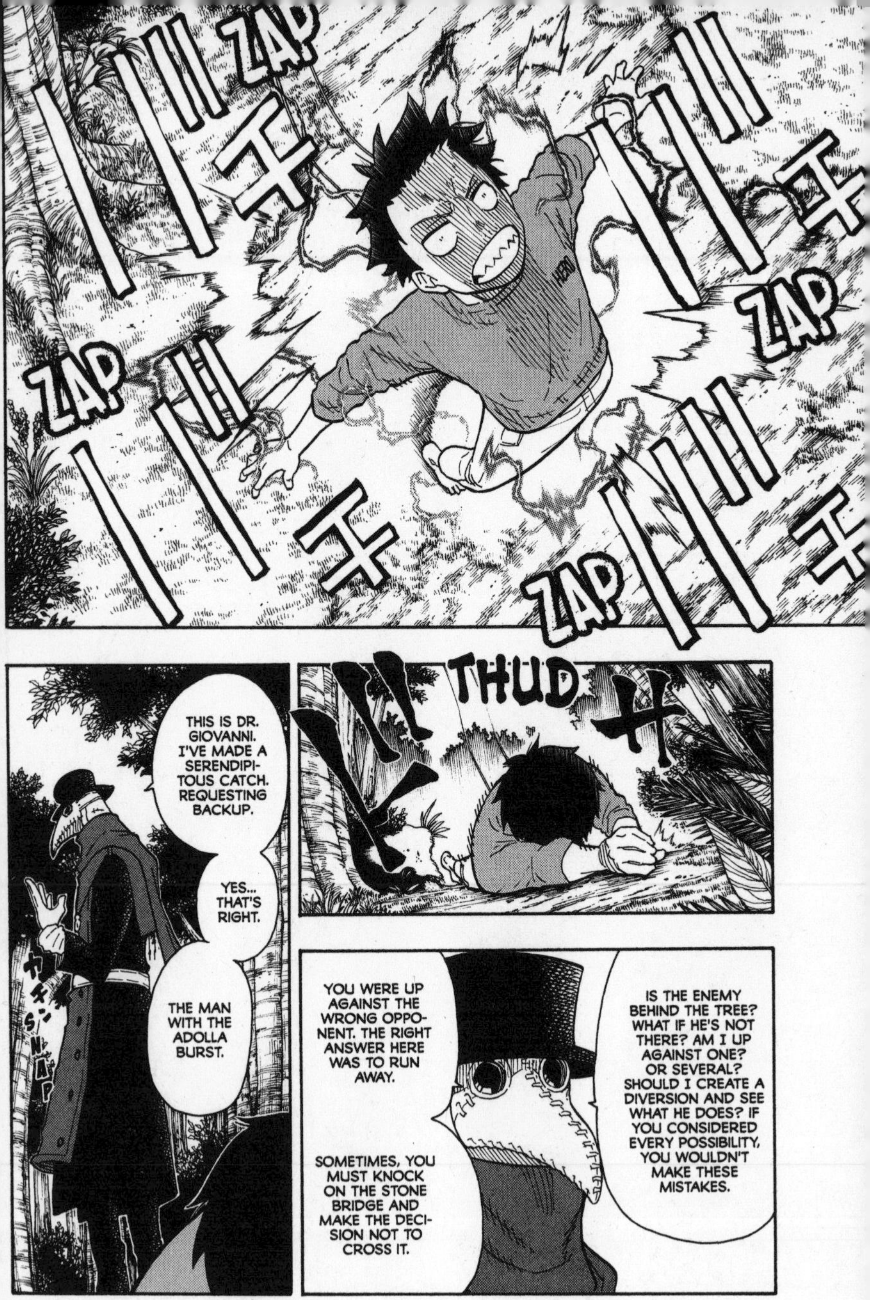
ZAP
ZAP
ZAP
ZAP
THUD
IS THE ENEMY BEHIND THE TREE? WHAT IF HE'S NOT THERE? AM I UP AGAINST ONE? OR SEVERAL? SHOULD I CREATE A DIVERSION AND SEE WHAT HE DOES? IF YOU CONSIDERED EVERY POSSIBILITY, YOU WOULDN'T MAKE THESE MISTAKES.
YOU WERE UP AGAINST THE WRONG OPPO-NENT. THE RIGHT ANSWER HERE WAS TO RUN AWAY.
SOMETIMES, YOU MUST KNOCK ON THE STONE BRIDGE AND MAKE THE DECI-SION NOT TO CROSS IT.
THIS IS DR. GIOVANNI. I'VE MADE A SERENDIPI-TOUS CATCH. REQUESTING BACKUP.
YES... THAT'S RIGHT.
THE MAN WITH THE ADOLLA BURST.
SNAP

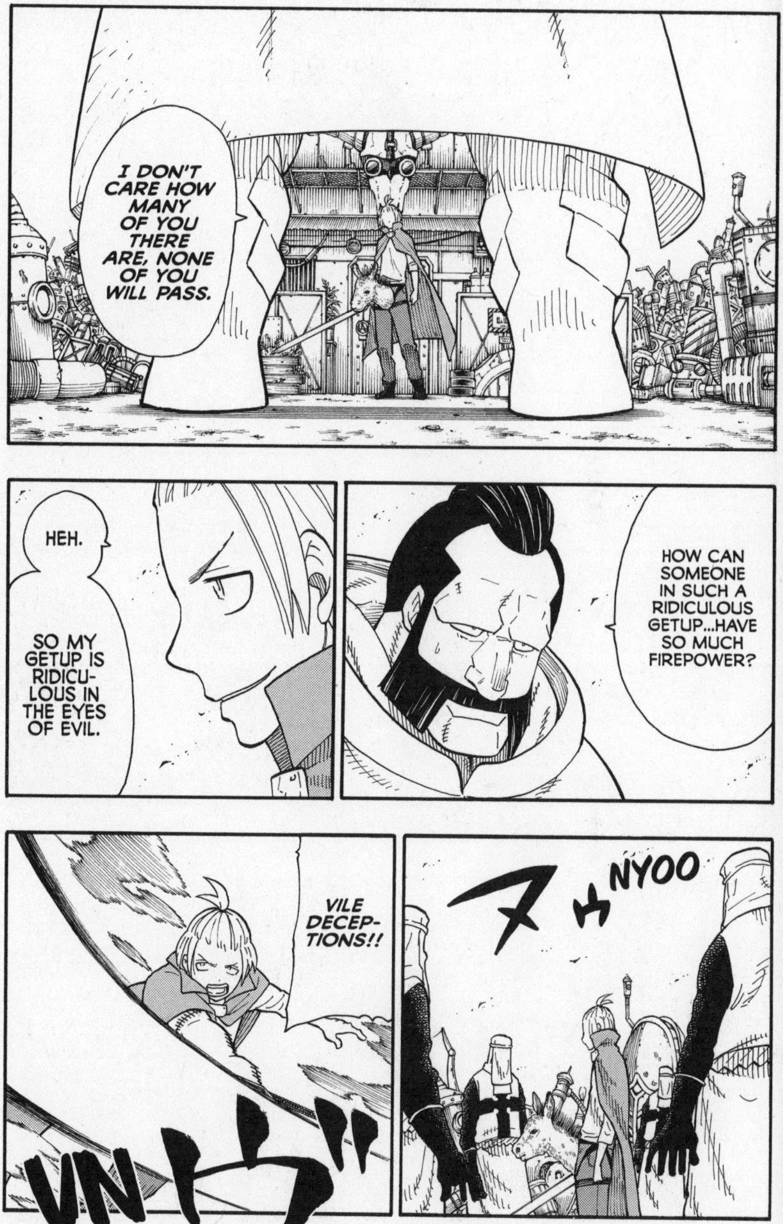
I DON'T CARE HOW MANY OF YOU THERE ARE, NONE OF YOU WILL PASS.
HOW CAN SOMEONE IN SUCH A RIDICULOUS GETUP...HAVE SO MUCH FIREPOWER?
HEH.
SO MY GETUP IS RIDICULOUS IN THE EYES OF EVIL.
NYOO
VILE DECEPTIONS!!

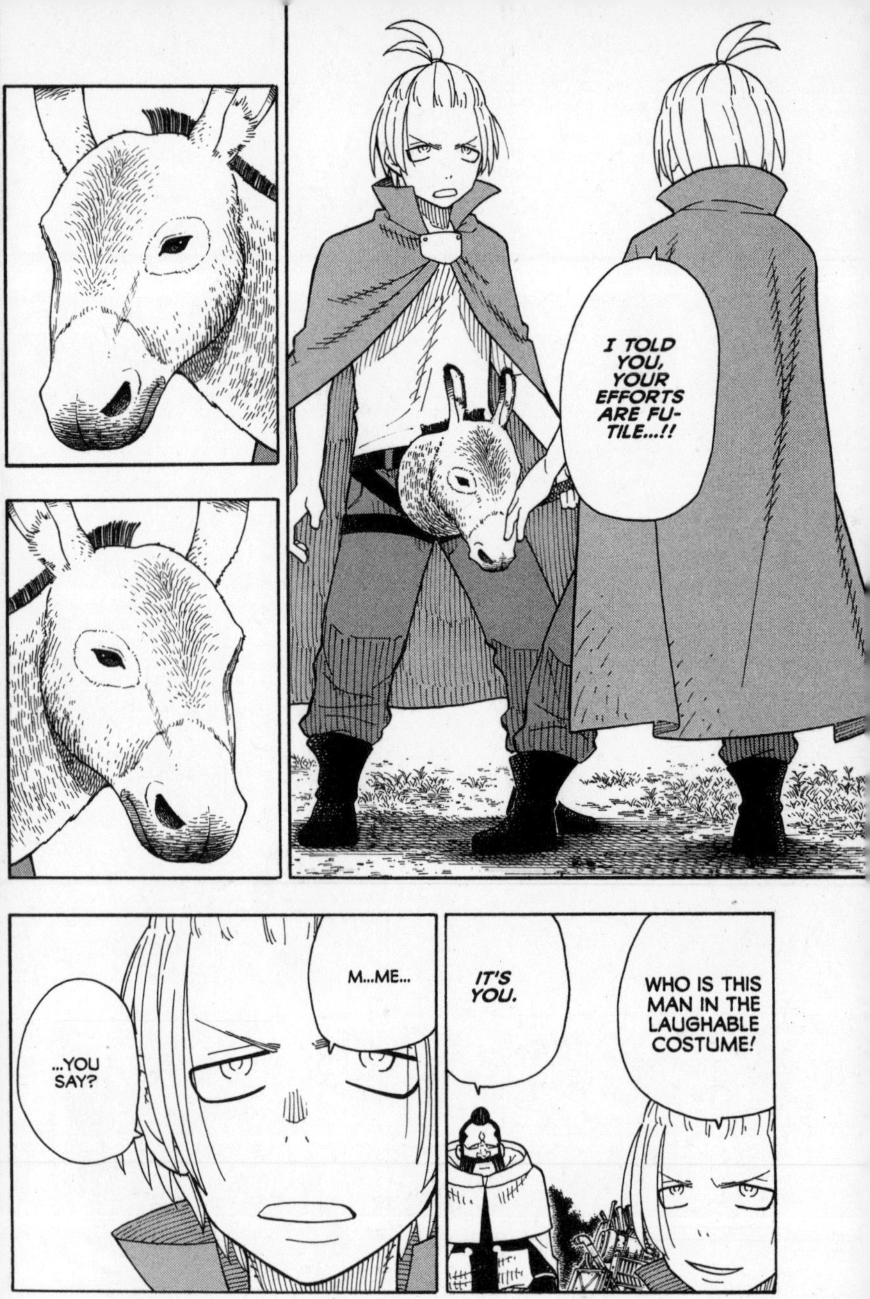
I TOLD YOU, YOUR EFFORTS ARE FU-TILE...!!
WHO IS THIS MAN IN THE LAUGHABLE COSTUME!
IT'S YOU.
M...ME...
...YOU SAY?

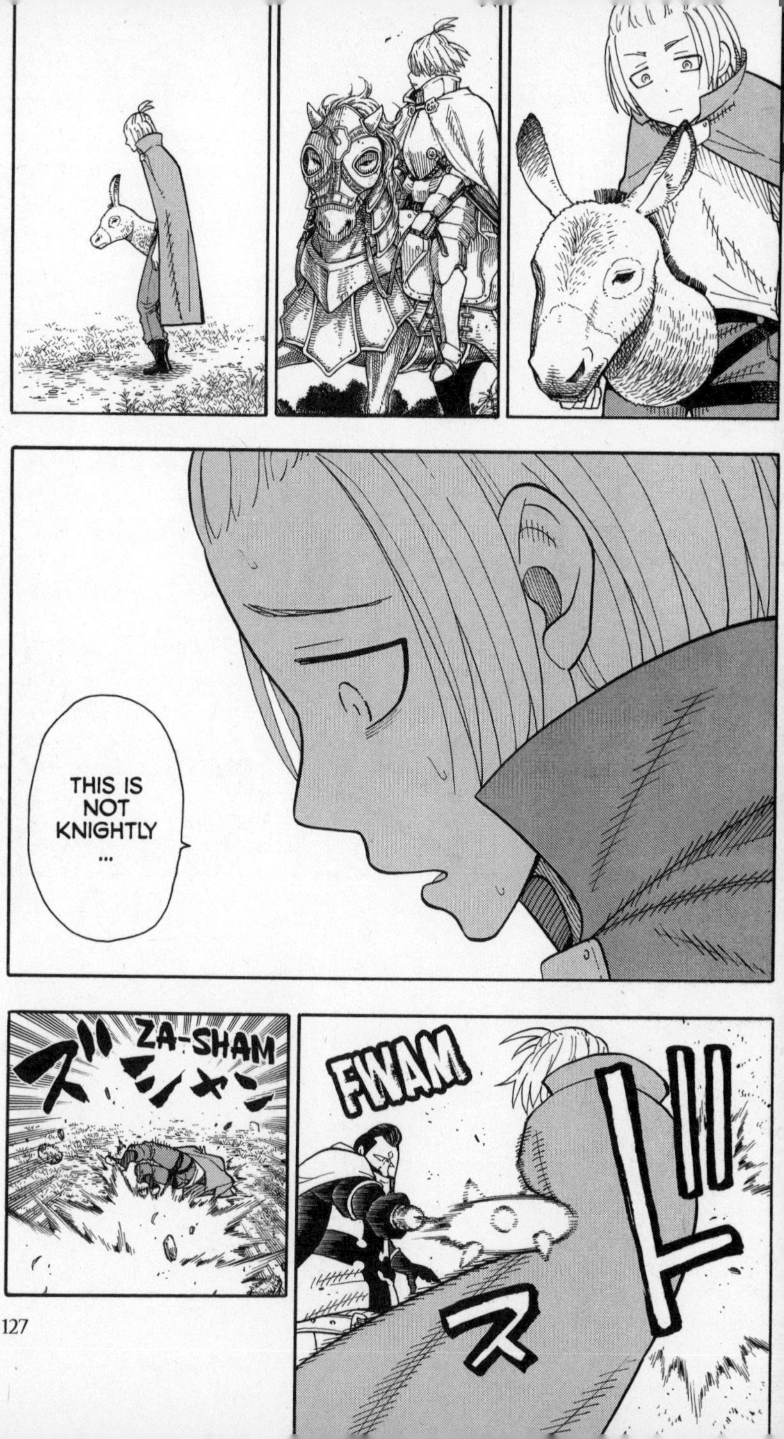
THIS IS NOT KNIGHTLY ...
FWAM
ドス
ZA-SHAM
ズシャン

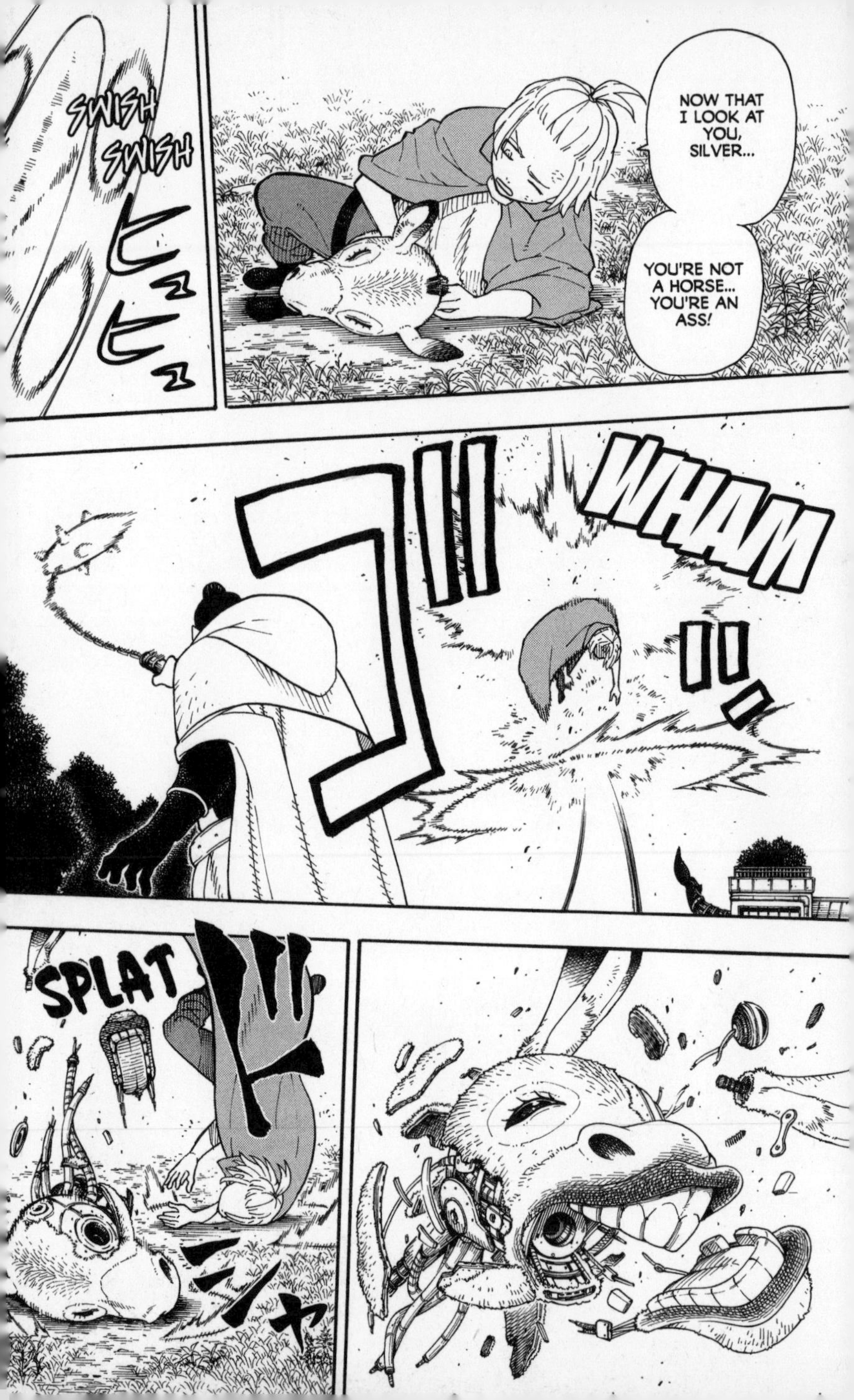
NOW THAT I LOOK AT YOU, SILVER...
YOU'RE NOT A HORSE... YOU'RE AN ASS!
SWISH SWISH
ヒュ ヒュ
WHAM
SPLAT

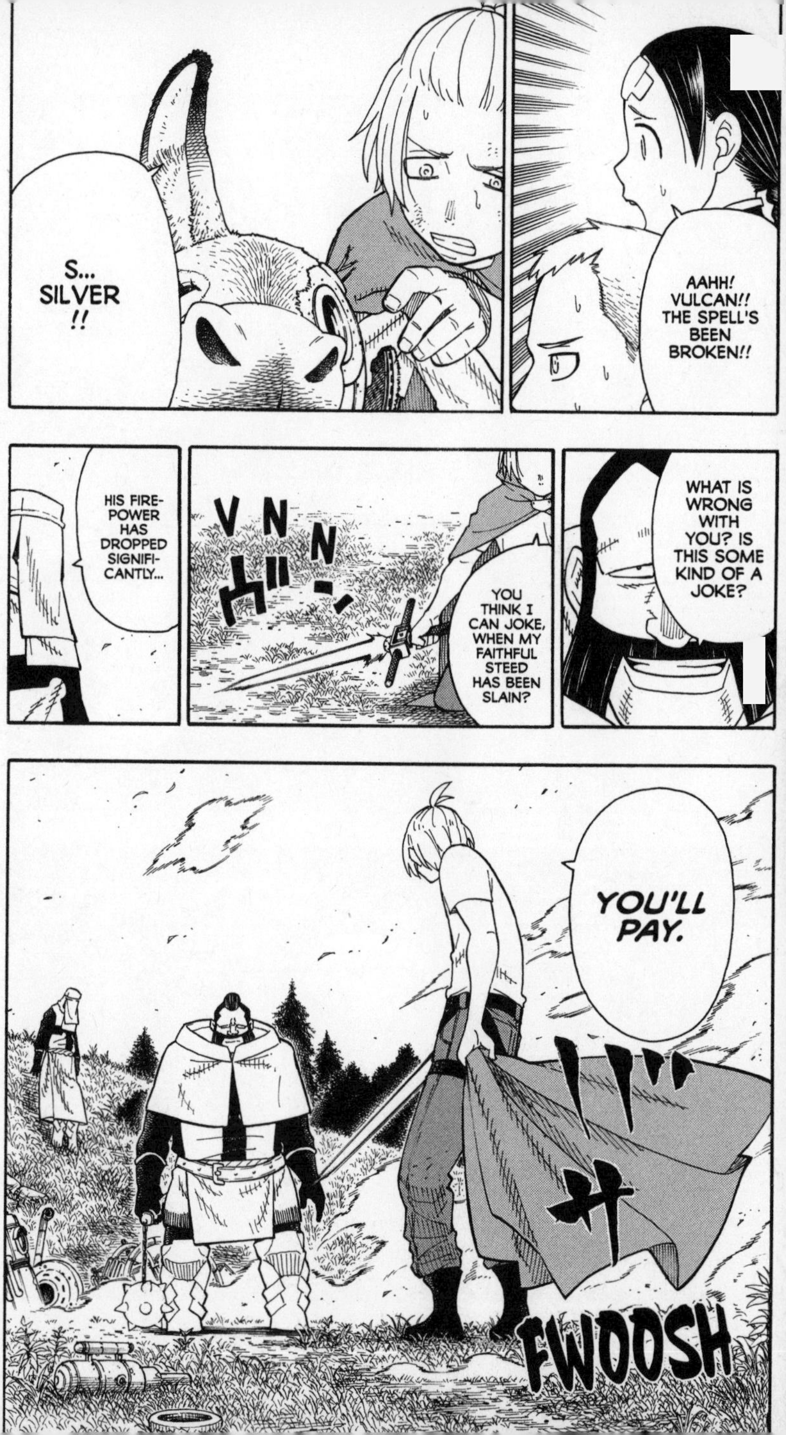
AAHH! VULCAN!! THE SPELL'S BEEN BROKEN!!
S... SILVER!!
WHAT IS WRONG WITH YOU? IS THIS SOME KIND OF A JOKE?
YOU THINK I CAN JOKE, WHEN MY FAITHFUL STEED HAS BEEN SLAIN?
VNN
HIS FIRE-POWER HAS DROPPED SIGNIFI-CANTLY...
YOU'LL PAY.
FWOOSH

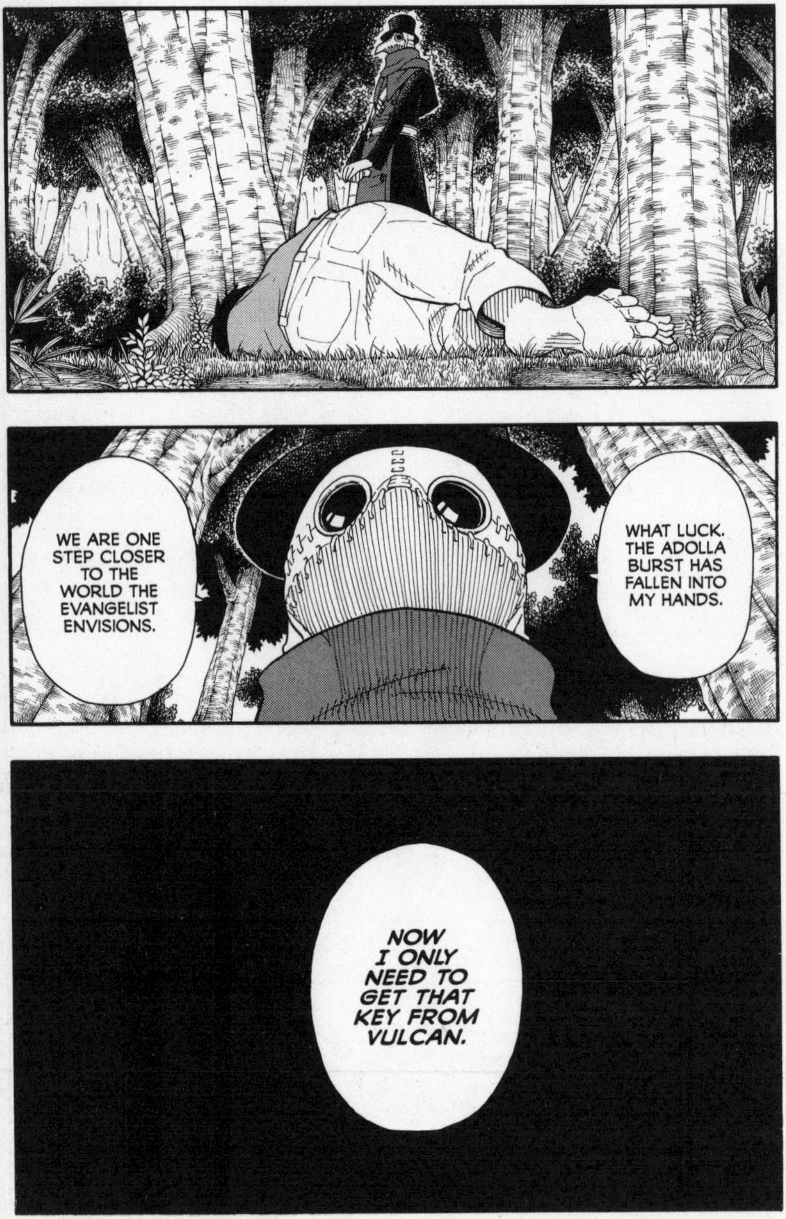
WHAT LUCK. THE ADOLLA BURST HAS FALLEN INTO MY HANDS.
WE ARE ONE STEP CLOSER TO THE WORLD THE EVANGELIST ENVISIONS.
NOW I ONLY NEED TO GET THAT KEY FROM VULCAN.

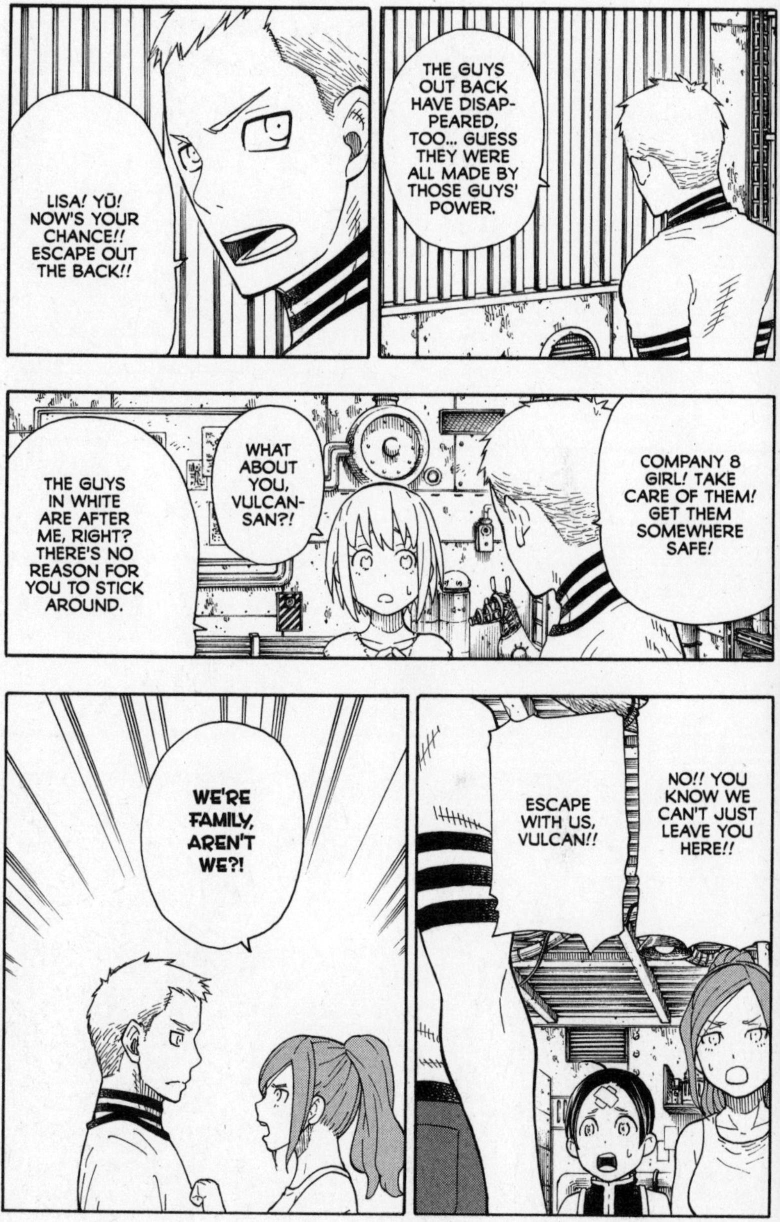
THE GUYS OUT BACK HAVE DISAPPEARED, TOO... GUESS THEY WERE ALL MADE BY THOSE GUYS' POWER.
LISA! YŪ! NOW'S YOUR CHANCE!! ESCAPE OUT THE BACK!!
COMPANY 8 GIRL! TAKE CARE OF THEM! GET THEM SOMEWHERE SAFE!
WHAT ABOUT YOU, VULCAN-SAN?!
THE GUYS IN WHITE ARE AFTER ME, RIGHT? THERE'S NO REASON FOR YOU TO STICK AROUND.
NO!! YOU KNOW WE CAN'T JUST LEAVE YOU HERE!!
ESCAPE WITH US, VULCAN!!
WE'RE FAMILY, AREN'T WE?!

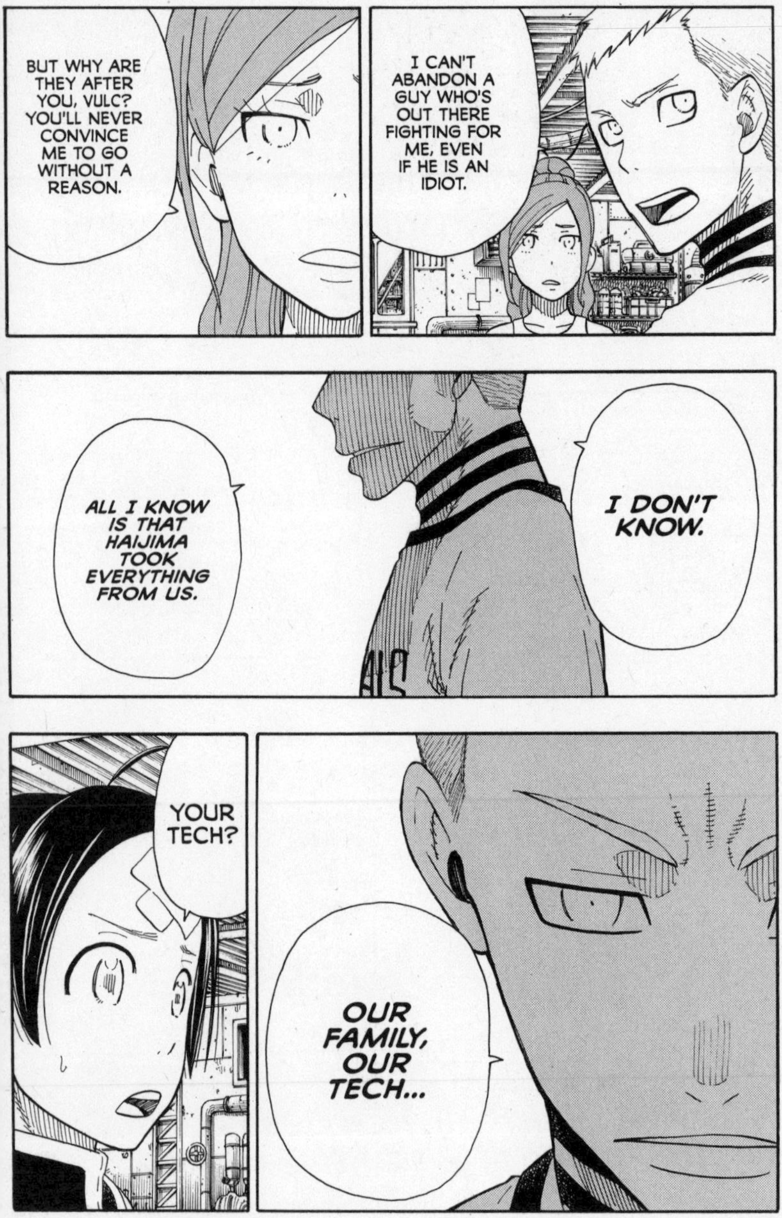
I CAN'T ABANDON A GUY WHO'S OUT THERE FIGHTING FOR ME, EVEN IF HE IS AN IDIOT.
BUT WHY ARE THEY AFTER YOU, VULC? YOU'LL NEVER CONVINCE ME TO GO WITHOUT A REASON.
I DON'T KNOW.
ALL I KNOW IS THAT HAIJIMA TOOK EVERYTHING FROM US.
OUR FAMILY, OUR TECH...
YOUR TECH?

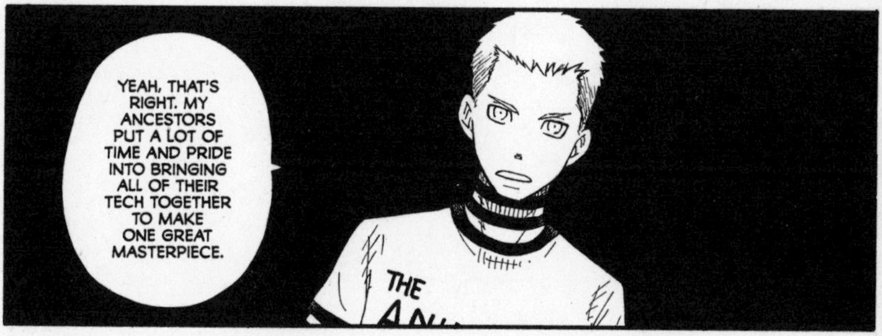
YEAH, THAT'S RIGHT. MY ANCESTORS PUT A LOT OF TIME AND PRIDE INTO BRINGING ALL OF THEIR TECH TOGETHER TO MAKE ONE GREAT MASTERPIECE.
THE
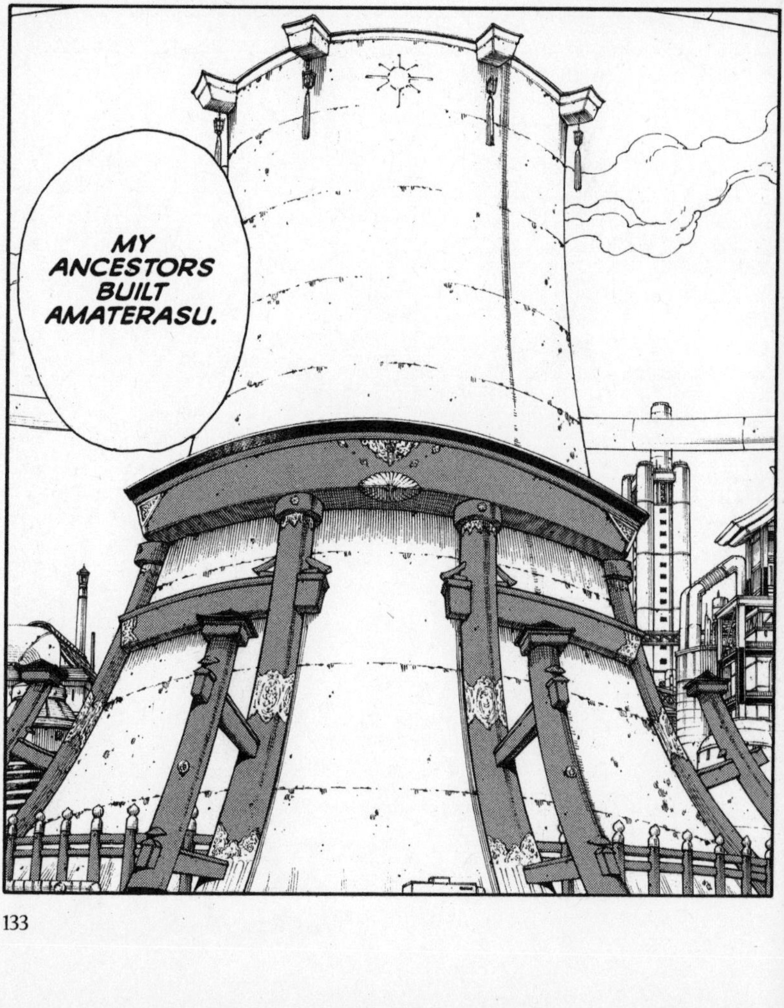
MY ANCESTORS BUILT AMATERASU.

FIRE FORCE

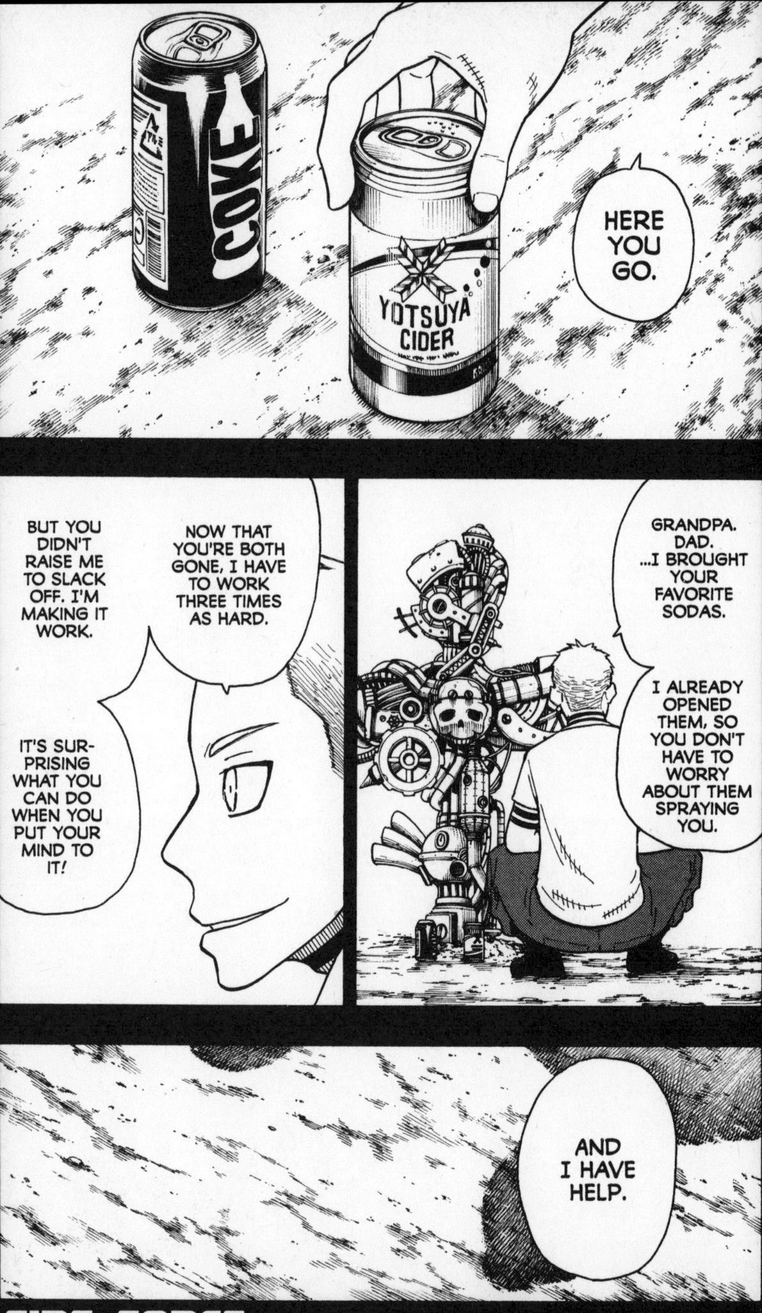
COKE
YOTSUYA CIDER
HERE YOU GO.
GRANDPA. DAD. ...I BROUGHT YOUR FAVORITE SODAS.
I ALREADY OPENED THEM, SO YOU DON'T HAVE TO WORRY ABOUT THEM SPRAYING YOU.
NOW THAT YOU'RE BOTH GONE, I HAVE TO WORK THREE TIMES AS HARD.
BUT YOU DIDN'T RAISE ME TO SLACK OFF. I'M MAKING IT WORK.
IT'S SURPRISING WHAT YOU CAN DO WHEN YOU PUT YOUR MIND TO IT!
AND I HAVE HELP.

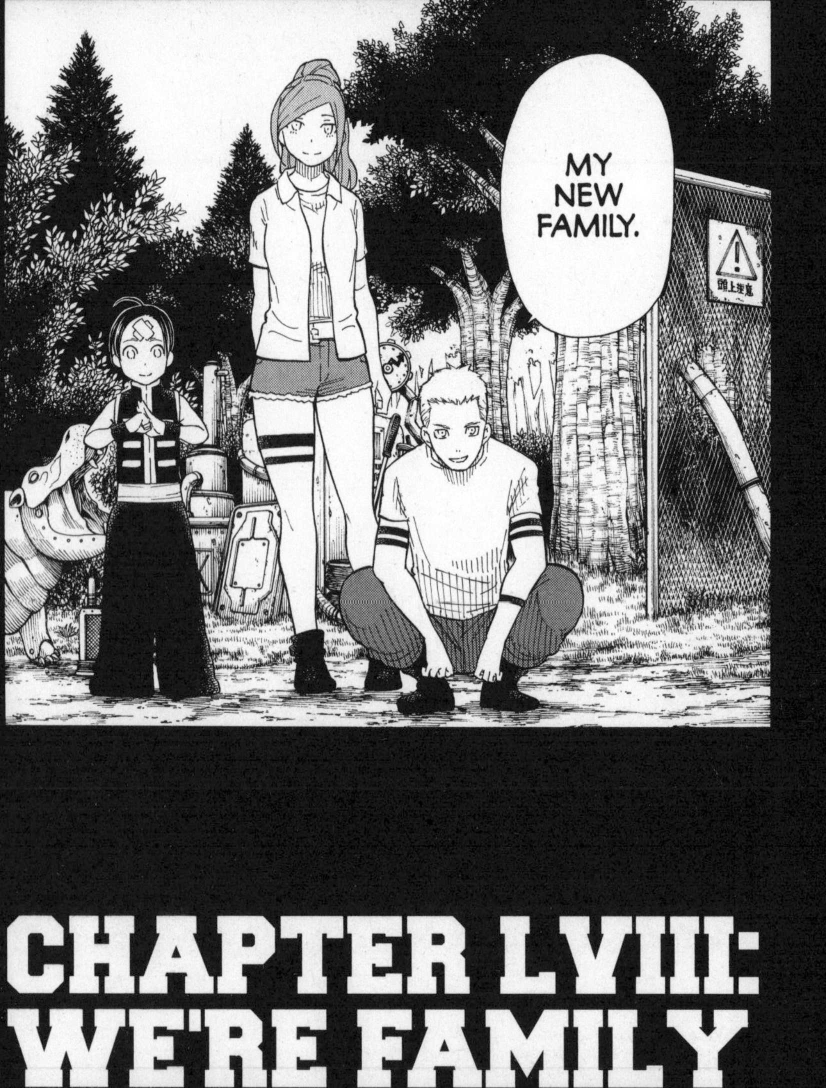
MY NEW FAMILY.

CHAPTER LVIII: WE'RE FAMILY

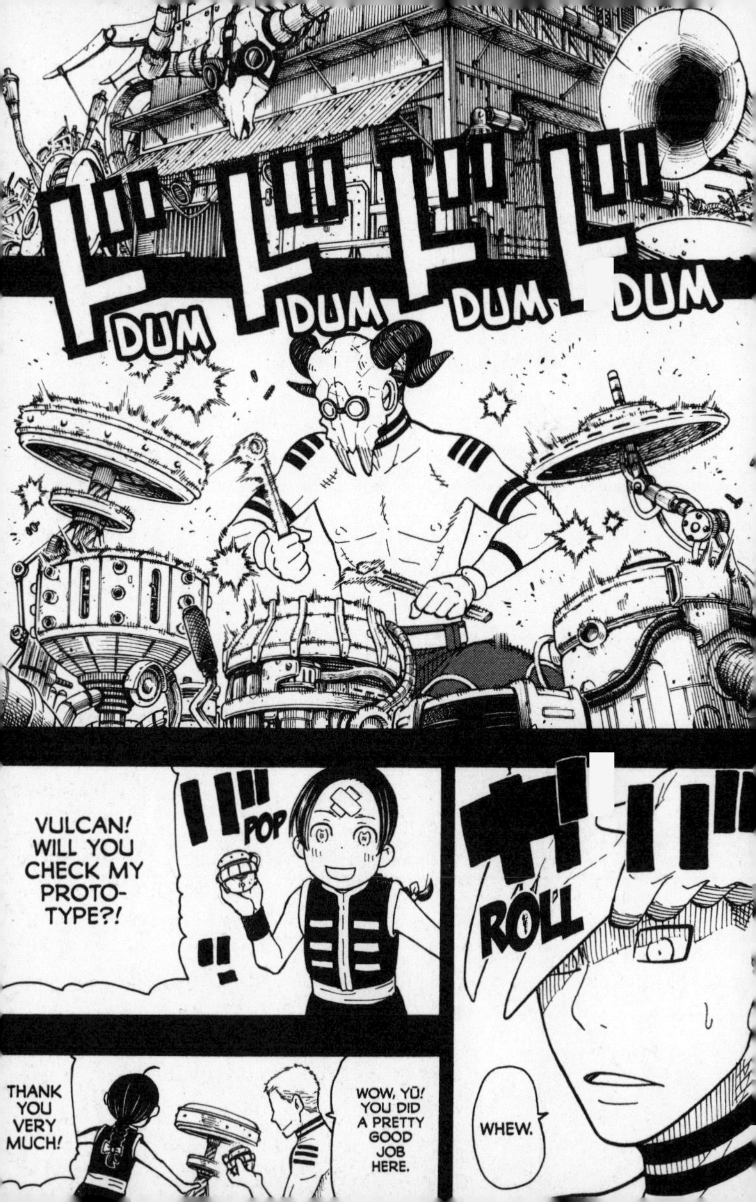
DUM
DUM
DUM
DUM
ROLL
WHEW.
VULCAN! WILL YOU CHECK MY PROTO-TYPE?!
POP
WOW, YŪ! YOU DID A PRETTY GOOD JOB HERE.
THANK YOU VERY MUCH!

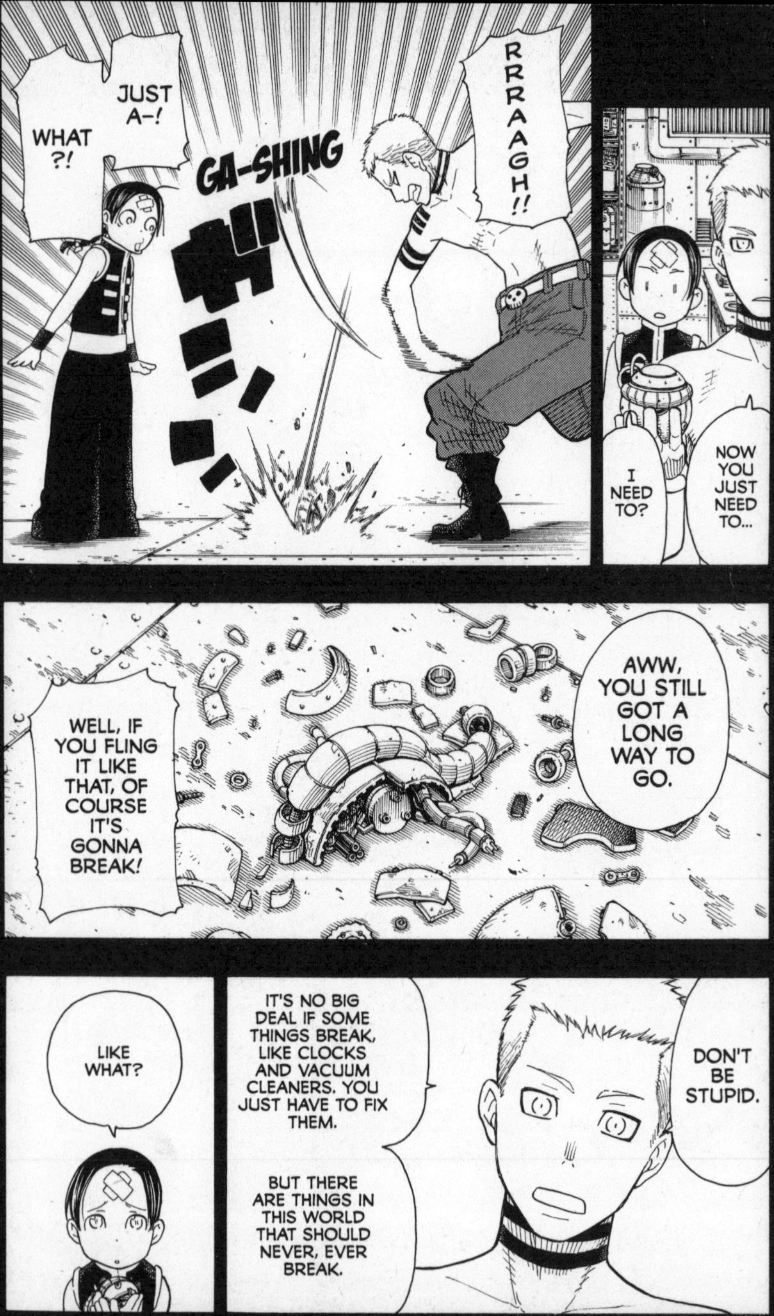
NOW YOU JUST NEED TO...
I NEED TO?
RRRAAGH!!
JUST A-! WHAT?!
GA-SHING
AWW, YOU STILL GOT A LONG WAY TO GO.
WELL, IF YOU FLING IT LIKE THAT, OF COURSE IT'S GONNA BREAK!
DON'T BE STUPID.
IT'S NO BIG DEAL IF SOME THINGS BREAK, LIKE CLOCKS AND VACUUM CLEANERS. YOU JUST HAVE TO FIX THEM.
BUT THERE ARE THINGS IN THIS WORLD THAT SHOULD NEVER, EVER BREAK.
LIKE WHAT?

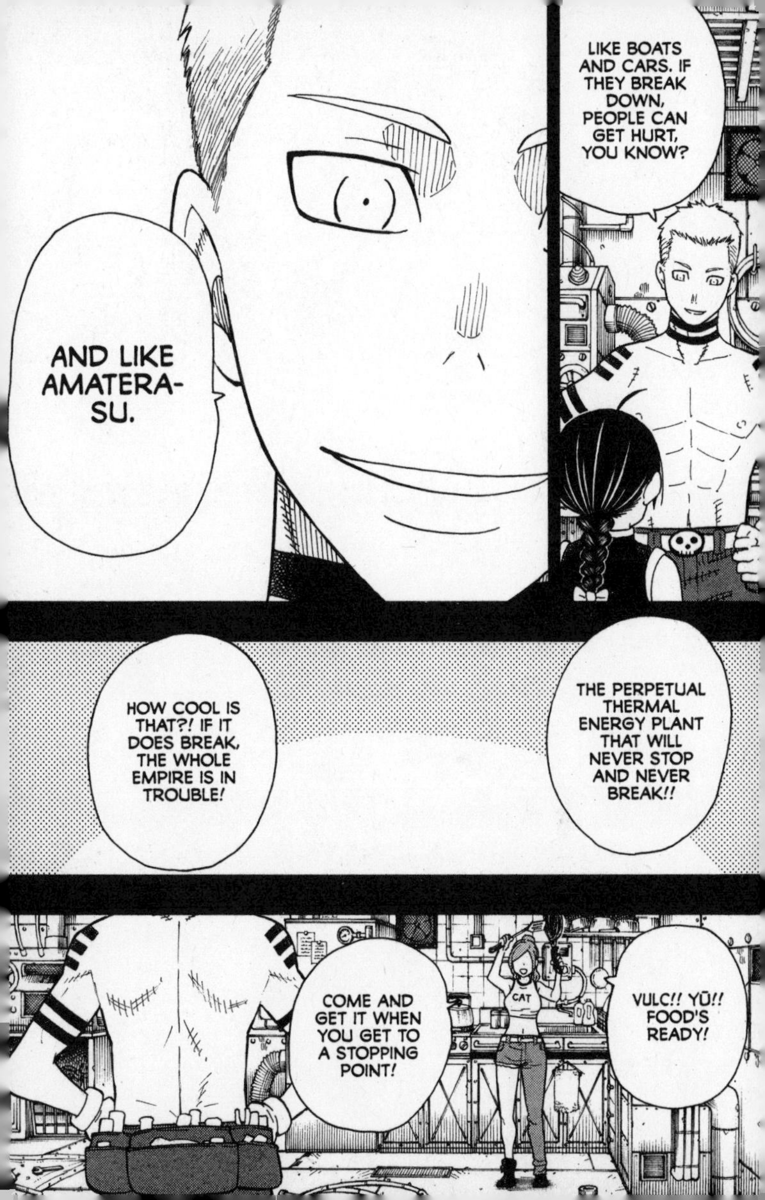
LIKE BOATS AND CARS. IF THEY BREAK DOWN, PEOPLE CAN GET HURT, YOU KNOW?
AND LIKE AMATERA-SU.
THE PERPETUAL THERMAL ENERGY PLANT THAT WILL NEVER STOP AND NEVER BREAK!!
HOW COOL IS THAT?! IF IT DOES BREAK, THE WHOLE EMPIRE IS IN TROUBLE!
VULC!! YŪ!! FOOD'S READY!
COME AND GET IT WHEN YOU GET TO A STOPPING POINT!
CAT

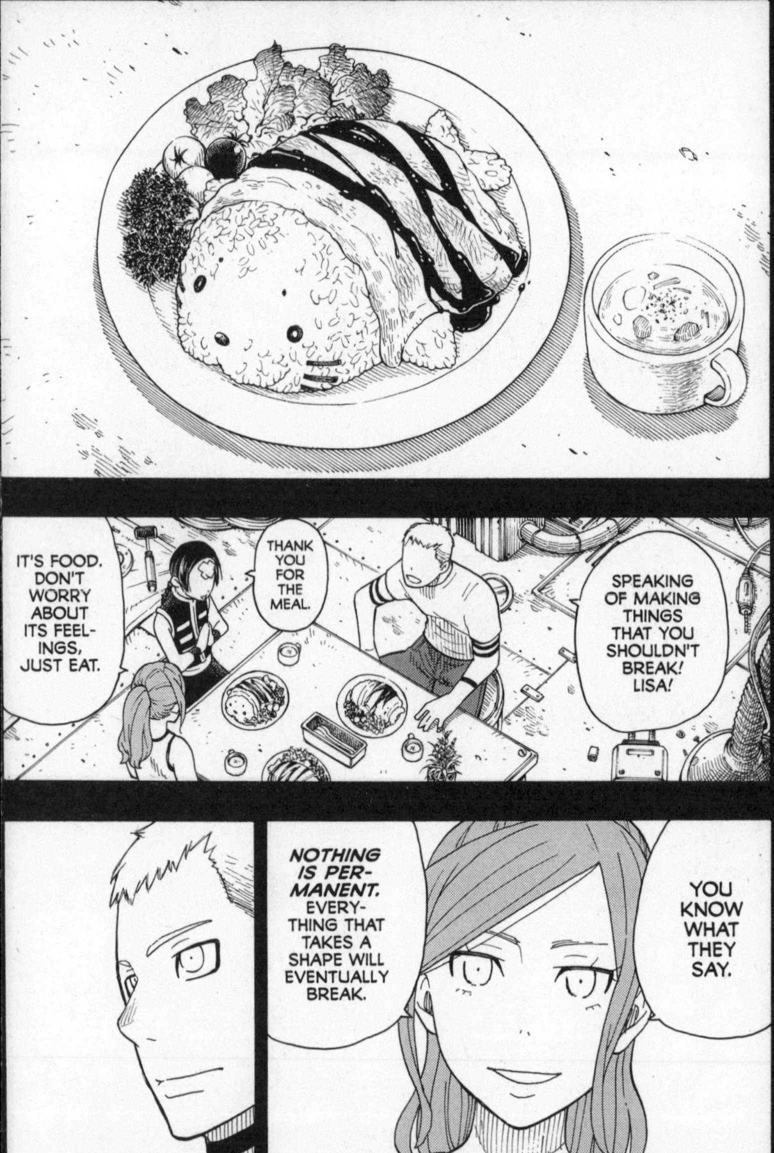
SPEAKING OF MAKING THINGS THAT YOU SHOULDN'T BREAK! LISA!
THANK YOU FOR THE MEAL.
IT'S FOOD. DON'T WORRY ABOUT ITS FEEL-INGS, JUST EAT.
YOU KNOW WHAT THEY SAY.
NOTHING IS PER-MANENT. EVERY-THING THAT TAKES A SHAPE WILL EVENTUALLY BREAK.

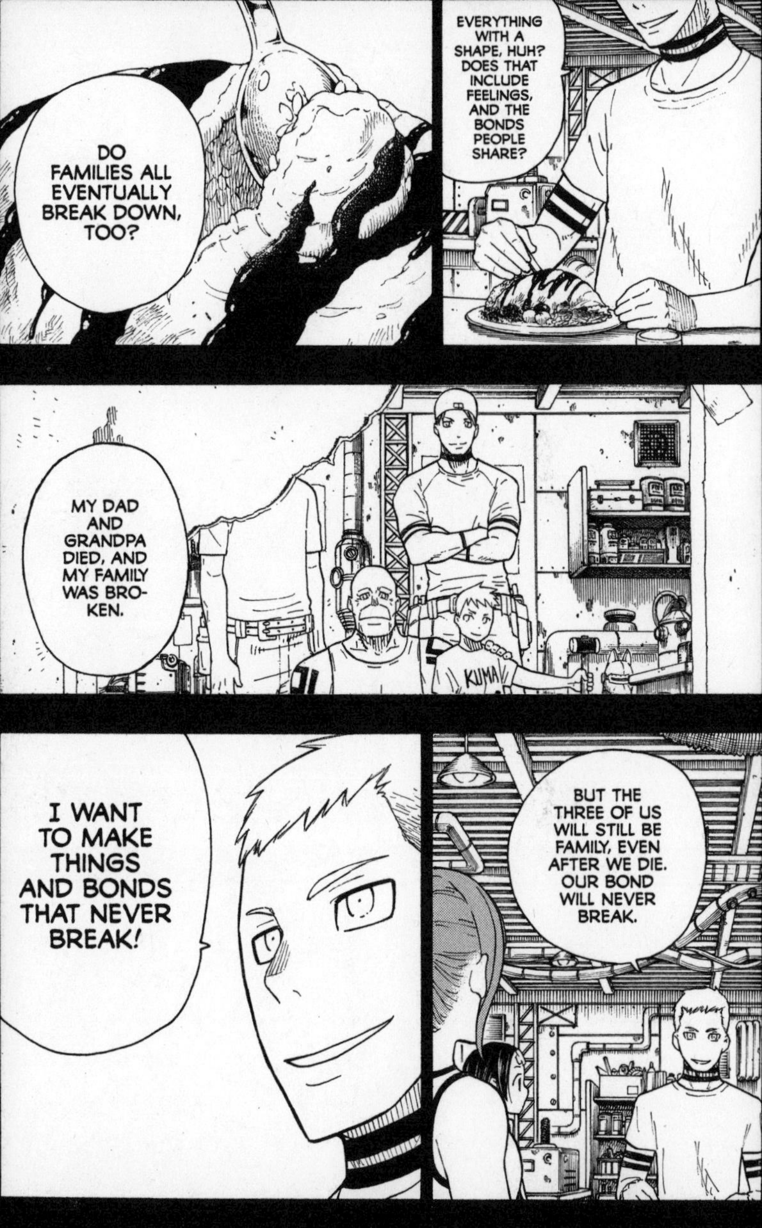
EVERYTHING WITH A SHAPE, HUH? DOES THAT INCLUDE FEELINGS, AND THE BONDS PEOPLE SHARE?
DO FAMILIES ALL EVENTUALLY BREAK DOWN, TOO?
MY DAD AND GRANDPA DIED, AND MY FAMILY WAS BRO-KEN.
KUMA
BUT THE THREE OF US WILL STILL BE FAMILY, EVEN AFTER WE DIE. OUR BOND WILL NEVER BREAK.
I WANT TO MAKE THINGS AND BONDS THAT NEVER BREAK!

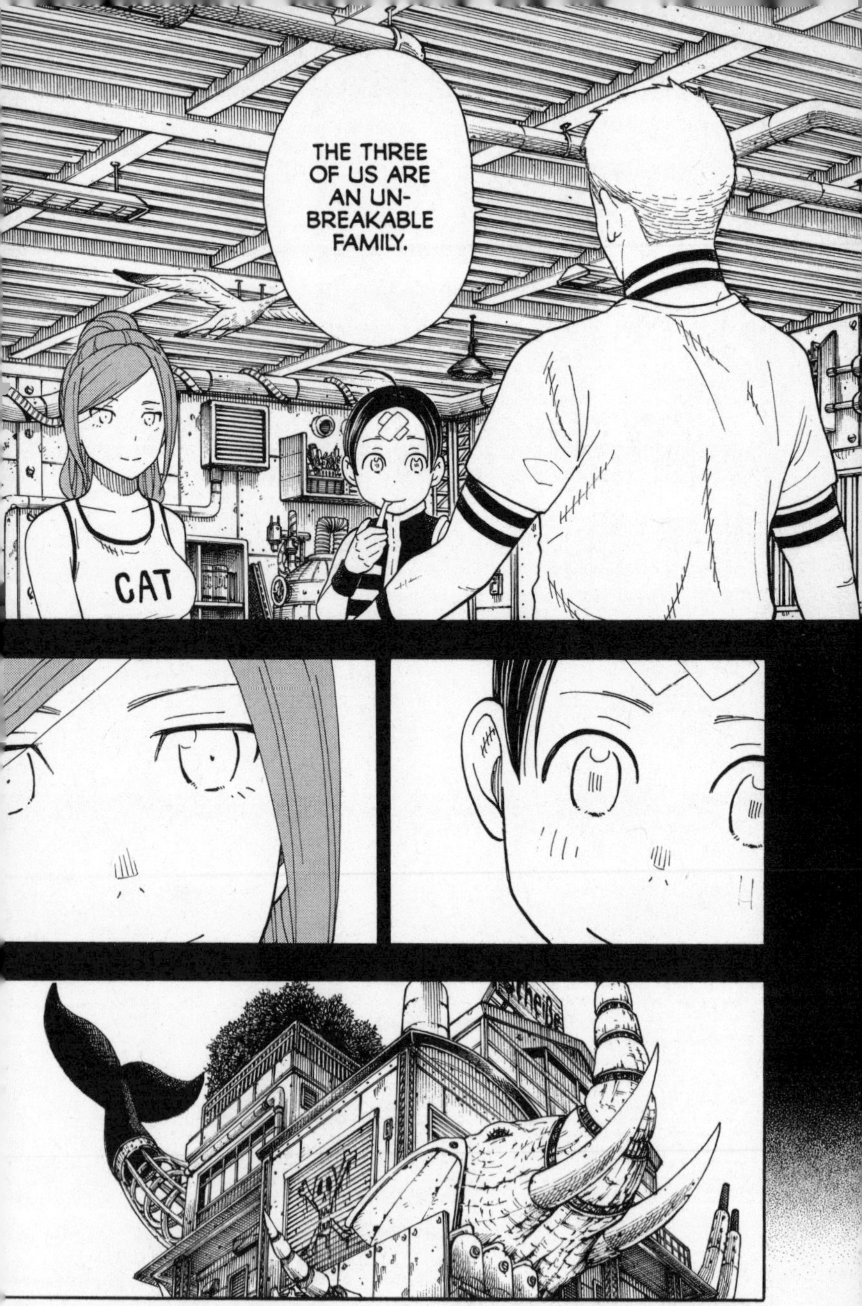
THE THREE OF US ARE AN UN-BREAKABLE FAMILY.
CAT

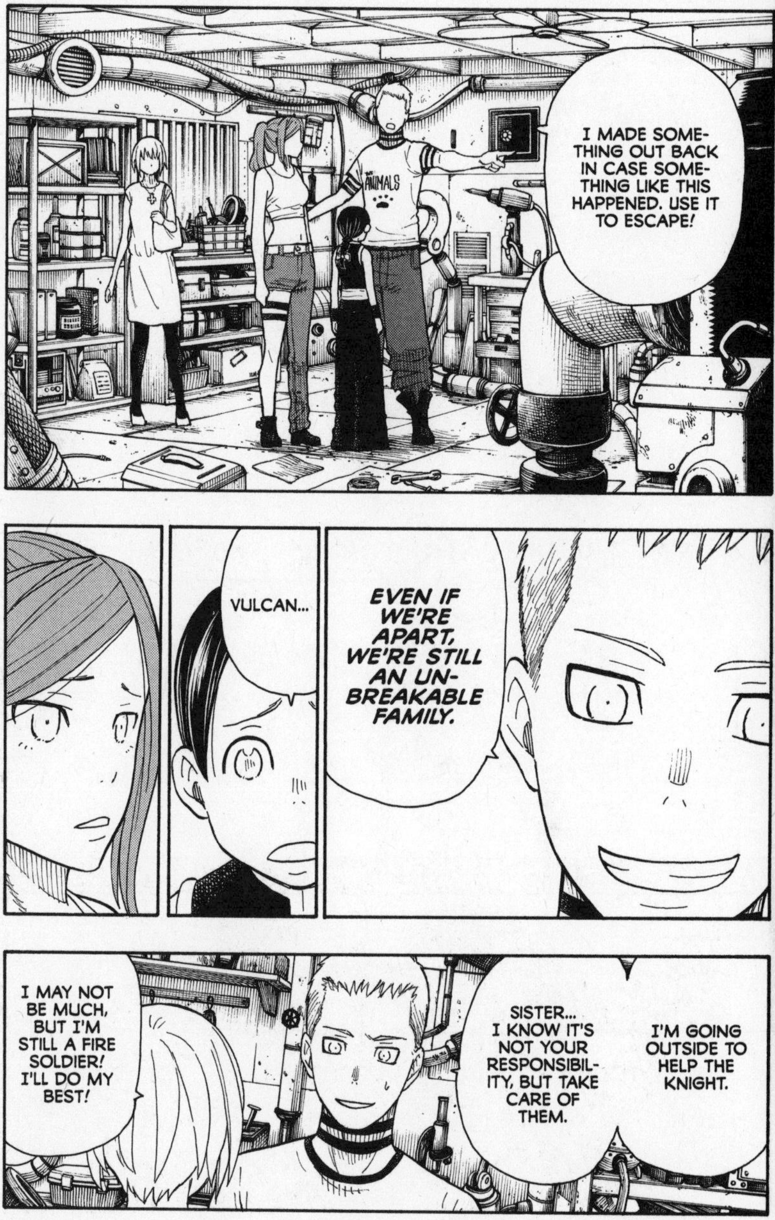
I MADE SOMETHING OUT BACK IN CASE SOMETHING LIKE THIS HAPPENED. USE IT TO ESCAPE!
EVEN IF WE'RE APART, WE'RE STILL AN UNBREAKABLE FAMILY.
VULCAN...
I'M GOING OUTSIDE TO HELP THE KNIGHT.
SISTER... I KNOW IT'S NOT YOUR RESPONSIBILITY, BUT TAKE CARE OF THEM.
I MAY NOT BE MUCH, BUT I'M STILL A FIRE SOLDIER! I'LL DO MY BEST!

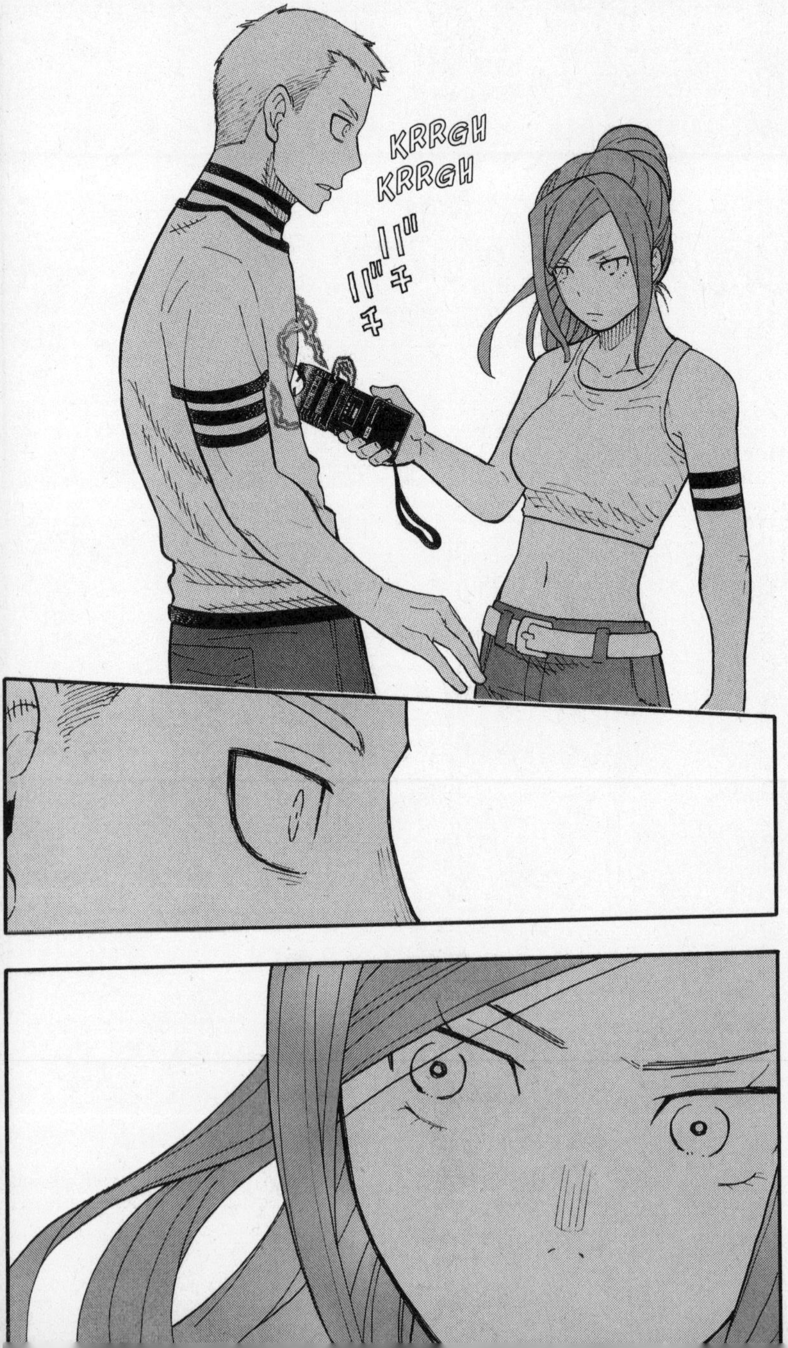
KRRGH
KRRGH
ジジ
ジジ

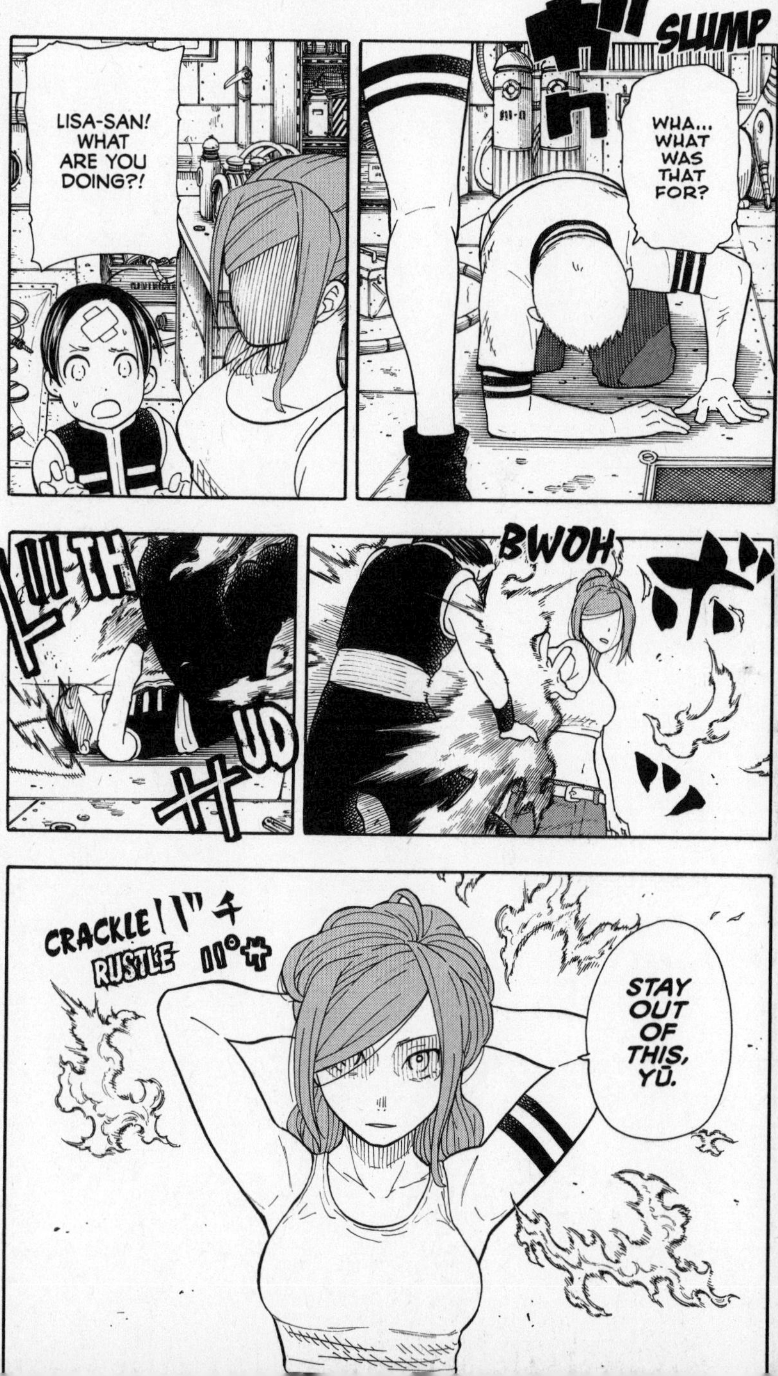
SLUMP
WHA... WHAT WAS THAT FOR?
LISA-SAN! WHAT ARE YOU DOING?!
BWOH
THUD
CRACKLE
RUSTLE
STAY OUT OF THIS, YŪ.

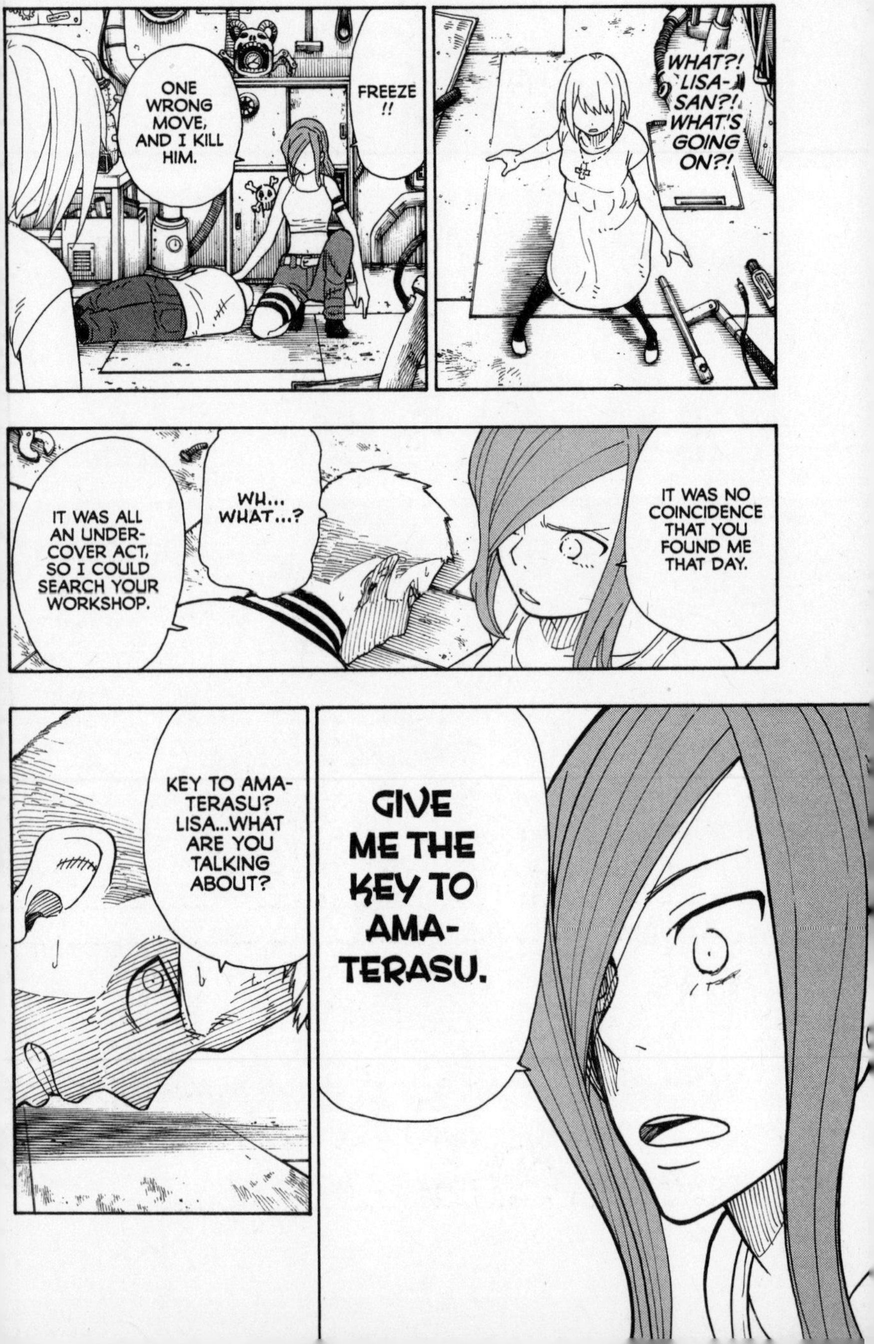

WHAT?! LISA-SAN?! WHAT'S GOING ON?!
FREEZE!!
ONE WRONG MOVE, AND I KILL HIM.
IT WAS NO COINCIDENCE THAT YOU FOUND ME THAT DAY.
WH... WHAT...?
IT WAS ALL AN UNDER-COVER ACT, SO I COULD SEARCH YOUR WORKSHOP.
GIVE ME THE KEY TO AMA-TERASU.
KEY TO AMA-TERASU? LISA...WHAT ARE YOU TALKING ABOUT?

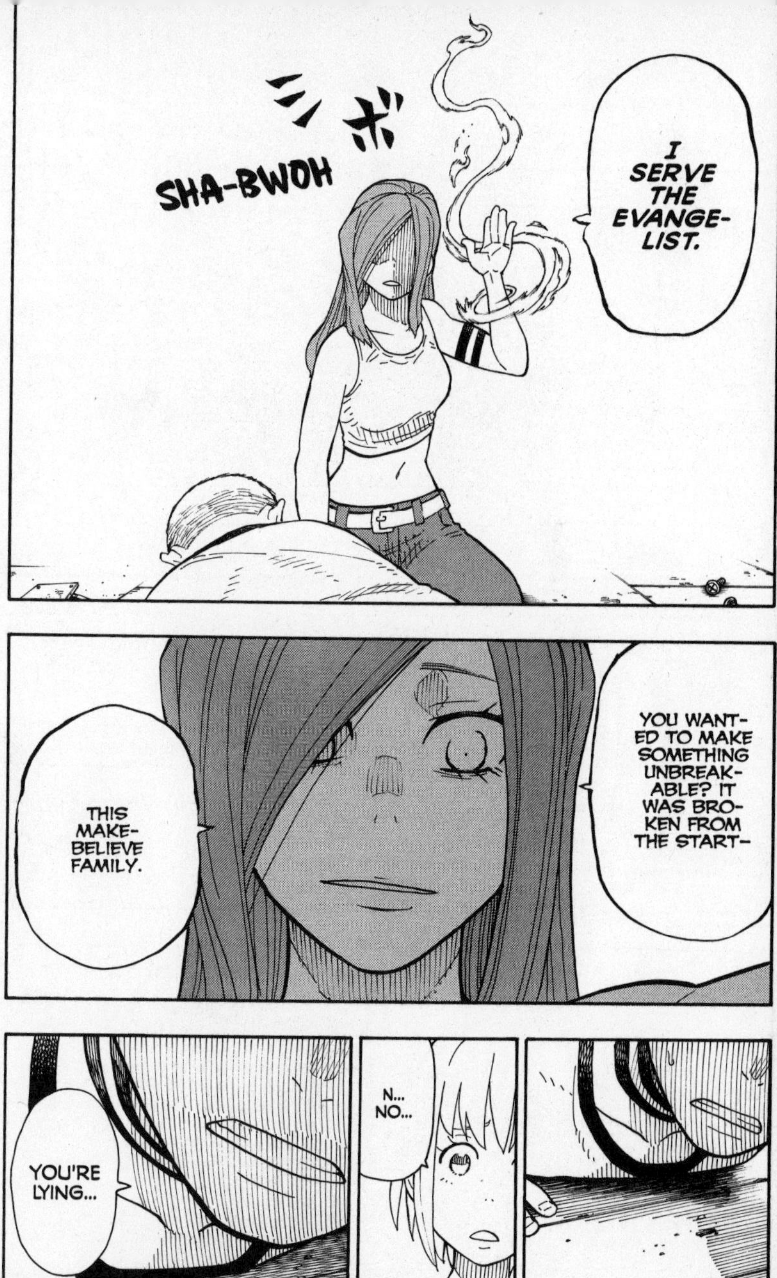
I SERVE THE EVANGE-LIST.
SHA-BWOH
YOU WANT-ED TO MAKE SOMETHING UNBREAK-ABLE? IT WAS BRO-KEN FROM THE START–
THIS MAKE-BELIEVE FAMILY.
N... NO...
YOU'RE LYING...

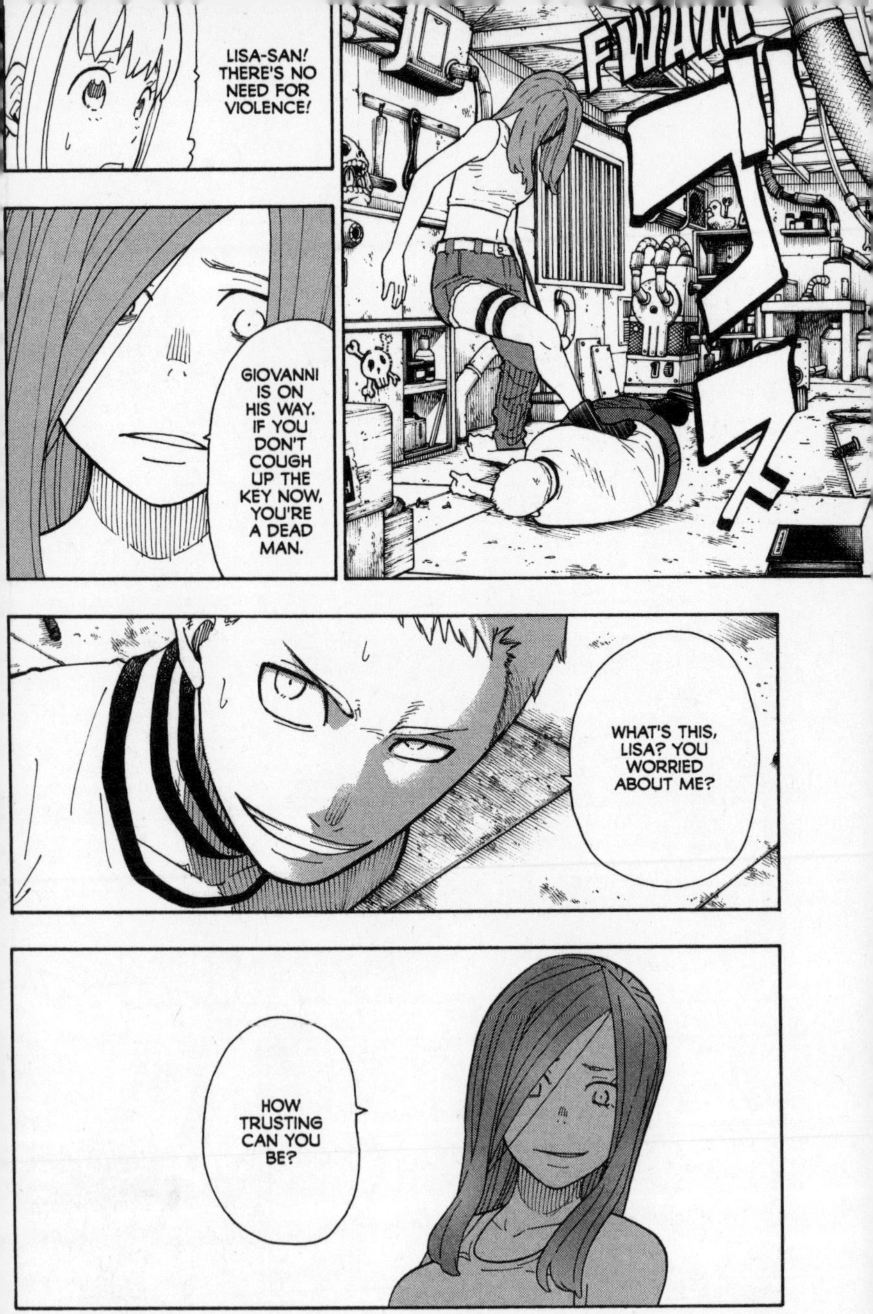
FWAM
LISA-SAN! THERE'S NO NEED FOR VIOLENCE!
GIOVANNI IS ON HIS WAY. IF YOU DON'T COUGH UP THE KEY NOW, YOU'RE A DEAD MAN.
WHAT'S THIS, LISA? YOU WORRIED ABOUT ME?
HOW TRUSTING CAN YOU BE?

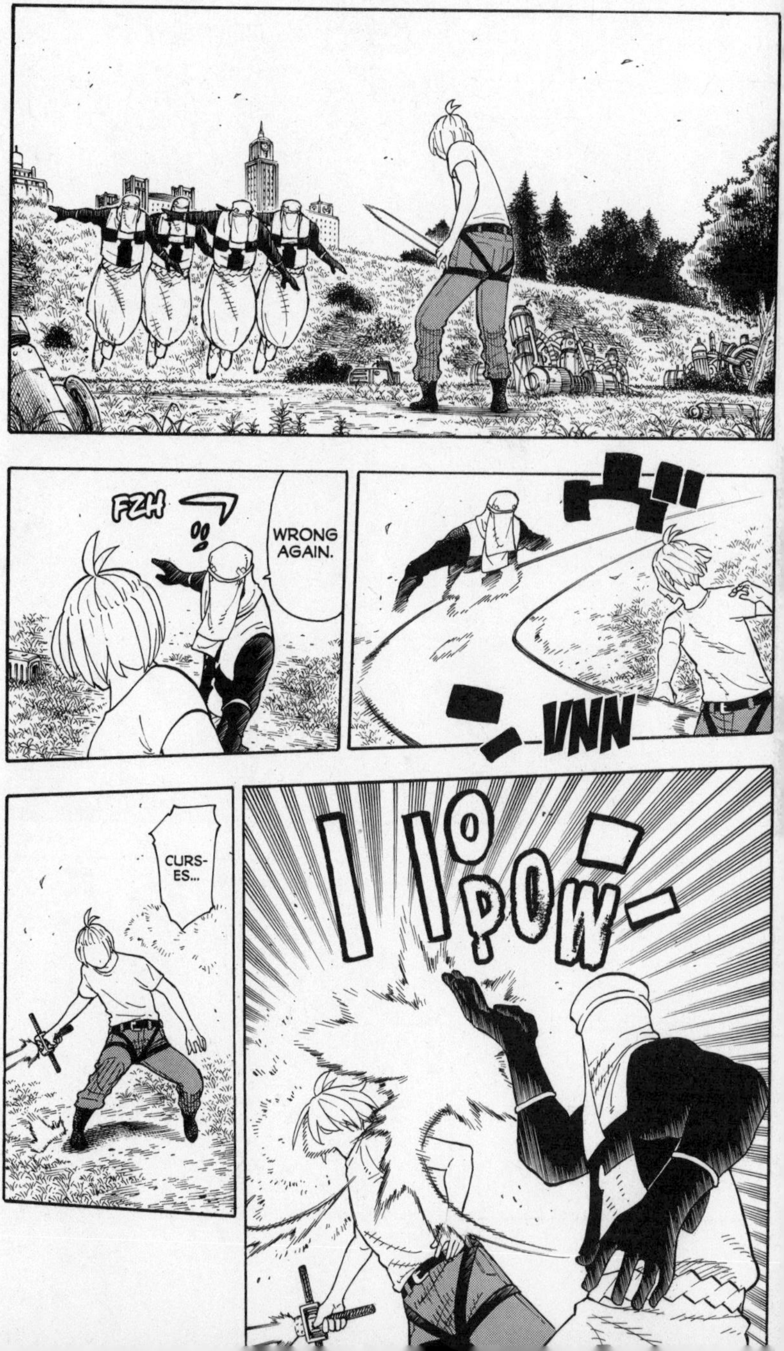
VNN
WRONG AGAIN.
FZH
POW
CURS-ES...

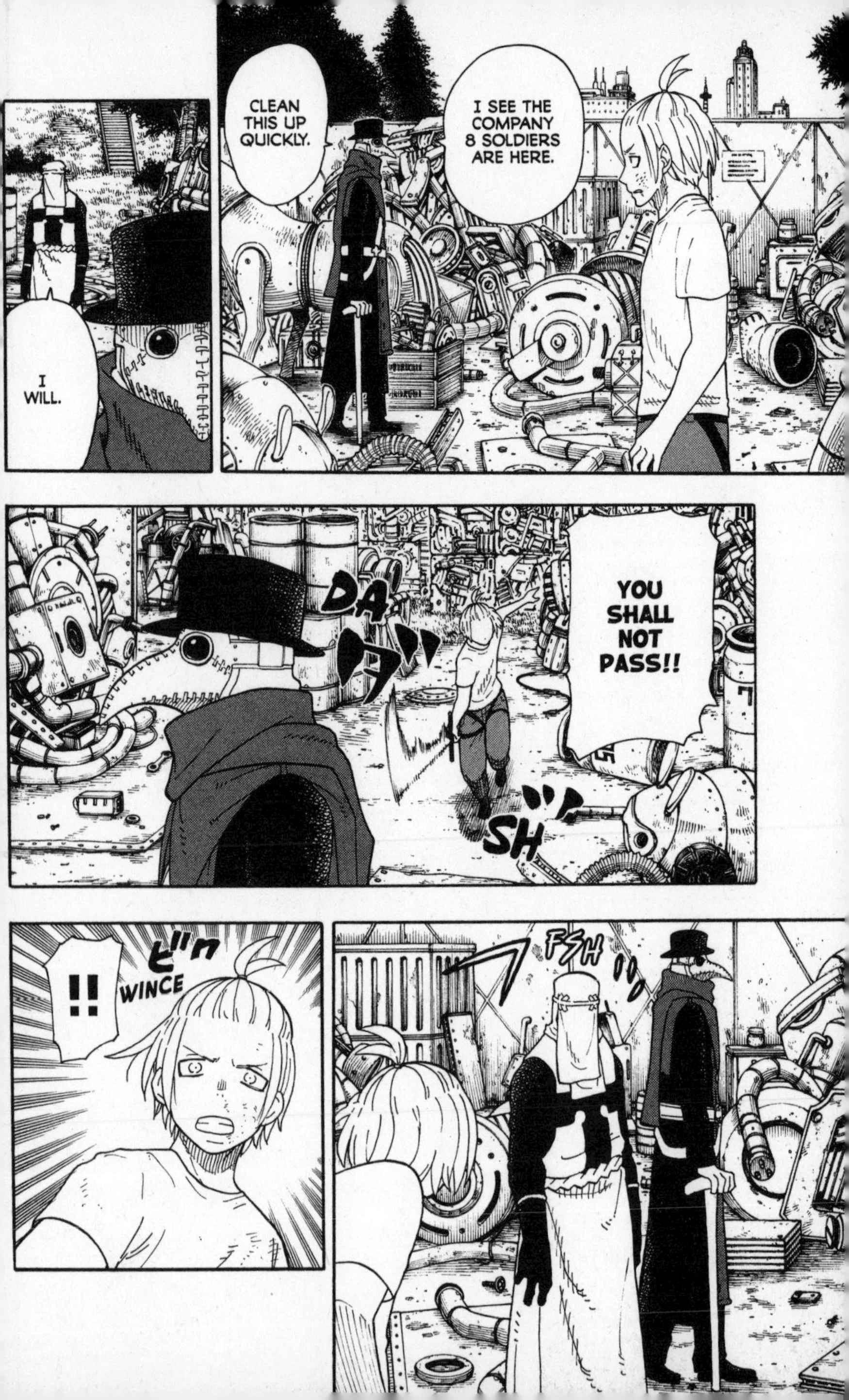
I SEE THE COMPANY 8 SOLDIERS ARE HERE.
CLEAN THIS UP QUICKLY.
I WILL.
YOU SHALL NOT PASS!!
DA
SH
FSH
!!
WINCE

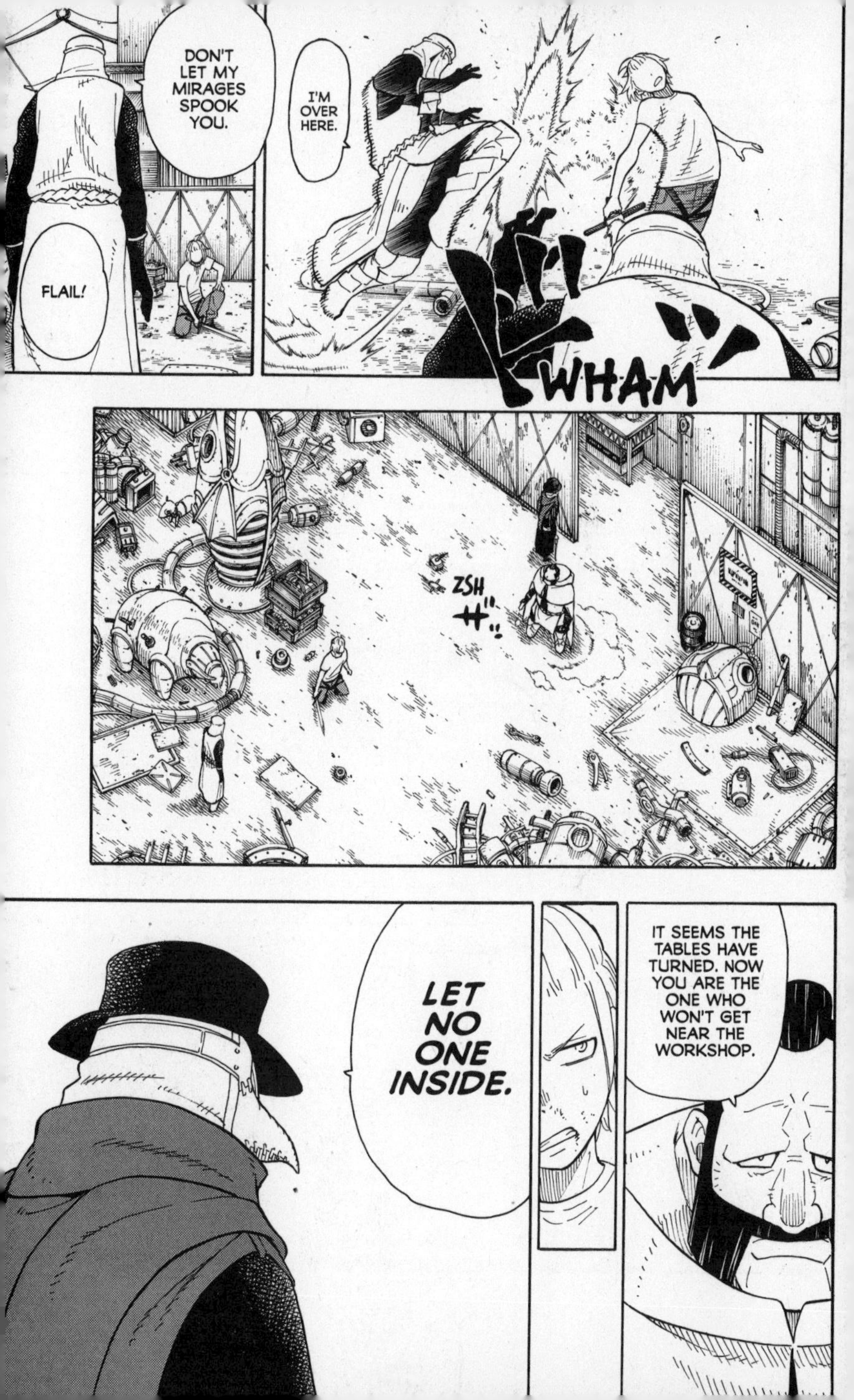
I'M OVER HERE.
WHAM
DON'T LET MY MIRAGES SPOOK YOU.
FLAIL!
ZSH
IT SEEMS THE TABLES HAVE TURNED. NOW YOU ARE THE ONE WHO WON'T GET NEAR THE WORKSHOP.
LET NO ONE INSIDE.

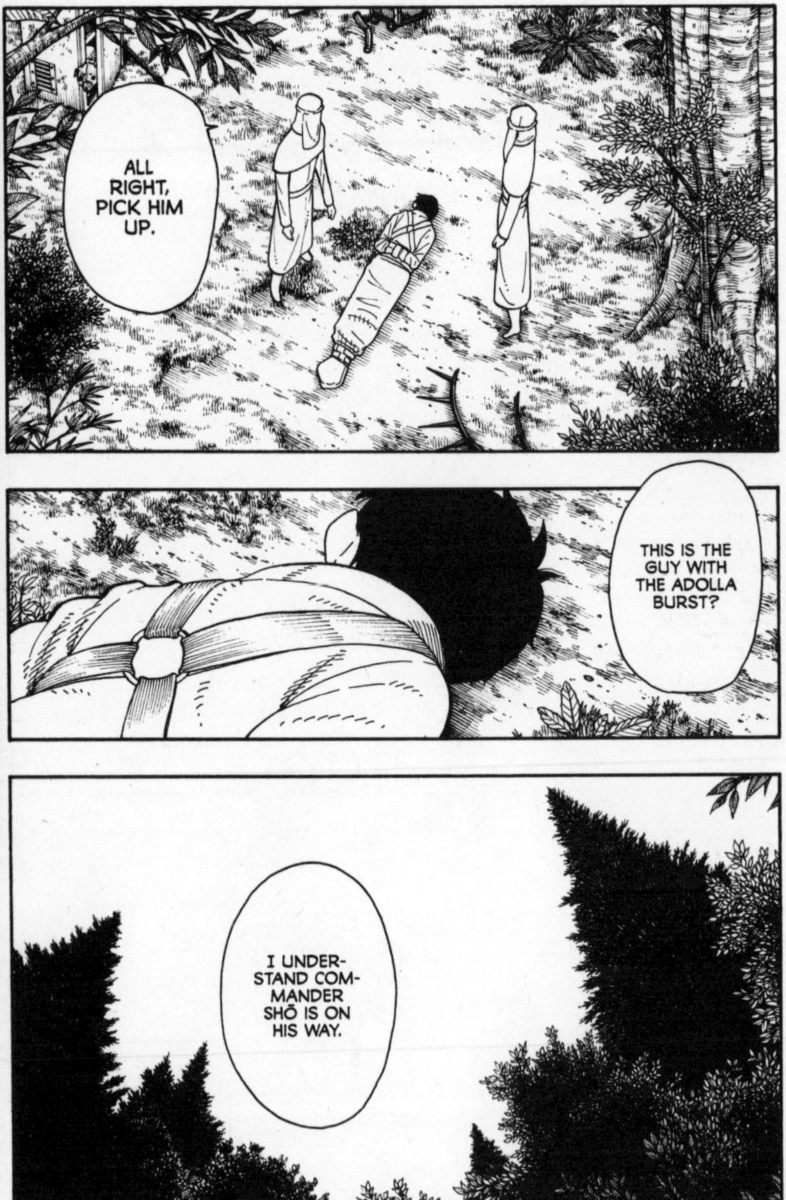
ALL RIGHT, PICK HIM UP.
THIS IS THE GUY WITH THE ADOLLA BURST?
I UNDER-STAND COM-MANDER SHŌ IS ON HIS WAY.

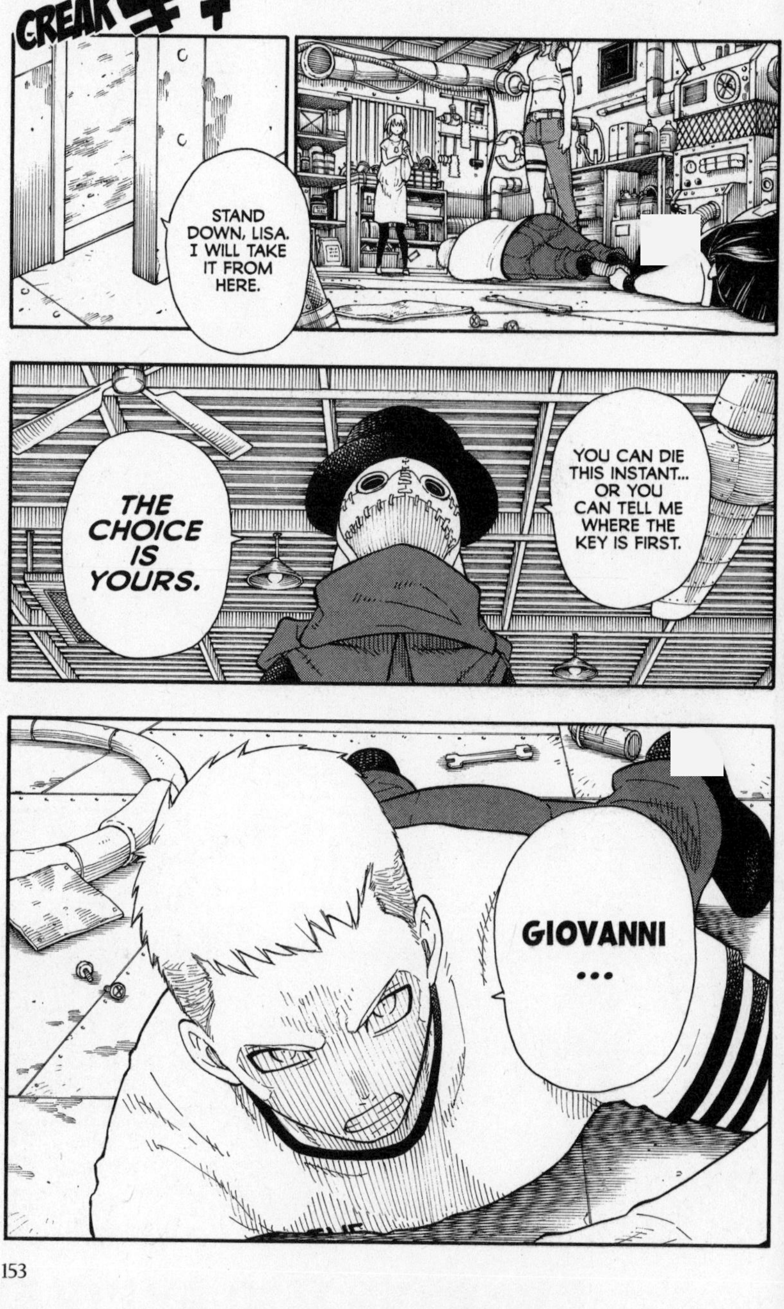
CREAK キィ
STAND DOWN, LISA. I WILL TAKE IT FROM HERE.
YOU CAN DIE THIS INSTANT... OR YOU CAN TELL ME WHERE THE KEY IS FIRST.
THE CHOICE IS YOURS.
GIOVANNI ...

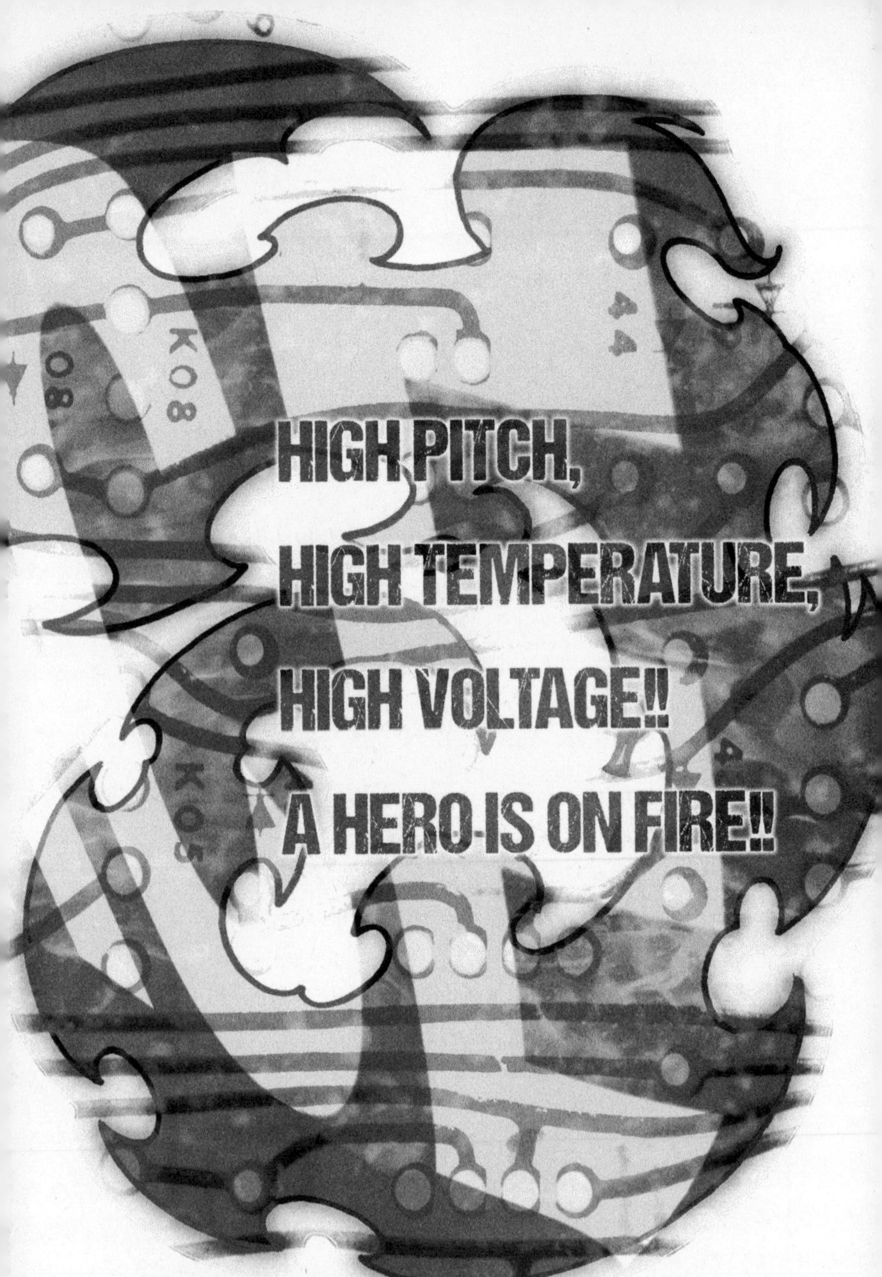
HIGH PITCH,
HIGH TEMPERATURE,
HIGH VOLTAGE!!
A HERO IS ON FIRE!!

CHAPTER LIX: ARRIVAL!

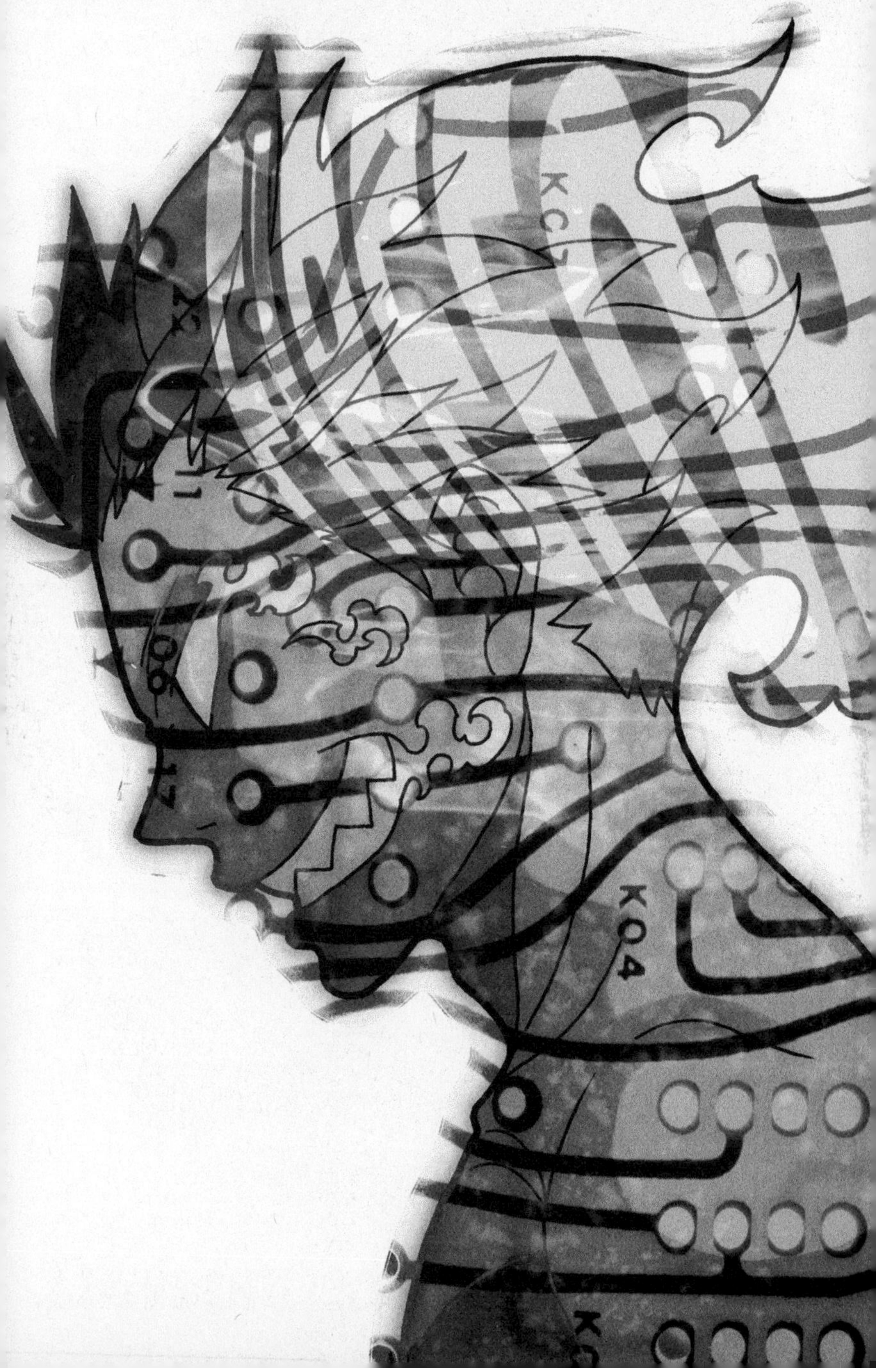
K04

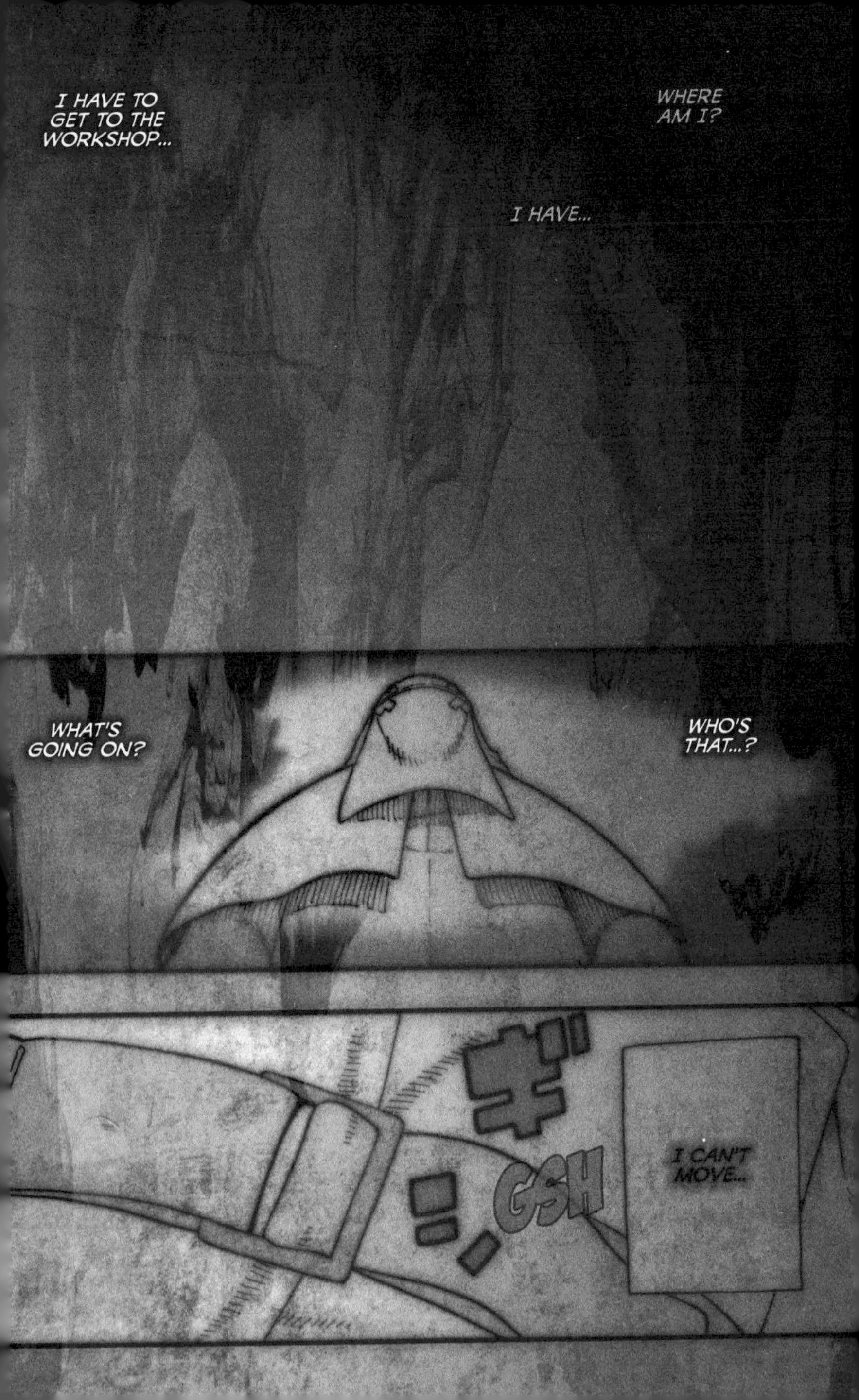
WHERE AM I?
I HAVE TO GET TO THE WORKSHOP...
I HAVE...
WHO'S THAT...?
WHAT'S GOING ON?
I CAN'T MOVE...
GSH

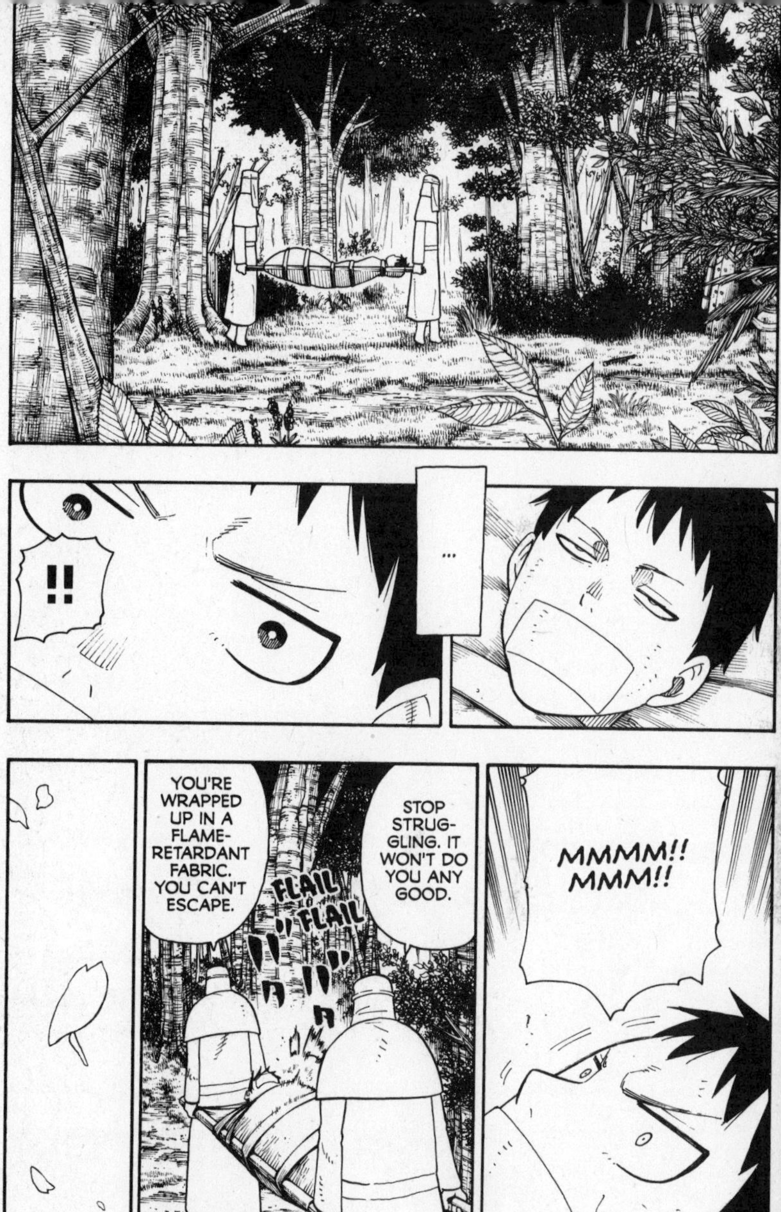
...
!!
MMMM!! MMM!!
STOP STRUG-GLING. IT WON'T DO YOU ANY GOOD.
YOU'RE WRAPPED UP IN A FLAME-RETARDANT FABRIC. YOU CAN'T ESCAPE.
FLAIL FLAIL

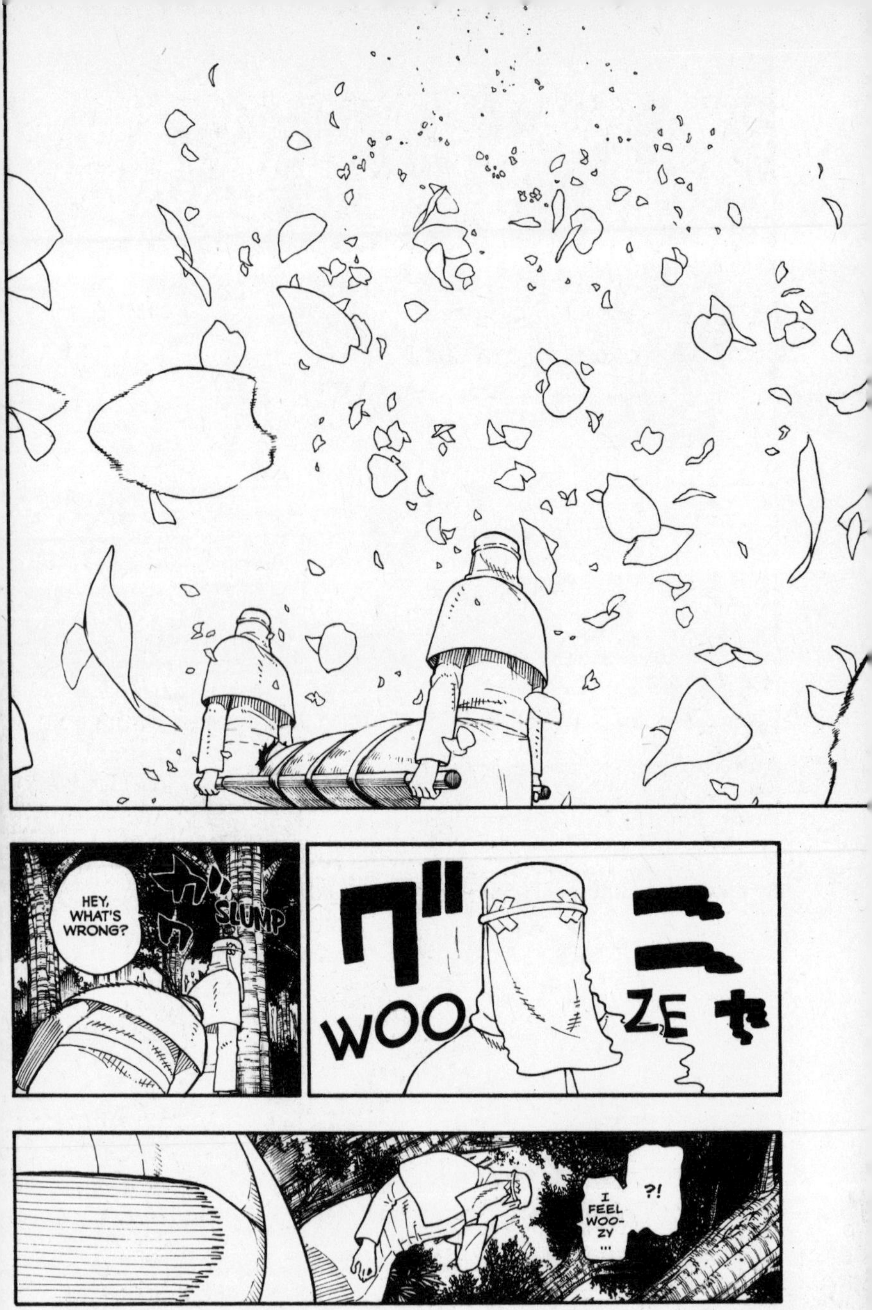
WOO
ZE
SLUMP
HEY, WHAT'S WRONG?
?!
I FEEL WOO-ZY...

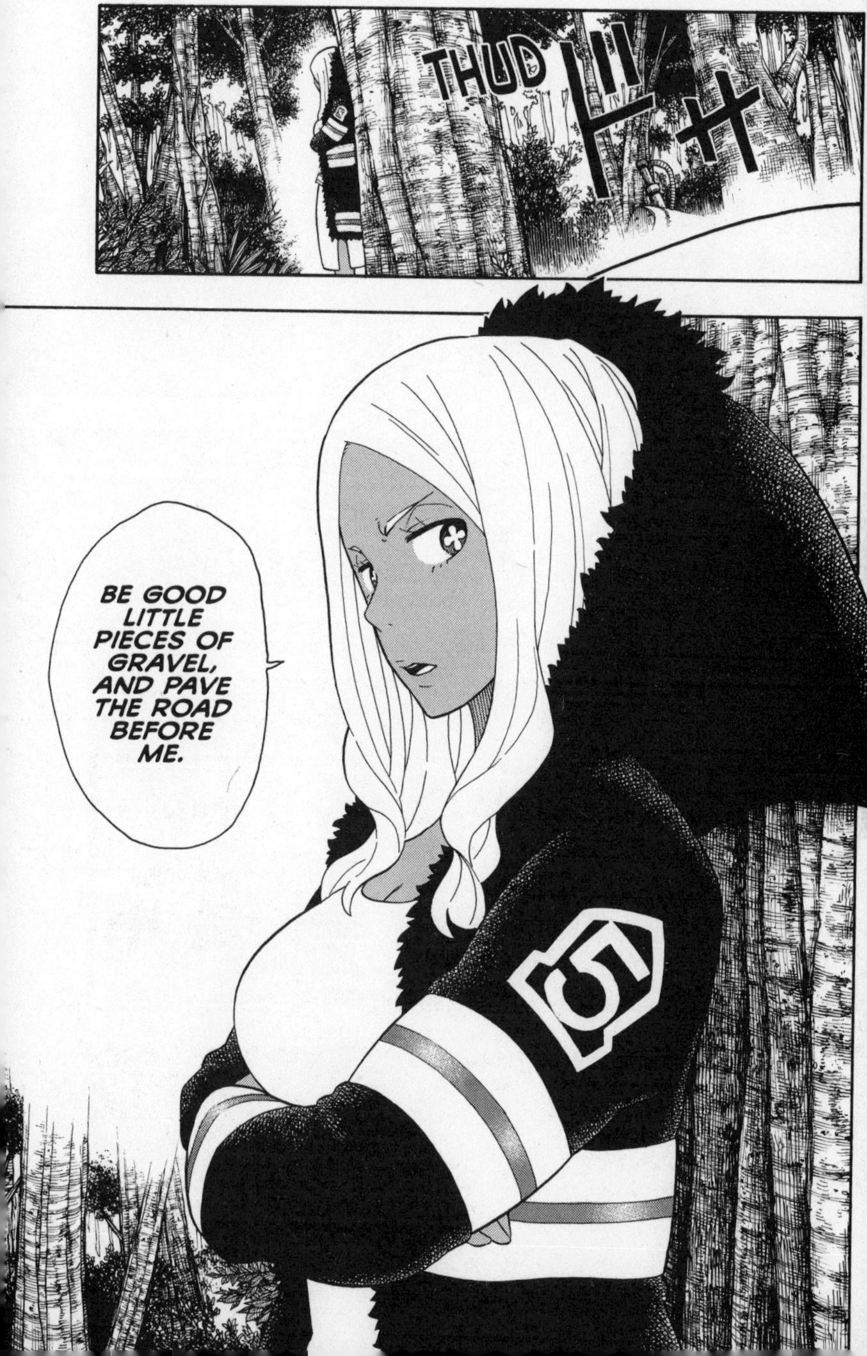
THUD
BE GOOD LITTLE PIECES OF GRAVEL, AND PAVE THE ROAD BEFORE ME.

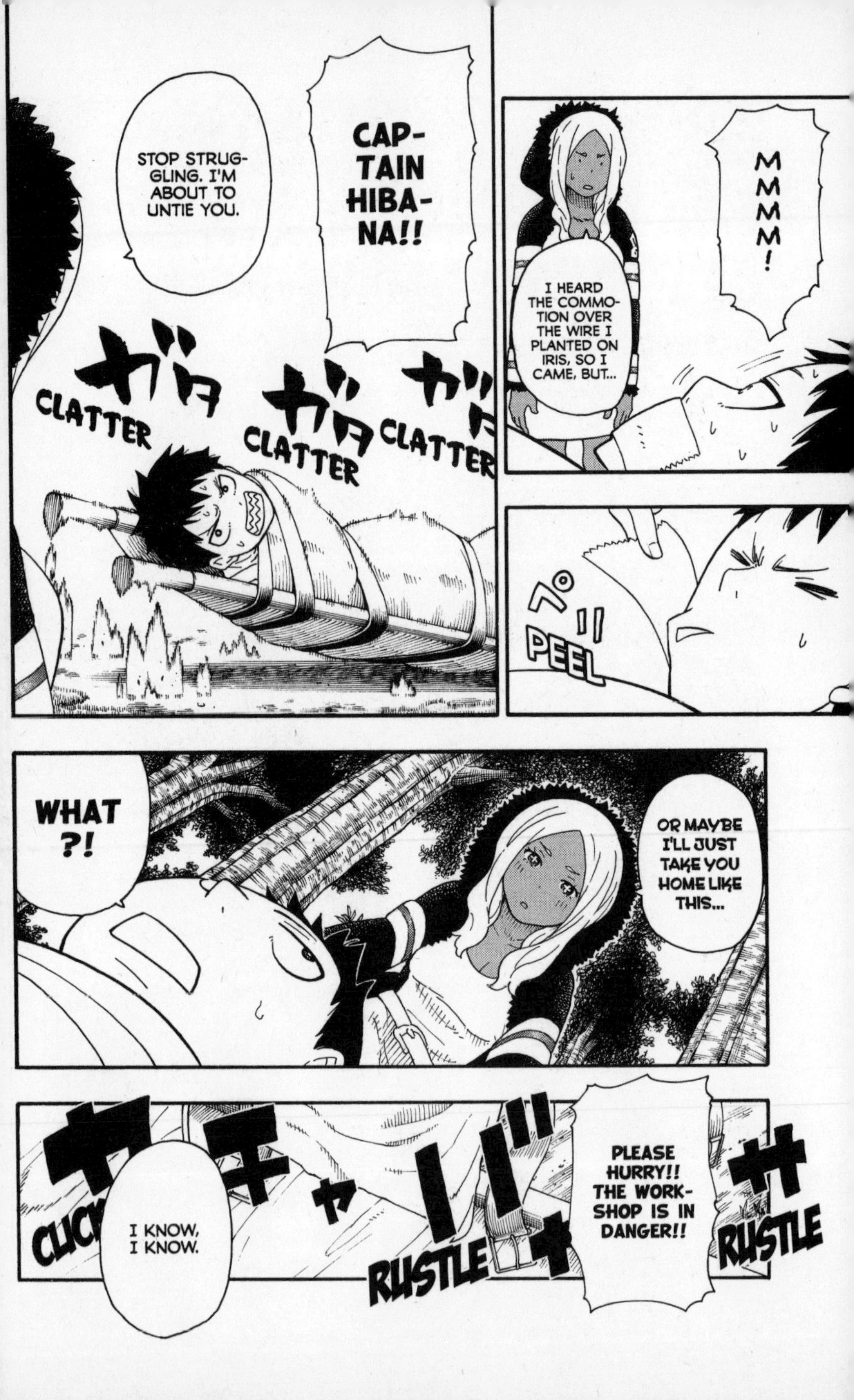
MMMM!
I HEARD THE COMMOTION OVER THE WIRE I PLANTED ON IRIS, SO I CAME, BUT...
PEEL
CAPTAIN HIBANA!!
STOP STRUGGLING. I'M ABOUT TO UNTIE YOU.
CLATTER
CLATTER
CLATTER
OR MAYBE I'LL JUST TAKE YOU HOME LIKE THIS...
WHAT?!
RUSTLE
PLEASE HURRY!! THE WORKSHOP IS IN DANGER!!
RUSTLE
I KNOW, I KNOW.
CLICK

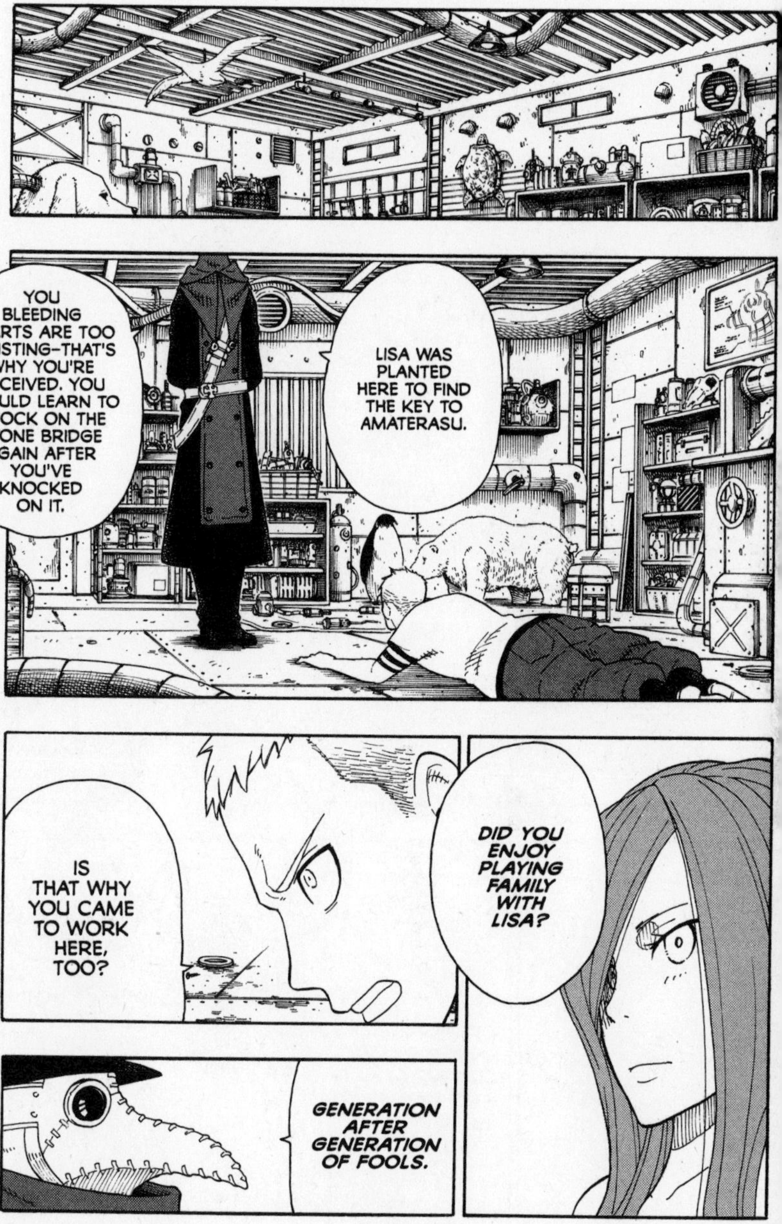
LISA WAS PLANTED HERE TO FIND THE KEY TO AMATERASU.
YOU BLEEDING HEARTS ARE TOO TRUSTING–THAT'S WHY YOU'RE DECEIVED. YOU SHOULD LEARN TO KNOCK ON THE STONE BRIDGE AGAIN AFTER YOU'VE KNOCKED ON IT.
DID YOU ENJOY PLAYING FAMILY WITH LISA?
IS THAT WHY YOU CAME TO WORK HERE, TOO?
GENERATION AFTER GENERATION OF FOOLS.

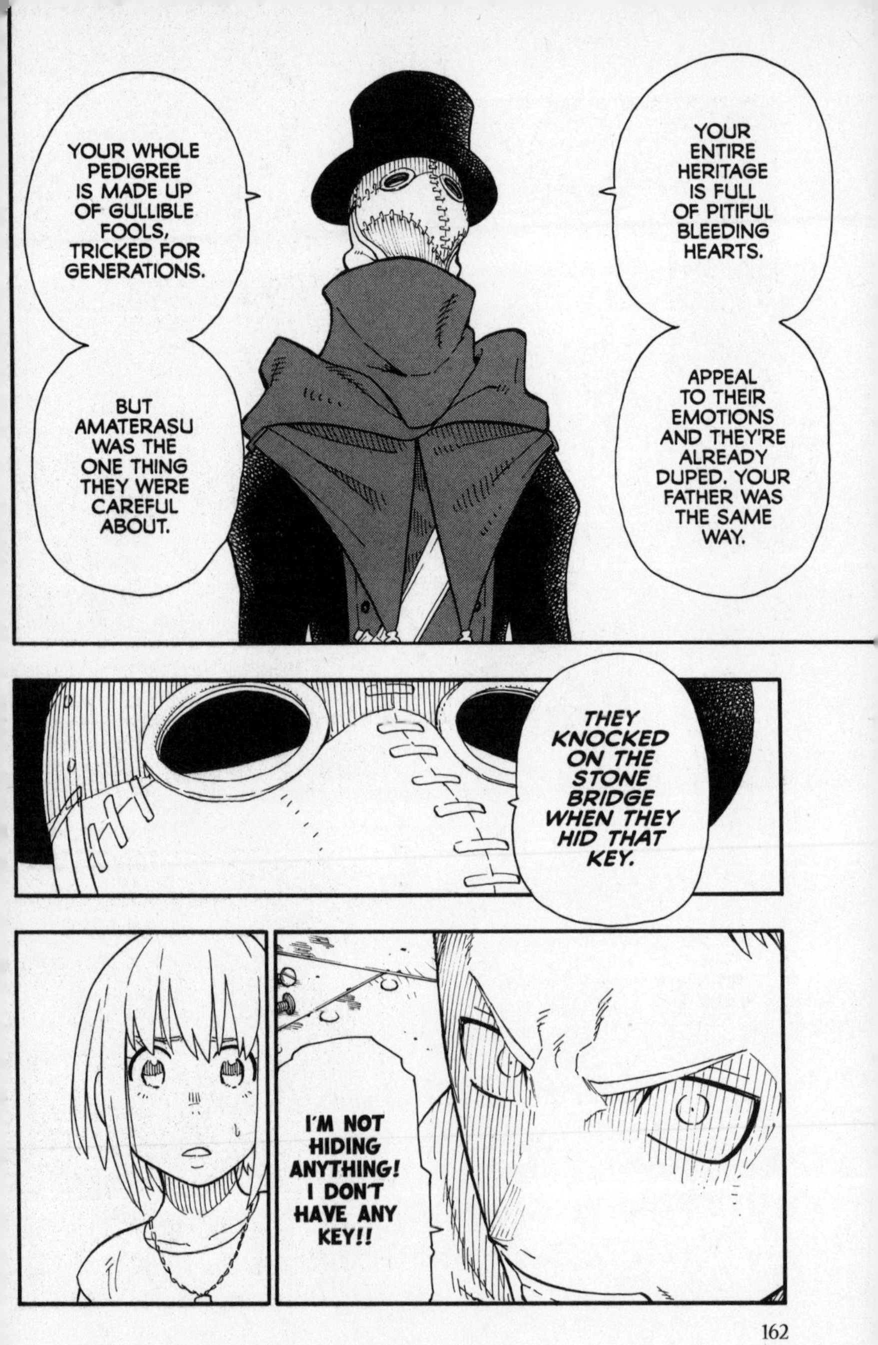
YOUR ENTIRE HERITAGE IS FULL OF PITIFUL BLEEDING HEARTS.
YOUR WHOLE PEDIGREE IS MADE UP OF GULLIBLE FOOLS, TRICKED FOR GENERATIONS.
APPEAL TO THEIR EMOTIONS AND THEY'RE ALREADY DUPED. YOUR FATHER WAS THE SAME WAY.
BUT AMATERASU WAS THE ONE THING THEY WERE CAREFUL ABOUT.
THEY KNOCKED ON THE STONE BRIDGE WHEN THEY HID THAT KEY.
I'M NOT HIDING ANYTHING! I DON'T HAVE ANY KEY!!

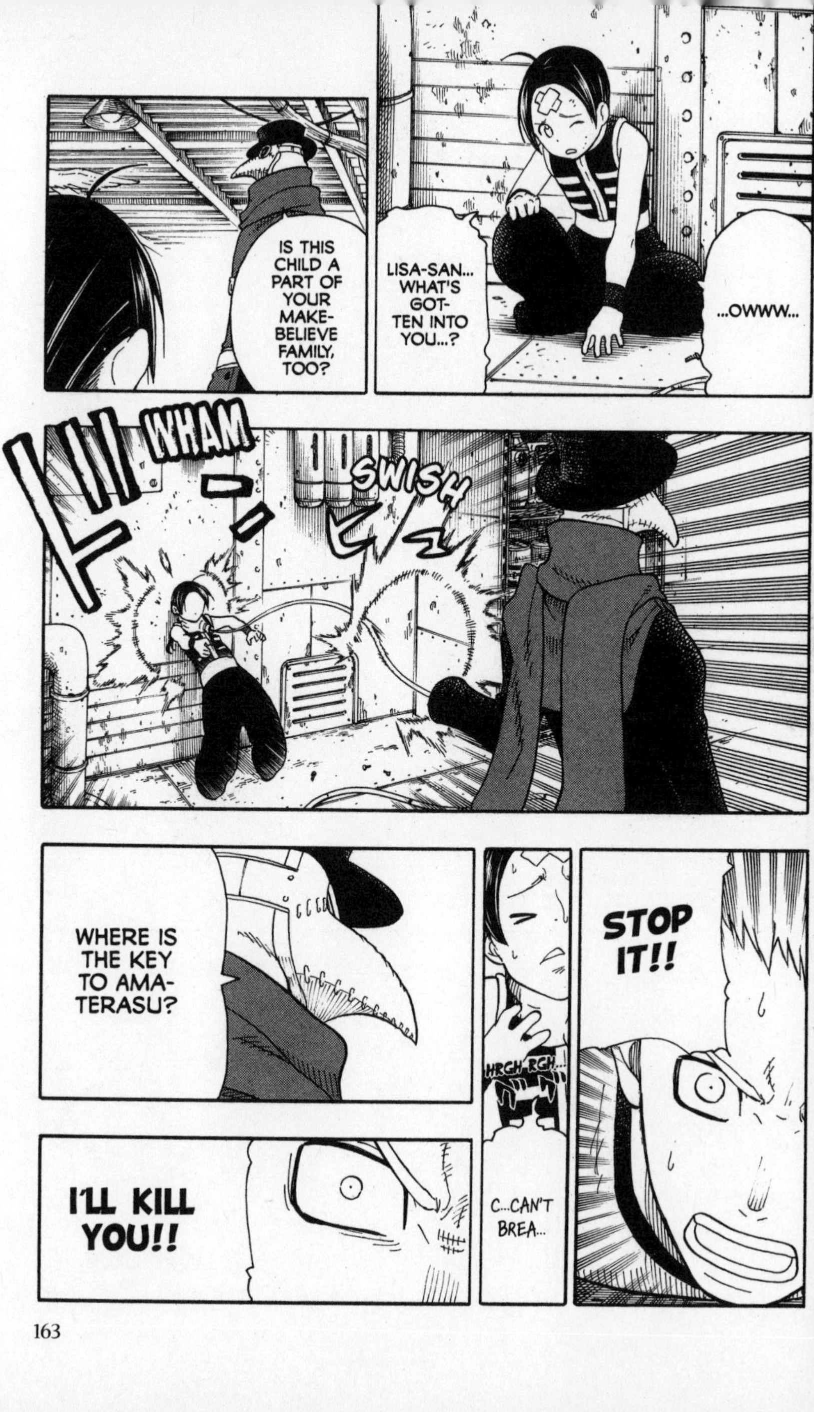
...OWWW...
LISA-SAN... WHAT'S GOT-TEN INTO YOU...?
IS THIS CHILD A PART OF YOUR MAKE-BELIEVE FAMILY, TOO?
SWISH
WHAM
STOP IT!!
HRGH RGH...
C...CAN'T BREA...
WHERE IS THE KEY TO AMA-TERASU?
I'LL KILL YOU!!

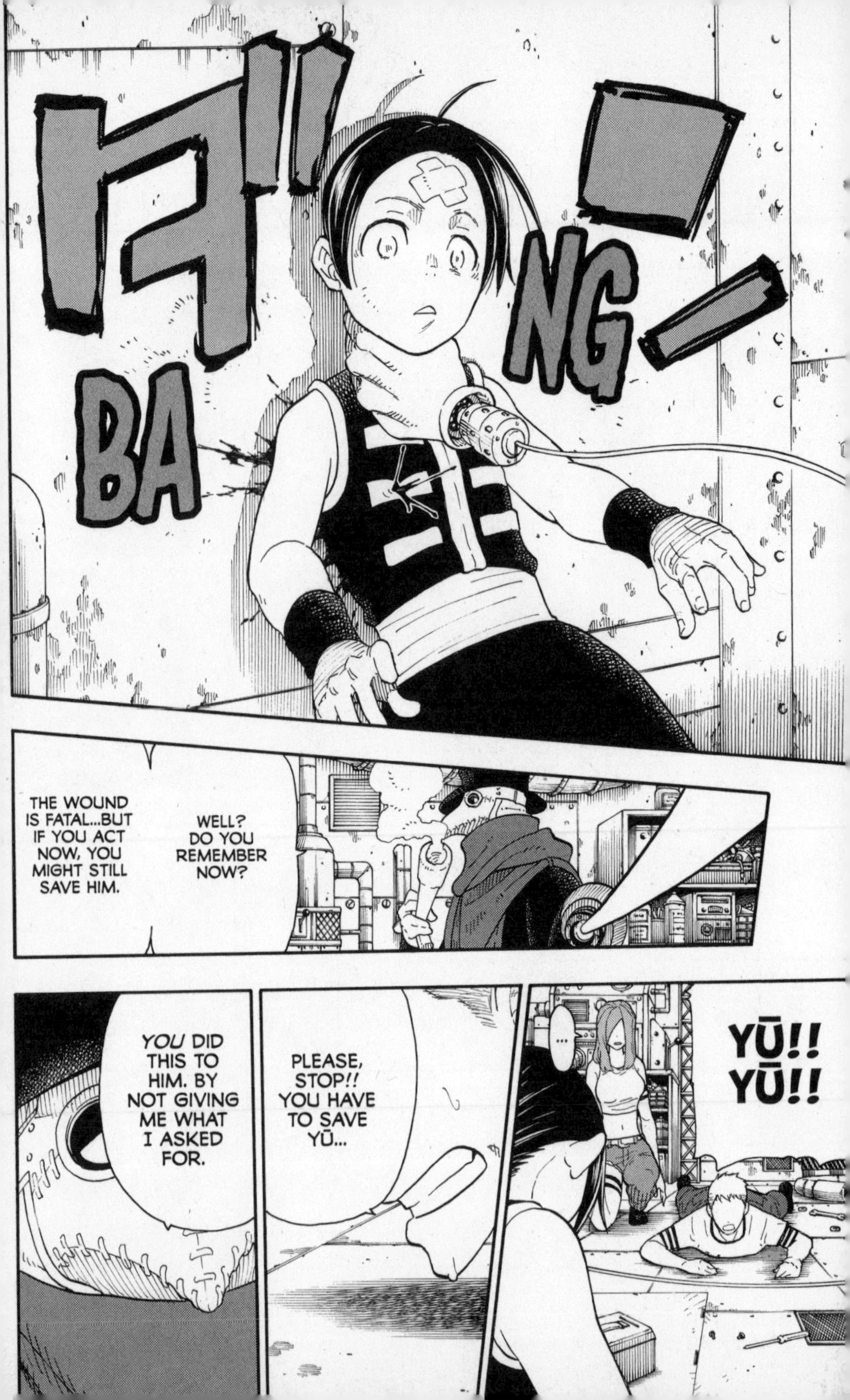
BANG
WELL? DO YOU REMEMBER NOW?
THE WOUND IS FATAL...BUT IF YOU ACT NOW, YOU MIGHT STILL SAVE HIM.
YŪ!! YŪ!!
...
PLEASE, STOP!! YOU HAVE TO SAVE YŪ...
YOU DID THIS TO HIM. BY NOT GIVING ME WHAT I ASKED FOR.

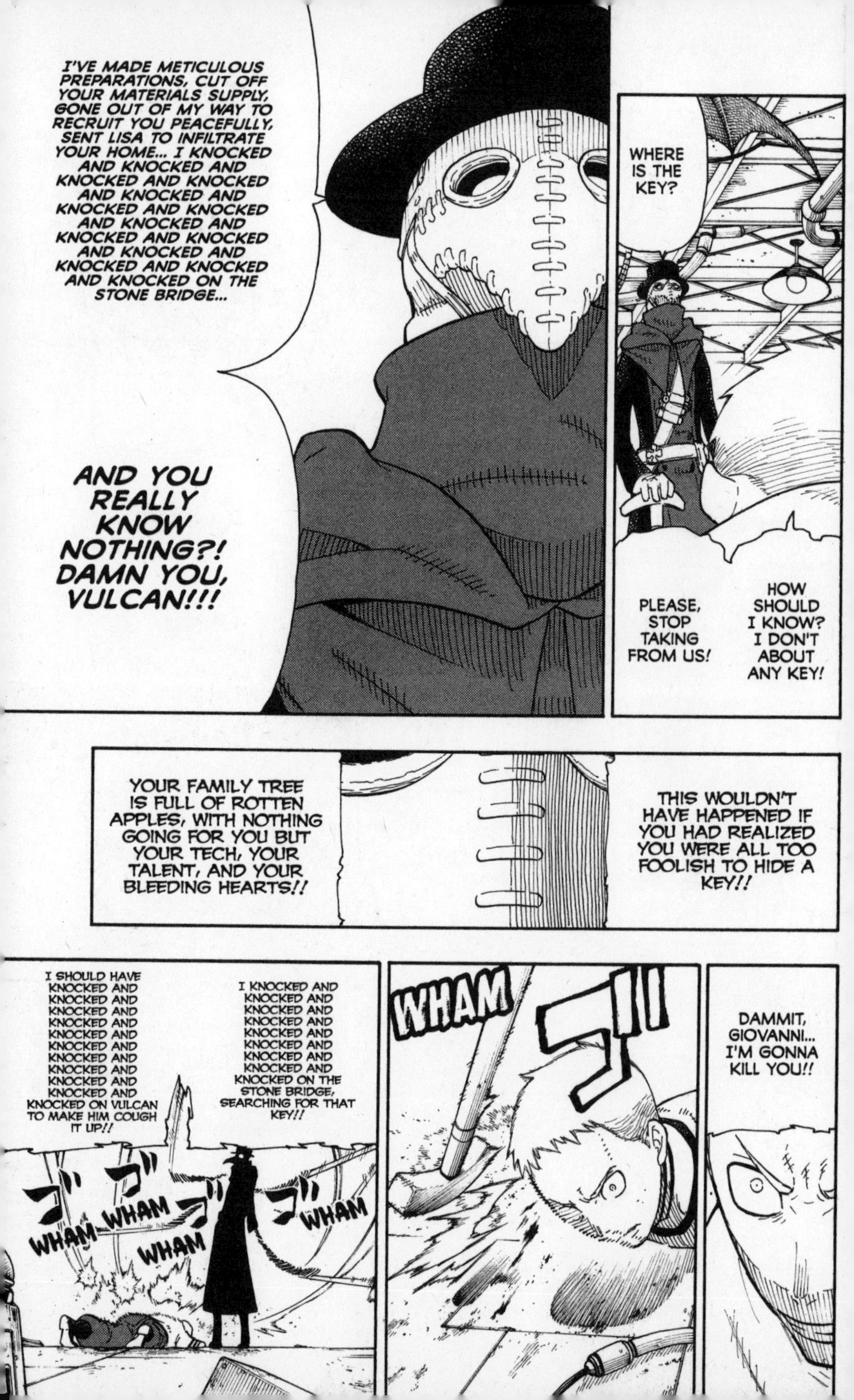
WHERE IS THE KEY?
HOW SHOULD I KNOW? I DON'T ABOUT ANY KEY!
PLEASE, STOP TAKING FROM US!
I'VE MADE METICULOUS PREPARATIONS, CUT OFF YOUR MATERIALS SUPPLY, GONE OUT OF MY WAY TO RECRUIT YOU PEACEFULLY, SENT LISA TO INFILTRATE YOUR HOME... I KNOCKED AND KNOCKED AND KNOCKED AND KNOCKED AND KNOCKED AND KNOCKED AND KNOCKED AND KNOCKED AND KNOCKED AND KNOCKED AND KNOCKED AND KNOCKED AND KNOCKED AND KNOCKED ON THE STONE BRIDGE...
AND YOU REALLY KNOW NOTHING?! DAMN YOU, VULCAN!!!
THIS WOULDN'T HAVE HAPPENED IF YOU HAD REALIZED YOU WERE ALL TOO FOOLISH TO HIDE A KEY!!
YOUR FAMILY TREE IS FULL OF ROTTEN APPLES, WITH NOTHING GOING FOR YOU BUT YOUR TECH, YOUR TALENT, AND YOUR BLEEDING HEARTS!!
DAMMIT, GIOVANNI... I'M GONNA KILL YOU!!
WHAM
I KNOCKED AND KNOCKED AND KNOCKED AND KNOCKED AND KNOCKED AND KNOCKED AND KNOCKED AND KNOCKED AND KNOCKED ON THE STONE BRIDGE, SEARCHING FOR THAT KEY!!
I SHOULD HAVE KNOCKED AND KNOCKED AND KNOCKED AND KNOCKED AND KNOCKED AND KNOCKED AND KNOCKED AND KNOCKED AND KNOCKED AND KNOCKED AND KNOCKED ON VULCAN TO MAKE HIM COUGH IT UP!!
WHAM
WHAM
WHAM
WHAM
WHAM

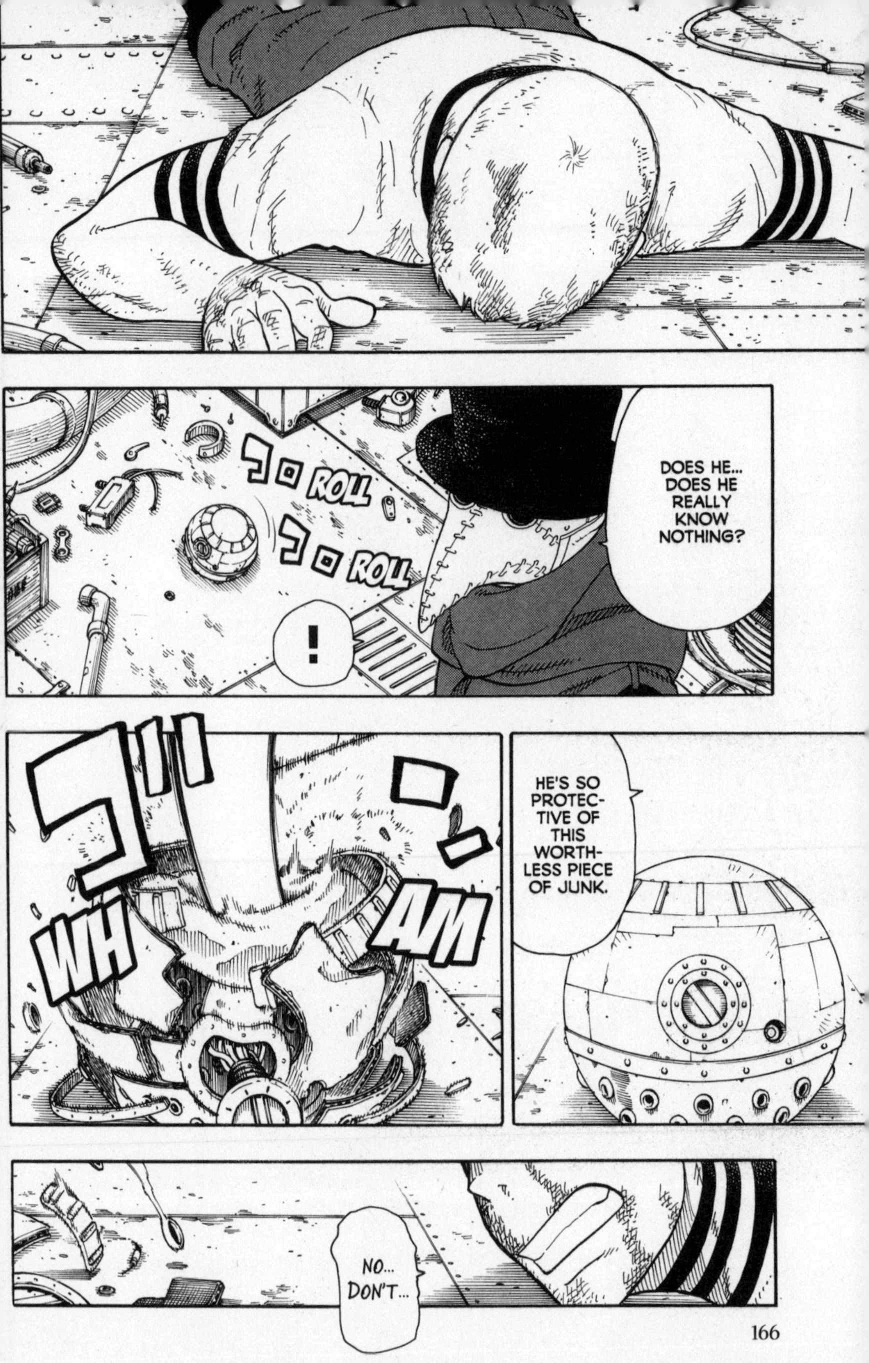
DOES HE... DOES HE REALLY KNOW NOTHING?
コロ ROLL
コロ ROLL
!
HE'S SO PROTECTIVE OF THIS WORTHLESS PIECE OF JUNK.
WHAM
NO... DON'T...

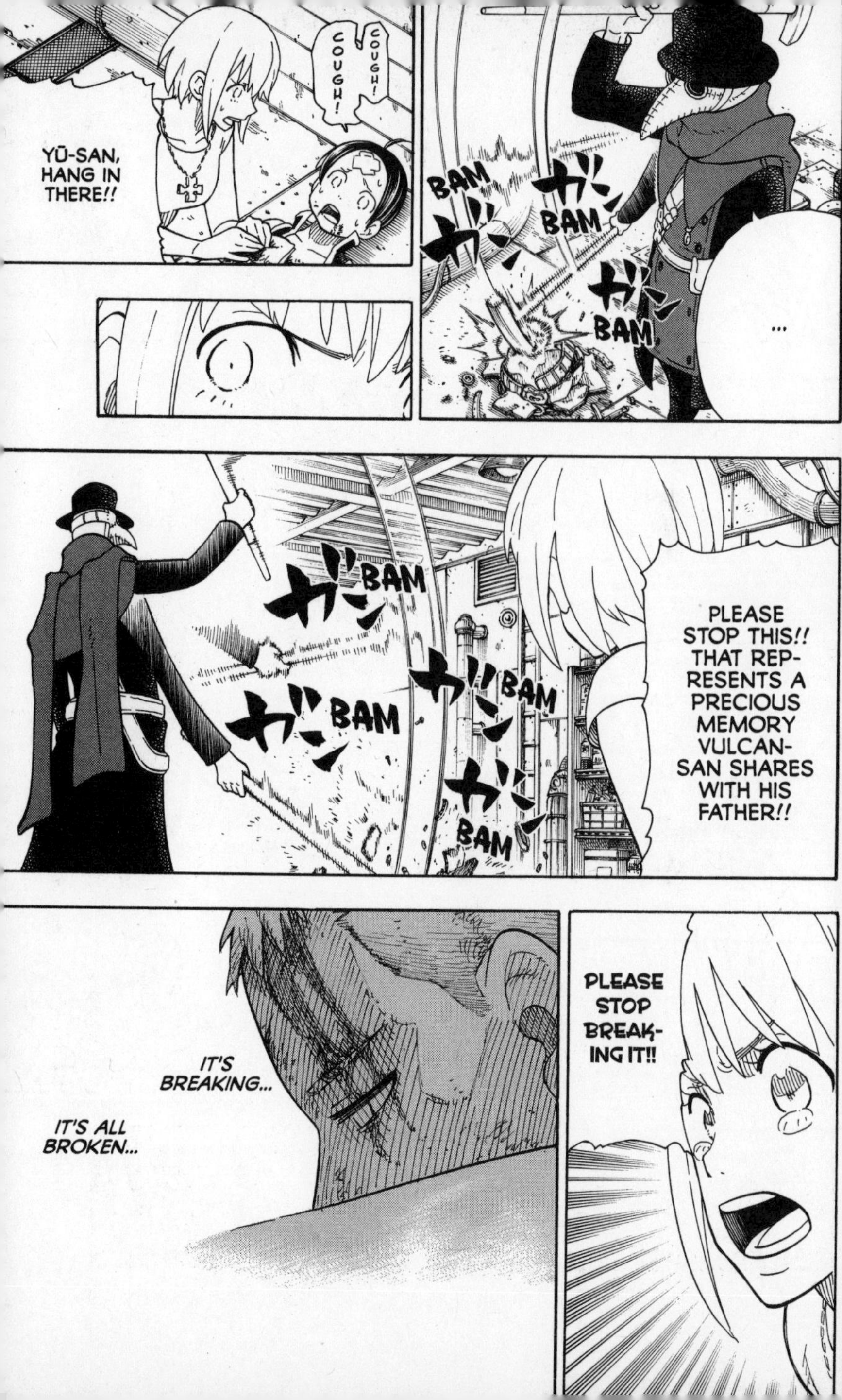
BAM
BAM
BAM
...
COUGH! COUGH!
YŪ-SAN, HANG IN THERE!!
PLEASE STOP THIS!! THAT REPRESENTS A PRECIOUS MEMORY VULCAN-SAN SHARES WITH HIS FATHER!!
BAM
BAM
BAM
BAM
PLEASE STOP BREAKING IT!!
IT'S BREAKING...
IT'S ALL BROKEN...

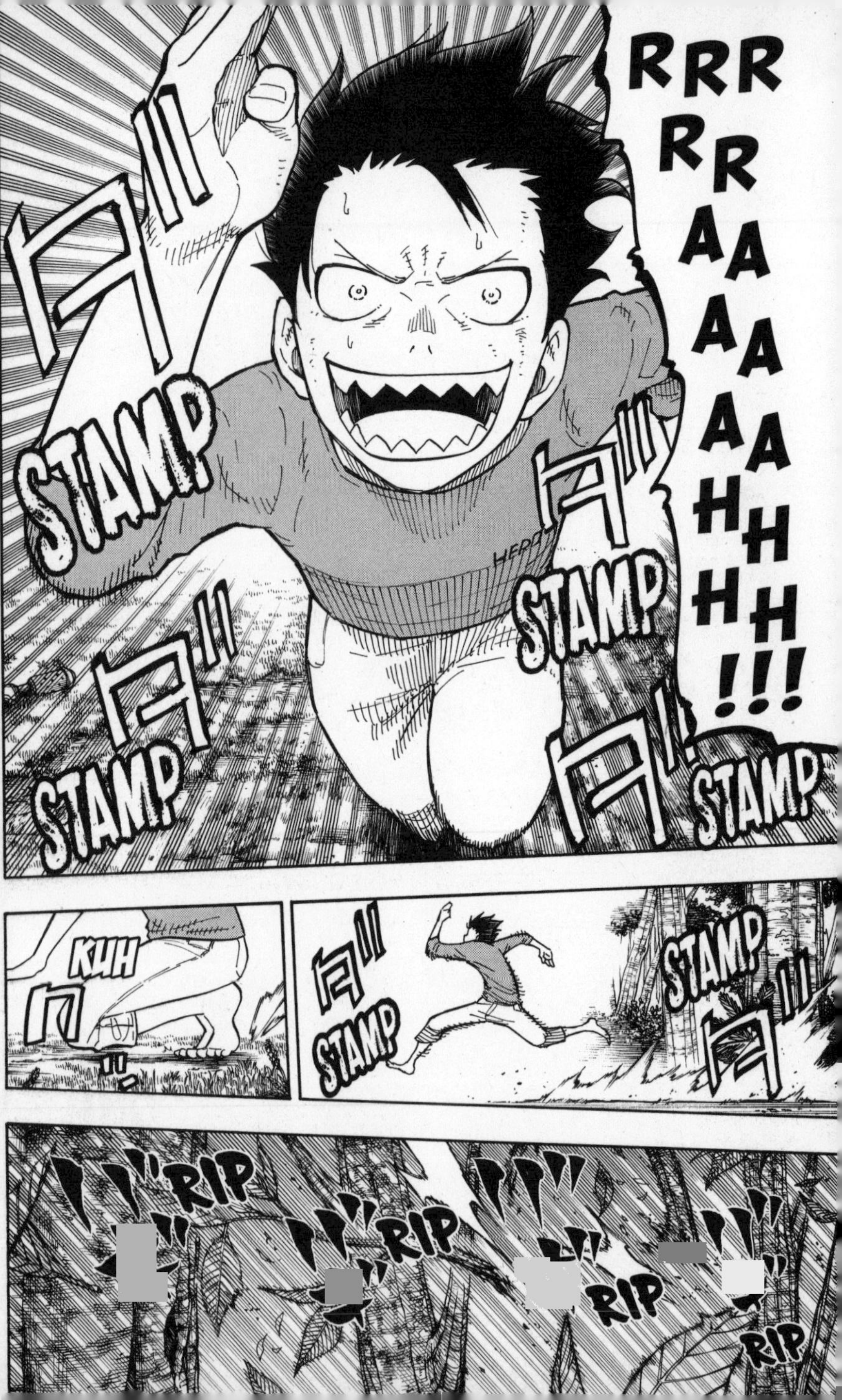
RRRRAAAAAAHHHH!!!
STAMP
STAMP
STAMP
STAMP
STAMP
STAMP
KUH
RIP
RIP
RIP
RIP

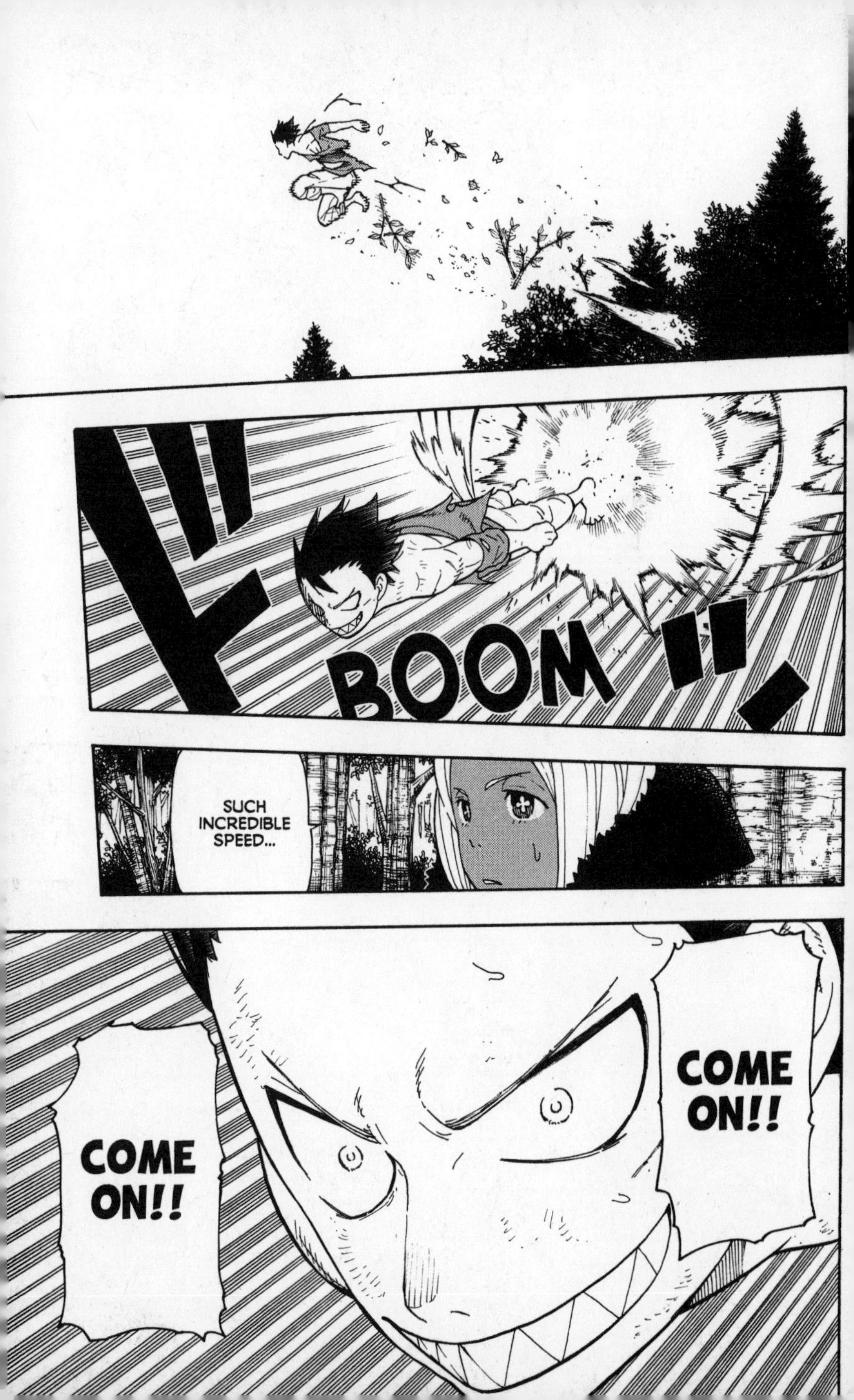
BOOM!!
SUCH INCREDIBLE SPEED...
COME ON!!
COME ON!!

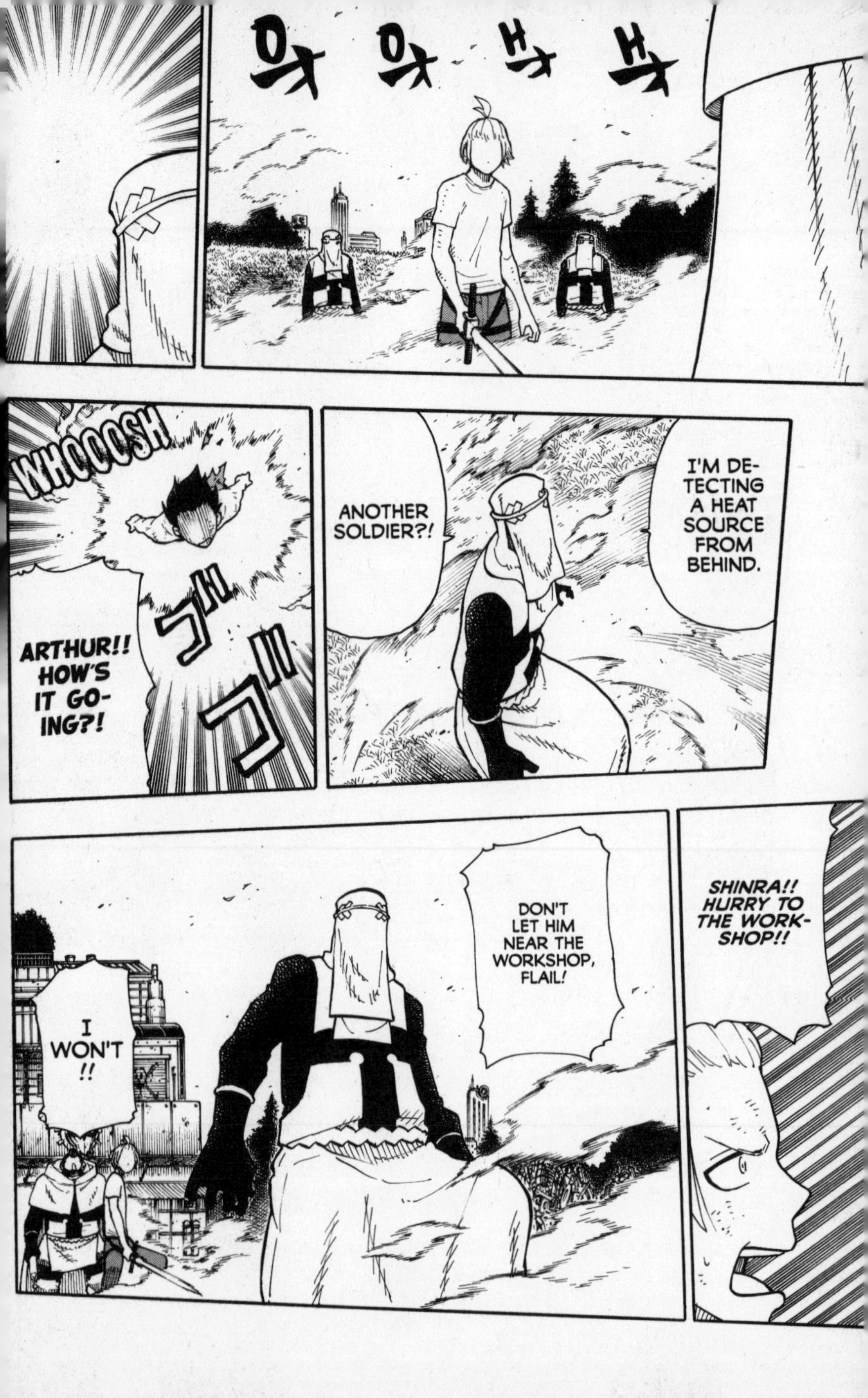
I'M DE-TECTING A HEAT SOURCE FROM BEHIND.
ANOTHER SOLDIER?!
WHOOOSH
ARTHUR!! HOW'S IT GO-ING?!
SHINRA!! HURRY TO THE WORK-SHOP!!
DON'T LET HIM NEAR THE WORKSHOP, FLAIL!
I WON'T!!

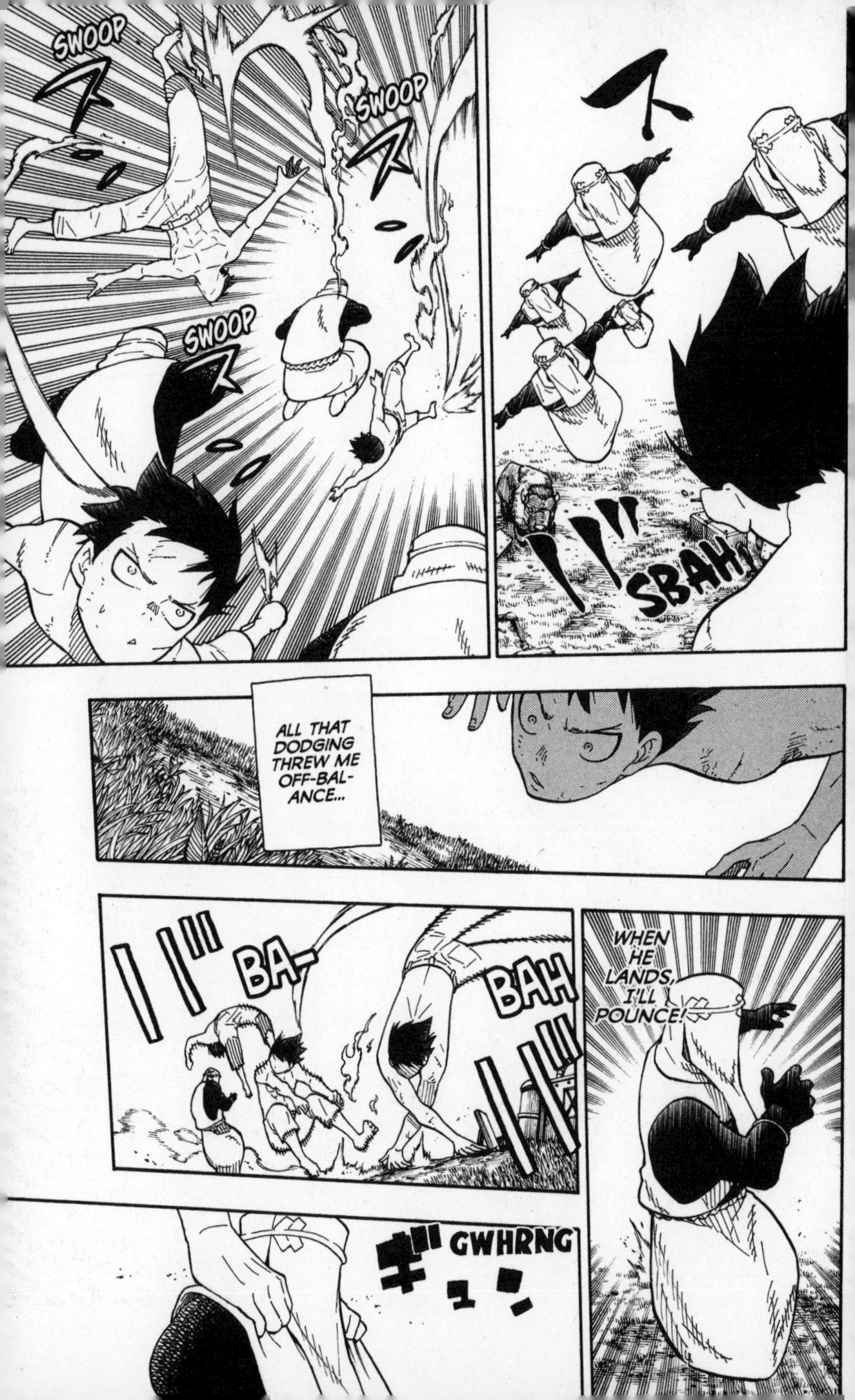
SBAH
SWOOP
SWOOP
SWOOP
ALL THAT DODGING THREW ME OFF-BAL-ANCE...
WHEN HE LANDS, I'LL POUNCE!
BA-
BAH
GWHRNG

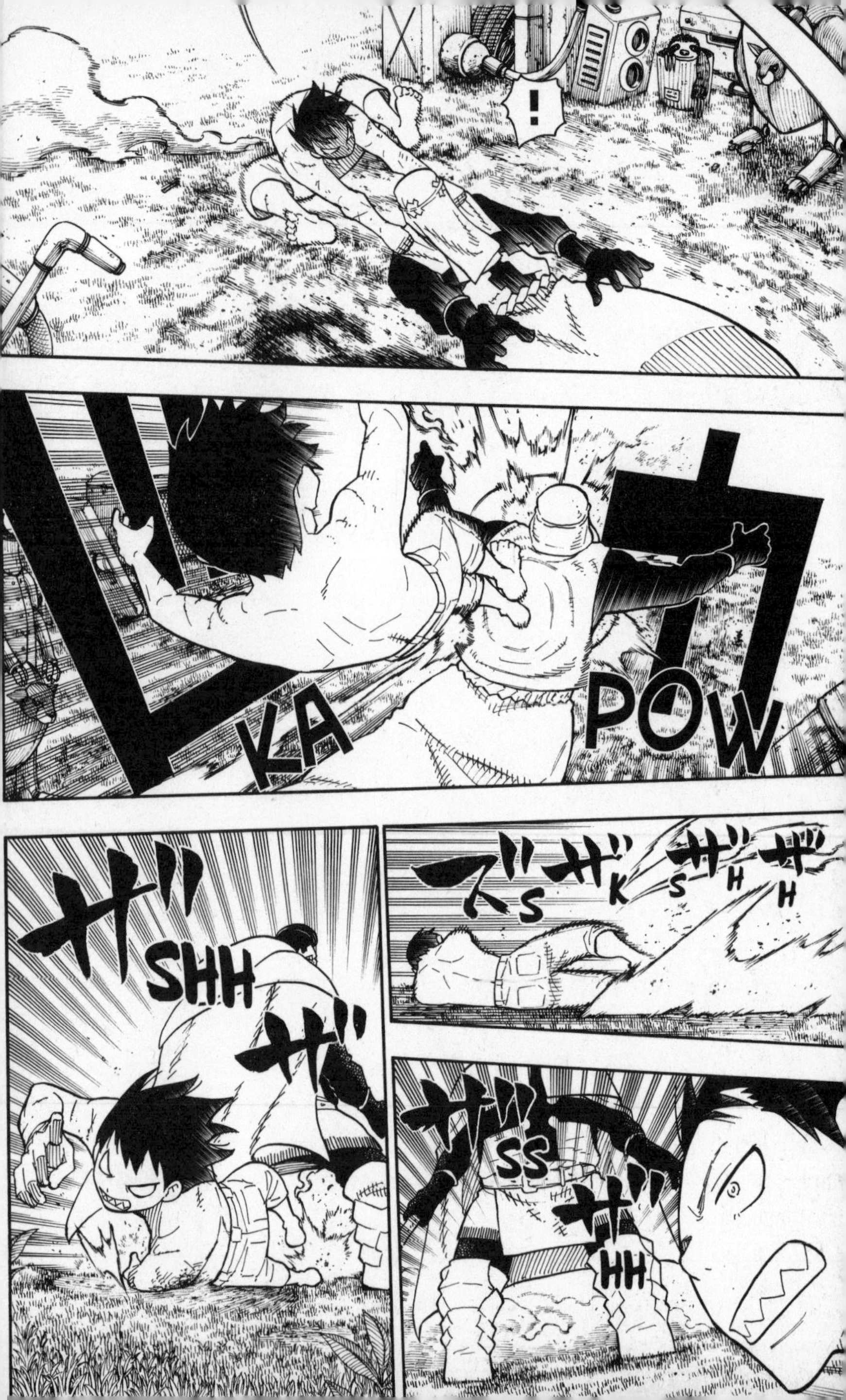
!
KA POW
SKSHH
SS
HH
SHH

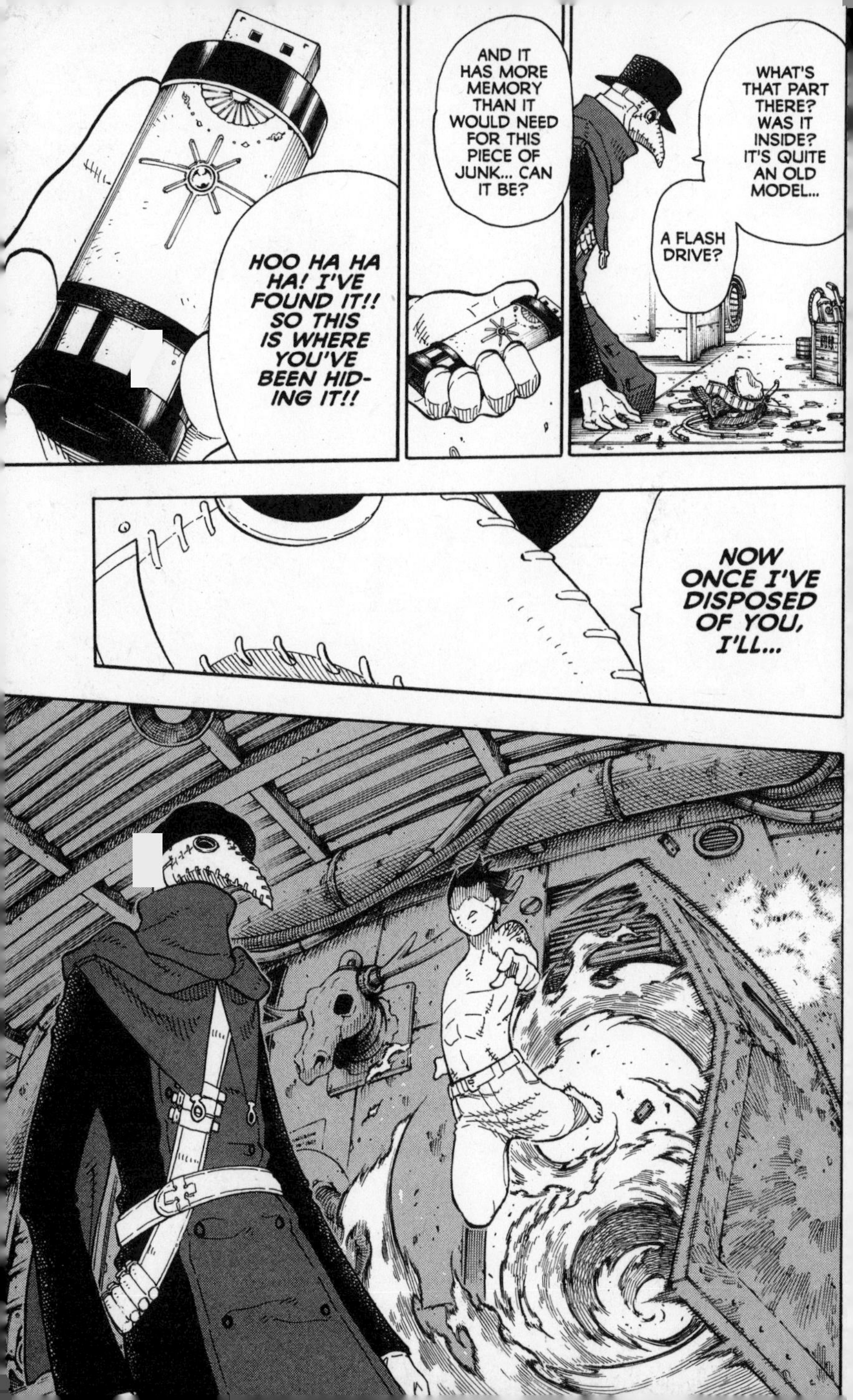
WHAT'S THAT PART THERE? WAS IT INSIDE? IT'S QUITE AN OLD MODEL...
A FLASH DRIVE?
AND IT HAS MORE MEMORY THAN IT WOULD NEED FOR THIS PIECE OF JUNK... CAN IT BE?
HOO HA HA HA! I'VE FOUND IT!! SO THIS IS WHERE YOU'VE BEEN HID-ING IT!!
NOW ONCE I'VE DISPOSED OF YOU, I'LL...

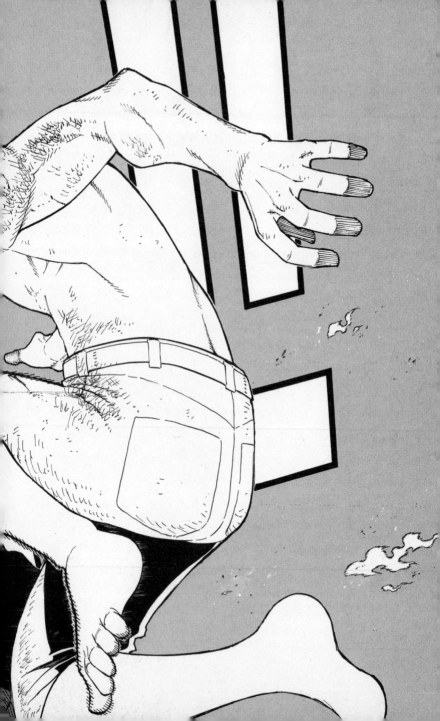

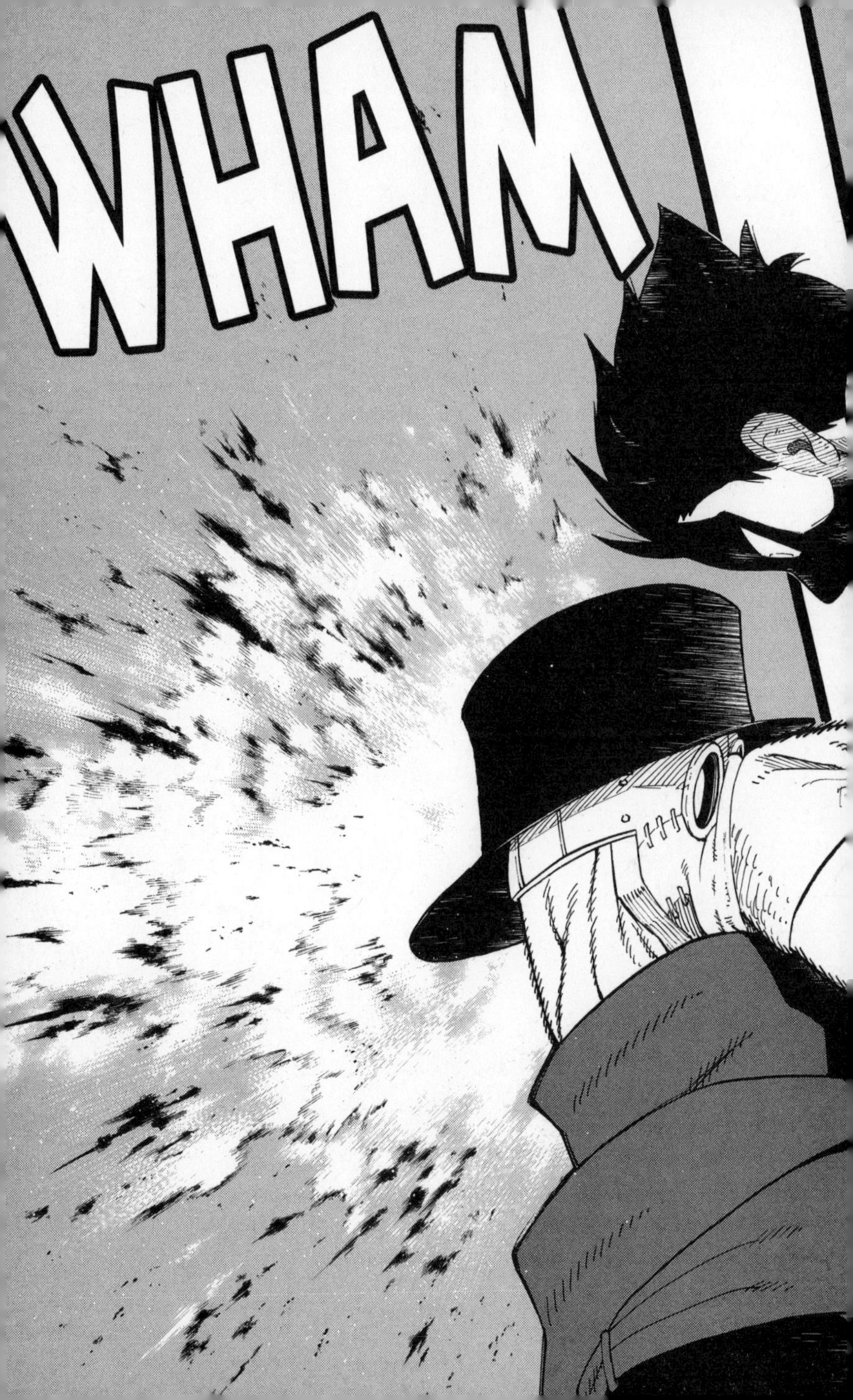
WHAM

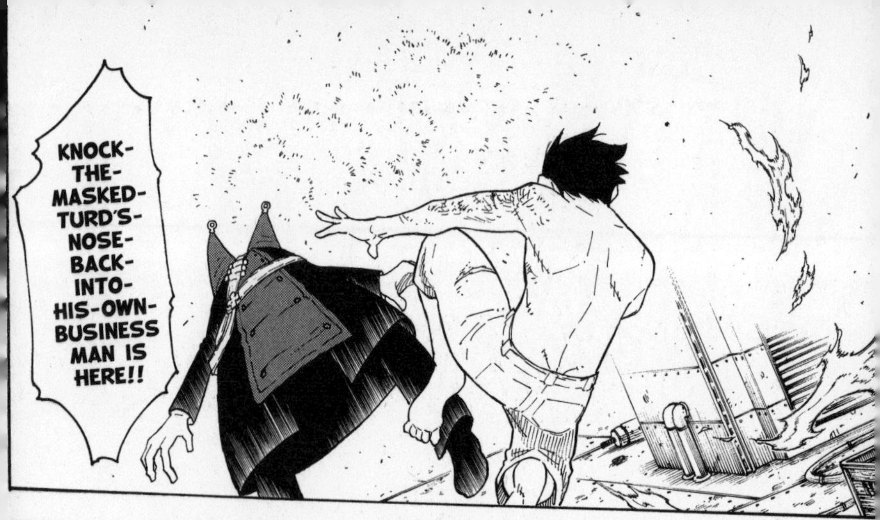
KNOCK-THE-MASKED-TURD'S-NOSE-BACK-INTO-HIS-OWN-BUSINESS MAN IS HERE!!
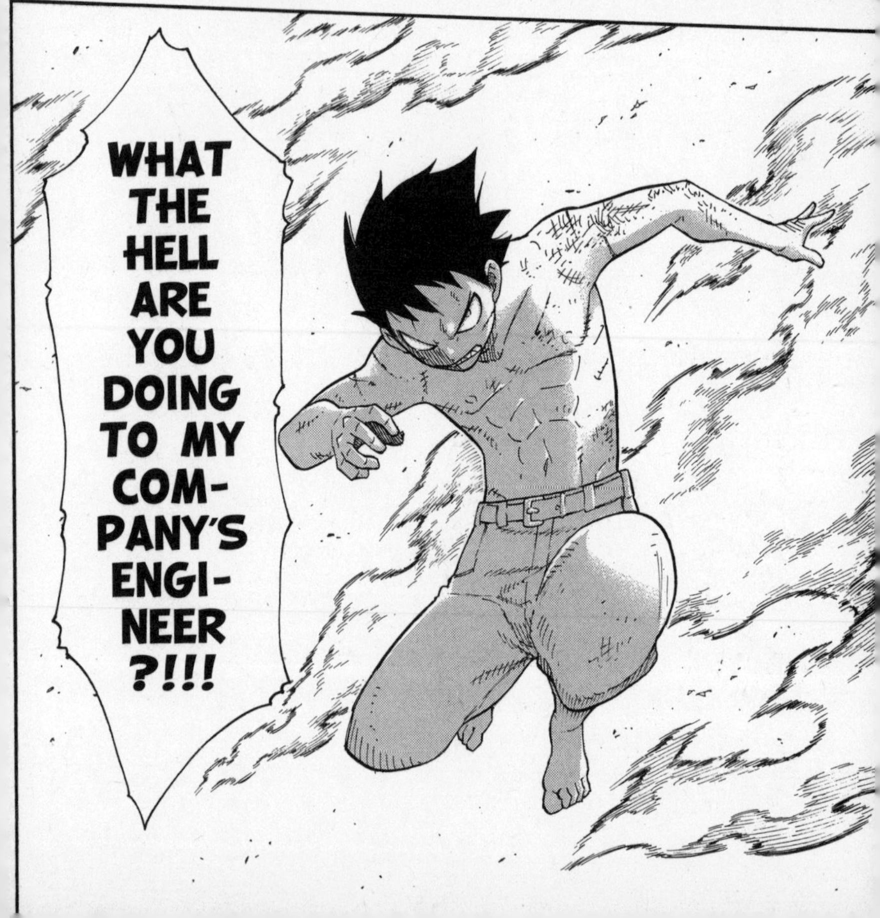
WHAT THE HELL ARE YOU DOING TO MY COMPANY'S ENGINEER?!!!

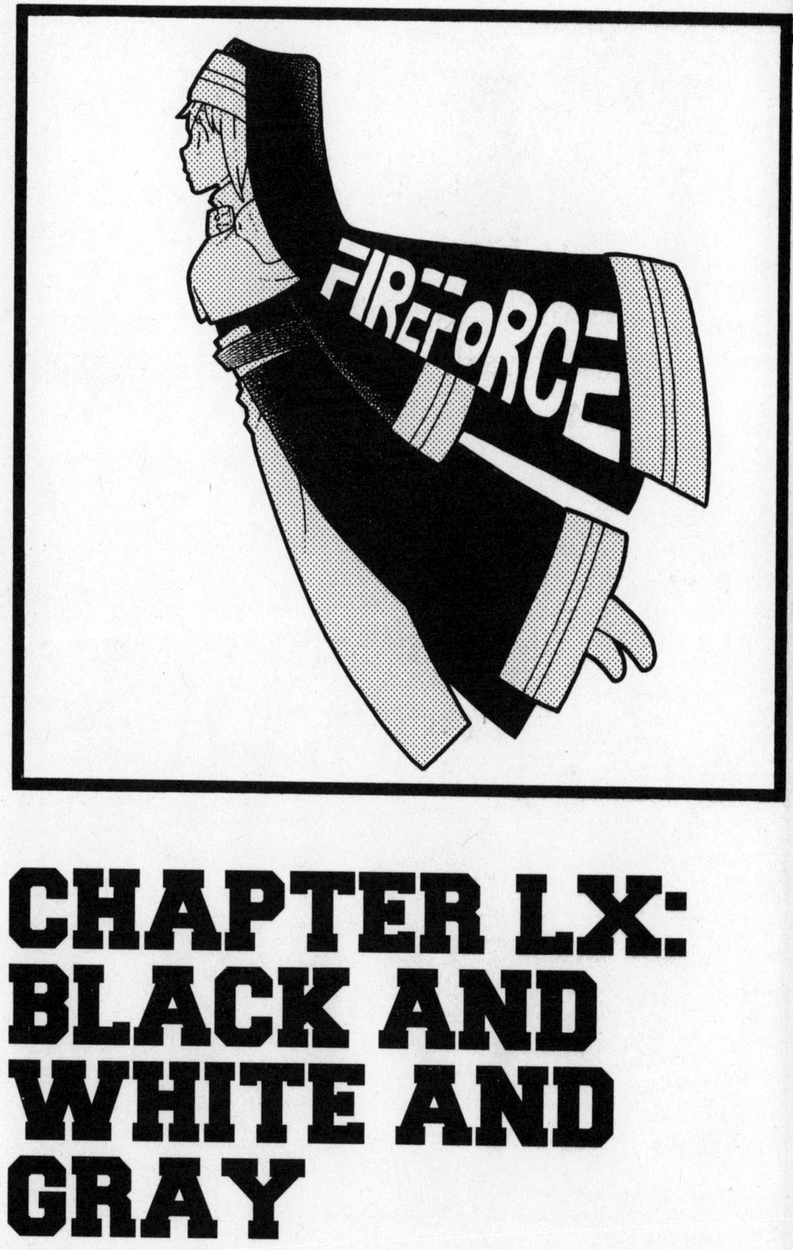
FIREFORCE

CHAPTER LX: BLACK AND WHITE AND GRAY

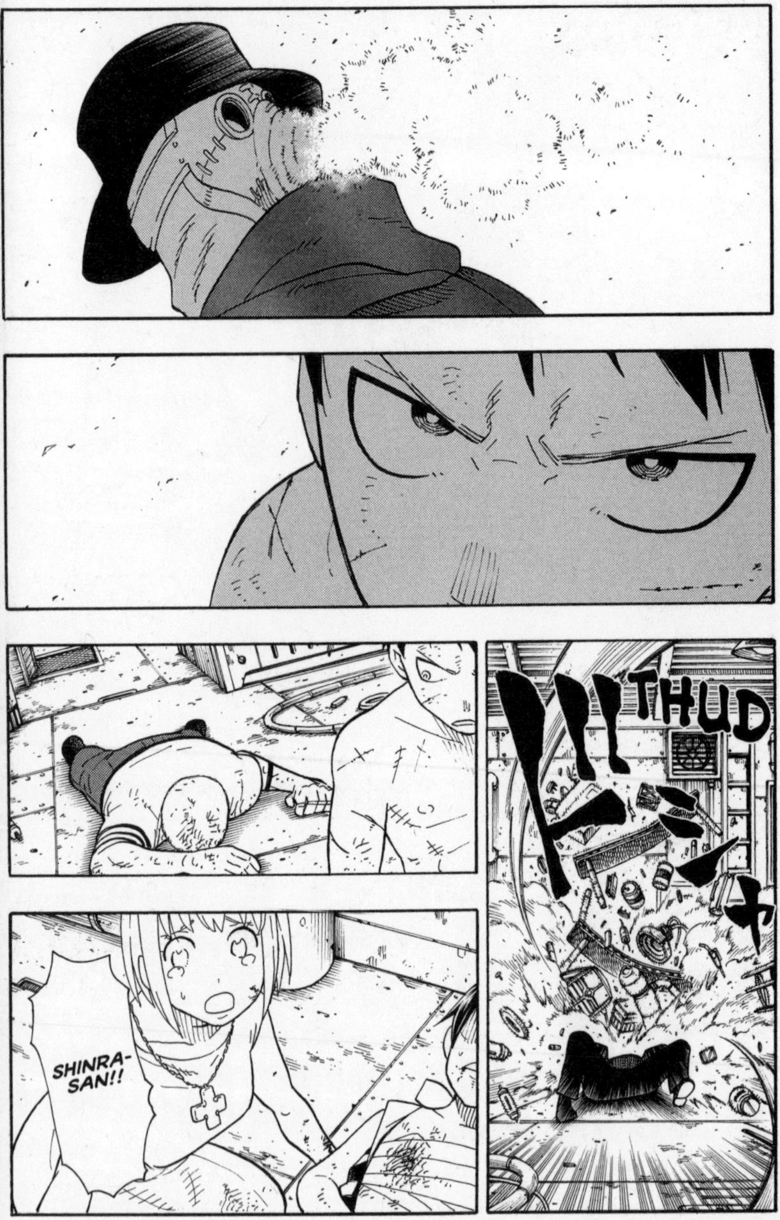
THUD
SHINRA-SAN!!

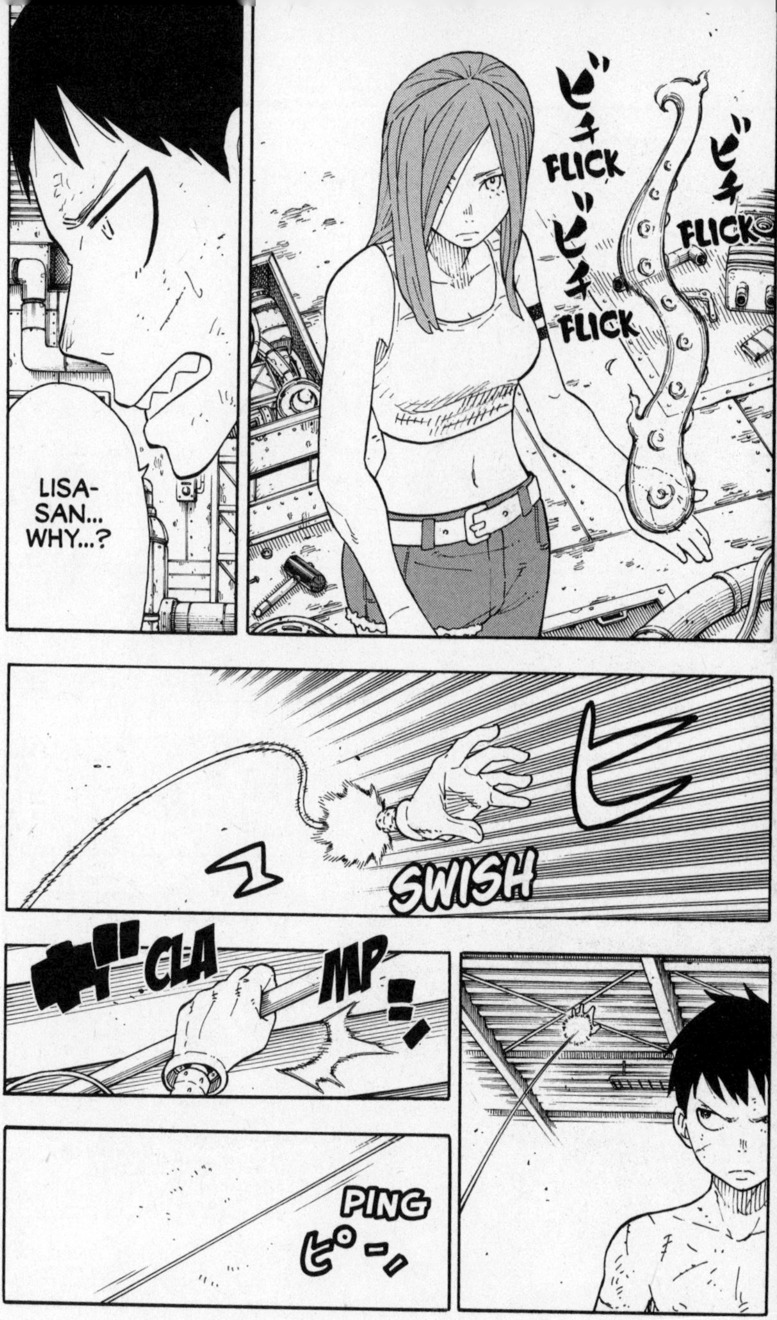
ビチ
FLICK
ビチッビチ
FLICK
FLICK
LISA-SAN... WHY...?
ヒ
SWISH
CLA MP
PING

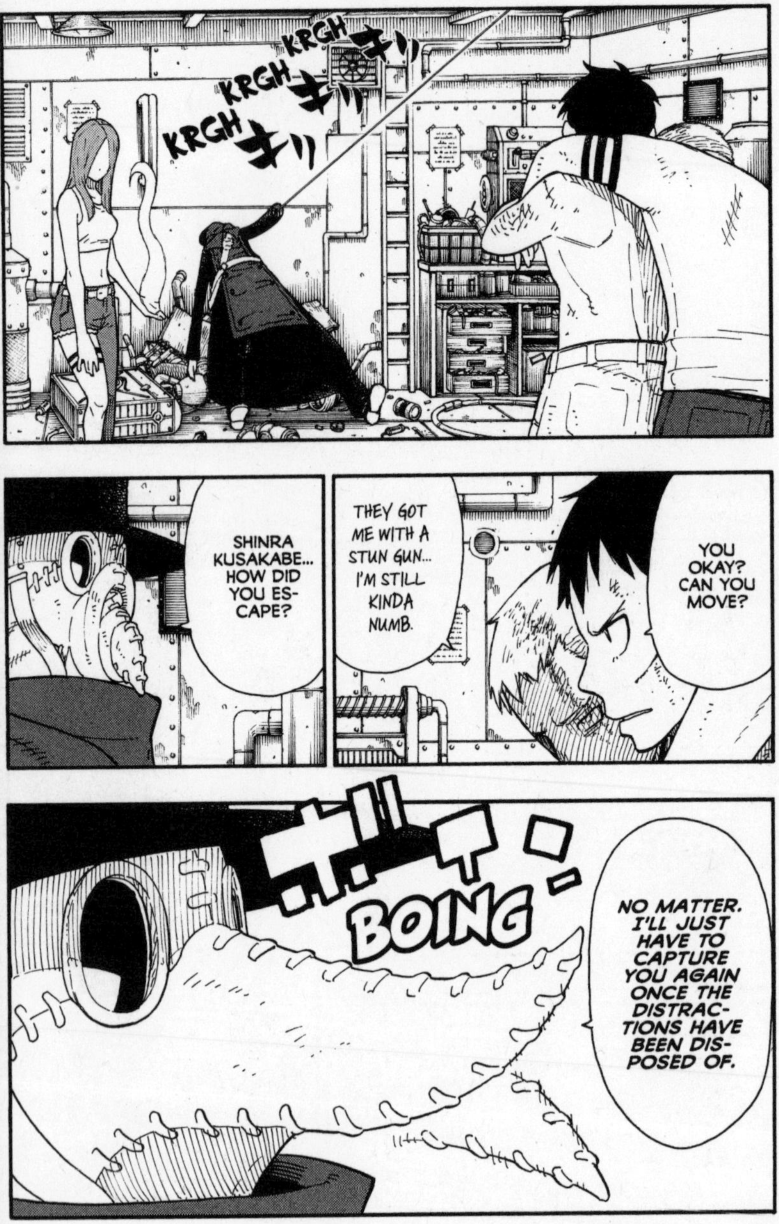
KRGH キリ
KRGH キリ
KRGH キリ
YOU OKAY? CAN YOU MOVE?
THEY GOT ME WITH A STUN GUN... I'M STILL KINDA NUMB.
SHINRA KUSAKABE... HOW DID YOU ES-CAPE?
NO MATTER. I'LL JUST HAVE TO CAPTURE YOU AGAIN ONCE THE DISTRAC-TIONS HAVE BEEN DIS-POSED OF.
BOING

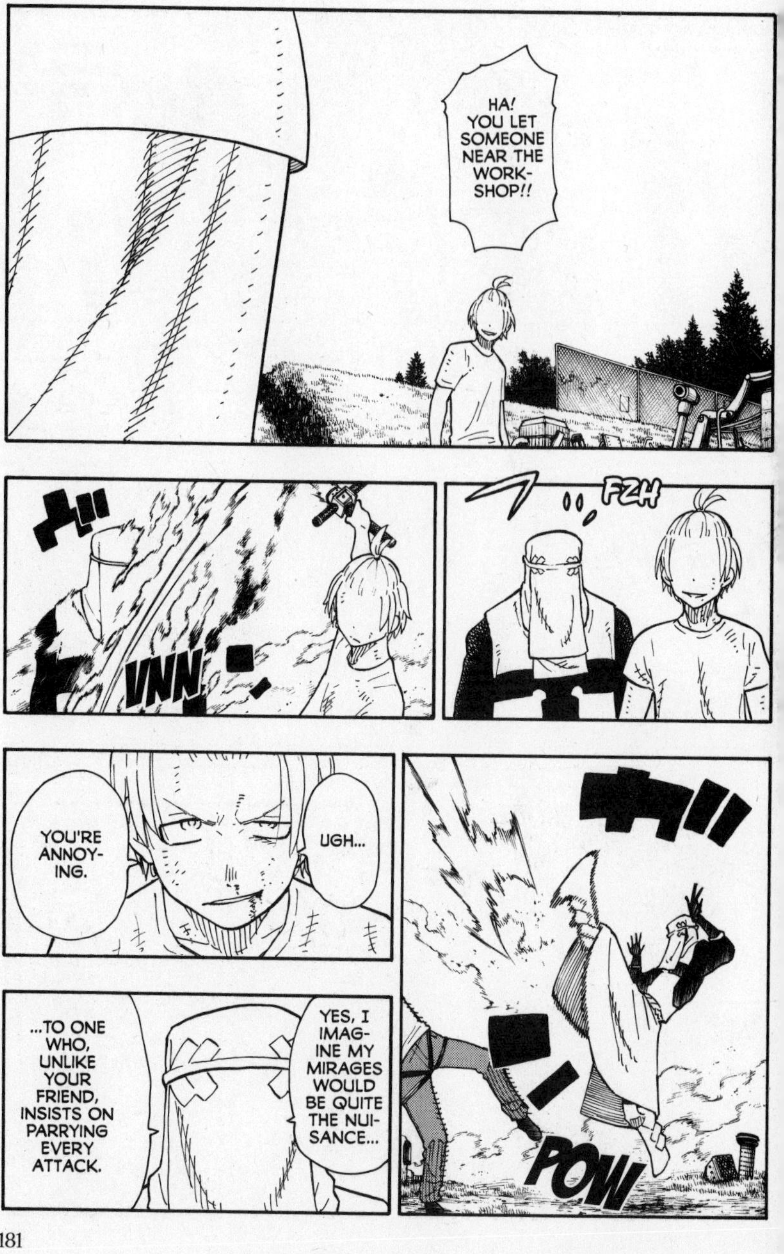
HA! YOU LET SOMEONE NEAR THE WORK-SHOP!!
FZH
VNN
POW
UGH...
YOU'RE ANNOY-ING.
YES, I IMAG-INE MY MIRAGES WOULD BE QUITE THE NUI-SANCE...
...TO ONE WHO, UNLIKE YOUR FRIEND, INSISTS ON PARRYING EVERY ATTACK.

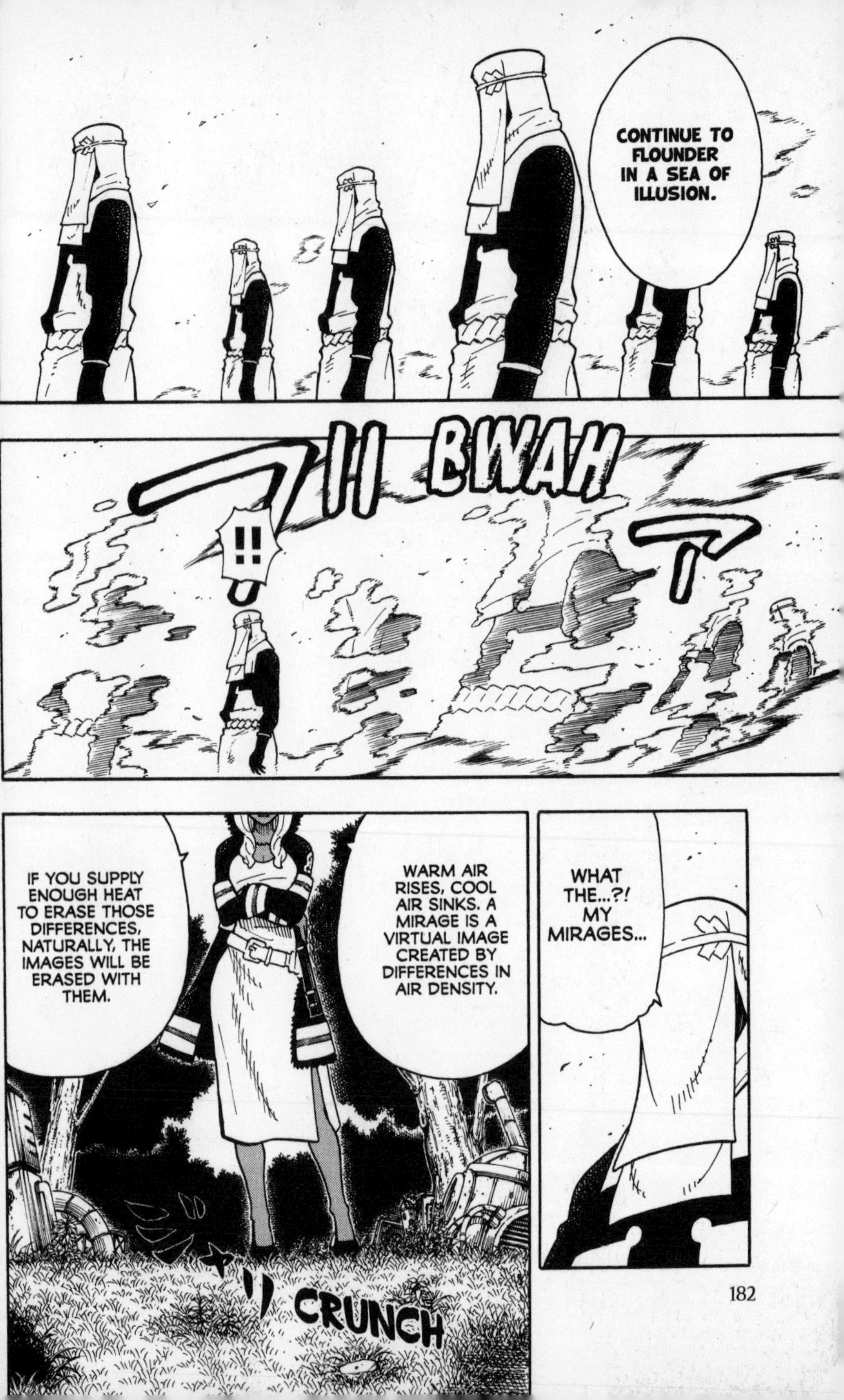
CONTINUE TO FLOUNDER IN A SEA OF ILLUSION.
BWAH
!!
WHAT THE...?! MY MIRAGES...
WARM AIR RISES, COOL AIR SINKS. A MIRAGE IS A VIRTUAL IMAGE CREATED BY DIFFERENCES IN AIR DENSITY.
IF YOU SUPPLY ENOUGH HEAT TO ERASE THOSE DIFFERENCES, NATURALLY, THE IMAGES WILL BE ERASED WITH THEM.
CRUNCH

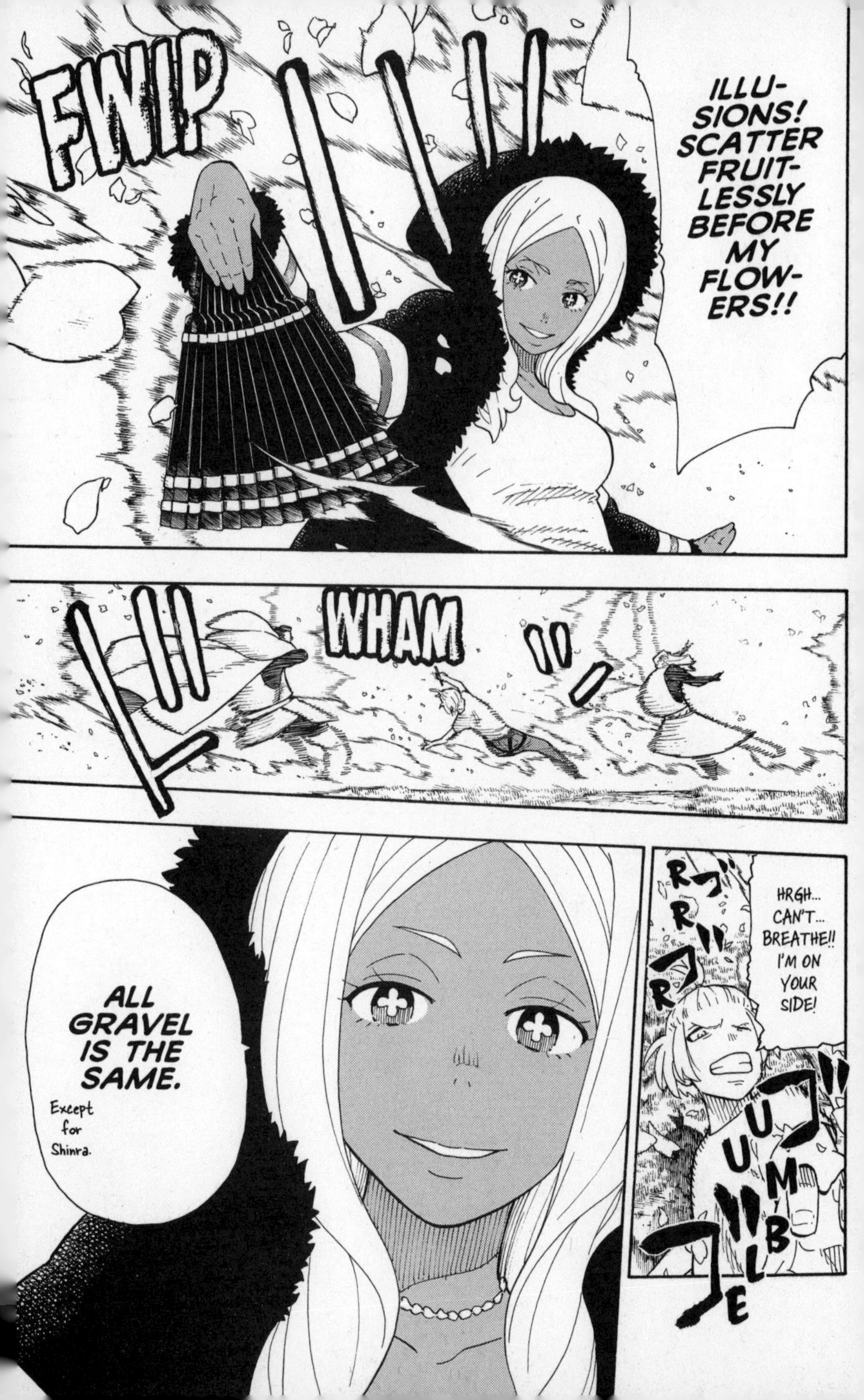
FWIP
ILLUSIONS! SCATTER FRUITLESSLY BEFORE MY FLOWERS!!
WHAM
RRR
HRGH... CAN'T... BREATHE!! I'M ON YOUR SIDE!
UUMBLE
ALL GRAVEL IS THE SAME.
Except for Shinra.

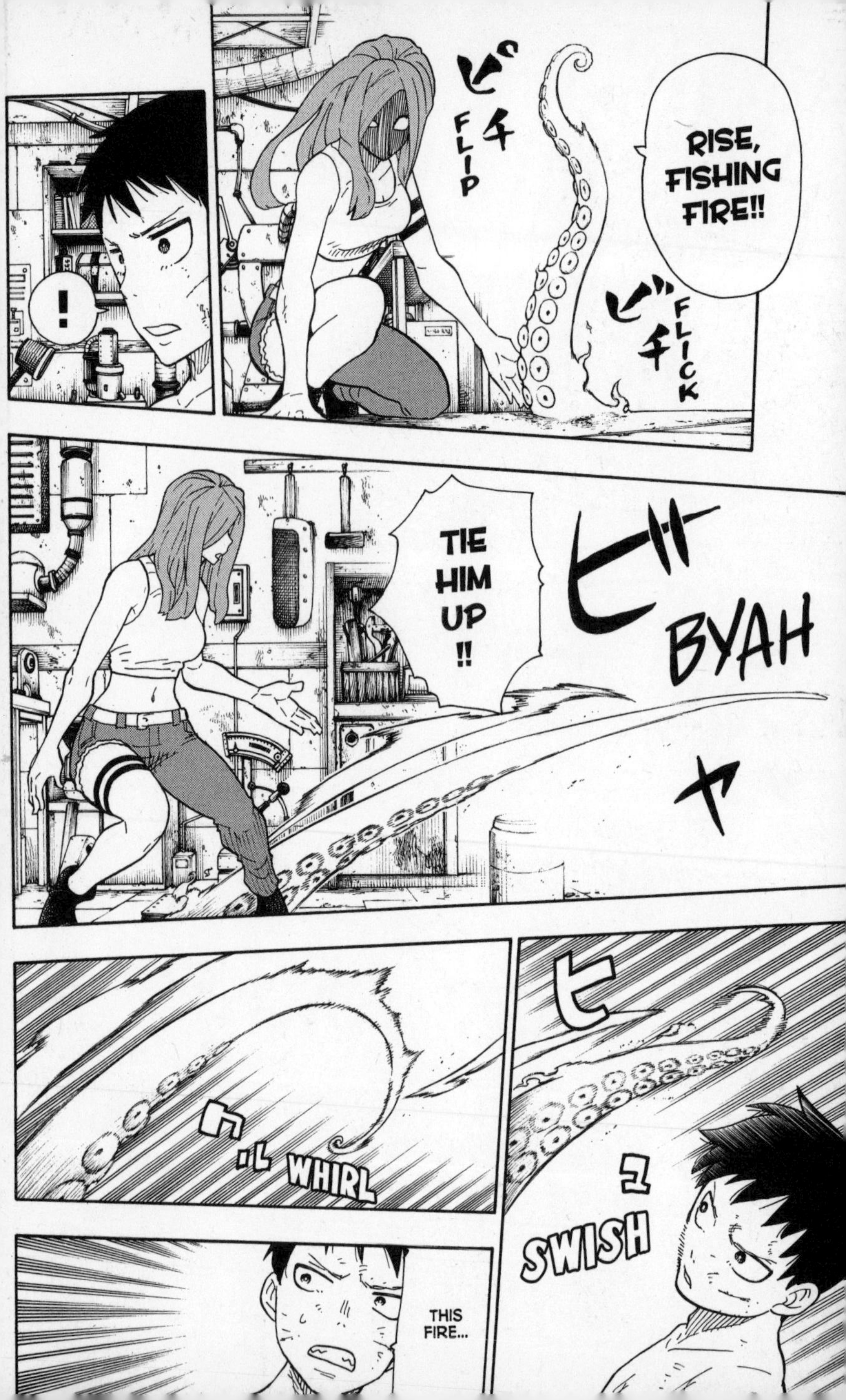
RISE, FISHING FIRE!!
ビチ FLIP
ビチ FLICK
!
TIE HIM UP !!
ビャ BYAH
ヒュ SWISH
クル WHIRL
THIS FIRE...

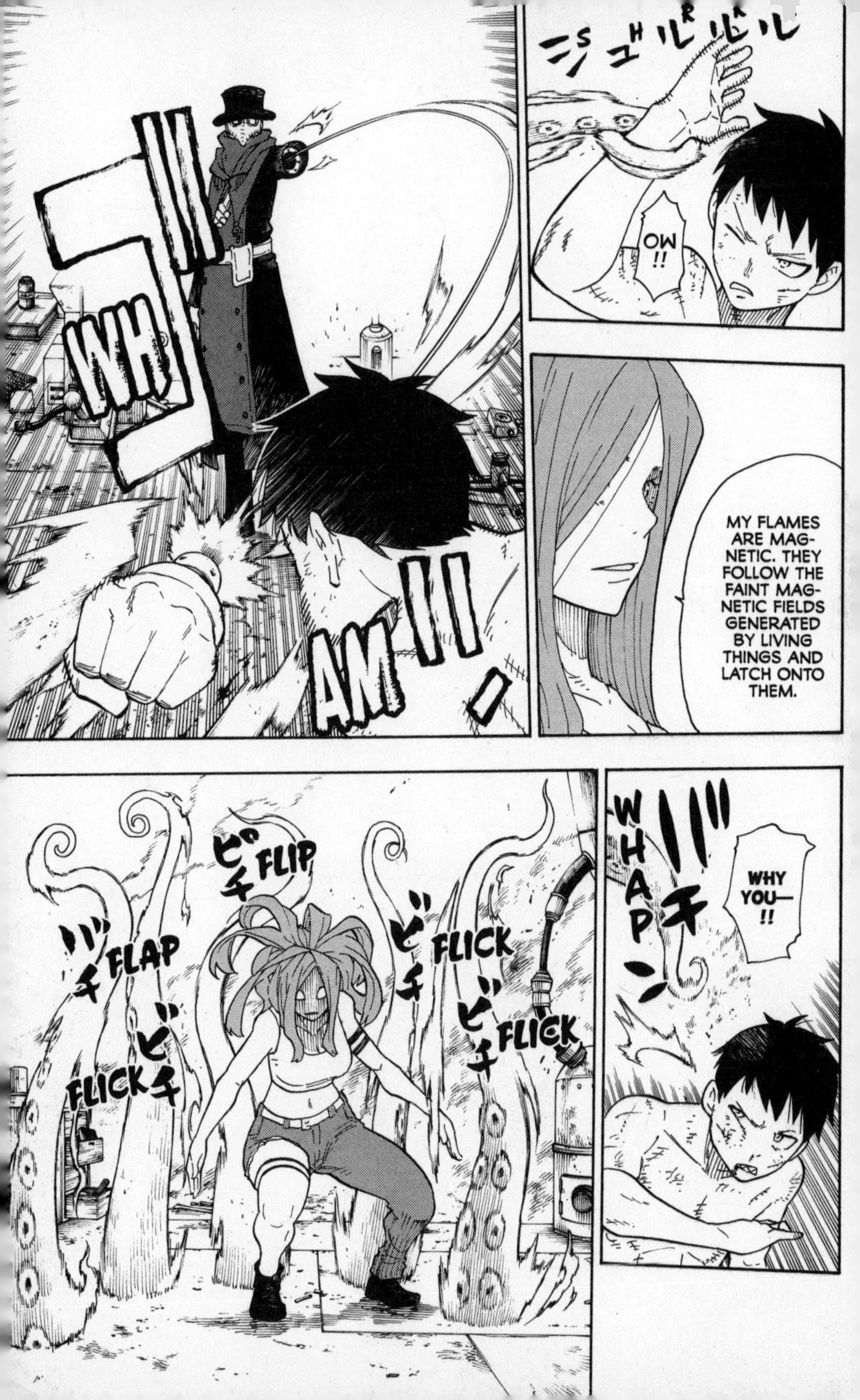
ジュルルル
OW!!
MY FLAMES ARE MAG-NETIC. THEY FOLLOW THE FAINT MAG-NETIC FIELDS GENERATED BY LIVING THINGS AND LATCH ONTO THEM.
WHAM!!
WHAP
ババチン
WHY YOU—!!
ビチ FLIP
ビチ FLICK
ビチ FLICK
バチ FLAP
ビチ FLICK

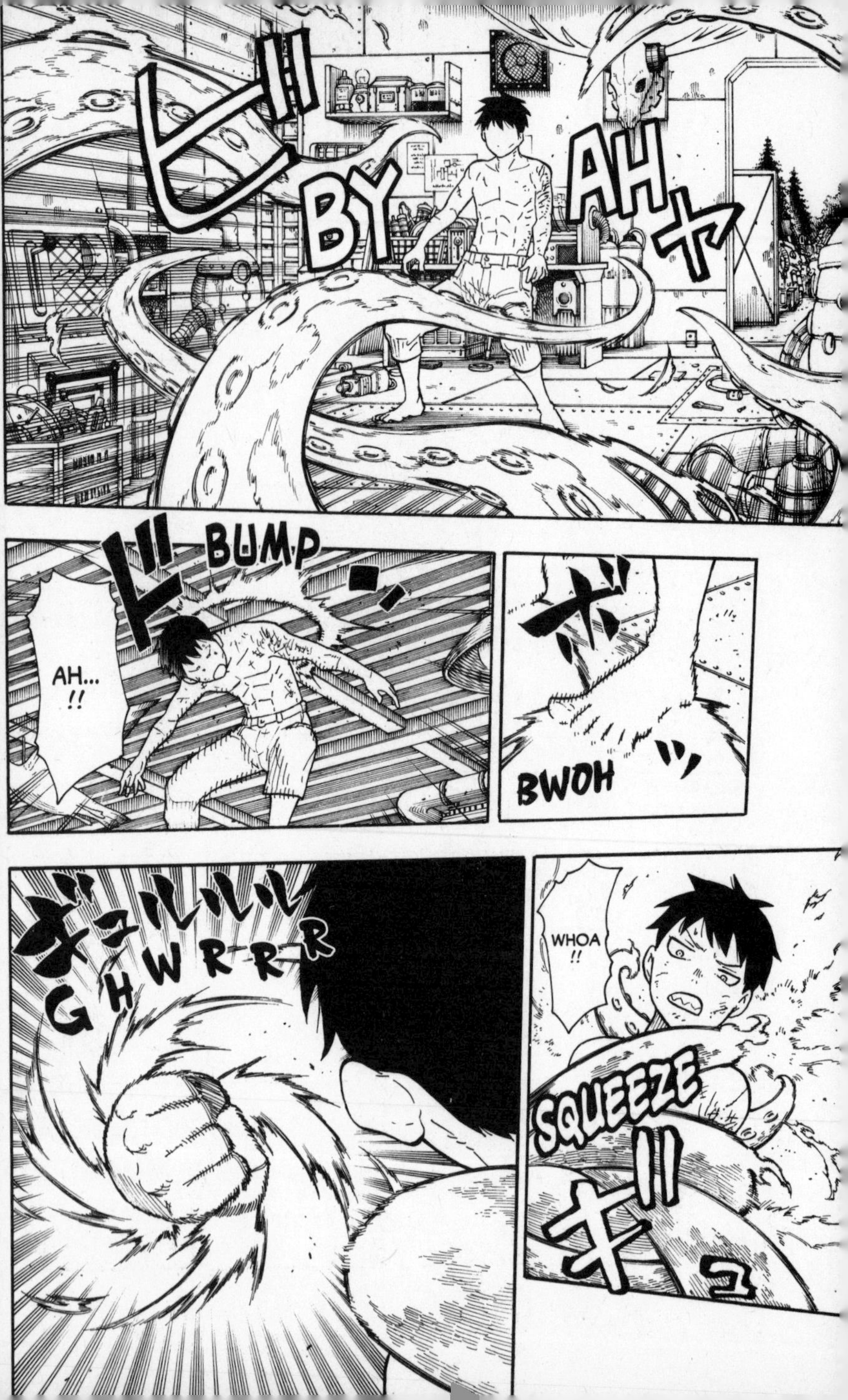
BY
AH
BUMP
AH... !!
BWOH
WHOA !!
SQUEEZE
GHWRRR

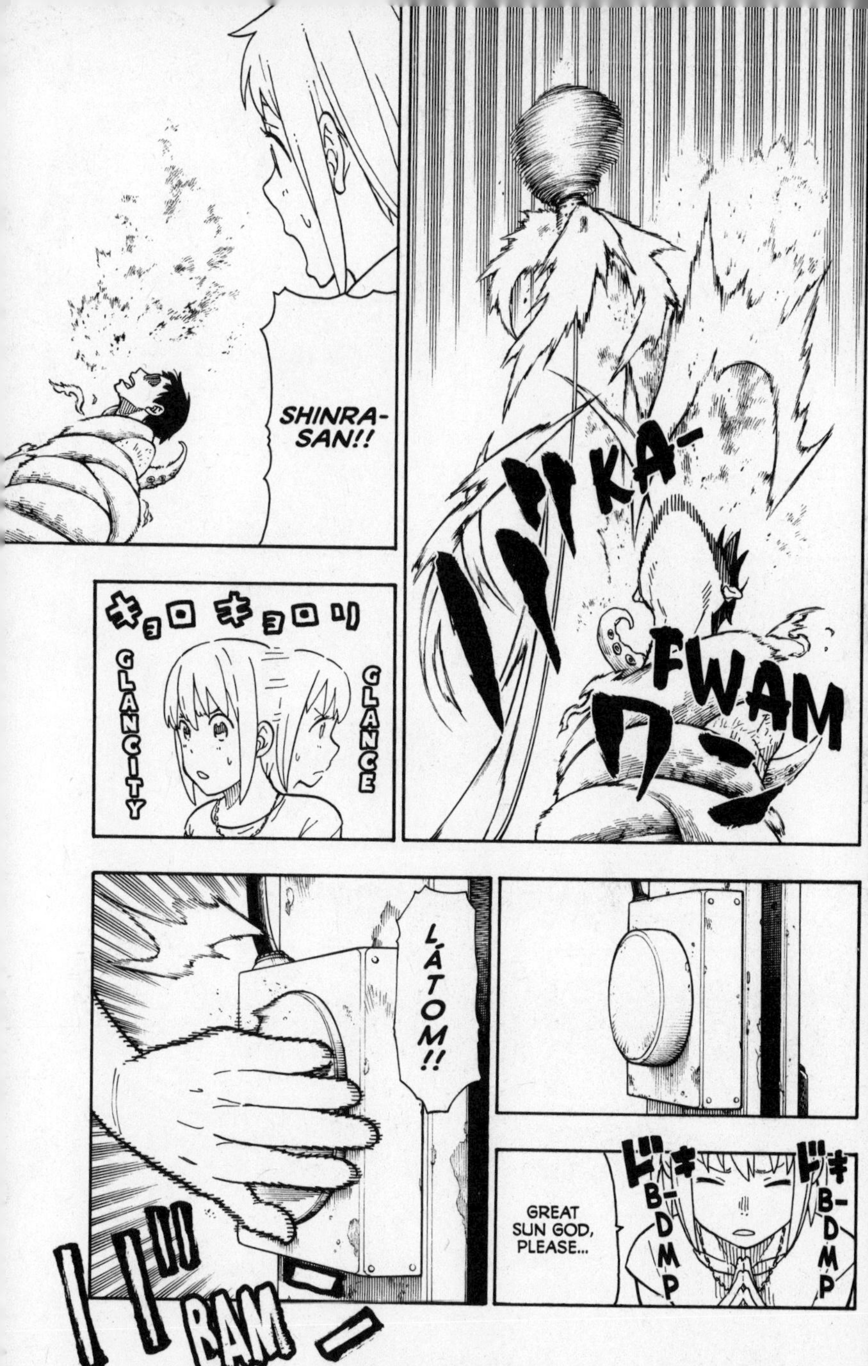

KA-
FWAM
SHINRA-SAN!!
キョロキョロッ
GLANCE
GLANCITY
B-DMP
B-DMP
GREAT SUN GOD, PLEASE...
LÁTOM!!
BAM

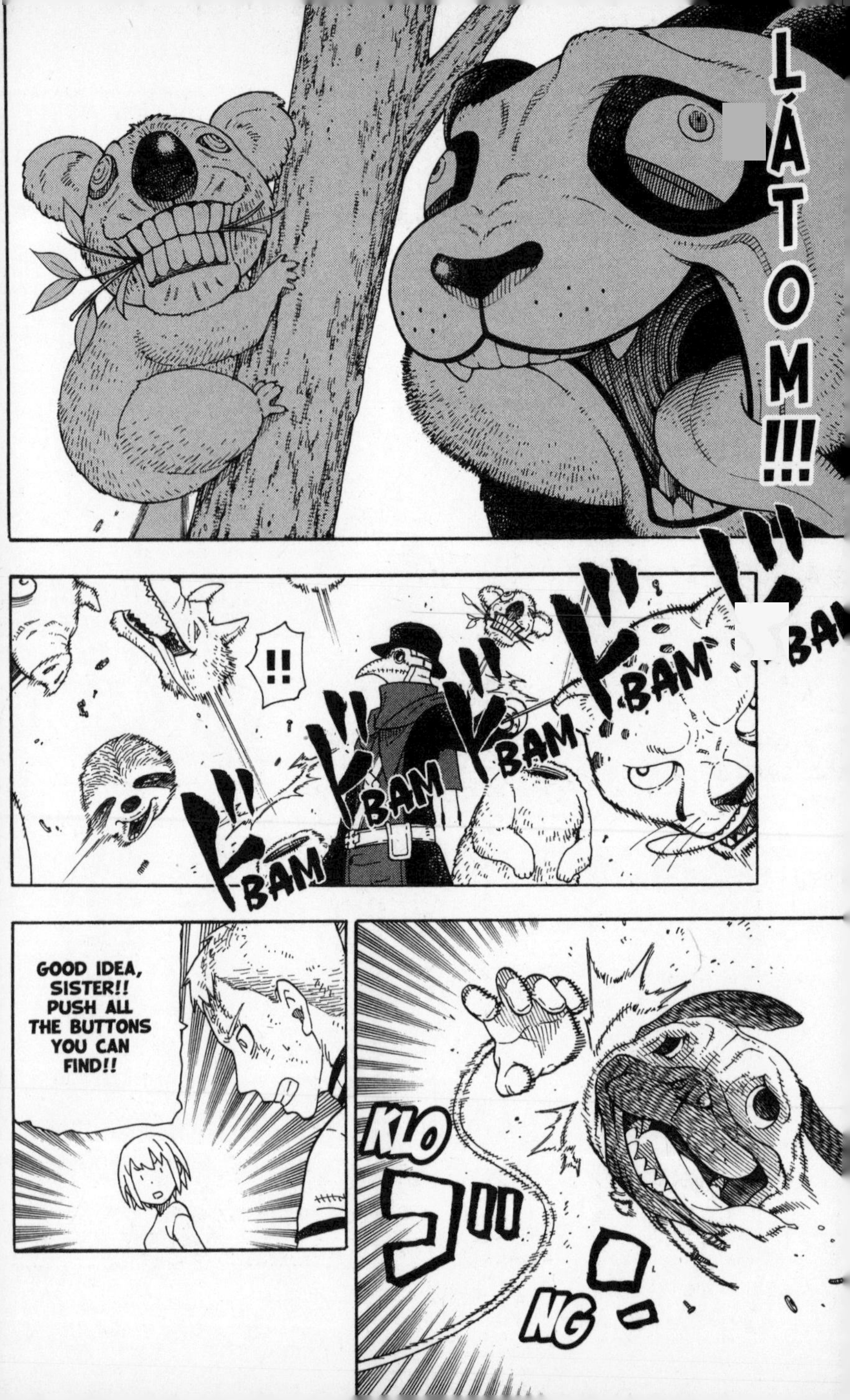
LÁTOM!!!
BAM
BAM
BAM
BAM
BAM
!!
BAM
KLO
NG
GOOD IDEA, SISTER!! PUSH ALL THE BUTTONS YOU CAN FIND!!

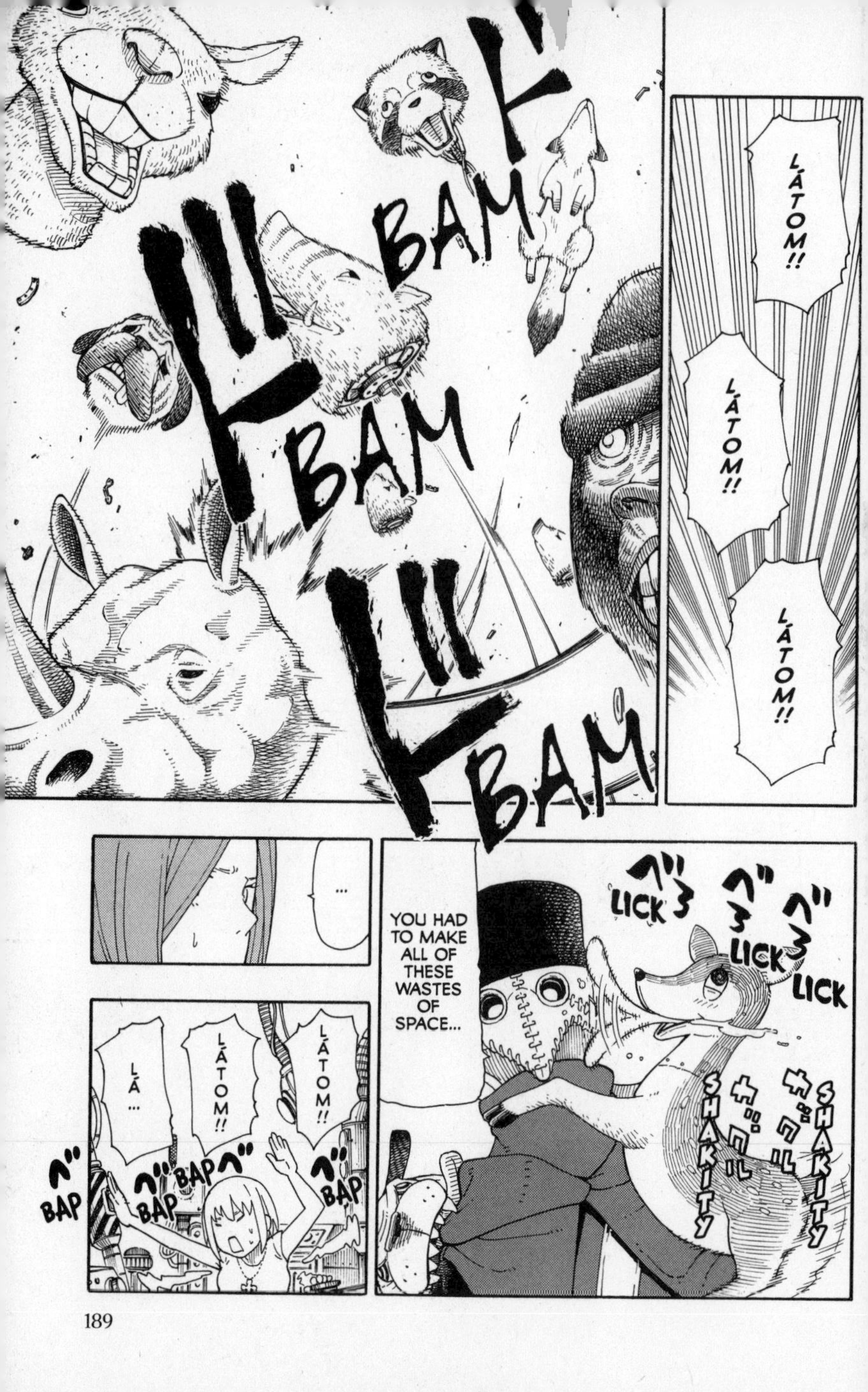

LÁTOM!!
LÁTOM!!
LÁTOM!!
BAM
BAM
BAM
YOU HAD TO MAKE ALL OF THESE WASTES OF SPACE...
LICK
LICK
LICK
SHAKITY
SHAKITY
...
LÁTOM!!
LÁTOM!!
LÁ...
BAP
BAP
BAP
BAP

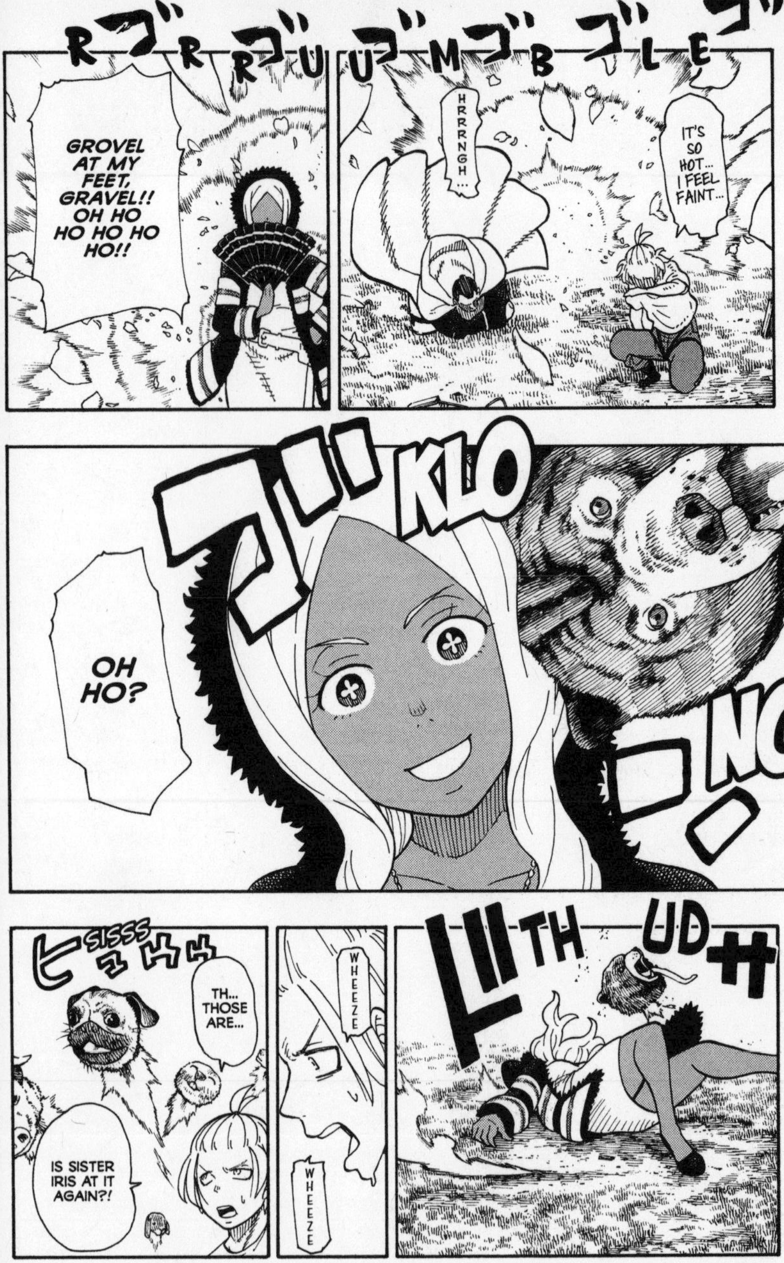
RRRUUMBLE
IT'S SO HOT... I FEEL FAINT...
HRRRNGH...
GROVEL AT MY FEET, GRAVEL!! OH HO HO HO HO HO!!
KLONG
OH HO?
THUD
WHEEZE
WHEEZE
SISSS
TH... THOSE ARE...
IS SISTER IRIS AT IT AGAIN?!

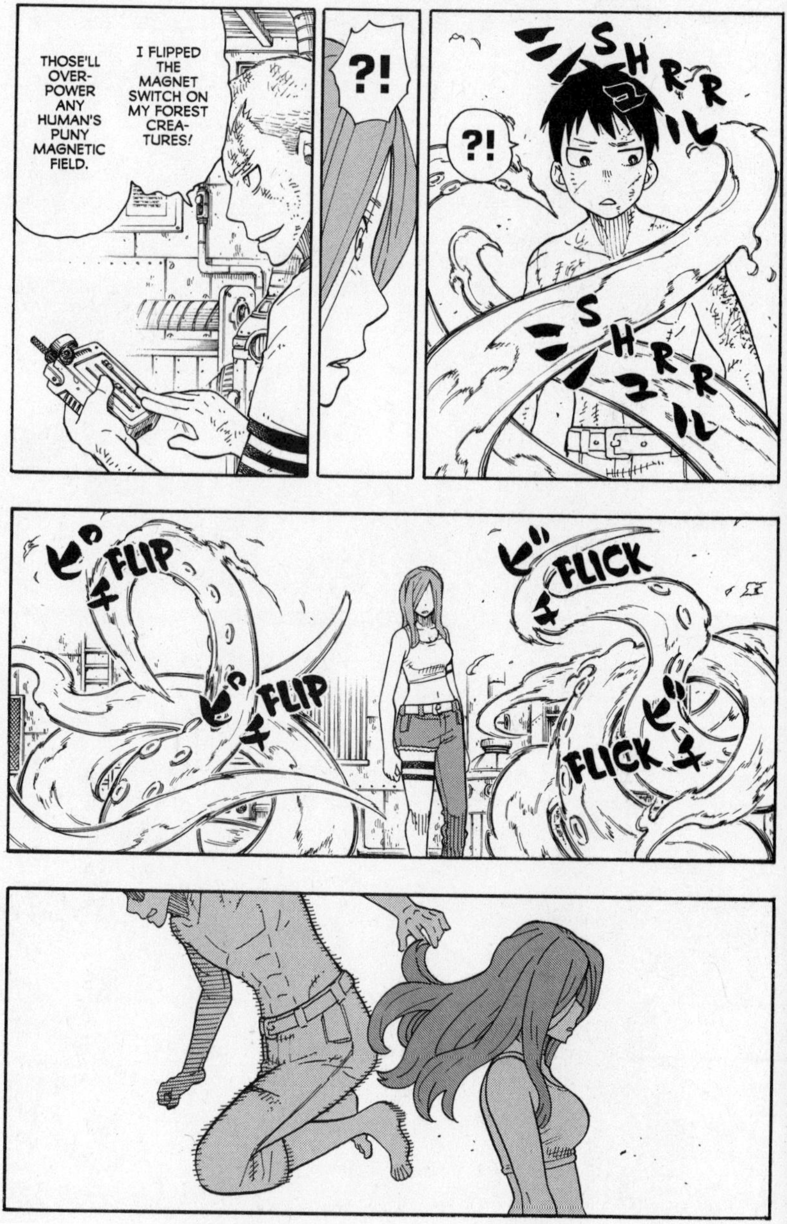
SHRRR
?!
SHRRR
?!
I FLIPPED THE MAGNET SWITCH ON MY FOREST CREA-TURES!
THOSE'LL OVER-POWER ANY HUMAN'S PUNY MAGNETIC FIELD.
FLICK
FLICK
FLIP
FLIP

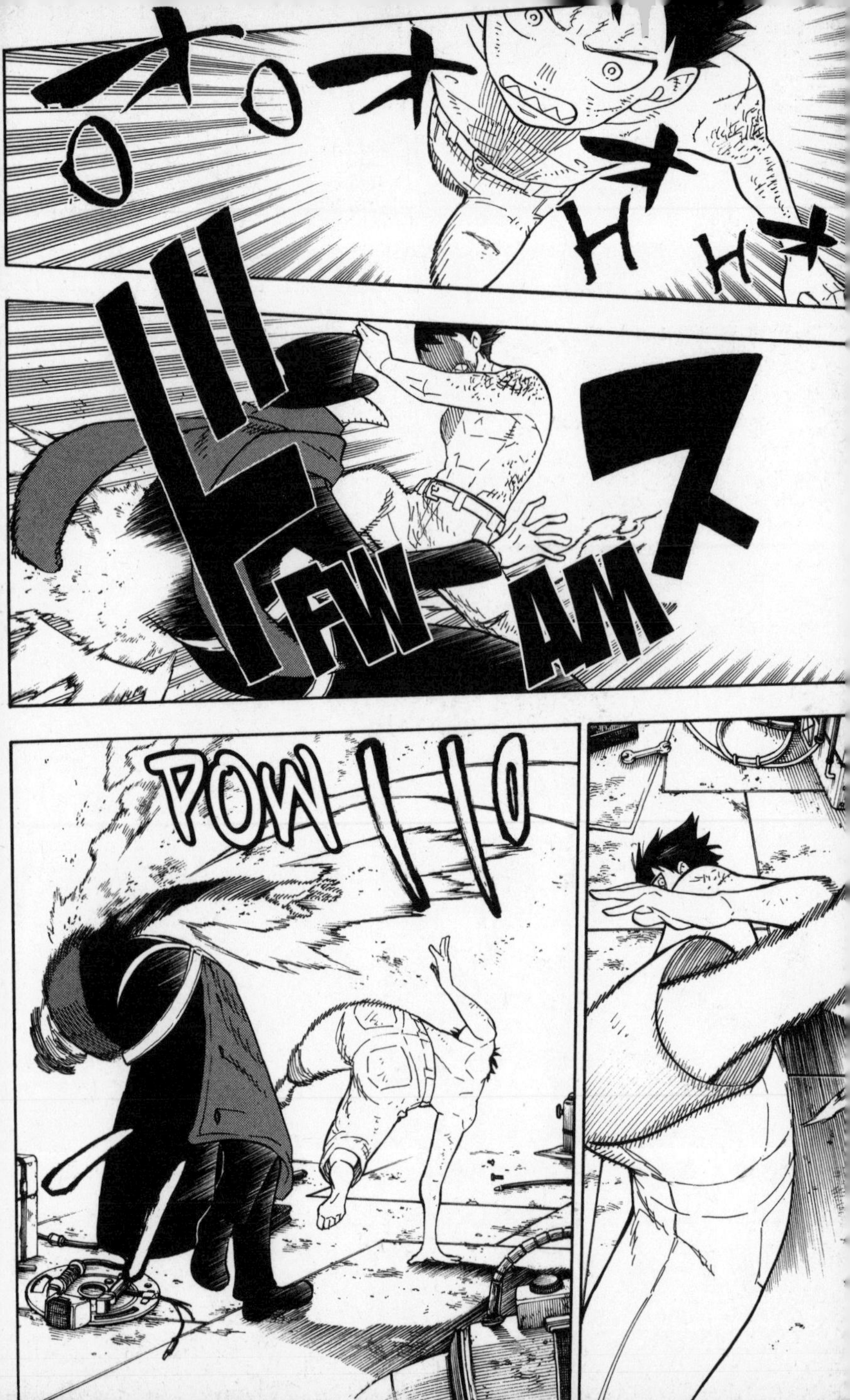

FWAM
POW!!

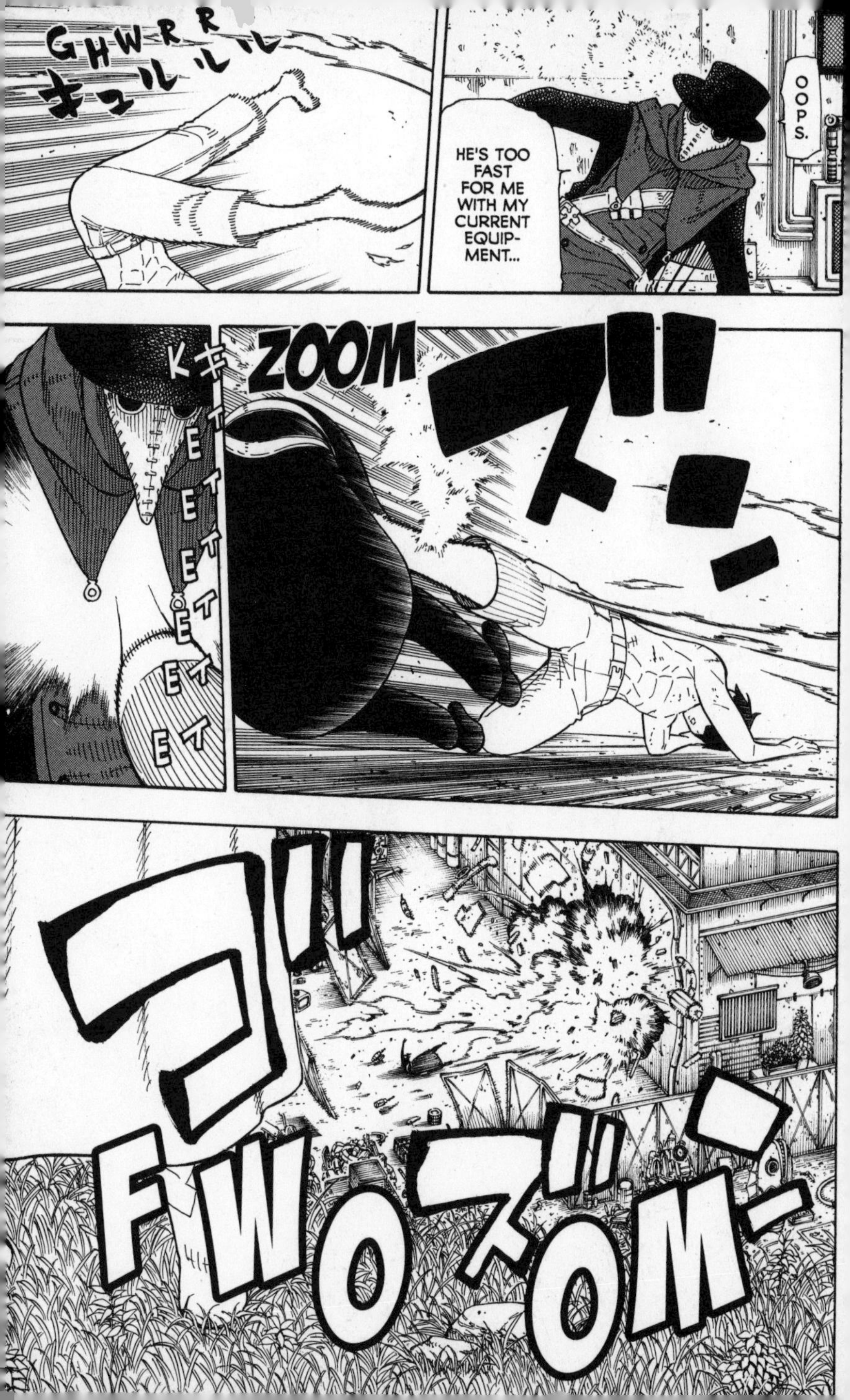
OOPS.
HE'S TOO FAST FOR ME WITH MY CURRENT EQUIPMENT...
GHWRR
ZOOM
KEEEEEE
FWOOM

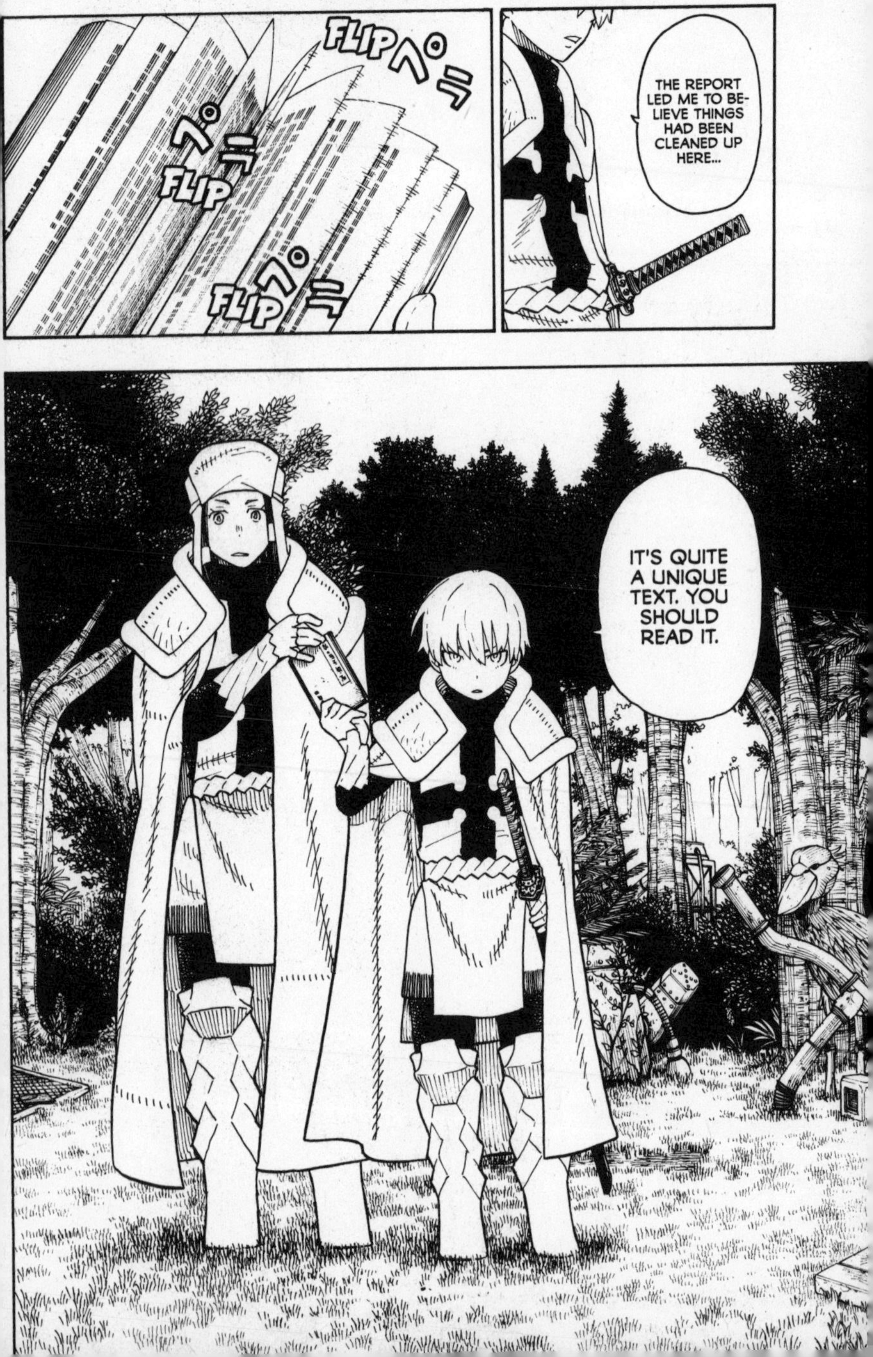
THE REPORT LED ME TO BE-LIEVE THINGS HAD BEEN CLEANED UP HERE...
FLIP ペラ
FLIP ペラ
FLIP ペラ
IT'S QUITE A UNIQUE TEXT. YOU SHOULD READ IT.

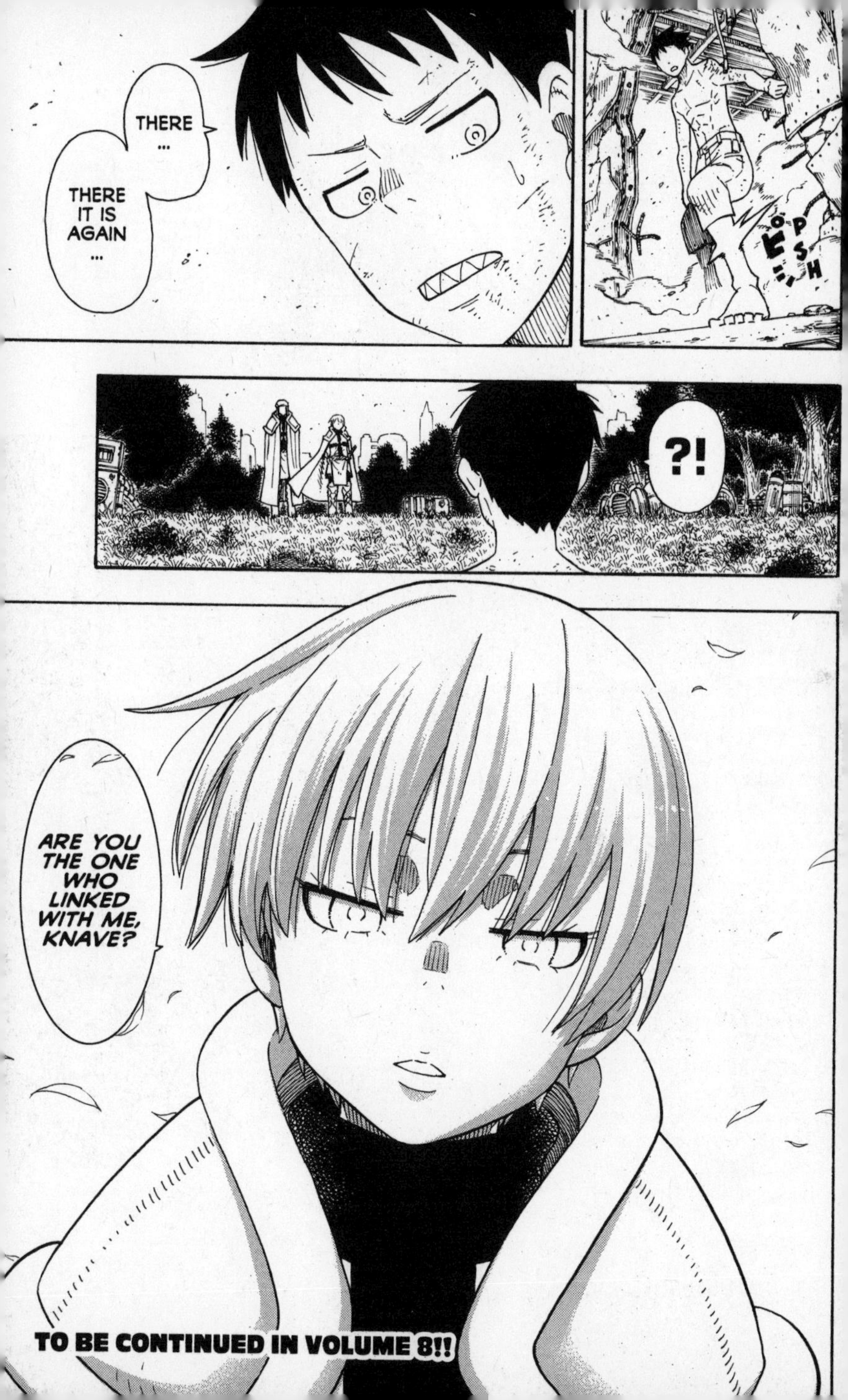
THERE ... THERE IT IS AGAIN ...
?!
ARE YOU THE ONE WHO LINKED WITH ME, KNAVE?
TO BE CONTINUED IN VOLUME 8!!

Translation Notes:

I follow ya, Big Cheese!, page 19

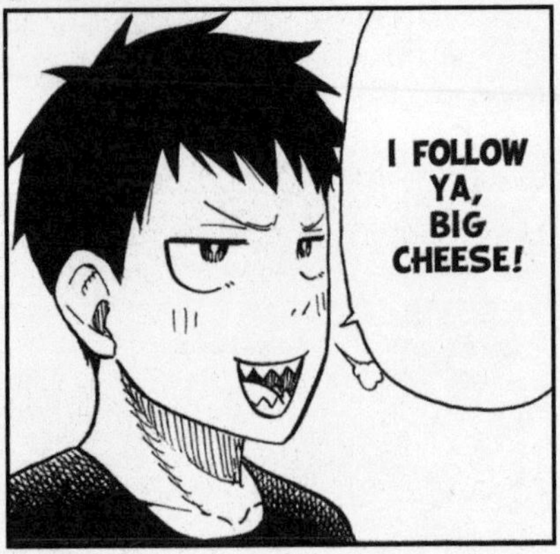
I FOLLOW YA, BIG CHEESE!

As Shinra tells Iris, this is how the proto-nationalists of Company 7 talk—or at least, the Japanese text represents how they talk. The Japanese phrase *gatten shōchi* is an Old Edo style of hearing and accepting an order, something like the "roger wilco" you might hear in a Hollywood film. Because Old Edo puts people in the mind of samurai, one way to deal with this style of speaking would be to make it sound like an old warrior, but surely the reader remembers that the fire brigade in Asakusa does not fit that formal samurai image, and their language is certainly nowhere near that polite. The translators have therefore chosen to attempt to recreate the attitude of this language by representing it through Prohibition-era slang.

Junk-Off, page 34

There is a famous chain of secondhand retailers in Japan where you can sell your items (or pick up used goods at a bargain) which are all appended "-off" — Book-Off (books), Mode-Off (clothes), Hard-off (electronics) and others. Apparently the Fire Force universe adds another store to the chain specifically for, well, junk.

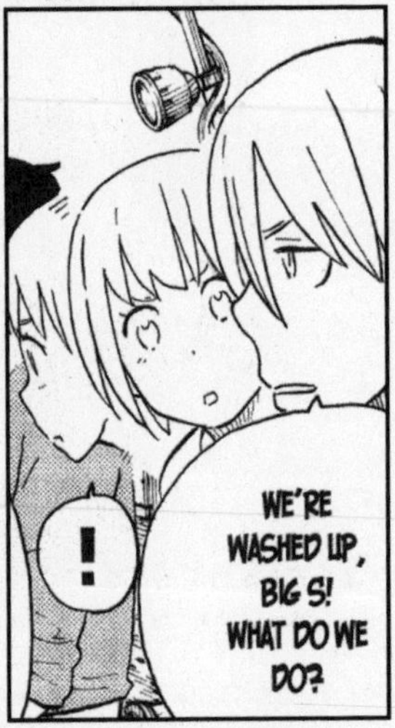
!
WE'RE WASHED UP, BIG S! WHAT DO WE DO?

Big S, page 54

Another habit Shinra and Arthur picked up in Asakusa is to call each other *Shin no Ji* and *Ar no Ji*, meaning roughly, "letter Shin" and "letter Ar." It makes more sense in Japanese, because, for example, there's only one written character for Shin in Shinra. This form of nickname is used among yakuza (gangsters) and other less than upstanding citizens, and generally is not used with any amount of respect. Because it takes the first written character of a person's name, the translators have opted to use the initials, which, being capitalized, are big versions of those letters.

Knock on the stone bridge, page 124

There's a saying in Japanese, "To knock on a stone bridge before crossing." The idea is that, because stone bridges are generally very sturdy, only a very cautious person would knock on it to test that sturdiness. Dr. Giovanni is suggesting that sometimes even the stone bridge isn't as sturdy as it looks, so one must have the judgment skills to refuse to cross if the bridge doesn't seem sound.

Knock-the-Masked-Turd's-Nose-Back-Into-His-Own-Business Man, page 176

Another saying, *hanappashira o heshioru*, literally means "to break someone's nose." In a figurative sense, it is used in reference to taking someone down a peg, cutting them down to size, or putting them back in their place. Unfortunately, none of the English idioms involve literally breaking noses, which is what Shinra does to Dr. Giovanni's mask. The translators opted to attempt to maintain the pun.

Fishing Fire, page 184

As the reader might expect, a "fishing fire," or *isaribi*, is a fire used for fishing in an old practice that has been used for centuries. In this case, the fire is also part fish. The word *isaribi* may also be related to Lisa's name—the L and R are pronounced the same in Japanese, so switching the *sa* and *ri* would form the name Lisa.

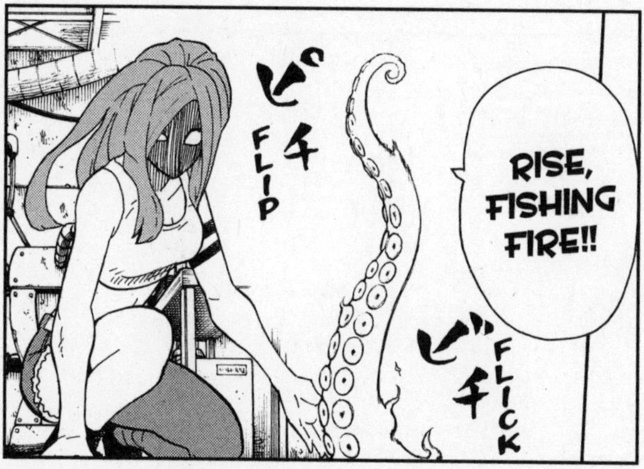
RISE, FISHING FIRE!!
FLIP
FLICK

Tamaki's birthday and nickname, page 200

In Japan, February 22, or 2/22 is Cat Day, because the word for "two," *ni*, is also a sound cats make. Her nickname, Tama-chan, is not only short for Tamaki—it also happens to be the stereotypical cat name in Japan, something like Fluffy. *Tama* means "ball," and is most likely a reference to the feline habit of curling up into very round shapes.

AFTERWORD MANGA: ATSUSHIYA

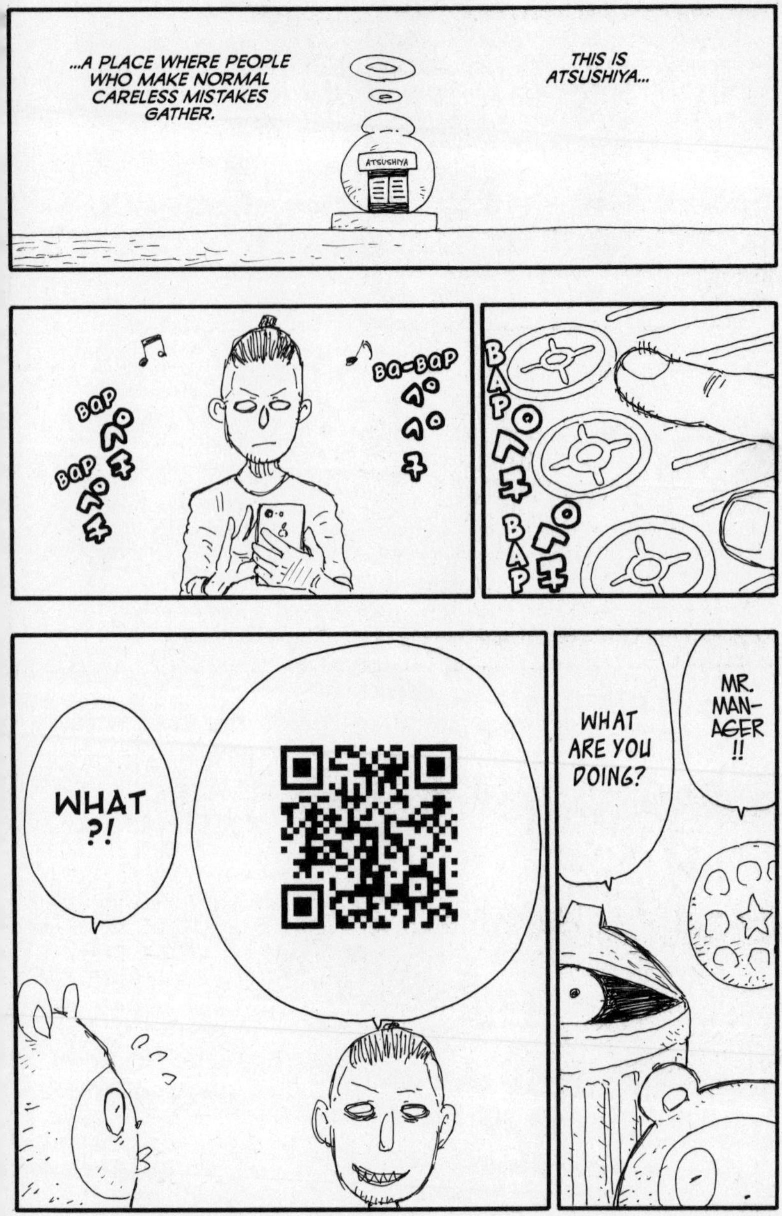
THIS IS ATSUSHIYA...
...A PLACE WHERE PEOPLE WHO MAKE NORMAL CARELESS MISTAKES GATHER.
ATSUSHIYA
BAP
BAP
Ba-Bap
Bap
Bap
MR. MANAGER!!
WHAT ARE YOU DOING?
WHAT?!

WHAT ARE YOU SAYING?!
WHAT IS WRONG WITH YOU, MAN? SPEAK HUMAN LANGUAGE! DON'T MOCK US JUST BECAUSE WE'RE NOT HUMAN!
I THINK THIS IS A QR CODE—THE KIND YOU TAKE A PICTURE OF WITH YOUR PHONE.
SAY IT AGAIN, MR. MANAGER.
BEE-BEEP
TH... THIS IS—?!
THE FREE-TO-PLAY SMARTPHONE AND TABLET OFFICIAL FIRE FORCE BATTLE RHYTHM GAME: BURNING BEAT?! PLAY AS SHINRA AND THE OTHER ROOKIE FIRE SOLDIERS IN A SUPER INTENSE TRAINING DRILL! PUT OUT FIRES AND INFERNALS IN TIME WITH THE BEAT OF THE BACKGROUND MUSIC! USE THE CODE INCLUDED INSIDE THE BELLY BAND OF VOLUME 7 TO UNLOCK ALL FOUR CHARACTERS! ON TOP OF THAT, YOU CAN PARTICIPATE IN THE RANKING WARS TO WIN ONE OF 100 SKETCHES BY OUR VERY OWN MANAGER!

PLAY THE GAME AND SEE THE OFFICIAL SITE USING USHER'S QR CODE OR BY GOING TO HTTP://ENEN-BEAT.COM/!

NOTE: THIS CAMPAIGN WAS JAPAN-ONLY, AND LASTED FROM FEBRUARY 15 THROUGH APRIL 17, 2017.

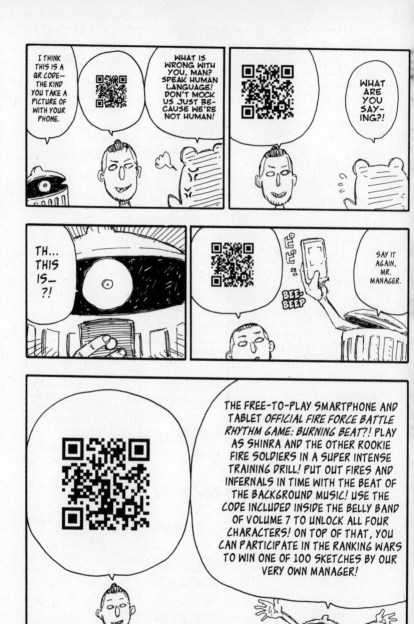

FIRE FORCE

TAMAKI KOTATSU

AFFILIATION: SPECIAL FIRE FORCE COMPANY 8

RANK: SECOND CLASS SOLDIER

ABILITY: THIRD GENERATION PYROKINETIC (CHANGES FLAMES INTO CAT EARS, TAIL, AND CLAWS)

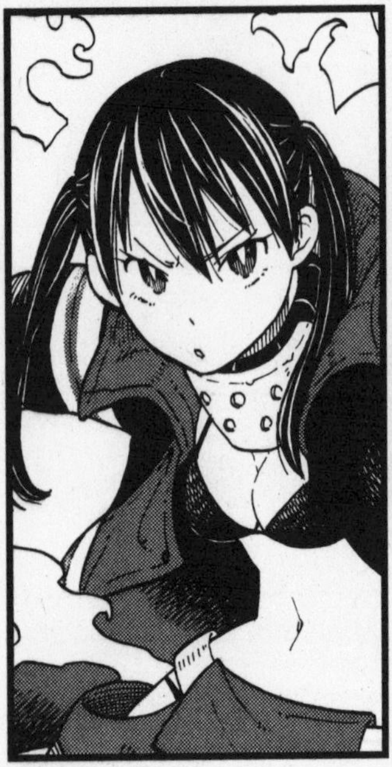

Height	156 cm [5'1"] (I wish I were a little taller!)
Weight	Weight: 41 kg [90.41 lbs.]
Age	I'm 17!
Birthday	February 22
Sign	Pisces
Bloodtype	A
Nickname	Cat Girl, Tama-chan
Self-Proclaimed	I don't wanna be a lucky lecher lure!
Favorite Foods	Fishies♥
Least Favorite Food	Celery, carrots, peppers...blegh
Favorite Music	Pop
Favorite Animal	Kitty♥
Favorite Color	Hmm...I can't choose! If I had to pick, white and yellow!
Her Type	Someone with no secrets, some-one who's not too fired up
Who She Respects	Daddy, Mommy, Captain Burns, Lieutenant Karim, Lieutenant Huo Yan
Who She Has Trouble Around	Lieutenant Rekka
Who She's Afraid Of	People who suddenly change their attitude, Lieutenant Rekka
Hobbies	Napping in the park (@¯ρ¯@) So soothing!
Daily Routine	Caring for my hair and fingernails. I never miss a day!
Dream	I want a kitty cat!!
Shoe Size	23.5 cm [7]
Eyesight	0.9 [20/22]
Favorite Subject	Music Any class where the girls and boys are separated.
Least Favorite Subject	Co-ed P.E. Seriously, it should be illegal#

Fire Force

WELCOME TO THE BALLROOM

By Tomo Takeuchi

eckless high school student Tatara Fujita wants to be good at omething—anything. Unfortunately, he's about as average as a slouchy een can be. The local bullies know this, and make it a habit to hit him up r cash, but all that changes when the debonair Kaname Sengoku sends hem packing. Sengoku's not the neighborhood watch, though. He's a rofessional ballroom dancer. And once Tatara Fujita gets ulled into the world of ballroom, his life will never be the ame.

KC KODANSHA COMICS

Japan's most powerful spirit medium delves into the ghost world's greatest mysteries!

Story by Kyo Shirodaira, famed author of mystery fiction and creator of *Spiral*, *Blast of Tempest*, and *The Record of a Fallen Vampire*.

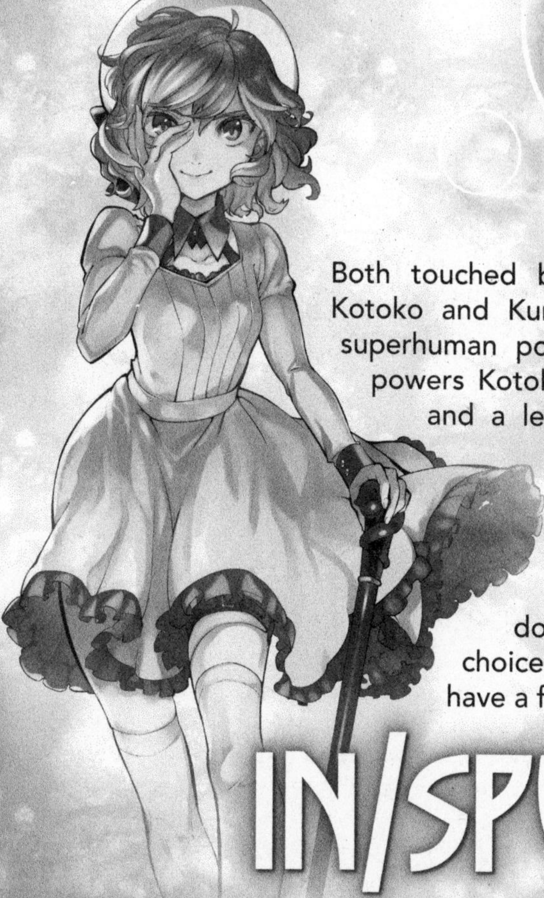

Both touched by spirits called yôka Kotoko and Kurô have gained uniqu superhuman powers. But to gain he powers Kotoko has given up an ey and a leg, and Kurô's persona life is in shambles. S when Kotoko suggest they team up to dea with renegades fron the spirit world, Kur doesn't have many othe choices, but Kotoko might jus have a few ulterior motives...

IN/SPECTRE

STORY BY KYO SHIRODAIRA
ART BY CHASHIBA KATASE

H·A·P·P·I·N·E·S·S

——ハピネス——

By **Shuzo Oshimi**

From the creator of *The Flowers of Evil*

Nothing interesting is happening in Makoto Ozaki's first year of high school. HIs life is a series of quiet humiliations: low-grade bullies, unreliable friends, and the constant frustration of his adolescent lust. But one night, a pale, thin girl knocks him to the ground in an alley and offers him a choice.

Now everything is different. Daylight is searingly bright. Food tastes awful. And worse than anything is the terrible, consuming thirst...

Praise for Shuzo Oshimi's *The Flowers of Evil*

"A shockingly readable story that vividly—one might even say queasily—evokes the fear and confusion of discovering one's own sexuality. Recommended." —The Manga Critic

"A page-turning tale of sordid middle school blackmail." —Otaku USA Magazine

"A stunning new horror manga." —Third Eye Comics

KODANSHA COMICS

The Black Museum: The Ghost and the Lady

By Kazuhiro Fujita

Deep in Scotland Yard in London sits an evidence room dedicated to the greate
mysteries of British history. In this "Black Museum" sits a misshapen hunk o
lead—two bullets fused together—the key to a wartime encounter between Florenc
Nightingale, the mother of modern nursing, and a supernatural Man in Grey. Th
story is unknown to most scholars of history, but a special guest of the museum wi
tell the tale of *The Ghost and the Lady*...

Praise for Kazuhiro Fujita's *Ushio and Tora*

"A charming revival that combines a classic look with modern depth and pacing... **Essential viewin
both for curmudgeons and new fans alike.**" — Anime News Network

"**GREAT!** The first episode of *Ushio and Tora* captures the essence of '90s anime." — IGN

KC
KODANSHA
COMICS

New action series from Hiroyuki Takei, creator of the classic shonen franchise Shaman King!

In medieval Japan, a bell hanging on the collar is a sign that a cat has a master. Norachiyo's bell hangs from his katana sheath, but he is nonetheless a stray — a ronin. This one-eyed cat samurai travels across a dishonest world, cutting through pretense and deception with his blade.

NEKOGAHARA

STRAY CAT SAMURAI

By

Hiroyuki Takei

Based on the critically acclaimed classic horror manga

The first new *Parasyte* manga in over 20 years!

NEO PARASYTE f

BY ASUMIKO NAKAMURA, EMA TOYAMA, MIKI RINNO, LALAKO KOJIMA, KAORI YUK
BANKO KUZE, YUUKI OBATA, KASHIO, YUI KUROE, ASIA WATANABE, MIKIMAN
HIKARU SURUGA, HAJIME SHINJO, RENJURO KINDAICHI, AND YURI NARUSHIMA

A collection of chilling new *Parasyte* stories from Japan's top shojo artist:

Parasites: shape-shifting aliens whose only purpose is to assimilate with and consum the human race... but do these monsters have a different side? A parasite becomes prince to save his romance-obsessed female host from a dangerous stalker. Anoth hosts a cooking show, in which the real monsters are revealed. These and 13 mor stories, from some of the greatest shojo manga artists alive today, together make up a chilling, funny, and entertaining tribute to one of manga's horror classics!

Fire Force volume 7 is a work of fiction. Names, characters, places, and incidents are the products of the author's imagination or are used fictitiously. Any resemblance to actual events, locales, or persons, living or dead, is entirely coincidental.

A Kodansha Comics Trade Paperback Original.

Published in the United States by Kodansha Comics, an imprint of Kodansha USA Publishing, LLC, New York.

Publication rights for this English edition arranged through Kodansha Ltd., Tokyo.

First published in Japan in 2017 by Kodansha Ltd., Tokyo.

ISBN 978-1-63236-479-1

Printed in the United States of America.

www.kodanshacomics.com

9 8 7 6 5 4 3 2 1

Translation: Alethea Nibley & Athena Nibley
Lettering: AndWorld Design
Editing: Lauren Scanlan
Kodansha Comics edition cover design: Phil Balsman